Industry 5.0 for Smart Healthcare Technologies

In this book, the role of Artificial Intelligence (AI), Internet of Things (IoT) and Blockchain in smart healthcare is explained through a detailed study of Artificial Neural Network, Fuzzy Set Theory, Intuitionistic Fuzzy Set, Machine Learning and Big Data technology.

Industry 5.0 for Smart Healthcare Technologies: Utilizing Artificial Intelligence, Internet of Medical Things and Blockchain focuses on interesting applications of AI, promising advancements in IoT and important findings in Blockchain technology. When applied to smart healthcare technologies, Industry 5.0 offers numerous benefits that can revolutionize the healthcare industry. This book provides readers with insights and tools for enhanced patient care, remote patient monitoring, predictive analytics and early intervention of diseases, seamless data sharing and interoperability, telemedicine and virtual care, and a safer and more secure healthcare ecosystem. The authors examine novel computational algorithms for the processing of medical images, as well as novel algorithms for the processing of biosignals in detection of diseases. This book also explores systems for processing physiological parameters and discusses applications of AI techniques in the broader healthcare industry. The authors also investigate the importance of Augmented Reality/Virtual Reality (AR/VR) in the healthcare sector and examine the futuristic applications of Industry 5.0 in the healthcare sector.

This book is intended for researchers and professionals working in interdisciplinary fields of computer engineering/science and healthcare. It will provide them with the tools to enhance diagnostics, optimize treatment plans, and empower patients to actively participate in their healthcare journey.

Edge AI in Future Computing

*Series Editors: Arun Kumar Sangaiah, SCOPE, VIT University, Tamil Nadu
Mamta Mittal, G. B. Pant Government Engineering College, Okhla, New Delhi*

AI-Driven IoT Systems for Industry 4.0
Deepa Jose, Paul Sanchita, Sachi Nandan Mohanty, and Preethi Nanjundan

Big Data and Edge Intelligence for Enhanced Cyber Defense: Principles and Research
Chhabi Rani Panigrahi, Victor Hugo C. de Albuquerque, Akash Kumar Bhoi, and
Hareesha K. S.

Soft Computing Techniques in Engineering, Health, Mathematical and Social Sciences
Pradip Debnath and S. A. Mohiuddine

Machine Learning for Edge Computing: Frameworks, Patterns and Best Practices
Amitoj Singh, Vinay Kukreja, and Taghi Javdani Gandomani

Internet of Things: Frameworks for Enabling and Emerging Technologies
Bharat Bhushan, Sudhir Kumar Sharma, Bhuvan Unhelkar, Muhammad Fazal Ijaz,
and Lamia Karim

*Soft Computing: Recent Advances and Applications in Engineering and Mathematical
Sciences*
Pradip Debnath, Oscar Castillo, and Poom Kumam

Computational Statistical Methodologies and Modeling for Artificial Intelligence
Priyanka Harjule, Azizur Rahman, Basant Agarwal, and Vinita Tiwari

*Industry 5.0 for Smart Healthcare Technologies: Utilizing Artificial Intelligence,
Internet of Medical Things and Blockchain*
Edited by Sherin Zafar, S. N. Kumar, A. Ahilan, and Gulsun Kurubacak Cakir

For more information about this series, please visit: https://www.routledge.com/
Edge-AI-in-Future-Computing/book-series/EAIFC

Industry 5.0 for Smart Healthcare Technologies

Utilizing Artificial Intelligence, Internet of Medical Things and Blockchain

Edited by
Sherin Zafar, S. N. Kumar, A. Ahilan,
and Gulsun Kurubacak Cakir

CRC Press
Taylor & Francis Group
Boca Raton London New York

CRC Press is an imprint of the
Taylor & Francis Group, an **informa** business

Designed cover image: © Shutterstock Images

First edition published 2025
by CRC Press
2385 NW Executive Center Drive, Suite 320, Boca Raton FL 33431

and by CRC Press
4 Park Square, Milton Park, Abingdon, Oxon, OX14 4RN

CRC Press is an imprint of Taylor & Francis Group, LLC

© 2025 selection and editorial matter, Sherin Zafar, S. N. Kumar, A. Ahilan, and Gulsun Kurubacak Cakir; individual chapters, the contributors

Library of Congress Cataloging-in-Publication Data
Names: Zafar, Sherin, editor.
Title: Industry 5.0 for smart healthcare technologies : utilizing
artificial intelligence, Internet of Medical Things and Blockchain /
edited by Sherin Zafar [and three others].
Description: First edition. | Boca Raton : CRC Press, [2024] | Series: Edge
AI in future computing | Includes bibliographical references and index. |
Identifiers: LCCN 2024008637 (print) | LCCN 2024008638 (ebook) |
ISBN 9781032632209 (hbk) | ISBN 9781032632216 (pbk) | ISBN 9781032632223 (ebk)
Subjects: LCSH: Medical informatics. | Medical technology. |
Artificial intelligence–Medical applications. | Internet in medicine.
Classification: LCC R858 .I528 2024 (print) | LCC R858 (ebook) |
DDC 610.285–dc23/eng/20240528
LC record available at https://lccn.loc.gov/2024008637
LC ebook record available at https://lccn.loc.gov/2024008638

ISBN: 978-1-032-63220-9 (hbk)
ISBN: 978-1-032-63221-6 (pbk)
ISBN: 978-1-032-63222-3 (ebk)

DOI: 10.1201/9781032632223

Typeset in Times
by codeMantra

Contents

Preface

In a time marked by rapid technological advancements across various sectors, healthcare is a pivotal domain undergoing profound changes. The fusion of Industry 4.0 innovations with healthcare, giving rise to what is now termed Industry 5.0, signifies a significant shift in how healthcare services are perceived and delivered. This book delves deeply into the captivating realm of Industry 5.0 for Smart Healthcare Technologies, exploring the intersection of state-of-the-art technological breakthroughs and the intricate landscape of healthcare provision. As we find ourselves on the brink of a new era of innovation, it becomes crucial to comprehend the synergies between industry practices and healthcare, leveraging their potential to improve patient care, streamline operational processes and catalyse remarkable advancements in medical research and treatments.

Through a thorough examination of fundamental concepts, emerging trends, and practical applications, this book serves as a guiding light for healthcare professionals, technologists, researchers, policymakers and enthusiasts alike. From the incorporation of artificial intelligence and machine learning in diagnostics to the deployment of the Internet of Medical Things (IoMT) for remote patient monitoring, each chapter illuminates the transformative influence of Industry 5.0 on reshaping the healthcare landscape. Furthermore, this book goes beyond theoretical discourse by providing practical insights, real-world case studies and actionable implementation strategies, empowering stakeholders to navigate the complexities of adopting and integrating smart healthcare technologies into existing frameworks effectively.

As we embark on this enlightening expedition into the realm of Industry 5.0 for Smart Healthcare Technologies, let us embrace a culture of innovation, collaboration and a shared vision for a future where technology serves as a driving force for enhancing healthcare outcomes and elevating the quality of life for individuals worldwide.

About the Editors

Dr. Sherin Zafar is Assistant Professor (Grade 2) of Computer Science & Engineering in the School of Engineering Sciences & Technology, Jamia Hamdard. With a decade of successful experience in teaching and research management, she specializes in Wireless Networks, Soft Computing, and Network Security. Dr. Zafar has a strong profile on platforms like Scopus, Mendeley, Google Scholar, Research Gate and Publons. She has published approximately 50 papers in Scopus, SCI, and peer-reviewed journals. She also serves on the Editorial Board and as the Editor in Chief of many reputed and Scopus-indexed journals. She has published six books and holds five patents on AI, ML and Blockchain technology. She served as Co-PI for the FIST project of DST and PI for two completed Unnat Bharat projects. A strong believer in the power of positive thinking in the workplace, Dr. Sherin regularly develops internship and career campaigns for students through Internshala and Epoch (Literary and Cultural Society) Groups and has guided a significant number of graduate, post graduate and also PhD students. Dr. Sherin has chaired session for more than 15 international conferences, delivered keynote speeches, served as a resource person for 120+ webinars and FDPs for renowned institutions, such as AICTE STTP and AICTE ATAL FDP. Dr. Zafar has received the best paper awards in renowned conferences and Master Award and Mentor Award from Spoken Tutorial IIT Bombay. She has organized 5+ International Conferences and is a fellow member of the I2Or India organization. Currently, three students have successfully completed PhD under her guidance and over 10 students are pursuing PhD having ICMR and Visveswaraya scholarship. Sherin enjoys a good Netflix and Cricket binge but can also be found on long drives along country roads.

Dr. S. N. Kumar received his BE degree from the Department of Electrical and Electronics Engineering, Sun College of Engineering and Technology in 2007, an ME degree in applied electronics from the Anna University of Technology, Tirunelveli, and a PhD degree from Sathyabama Institute of Science and Technology in 2019. Currently, he serves as an Associate Professor in the Department of Electrical and Electronics Engineering at Amal Jyothi College of Engineering, Kanjirappally. His research areas include medical image processing and embedded systems. He has delivered several lectures on medical image processing in seminars, workshops, and Faculty Development Programs of AICTE Training and Learning (ATAL) Academy. He has edited two books and authored 12 textbooks for the engineering community.

Dr. A. Ahilan received his PhD degree from Anna University, India. He has worked as a Research Consultant with TCS, Bengaluru, where he has guided numerous computer vision projects and Bluetooth low-energy projects. He has experience in hands-on programming in MATLAB, Verilog, and Python at various technical institutions around India. He is an Associate Professor in the Department of Electronics and Communication Engineering, PSN College of Engineering and Technology, India. His research interests include FPGA prototyping, computer vision, Internet of Things, cloud computing in medical applications, biometrics and automation.

Dr. Gulsun Kurubacak Cakir is a Professor of Distance Education at the College of Open Education, Anadolu University. She undertook graduate studies at Anadolu University, Turkey (MA in Educational Technology) and the University of Cincinnati, USA (EdD in Curriculum & Instruction). She also worked as a post-doctoral fellow at the College of Education, New Mexico State University, USA (2001–2002). Dr. Cakir earned her BS degree in Computer Engineering from the College of Informatics Technologies and Engineering, Hoca Ahmet Yesevi International Turk-Kazakhstani University in 2012–2013. Dr. Cakir has over 35 years of experience in focusing on the egalitarian and ecological aspects of open and distance learning; finding new answers, viewpoints and explanations to online communication problems through critical pedagogy; and improving learners' critical and creative thinking skills through project-based online learning, universal design principles and new communication technologies (ubiquities technologies, mobile technologies, virtual reality, augmented reality, mixed reality, etc.).

Contributors

Mohd Abdul Ahad
Department of Computer Science &
Engineering
School of Engineering Sciences &
Technology
New Delhi, India

Imtiaj Ahmed
Department of CSE
East West University
Dhaka, Bangladesh

M. Afshar Alam
Jamia Hamdard University
New Delhi, India

Quazi Mohmmad Alfred
Department of ECE
Aliah University
Kolkata, India

Mehtap Altunel
CPA Office
Eskişehir, Turkey

A. Anandkumar
Jai Shriram Engineering College
Tamil Nadu, India

S. Anjali
Lovely Professional University
Punjab, India

Simber Atay
Faculty of Fine Arts
Dokuz Eylül University
İzmir, Turkey

Yasemin Demir Avcı
Department of Public Health Nursing,
Faculty of Nursing
Akdeniz University
Antalya, Turkey

Gulsun Kurubacak Cakir
Faculty of Communication
Ankara Haci Bayram Veli
University Ankara, Turkey

Serhat Cakir
Department of Technology and
Knowledge Management
Baskent University
Ankara, Turkey

Meghna Chaudhary
Department of CSE
SEST
Jamia Hamdard, India

Gagan Deep
Chitkara Business School
Chitkara University, Punjab, India

A. Dhanamathi
Roever Engineering College
Perambalur, India

G. Fathima
Adhiyamaan College of Engineering
Hosur, India

S. Gharib
Institute of National Planning
Salah Salem intersection with Al Tayran
Nasr City
Cairo, Egypt

Selin Göçen
Faculty of Education
Dicle University
Diyarbakır, Turkey

D. Godwinraj
Department of ECE
Amal Jyothi College of Engineering
Kanjirappally, India

Sebahat Gözüm
Department of Public Health Nursing,
    Faculty of Nursing
Akdeniz University
Antalya, Turkey

C. Gunasundari
Roever Engineering College
Perambalur, India

P. Hema
Department of EEE
Jai Shriram Engineering College
Tamil Nadu, India

Rafidah Abd Karim
Academy of Language Studies
Universiti Teknologi MARA Perak
    Branch Tapah Campus
Perak, Malaysia

Samia Khan
Department of Computer Science &
    Engineering
School of Engineering Sciences &
    Technology
Jamia Hamdard, India

N. Labib
Institute of National Planning
Salah Salem intersection with Al Tayran
    Nasr City
Cairo, Egypt

M. Marimuthu
School of Computer Science and
    Engineering
VIT University
Chennai, India

S. Menaga
Jai Shriram Engineering College
Tamil Nadu, India

Sawant Mitali
Department of Economics
K.P.B Hinduja College
Mumbai, India
and
Department of Economics
B. K. Birla College
University of Mumbai
Mumbai, India

K. Pradeepa
Department of Computer Science
KPR College of Arts Science and
    Research
Coimbatore, India

R. Rathna
Jai Shriram Engineering College
Tamil Nadu, India

Jayanta Kumar Ray
Department of ETCE
Gobindapur Sephali Memorial
    Polytechnic
Purba Bardhaman, India

I. Sakthidevi
Adhiyamaan College of Engineering
Hosur, India

P. Saravanan
School of Computer Science and
    Engineering
VIT University
Chennai, India

Seval Kardeş Selimoğlu
Department of Accounting and Finance
Anadolu University
Tepebaşı/Eskişehir, Turkey

Prabu Selvam
Department of Computer Science
SRM Institute of Science and
    Technology
Tiruchirappali, India

Farheen Siddiqui
Department of Computer Science &
    Engineering
School of Engineering Sciences &
    Technology
Jamia Hamdard, India

C. Sreeja
Department of EEE
Amal Jyothi College of Engineering
Kerala, India

S. Srividhya
Department of Computer Science
KPR College of Arts Science and
    Research
Coimbatore, India

Rogina Sultana
Department of ECE
Aliah University
Kolkata, India

M. Sumathi
School of Computing
SASTRA University
Thanjavur, India

R. Swaranambigai
Jai Shriram Engineering College
Tamil Nadu, India

A. Tedla Berhane
Data Science, College of Health and
    Sciences
Eastern University
St. Davids, PA

Swabra Yahya Umutoni
Department of Business Administration
Anadolu University
Tepebaşı/Eskişehir, Turkey

R. Vanithamani
Department of BME
Avinashilingam Institute for Home
    Science and Higher Education for
    Women
Tamil Nadu, India

V. Jyoti
Chitkara Business School, Chitkara
    University
Punjab, India

B. Gaikar Vilas
Smt. CHM. College, Member, Board of
    Studies in Economics
University of Mumbai
Mumbai, India

Gül Yeşilçelebi
Healthcare Management
Gümüşhane University
Gümüşhane, Turkey

Sherin Zafar
Department of CSE
SEST
Jamia Hamdard, India

1 Industry 5.0 in the Smart Healthcare Sector

S. N. Kumar, Kannadhasan Suriyan,
I. Christina Jane, Jomin Joy, and H. Ajay Kumar

1.1 INTRODUCTION

In Sector 1.0, the First Industrial Revolution, coal and steam-powered machinery greatly increased productivity across manufacturing processes [1], altering transportation, industry, and the idea of labor. Petroleum and electrical technology are involved in Industry 2.0 [2]. The invention of new technologies during this era, including the combustion engine, the electric power grid, and production lines, revolutionized manufacturing processes and paved the way for the growth of new industries like telecommunications, chemicals, and automobiles. Workforce computer usage increased, leading to the evolution of Industry 3.0 [3]. A fresh wave of industrialization was initiated by robots, PLCs (programmable logic controllers), ICTs (in-circuit testers) gadgets, and other information technologies. The emergence of renewable energy and internet connectivity ushered in a new era marked by globalization, automation, and manufacturing advancements. Nowadays, terms like "Industry 4.0" and "5.0" are frequently used [4]. Although artificial intelligence (AI), machine learning (ML), and robots are already beginning to completely change our perspectives, Internet of Things (IoT), big data, and automation continue to offer new opportunities for users and designers. Understanding the shift that we're undergoing and our role in the overall scheme of things as architects and engineers today can help us better understand the industry. A new manufacturing model called "Industry 5.0" strongly emphasizes the interaction between humans and machinery. The advent of automated technology, IoT, and intelligent factories gave rise to the preceding layer known as Industry 4.0. The next phase, Industry 5.0, entails harnessing the unique creative potential of humans alongside increasingly powerful and accurate devices.

The use of ML algorithms and other cognitive technology [5] in medical scenarios is referred to as AI in healthcare. Artificial intelligence, also known as AI, may be characterized by the ability of computers and other technologies to imitate human cognition, particularly learning, thinking, and acting. AI could reduce mistakes made by humans, assist healthcare workers and professionals, and offer constant patient care. AI has the potential to be used much more in evaluating medical images, X-rays, and tests, diagnosing medical issues [6], as well as creating treatment plans. As these tools continue to advance, AI has the potential to save billions of dollars in healthcare costs by automating healthcare administration and relieving providers of administrative constraints. Claims management and clinical decision support are two areas it can improve.

DOI: 10.1201/9781032632223-1

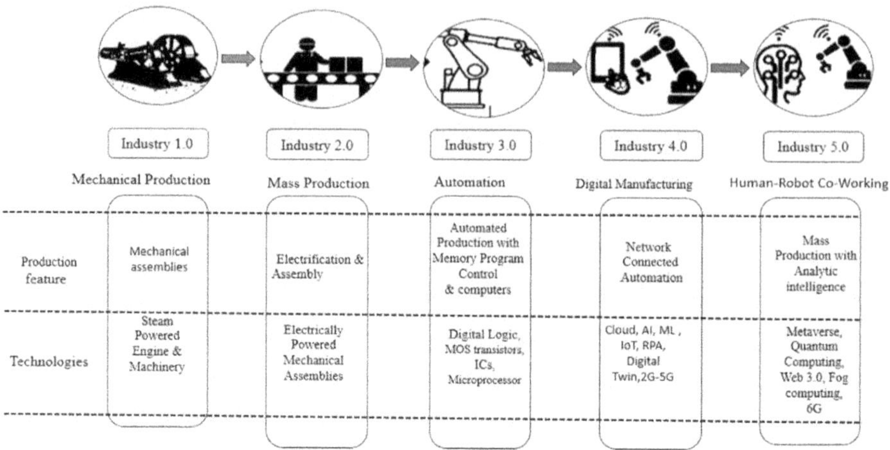

FIGURE 1.1   Industry 5.0 evolution.

The Internet of Medical Things (IoMT), a collection of software programs, hardware, and other digital solutions developed specifically for the healthcare industry [7], is wirelessly connected. These components can interact with each other and instantaneously collect, process, and evaluate huge amounts of data, thanks to cloud computing. The term "Internet of Medical Things" refers to the group of medical software [8] and gadgets connected to online computer networks and healthcare IT systems. The basic concept of IoMT, machine-to-machine communication, is facilitated by medical devices that incorporate Wi-Fi. Using remote patient monitoring (RPM) [9] for long-term and persistent illness patients, tracking medication orders for patients and monitoring the whereabouts of those in hospitals, collecting data gathered from wearable mobile health devices owned by patients, and establishing an affiliation between doctors, nurses, and ambulances traveling to the hospital are functionalities of IoMT devices. IoMT devices connect to cloud platforms so that data gathered may be saved and examined. One term for IoMT is the "healthcare Internet of Things" (H-IoT). The Industry 5.0 evolution is depicted in Figure 1.1 [10].

1.2 INDUSTRY 5.0 IN SMART HEALTHCARE SECTOR: FOCUSING ON AI

In [11], the authors explore how Industry 5.0, which combines smart technology with human-centered collaboration, has the potential to completely transform healthcare delivery. Opportunities such as robotic surgery, telemedicine, enhanced diagnostics, personalized medicine, and patient-centered care are highlighted. It also draws attention to problems including integration, cybersecurity risks, the digital divide, ethical issues, and the necessity of large investments in infrastructure development. A revolutionary AI architecture for Industry 5.0, with a focus on safety and human-machine cooperation, was proposed in [12]. This architecture prioritizes transparency and user control, combining virtual reality, explainable AI (XAI), and active learning. Additionally, it utilizes data-driven insights for quality assurance and predictive maintenance, promoting trust by giving AI and safety procedures first priority. Benefits of the architecture include improved decision-making, increased worker safety, increased efficiency, and greater adaptability. Nevertheless, there are obstacles to overcome, such as creating efficient XAI tools, incorporating AI into current systems, and handling moral dilemmas [12]. The shift to mass customization known as Industry 5.0 is centered on specialized parts for medical applications, including transplants, artificial organs, and medical implants. AI-enabled sensors improve productivity and reliability by enabling quick data processing. Industry 5.0 advancements facilitate personalized healthcare through accurate measurement and monitoring of human body factors [13]. The Security Risk Assessment Framework for Healthcare Industry 5.0 (SRVF HI5.0) is presented in [14]. It consists of five phases: mitigation, preparation, identification, analysis, and evaluation. This framework considers Industry 5.0 characteristics such as big data and AI in addition to industry best practices. A case study of a fictional hospital deploying Industry 5.0 technology is used to assess the framework, demonstrating its efficiently in recognizing and addressing security threats and supporting a comprehensive approach to risk assessment for healthcare institutions [14].

The study [15] focuses on Industry 5.0's AI-based imperatives for creating robust supply chains after COVID-19 such as intelligent decision-making systems, predictive maintenance, and real-time activity tracking. These imperatives are prioritized using the Bayesian Best-Worst Method (BBWM). According to the report, the most important aspect is employing the IoT to track supply chain activity in real-time. Predictive maintenance, sophisticated demand forecasting, and clever logistics optimization are additional top priorities. Conclusions recommend giving investments in AI for flexible supply chains priority [15]. The goal of Huai-Wei Lo's research is to create an Industry 5.0 sustainable supplier evaluation system using data-driven decision support [16]. The quality, dependability, cost-effectiveness, and environmental impact of suppliers are among the quantitative metrics that the system uses to evaluate their performance. The technology finds sustainable suppliers based on real-world data and makes suggestions to improve the effectiveness of the supply chain. This supports environmentally friendly procedures in the medical equipment sector [16]. A wide range of potential advantages is provided by Industry 5.0 technologies, such as improved patient care, remote healthcare, enhanced diagnostics, personalized medicine, and cutting-edge research. But it's important to give ethical issues like data privacy and possible job displacement serious thought. Healthcare inequities already exist, and the digital divide may make them worse. Cybersecurity risks also need to be taken seriously. For effective data interchange, integration and interoperability are essential. Large financial resources are needed to implement these technologies, which presents difficulties for developing nations and smaller organizations. Society 5.0 has the potential to advance human-centered healthcare, create more equal healthcare systems, improve international cooperation, encourage ethical AI use, and create sustainable healthcare systems [17].

In [18], the authors investigate how sensors and digital health technology can revolutionize virtual care in the context of Healthcare 5.0. Wearable technology and biosensors are examples of sensor-based technologies that offer real-time activity levels and vital sign monitoring. Healthcare professionals can evaluate patient status, modify treatment regimens, and take early action through remote monitoring. Personalized care and increased patient engagement are made possible by sensor data analysis and AI algorithms. Difficulties such as data privacy, cybersecurity, accessibility, and moral issues are among the challenges. Sensor-based technology can lower hospital readmission rates, increase patient happiness, and improve chronic illness management and accessibility at an affordable cost [18]. With an emphasis on AI, big data, robotics, automation, and virtual reality, the study examines the possibilities of Industry 5.0 technologies in trauma and orthopedics. Personalized rehabilitation plans, surgical robots, and AI-powered diagnostics are identified. Big data and analytics aid in care optimization and the avoidance of issues. Automation and robotics improve control and precision during difficult processes. In a secure setting, virtual and augmented reality improve abilities and practice. The study concludes that Industry 5.0 technologies have the potential to completely transform orthopedics and trauma care, resulting in better patient outcomes, more individualized treatment, greater productivity, and lower costs [19]. In order to better understand Industry 5.0 trends in healthcare, Asim's [20] research focuses on collaborative robots, telemedicine, remote monitoring, personalized medicine, and health data analytics. With an emphasis on lifestyle, health history, and genetic makeup, these trends are reshaping the way healthcare is delivered in the future.

The role of XAI in Healthcare 5.0 is discussed in the study, along with some of its possible advantages and disadvantages [20]. The advantages of XAI in augmenting transparency, trust, tailored care, and enhanced diagnosis and treatment are emphasized. It also draws attention to issues including the absence of established practices, the need to strike a balance between technological complexity and user comprehension, and the need to ensure ethical usage. The study concludes that while XAI is critical for Healthcare 5.0, resolving issues is necessary to realize its full potential and foster confidence in AI-powered medical treatment [21].

A paradigm shift in healthcare systems, Healthcare 5.0 makes use of cutting-edge technology such as AI, IoT, and 5G communication. Predictive analytics, remote healthcare, real-time monitoring, and personalized treatment are all provided. AI is capable of analyzing medical data to provide individualized treatment regimens, diagnoses, and prophylactics. Nevertheless, there are obstacles to overcome, such as labor adaptation, infrastructure investments, ethical issues, security, and data privacy. Despite these obstacles, Healthcare 5.0 offers a bright future for changing the way healthcare is provided and enhancing patient outcomes. Proactive measures taken to solve these issues may result in a healthcare system that is more accessible, effective, and individualized [22].

1.3 INDUSTRY 5.0 IN SMART HEALTHCARE SECTOR: FOCUSING ON IoMT

In [23], the authors put forward a blockchain-based safe healthcare solution for IoMT systems in developing nations, to resolve privacy and data security issues and enhance access to healthcare in these areas. Blockchain technology is utilized in the system to guarantee data exchange and interoperability, store and manage patient

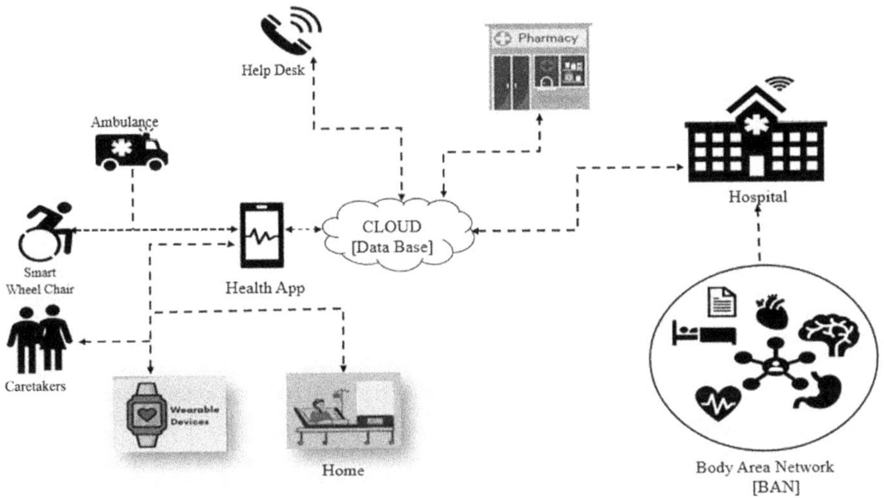

FIGURE 1.2 IoMT in healthcare sector.

data, and automate insurance claims, payments, and healthcare service delivery. Utilizing the peer-to-peer architecture of blockchain, it also lowers infrastructure expenses. Through resource allocation optimization, cost reduction in administrative expenses, and the facilitation of remote healthcare services, the suggested approach seeks to improve healthcare affordability and accessibility. The study identifies possible obstacles such as user adoption, digital literacy, and legal restrictions and recommends more study and development to improve the answer for practical implementation [23] (Figure 1.2).

The integration of transfer learning techniques with secure IoMT for disease prediction in Healthcare 5.0 is the topic of this research. It focuses on gathering precise patient data from medical equipment and sensors utilizing safe IoMT platforms. IoMT data is analyzed using transfer learning algorithms to estimate the likelihood of contracting particular diseases. The framework, which comprises data pre-processing, feature extraction, transfer learning model selection, fine-tuning, and model evaluation, is proposed in [24] for secure IoMT data collection and analysis using transfer learning for disease prediction. Personalized disease risk assessment, reduced training time and computational resources, and increased illness prediction accuracy are some of the possible advantages. However, further study is required to address issues including data security, privacy concerns, and biases in healthcare data [24]. The application of steganography in Smart Society 5.0 to secure data gathered by the IoMT is examined in this study. It examines two steganography techniques: Discrete Wavelet Transform (DWT) Domain Steganography and Least Significant Bit (LSB) Steganography. The findings indicate that although LSB steganography greatly reduces image quality, it has very little visual distortion. Higher embedding capability and improved defense against steganalysis attacks are two benefits of DWT steganography. A real-world case study demonstrates effective data extraction and embedding with little distortion and high PSNR (Peak Signal to

Noise Ratio) values. Challenges include data integrity, computational complexity, and susceptibility to steganalysis [25]. The IoMT and its application to sustainable smart city healthcare delivery are examined in [26]. It discusses the current state of IoMT healthcare as well as its potential advantages, difficulties, and opportunities. The study emphasizes how IoMT can enhance sustainability, public health readiness, and healthcare access. It also draws attention to issues with accessibility, interoperability, privacy, and data security. The study makes the case that strong cybersecurity defenses, ethical guidelines, and established practices can all aid in safeguarding private patient information. To ensure broad adoption, the study also emphasizes the necessity of bridging gaps in digital literacy and providing equal access to technology [26].

The research proposed in [27] focuses on disease prediction accuracy in the context of the smart healthcare industry 5.0 by utilizing transfer learning and a secure IoMT-based technique. To improve the precision of illness prediction, the researchers employ Google Net deep ML models and pre-trained deep learning models. In the era of Healthcare 5.0, the secure IoMT-based transfer learning method bridges the gap between sophisticated technology and healthcare by accurately predicting deadly cancer conditions [27]. Chourasia et al. (2023) explore the potential of Industry 5.0 in ophthalmology and digital metrology. Their research highlights the importance of AI, big data, and robotics in improving disease diagnosis, treatment, and surgical precision. The paper also examines the use of AI in ophthalmology and digital metrology, focusing on its applications in various sectors. It highlights the challenges and opportunities of implementing Industry 5.0 in different regions and cultures. The paper suggests potential future advancements, such as increased integration of AI and robotics in ophthalmic surgery, real-time data analysis and predictive models in digital metrology, and cross-industry collaboration for accelerated development and equitable implementation of Industry 5.0 solutions [28]. AI's capabilities for better diagnosis, prediction, and therapy in healthcare delivery are combined in AiIoMT. IoMT, a network of sensors and medical devices that gathers patient data in real-time, allows for remote care and ongoing monitoring. AI systems examine medical data to assist with diagnosis, forecast the likelihood of illness, customize treatment regimens, and guide professional judgment. When IoMT data is combined with AI capabilities, the results are better patient outcomes, proactive interventions, optimized care delivery, and more accurate diagnoses. AiIoMT offers several advantages, such as increased efficiency in healthcare, proactive disease prediction, individualized treatment, and better diagnostic accuracy [29].

The research work [31] investigates novel approaches to counteract COVID-19 in the medical field by utilizing edge-IoMT-based technologies. Utilizing wearable sensors and IoMT will reduce workload, assist carers, and promote independence. For COVID-19 patient monitoring, the authors suggest an intelligent edge-IoMT architecture that guarantees safe data collection and well-informed decision-making. Real-time health condition advice and preventive measure recommendations can be given to patients using the system [30]. The IoMT, a network of wearables, sensors, and medical equipment, gathers and shares real-time health data to provide better healthcare delivery, individualized treatment, and remote monitoring.

Numerous uses for it exist in the healthcare industry, such as medication adherence, emergency response, remote patient monitoring, chronic illness management, and customized treatment programs. Benefits include better patient outcomes, more cost-effective healthcare delivery, fewer readmissions to hospitals, and a rise in patient empowerment. Nonetheless, there are obstacles such as worries about data security and privacy, issues with interoperability, a lack of standardized protocols, and ethical dilemmas [31]. An IoMT-enabled smart healthcare model that uses ML algorithms to monitor senior citizens was proposed in [32]. The strategy seeks to increase patient autonomy while reducing the strain on medical professionals. Implantable and wearable technology is essential to ongoing patient monitoring. The model's efficacy was evaluated and examined with traditional ML methods on IoMT datasets [32]. To remotely monitor senior citizens, the research work [33] suggests a smart healthcare model that makes use of XAI and the IoMT. Early health issue detection is made possible by the model's usage of wearables and sensors to gather real-time health data. While processing this data, AI models maintain patient and healthcare provider anonymity, while offering insights on possible health hazards. The concept seeks to maximize resources available to the healthcare system, improve carers' quality of life, and enhance health outcomes. The advantages encompass prompt identification of health hazards, preemptive measures, heightened patient involvement, and efficient distribution of resources [33]. How ML algorithms can be used to improve the diagnosis of ovarian cancer by utilizing feature optimization approaches and IoMT data was proposed in [34]. Its goal is to provide a personalized, accurate, and non-invasive diagnostic tool for the identification of ovarian cancer. Data collection, pre-processing, feature selection, ML model creation, and model evaluation are all included in the research framework. Anticipated advantages include improved diagnostic precision, early identification, customized care, and a non-invasive and economical method. Challenges include the integration of clinical knowledge with AI, data quality and standardization, and ethical issues such as data security and privacy. The study recognizes that to achieve appropriate clinical application, medical practitioners and data scientists must collaborate [34].

1.4 INDUSTRY 5.0 IN SMART HEALTHCARE SECTOR: FOCUSING ON BLOCKCHAIN

The potential of blockchain technology in the healthcare sector is discussed in [35], with an emphasis on how it could solve issues such as data security, privacy, and ineffective supply chains. The distributed ledger technology, immutability, and cryptographic security of blockchain can enhance efficiency, transparency, and data management. Applications include prescription tracking, fraud prevention, personalized medicine, safe medical record keeping, and joint research. The research analyzes important features, including decentralization, immutability, and consensus processes, using a conceptual and review-based methodology. It draws attention to the potential advantages of blockchain adoption in the medical field, such as better patient care, increased effectiveness, and cost savings. Nonetheless, the study recognizes difficulties with user acceptance, scalability, and regulatory issues [35]. The blockchain features in healthcare are depicted in Figure 1.3.

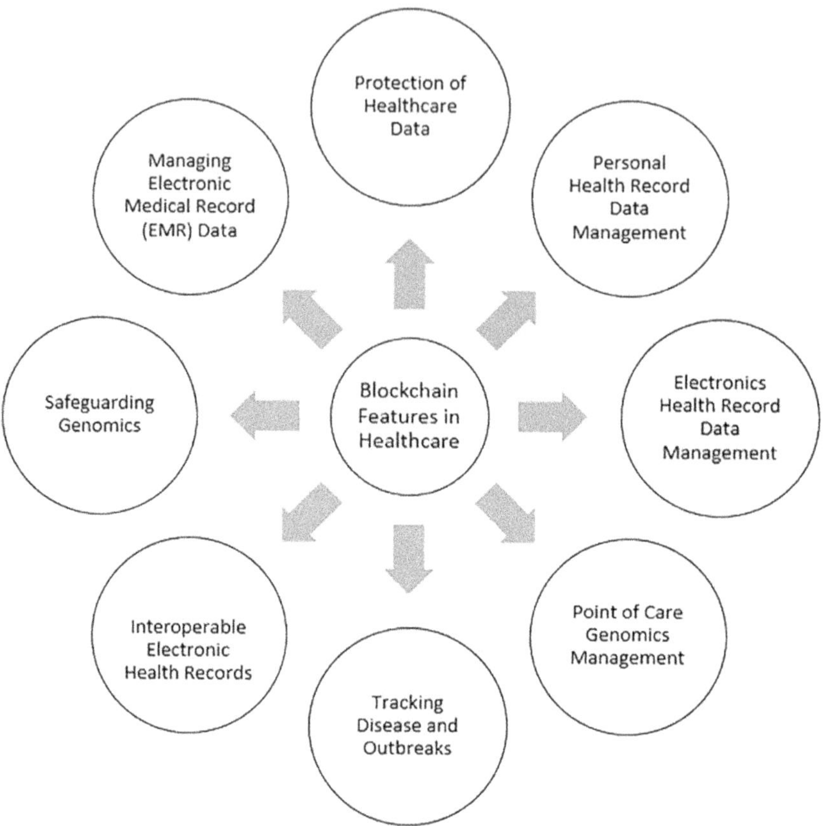

FIGURE 1.3 Blockchain features in healthcare.

GaRuDa, a blockchain-based drone delivery system for Healthcare 5.0 applications, is presented in [36]. The program combines traditional medical logistics with drone technology to increase accessibility and efficiency in healthcare. GaRuDa combines smart contracts for safe transactions, AI algorithms for effective delivery management, and a distributed ledger to maintain medical orders. GaRuDa offers cost-effectiveness, improved security, quicker delivery times, and better transparency. Clear legislation, technological limitations, public acceptability issues, and privacy considerations are some of the problems. In order to guarantee safe and moral drone operation in medical delivery applications, the report admits the necessity for more development and regulation [36]. To enhance medical diagnosis and disease prediction, the report suggests a healthcare system for Healthcare 5.0 that integrates blockchain technology with federated learning. By addressing security and privacy issues, the system hopes to enhance healthcare results and enable accurate diagnosis. The system gathers patient data through wearables and medical sensors, and federated learning protects patient privacy by preventing unwanted access. Proactive therapies and real-time monitoring are also made possible by the system, allowing prompt measures to stop the progression of the disease. Still, there are challenges with scalability, user adoption, and ethical considerations [37]. Blockchain technology (BC) and ML are being used in the field of smart healthcare, with a particular emphasis on important areas including medication adherence, disease diagnosis, remote patient monitoring, and body sensor data analysis. It also emphasizes BC's potential in fields including drug supply chain management, patient record interoperability, and privacy protection for medical data. Based on 112 publications published between 2010 and 2020, the study emphasizes the value of ML in telemedicine, disease diagnosis, and monitoring, as well as the function of the IoT in smart healthcare. The report also discusses ethical issues with data security and privacy, as well as new trends like XAI for healthcare applications [38]. The research work [39] discusses blockchain applications in healthcare, focusing on its key characteristics like decentralization, immutability, consensus mechanisms, and distributed ledger technology. It highlights the challenges of traditional systems in managing medical records, such as data security, accessibility, and interoperability. The paper also explores the potential benefits of blockchain adoption in healthcare, including improved data security, patient empowerment, and healthcare efficiency. However, it acknowledges challenges such as scalability, regulatory considerations, and user adoption [39].

The research article [40] suggests a blockchain-based application for patient identity management to enhance care transitions, particularly during crucial stages such as hospital discharge. There is a need for a safe and convenient alternative to traditional patient data management techniques because they can result in errors and fragmented care. Patient-controlled data, safe access and sharing, integration with current healthcare systems, auditability, and transparency are all provided by the suggested blockchain application. Using a design-thinking methodology, the article gathers requirements, analyzes obstacles encountered in care transitions, defines the architecture of the application, and assesses it through user feedback and expert review. Improved care coordination, fewer mistakes, patient empowerment, increased trust, higher efficiency, and cost savings are among the anticipated advantages [40]. According to this paper, "Secure Health" is a decentralized patient data storage system that uses blockchain technology to store medical information, permits patient ownership and auditability, and permits authorized healthcare practitioners to access data with patient authorization. The program is designed to seamlessly exchange data with the current healthcare infrastructure through integration. Preliminary results indicate positive user-friendliness, safe data integrity, enhanced data access and control, and the potential for better treatment outcomes [41]. By fusing blockchain technology, byzantine agreement, and quantum principles, the Brooks Iyengar Quantum Byzantine Agreement-Centered Blockchain Networking (BIQBA-BCN) architecture aims to safeguard IoT healthcare data. For transparency and integrity, the approach combines blockchain storage, Byzantine fault tolerance, and quantum communication. The model outperformed current methods in terms of encryption, decryption, execution, error rate, and confidentiality rates when validated using Python software [42]. EHDHE (enhanced healthcare documents in IoT-enabled healthcare ecosystems), a blockchain-based architecture intended to enhance the security of medical records in digital healthcare ecosystems enabled by the IoT, was put forward in [43]. To protect data privacy and stop unwanted changes, the framework addresses vulnerabilities in data exchange and storage. It includes multi-layered security using cryptographic techniques, smart contracts for document production and access management, a proposed application (PA) for generating and validating medical certificates, and IoT device integration for all-encompassing health monitoring. The study covers system design, security analysis, prototype development, and performance evaluation processes involved in creating and assessing the EHDHE framework. Promising outcomes include improved security and data integrity, performance efficiency, and technical viability [43].

In [44], the author discusses the importance of patient empowerment in smart health technologies, proposing a blockchain-based framework that enhances engagement, data ownership, and privacy. The framework includes decentralization, data ownership, privacy, interoperability, and smart contracts. The authors conducted a comprehensive review of blockchain in healthcare, highlighting its potential benefits and challenges. They suggest that future smart health technologies should consider integrating blockchain solutions [44]. To improve safe and intelligent healthcare as a service (HCaaS), this paper presents the Blockchain-based Healthcare Service System (BOSS) framework, which places a strong emphasis on Quality of Service (QoS). The platform includes a reputation and rating system, a decentralized service marketplace, smart contracts, and patient-centric data management. The creation and assessment of BOSS, including security analysis, simulation and performance evaluation, system design, and QoS assurance methodology, are described in the paper. Promising outcomes include improved security, performance efficiency, and technical viability. Enhancing patient access to healthcare services while guaranteeing data security, openness, and dependable service delivery is the goal of the BOSS framework [45]. A blockchain-based federated learning system for safe EHR (Electronic Health Record) analysis in intelligent healthcare is presented in [46]. While federated learning enables ML models to train on data saved on individual devices, the framework uses data fragmentation and encryption to safeguard specific patient data. The decentralized structure of blockchain and its secure record-keeping capabilities improve security and transparency. System design, privacy analysis, security analysis, and performance evaluation are all part of the framework's design and evaluation process. Promising outcomes include performance efficiency, improved security and transparency, and privacy preservation. Simulations are also used to show the performance of the framework, demonstrating its practicability for real-world applications [46].

1.5 CONCLUSION

Industry 5.0 advocates for collaborative ecosystems, where AI, IoMT, and blockchain seamlessly work together in healthcare. Decentralized decision-making empowers healthcare professionals and patients with AI-driven insights. Telemedicine and virtual care, enabled by AI and IoMT, offer convenient access to healthcare services. AI-driven insights contribute to personalized wellness plans, improving the overall patient experience. The outcome of this chapter paves the way for the researchers working on smart healthcare applications.

REFERENCES

1. Bruland, K., & Smith, K. (2013). Assessing the role of steam power in the first industrial revolution: The early work of Nick von Tunzelmann. *Research Policy, 42*(10), 1716–1723.
2. Yin, Y., Stecke, K. E., & Li, D. (2018). The evolution of production systems from Industry 2.0 through Industry 4.0. *International Journal of Production Research, 56*(1–2), 848–861.
3. Jiang, Z., Yuan, S., Ma, J., & Wang, Q. (2022). The evolution of production scheduling from Industry 3.0 through Industry 4.0. *International Journal of Production Research, 60*(11), 3534–3554.
4. Skobelev, P. O., & Borovik, S. Y. (2017). On the way from industry 4.0 to industry 5.0: From digital manufacturing to digital society. *Industry 4.0, 2*(6), 307–311.
5. Bini, S. A. (2018). Artificial intelligence, machine learning, deep learning, and cognitive computing: What do these terms mean and how will they impact health care? *The Journal of Arthroplasty, 33*(8), 2358–2361.
6. Babar, Z., van Laarhoven, T., Zanzotto, F. M., & Marchiori, E. (2021). Evaluating diagnostic content of AI-generated radiology reports of chest X-rays. *Artificial Intelligence in Medicine, 116*, 102075.
7. Guo, C., Ashrafian, H., Ghafur, S., Fontana, G., Gardner, C., & Prime, M. (2020). Challenges for the evaluation of digital health solutions–A call for innovative evidence generation approaches. *NPJ Digital Medicine, 3*(1), 110.
8. Razdan, S., & Sharma, S. (2022). Internet of medical things (IoMT): Overview, emerging technologies, and case studies. *IETE Technical Review, 39*(4), 775–788.
9. Abdullah, A., Ismael, A., Rashid, A., Abou-ElNour, A., & Tarique, M. (2015). Real time wireless health monitoring application using mobile devices. *International Journal of Computer Networks & Communications (IJCNC), 7*(3), 13–30.
10. Anantharaman, V., & Han, L. S. (2001). Hospital and emergency ambulance link: Using IT to enhance emergency pre-hospital care. *International Journal of Medical Informatics, 61*(2–3), 147–161.
11. Gomathi, L., Mishra, A. K., & Tyagi, A. K. (2023, April). Industry 5.0 for healthcare 5.0: Opportunities, challenges and future research possibilities. In: *2023 7th International Conference on Trends in Electronics and Informatics (ICOEI)* Tirunelveli, India (pp. 204–213). IEEE.
12. Rožanec, J. M., Novalija, I., Zajec, P., Kenda, K., Tavakoli Ghinani, H., Suh, S., ... & Soldatos, J. (2023). Human-centric artificial intelligence architecture for industry 5.0 applications. *International Journal of Production Research, 61*(20), 6847 6872.
13. Dalal, S., Seth, B., & Radulescu, M. (2023). Driving technologies of industry 5.0 in the medical field. In: Surjeet Dalal, Bijeta Seth, and Magdalena Radulescu (eds). *Digitalization, Sustainable Development, and Industry 5.0: An Organizational Model for Twin Transitions* (pp. 267–292). Emerald Publishing Limited.
14. Baz, A., Ahmed, R., Khan, S. A., & Kumar, S. (2023). Security risk assessment framework for the healthcare industry 5.0. *Sustainability, 15*(23), 16519.
15. Ahmed, T., Karmaker, C. L., Nasir, S. B., Moktadir, M. A., & Paul, S. K. (2023). Modeling the artificial intelligence-based imperatives of industry 5.0 towards resilient supply chains: A post-COVID-19 pandemic perspective. *Computers & Industrial Engineering, 177*, 109055.
16. Lo, H. W. (2023). A data-driven decision support system for sustainable supplier evaluation in the Industry 5.0 era: A case study for medical equipment manufacturing. *Advanced Engineering Informatics, 56*, 101998.

17. Tyagi, A. K., Lakshmi Priya, R., Mishra, A. K., & Balamurugan, G. (2023). Industry 5.0: Potentials, issues, opportunities, and challenges for society 5.0. In: Amit Kumar Tyagi (ed). *Privacy Preservation of Genomic and Medical Data*, 409–432.

18. Mbunge, E., Muchemwa, B., & Batani, J. (2021). Sensors and healthcare 5.0: Transformative shift in virtual care through emerging digital health technologies. *Global Health Journal*, 5(4), 169–177.

19. Iyengar, K. P., Pe, E. Z., Jalli, J., Shashidhara, M. K., Jain, V. K., Vaish, A., & Vaishya, R. (2022). Industry 5.0 technology capabilities in Trauma and Orthopaedics. *Journal of Orthopaedics*, 32, 125–132.

20. Asim, Z. (2022). Shaping healthcare system under industry 5.0: Trends and barriers. *Sudan Journal of Medical Sciences*, 17(3), 362–364.

21. Saraswat, D., Bhattacharya, P., Verma, A., Prasad, V. K., Tanwar, S., Sharma, G., ... & Sharma, R. (2022). *Explainable AI for Healthcare 5.0: Opportunities and Challenges*. IEEE.

22. Mohanta, B., Das, P., & Patnaik, S. (2019, May). Healthcare 5.0: A paradigm shift in digital healthcare system using artificial intelligence, IOT and 5G communication. In: *2019 International Conference on Applied Machine Learning (ICAML)* Bhubaneswar, India (pp. 191–196). IEEE.

23. Ray, S., Korchagina, E. V., Nikam, R. U., & Singhal, R. K. (2023). A blockchain-based secure healthcare solution for povertyled economy of IoMT under industry 5.0. In: Das, R.C. (ed.). *Inclusive Developments through Socio-economic Indicators: New Theoretical and Empirical Insights* (pp. 269–280). Emerald Publishing Limited.

24. Abbas, T., Fatima, A., Shahzad, T., Alissa, K., Ghazal, T. M., Al-Sakhnini, M. M., ... & Ahmed, A. (2023). *Secure IoMT for Disease Prediction Empowered with Transfer Learning in Healthcare 5.0, the Concept and Case Study*. IEEE.

25. Dhawan, S., Gupta, R., Rana, A. K., & Sharma, S. (2022). Internet of medical things (IoMT) & secured using steganography for development of smart society 5.0. In: Sachin Dhawan, Rashmi Gupta, Arun Kumar Rana, and Sharad Sharma (eds.). *Decision Analytics for Sustainable Development in Smart Society 5.0: Issues, Challenges and Opportunities* (pp. 173–189). Springer.

26. Mishra, P., & Singh, G. (2023). Internet of medical things healthcare for sustainable smart cities: Current status and future prospects. *Applied Sciences*, 13(15), 8869.

27. Murphy, K., Di Ruggiero, E., Upshur, R., Willison, D. J., Malhotra, N., Cai, J. C., ... & Gibson, J. (2021). Artificial intelligence for good health: A scoping review of the ethics literature. *BMC Medical Ethics*, 22(1), 1–17.

28. Chourasia, S., Pandey, S. M., Murtaza, Q., Agrawal, S., & Gupta, K. (2023). Redefining industry 5.0 in ophthalmology and digital metrology: A global perspective. *MAPAN*, 38, 527–545.

29. Awotunde, J. B., Folorunso, S. O., Ajagbe, S. A., Garg, J., & Ajamu, G. J. (2022). AiIoMT: IoMT-based system-enabled artificial intelligence for enhanced smart health-care systems. In: Al-Turjman, F., and Nayyar, A. (eds.). *Machine Learning for Critical Internet of Medical Things*. Springer, Cham (pp. 229–254).

30. Awotunde, J. B., Jimoh, R. G., Matiluko, O. E., Gbadamosi, B., & Ajamu, G. J. (2021). Artificial intelligence and an edge-IoMT-based system for combating COVID-19 pandemic. In: Tyagi, A.K., Abraham, A., and Kaklauskas, A. (eds). *Intelligent Interactive Multimedia Systems for e-Healthcare Applications* (pp. 191–214). Springer, Singapore.

31. Joyia, G. J., Liaqat, R. M., Farooq, A., & Rehman, S. (2017). Internet of medical things (IoMT): Applications, benefits and future challenges in healthcare domain. *Journal of Communications*, 12(4), 240–247.

32. Khan, M. F., Ghazal, T. M., Said, R. A., Fatima, A., Abbas, S., Khan, M. A., ... & Khan, M. A. (2021). An iomt-enabled smart healthcare model to monitor elderly people using machine learning technique. *Computational Intelligence and Neuroscience*, vol. 2021, Article ID 2487759, 10 pages.

33. Raza, H., Abbas, N., Amir, S., Arshad, K., Siddiqui, M. R. U., & Khan, S. I. (2022). An IoMT enabled smart healthcare model to monitor elderly people using explainable artificial intelligence (EAI). *Journal of NCBAE*, *1*(2), 16–22.

34. Ghazal, T. M., & Taleb, N. (2022). Feature optimization and identification of ovarian cancer using internet of medical things. *Expert Systems*, *39*(9), e12987.

35. Kaswan, K. S., Dhatterwal, J. S., & Singh, S. P. (2021). Blockchain technology for health care. In: Vineet Kansal, Raju Ranjan, Sapna Sinha, Rajdev Tiwari, and Nilmini Wickramasinghe. *Healthcare and Knowledge Management for Society 5.0* (pp. 1–20). CRC Press.

36. Gupta, R., Bhattacharya, P., Tanwar, S., Kumar, N., & Zeadally, S. (2021). GaRuDa: A blockchain-based delivery scheme using drones for healthcare 5.0 applications. *IEEE Internet of Things Magazine*, *4*(4), 60–66.

37. Rehman, A., Abbas, S., Khan, M. A., Ghazal, T. M., Adnan, K. M., & Mosavi, A. (2022). A secure healthcare 5.0 system based on blockchain technology entangled with federated learning technique. *Computers in Biology and Medicine*, *150*, 106019.

38. Li, Y., Shan, B., Li, B., Liu, X., & Pu, Y. (2021). Literature review on the applications of machine learning and blockchain technology in smart healthcare industry: A bibliometric analysis. *Journal of Healthcare Engineering*, Article ID 9739219, 1–11.

39. Sharma, V., & Divivedi, R. R. (2021). Blockchain-based medical records for the health care industry. In: Vineet Kansal, Raju Ranjan, Sapna Sinha, Rajdev Tiwari, and Nilmini Wickramasinghe (ed.). *Healthcare and Knowledge Management for Society 5.0* (pp. 77–88). CRC Press.

40. Abdul-Moheeth, M., Usman, M., Harrell, D. T., & Khurshid, A. (2022). Improving transitions of care: Designing a blockchain application for patient identity management. *Blockchain in Healthcare Today*, *5*. PMID: 36779020; PMCID: PMC9907417.

41. Khurshid, A., Holan, C., Cowley, C., Alexander, J., Harrell, D. T., Usman, M., ... & Meyer, E. (2021). Designing and testing a blockchain application for patient identity management in healthcare. *JAMIA Open*, *4*(3), ooaa073.

42. Zhao, Z., Li, X., Luan, B., Jiang, W., Gao, W., & Neelakandan, S. (2023). Secure internet of things (IoT) using a novel brooks Iyengar quantum byzantine agreement-centered blockchain networking (BIQBA-BCN) model in smart healthcare. *Information Sciences*, *629*, 440–455.

43. Sharma, P., Namasudra, S., Crespo, R. G., Parra-Fuente, J., & Trivedi, M. C. (2023). EHDHE: Enhancing security of healthcare documents in IoT-enabled digital healthcare ecosystems using blockchain. *Information Sciences*, *629*, 703–718.

44. Anik, F. I., Sakib, N., Shahriar, H., Xie, Y., Nahiyan, H. A., & Ahamed, S. I. (2023). Unraveling a blockchain-based framework towards patient empowerment: A scoping review envisioning future smart health technologies. *Smart Health*, *29*, 100401.

45. Singh, P. D., Kaur, R., Dhiman, G., & Bojja, G. R. (2023). BOSS: A new QoS aware blockchain assisted framework for secure and smart healthcare as a service. *Expert Systems*, *40*(4), e12838.

46. Guduri, M., Chakraborty, C., & Margala, M. (2023). Blockchain-based federated learning technique for privacy preservation and security of smart electronic health records. *IEEE Transactions on Consumer Electronics*, *70*(1), 2608–2617.

2 Technology Foresight for Better Healthcare

Serhat Cakir and Gulsun Kurubacak Cakir

2.1 INTRODUCTION

Technology foresight is a systematic approach to anticipate and explore future technological developments, their potential impacts, and how they can be harnessed to drive progress and innovation in a particular field, such as healthcare. Technology foresight aims to identify emerging trends, predict their future trajectory, and inform strategic decision-making to ensure that organizations and societies are better prepared to leverage these advancements. Technology foresight plays a critical role in shaping the future of medical practices, patient care, and healthcare systems. Foresight techniques were examined in the study. In the context of health, technology foresight study systematics were discussed. The steps to be taken for model development were explained in detail. As a result, a roadmap for technology foresight study was developed for researchers and managers interested in the subject. In the first section, general information about technology foresight will be given. Key technology foresight methods will be explained. The methods will be compared among themselves. Collaborative efforts among all stakeholders (health professionals, technologists, policymakers, and researchers) are essential for successful technology foresight in healthcare. The second section will explain the relationship and importance of healthcare and technology foresight. Previous foresight studies on healthcare technologies will be summarized. The stages of the widely used Delphi technique will be explained in the third section. These are, in order: (a) identifying the problem and requirements, (b) analyzing the current situation, (c) preparing the list of experts, (d) creating the Delphi statements, (e) preparing the format of the Delphi survey, (f) determining the personal information to be asked to the experts, (g) questioning the impact of each Delphi statement, (h) time intervals, (i) preparation of the first round (software), (j) analysis of the results of the first round, (k) preparation of the results of the first round for the second, (l) preparation of the second round, and (m) analysis of the results.

In healthcare, Delphi statements are a structured way to gather expert opinions and insights on various topics related to technology. The Delphi technique is a consensus-building technique that involves multiple rounds of surveys with a panel of experts. The following section will include a sample Delphi application study related to healthcare. The model developed in this section will serve as a roadmap for practitioners. In the appendix of this section, sample Delphi statements related to healthcare technologies will be given. In Section 2.5, expert evaluation (panel) and focus group work methods will be examined. This section will explain the

DOI: 10.1201/9781032632223-2

development process of roadmaps for both methods. Examples from previous work will also be given. Section 2.6 will provide examples of areas where technology foresight studies for healthcare can be cited. The final selection will include analysis and recommendations of technology foresight studies in healthcare.

2.2 GENERAL INFORMATION ABOUT TECHNOLOGY FORESIGHT

Future studies have been carried out for the last 30–40 years. The methods used were also used in prediction studies. Prospective studies (beyond foresight and forecasting) also suggest options rather than just a future [1,2]. The purpose of these studies is to help shape the future [3–5]. Broad definitions of technology foresight studies are given by Martin and Georghiou as follows [6]. Foresight research systematically looks into the long-term future of science and technology to identify strategic areas and emerge generic technologies that will generate enormous social and economic gains [7]. Technology foresight is the systematic evaluation of scientific and technological developments that can have a substantial impact on the improvement of quality of life, welfare, and industrial competitiveness [8]. Technology foresight is emerging as the most crucial field of activity of the 1990s. It primarily determines national Science, Technology, and Innovation (STI) programs [9]. We can list the reasons for the widespread use of technology foresight studies as follows:

- Understanding the importance of technological innovation for competitiveness, economic growth, and social welfare.
- The crisis in public IT funding. Difficulties in support decisions. The question of which subjects should be invested. The necessity of using limited budgets in one or a few strategic areas.
- Scientific knowledge, technology commercialization, setting standards, etc., within European innovation systems. Awareness of connectivity problems between processes and the ensuing techno-science crisis.
- The knowledge economy emphasizes "distributed information."
- Decentralization.

The purposes of technology foresight are:

- Direction determination; setting priorities (roadmaps)
- What is expected in the future, future thoughts/policies
- Communication/Training
- Increasing participation—adoption of decisions by all stakeholders
- Creation of relevant networks

The outputs of the technology foresight study, besides the determination of priorities, actions, reports, and publications, include the development of coordination, partnerships, and cooperation networks among the actors of the economy and STI, creating new strategic foresight tools and understanding among stakeholders, the creation of new employment areas and the emergence of projects, priority determination studies, and action plans based on disseminated information, with unusual legal regulations [10,11]. Technology foresight studies provide significant inputs in the formation of STI policies. We can list the possible effects in terms of the public, companies, and developing regions as follows:

- **From the public perspective**: Tools to broaden the perspective in industrial R&D policies. Foresight studies pull companies beyond the business planning process, thus providing a rationale for innovation, increasing R&D studies, and enabling more collaboration with the public research system (Public-University-Industry cooperation) [12].
- **For firms**: Firms must innovate in their cooperation network (customers, resource providers, regulatory agencies, etc.). Foresight is a tool that reduces uncertainties by creating a shared strategic vision. In the cooperation network that includes knowledge producers and resources, companies will put long-term issues on their agenda for the future.
- **In terms of developing economies/regions**: As STI systems are often not developed enough, new priorities must be set: Foresight studies help revise the STI system. It also leads to an understanding of the importance of research in political and economic circles and an increase in awareness.

  It is possible to say that there are many types of foresight. Some of these are given below:
  - Technology foresight (Regional, Environmental, etc.)
  - Geographic focus
  - Time/Horizon review
  - Large-scale studies—microscopic size studies
  - State initiatives at the national level—initiatives at the institutional level
  - Various sources of funding
  - For different purposes other than the above

The critical areas of activity of foresight studies are as follows:
- Evaluation of the present and the past
- Determination of foresight options by reviewing previous studies and piloting if necessary
- Evaluation of requirements against current capacity
- Identifying the requirements for the establishment of a new structure and arrangement
- Determination of the most appropriate method

Figure 2.1 shows the typical foresight process. Here, the time intervals are written as average values, and the times may vary depending on the sectoral foresight study.

The reasons for conducting technology foresight studies in the public and private sectors are as follows:

- The public mainly uses it to form national policies about the future. The time scope is between 5–30 years. Update periods are typically 3–4 years, depending on the industry.

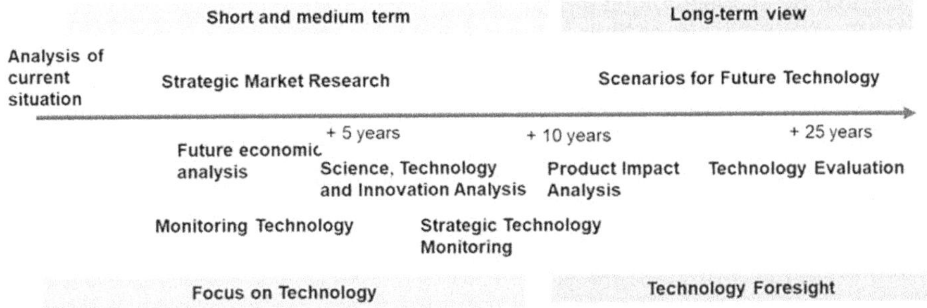

FIGURE 2.1 Typical technology foresight process.

- On the other hand, it also includes identifying strategic options, creating strategic planning units, conducting research and technology programs, and cooperating with corporate think tanks.

Typical technology foresight steps might be as follows:

1. Introducing and explaining the foresight (written, verbal, visual)
2. Identification of those concerned
3. Determining the first draft summary of the project (purpose, focus area)
4. Searching for sponsors
5. Participation of stakeholders (meeting)
6. Identification of sponsors
7. Selection of experts among the stakeholders (nomination)
8. Supporting the foresight process
9. Consultation with stakeholders (possible owners of outputs and processes)
10. Establishment of the Board of Directors from Stakeholders
11. Confirmation of the purpose and objectives of the TF (technology foresight) program
12. Approval of the work program, acceptance of the strategy, presentation of results, and selection of communication tools
13. Defining/adjusting evaluation criteria and determining outputs
14. Monitoring the project to maintain its quality
15. Raising awareness
16. Circulation of experts
17. Experts are nominated for panels
18. Access of experts to panels
19. Continuous management of the project
20. Keeping records of the project in terms of time, resources, and material
21. Following the technical objectives of the project
22. Maintaining the direction of the project in communication with stakeholders
23. Maintaining the direction of the project in communication with the Board of Directors
24. Holding meetings with panel managers

25. Sharing and integration of management reports with the Board of Directors
26. Ensuring the compatibility of the project with other regional studies
27. Gathering appropriate information and information
28. By participating in the meetings of the Board of Directors, transferring the ideas, success stories, and external opinions to the Executive Board
29. Transfer ideas, success stories, and external views to the project coordinator
30. Revising the work program, taking into account certain activities
31. Participation in consensus-building events

2.3 HEALTHCARE AND TECHNOLOGY FORESIGHT

Healthcare refers to the system and services provided for maintaining and improving people's health, preventing and treating illness, and overall well-being. It encompasses various medical, social, and public health activities that aim to promote, protect, and restore health in individuals and populations. Healthcare is a fundamental aspect of modern society and plays a critical role in enhancing the quality of life and increasing life expectancy [13,14] on the policy. The key components of healthcare are depicted in Figure 2.2.

Public health: Public health initiatives focus on preventing and controlling diseases on a population level. This includes disease surveillance, vaccination programs, health education, and promoting healthy behaviors.

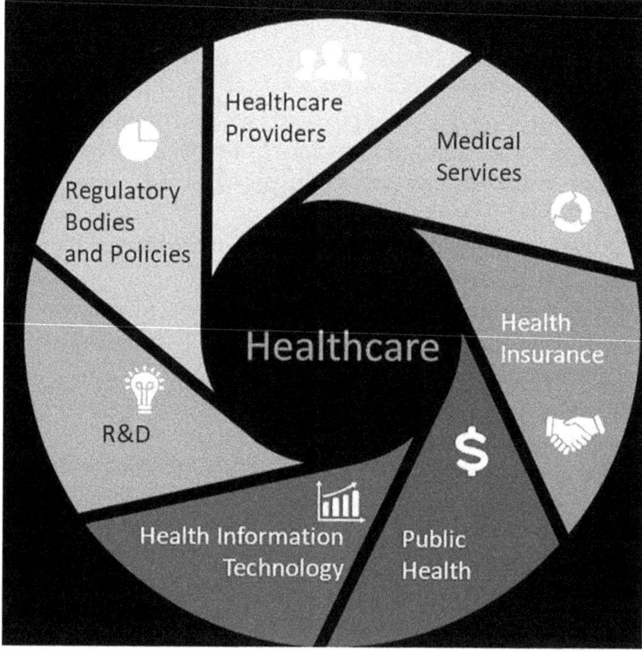

FIGURE 2.2 Key components of healthcare.

Research and development: Continuous research in medicine and healthcare leads to advancements in treatments, drugs, medical devices, and technologies, ultimately improving patient care and outcomes.

Health information technology (health IT): Integrating technology into healthcare processes, such as electronic health records (EHRs), telemedicine, health apps, and wearable devices, aims to improve efficiency and communication within the healthcare system.

State institutions and policies: The state determines the standards of the society's health security and health services and controls the laws and regulations. Plans and implements applications for health systems, culture, administrative structure, and traditions vary according to the country's regions. These factors are taken into account.

Countries may have different systems. In some countries, healthcare is publicly funded and has government-managed healthcare systems, while others rely on private healthcare providers and insurance. Significant difficulties may be encountered while providing health services. For example, access to patient care, expensive health costs, societal health inequalities, aging population, excess burden of chronic diseases, epidemic diseases, and ethical values can be counted. Countries make efforts to improve their health services. Increasing the number and quality of patient care centers, taking preventive measures, benefiting from advanced technologies, and ensuring equal conditions in society's access to health services are among the essential health policies of the state. Technology foresight studies include identifying industry trends and possible paradigm shifts. Various foresight studies are carried out to shape the future of the health sector. The results obtained play a vital role in preparing strategies and roadmaps.

The main objectives of technology foresight studies in the healthcare industry are:

Analyzing advanced emerging technologies: Monitor developments in advanced technologies such as artificial intelligence, genomics, nanotechnology, robotics, blockchain, virtual reality, and wearable devices. Plan the potential use of cutting-edge technology trends in health services at the end of the analyses.

Planning health trends according to needs: Identify demographic changes, epidemiological data, and global health problems and impacts to anticipate the future health needs of society and design new practices.

Developing policies and regulations: Determine how advanced technologies will affect existing ones, and design the necessary policies and regulations. Communicate these new policies and regulations to decision-makers.

Improving healthcare: Use the results of the foresight study to make reports to increase society's access to health services, the quality and efficiency of the service provided. Implement innovations such as telemedicine, remote diagnosis and monitoring, and personalized healthcare.

Improving diagnostic accuracy: Improve the accuracy of diagnosis and the effectiveness of treatment by using new technologies. Design to leverage advanced technologies to improve patient engagement and overall healthcare outcomes. Addressing Ethical and Social Implications: Consider emerging healthcare technologies' ethical, legal, and social implications to ensure responsible and equitable deployment.

Encouraging innovation and collaboration: Foster collaboration between healthcare institutions, technology companies, research organizations, and policymakers to drive innovation and create synergies between sectors.

Various methods can be employed to conduct healthcare and technology foresight, such as scenario planning, expert interviews, literature reviews, technology road mapping, and data analysis. By combining these approaches, stakeholders in the healthcare industry can gain valuable insights into future developments, enabling them to respond to challenges and seize opportunities proactively.

It's essential to recognize that while foresight methodologies can provide valuable guidance, the future is inherently uncertain, and unexpected developments may occur. Therefore, regular reassessment and adaptability are crucial to an effective healthcare and technology foresight strategy.

Delphi Technique: The Delphi technique is a foresight method based on the evaluations of subject experts. This technique creates strategies and prepares roadmaps to shape the future. The Delphi technique was developed by the Rand Corporation after World War II to monitor technological developments and predict future defense industry requirements [15,16]. You've probably heard, "Two hands are better than one." The Delphi technique is an expert survey. It consists of at least two or more rounds. The aim is for experts to reach a consensus on some issues. It is aimed to find the ones that get the consensus of the experts from the Delphi statements (the number varies according to the topic) prepared to shape the future.

First, you need to know whether the area where you will apply the Delphi technique needs this technique. Using this technique without justification is often problematic. There is no doubt that the reasoned Delphi technique, which is widely used today, is valid.

Identifying Technology Priorities: It determines technology priority at the national, sectoral, regional, or company level. It determines which technologies the country needs at the national level. Similarly, it is essential for setting priorities in other dimensions [17].

Policy Development: In the dimensions mentioned above, it is one of the most critical inputs in the policy development process. Countries are doing this kind of work for sustainable development.

Shaping the Future: The Delphi technique is widely used to shape the future [18]. Generally, various conditions are considered in the study where more than one scenario is produced. In this way, at least three scenarios (good, medium, and bad) are created. In some subjects, the number of scenarios may increase [19].

Figure 2.3 shows the stages of the Delphi survey.

The first step should be to prepare the subject and rationale of the study. The project group should be created, and the requirements determined. The current situation analysis is the first analysis of the project and includes collecting relevant information (whether it has been done before, human resources, infrastructure, etc.). Then (Step 3), it is necessary to collect the contact information of the experts who will

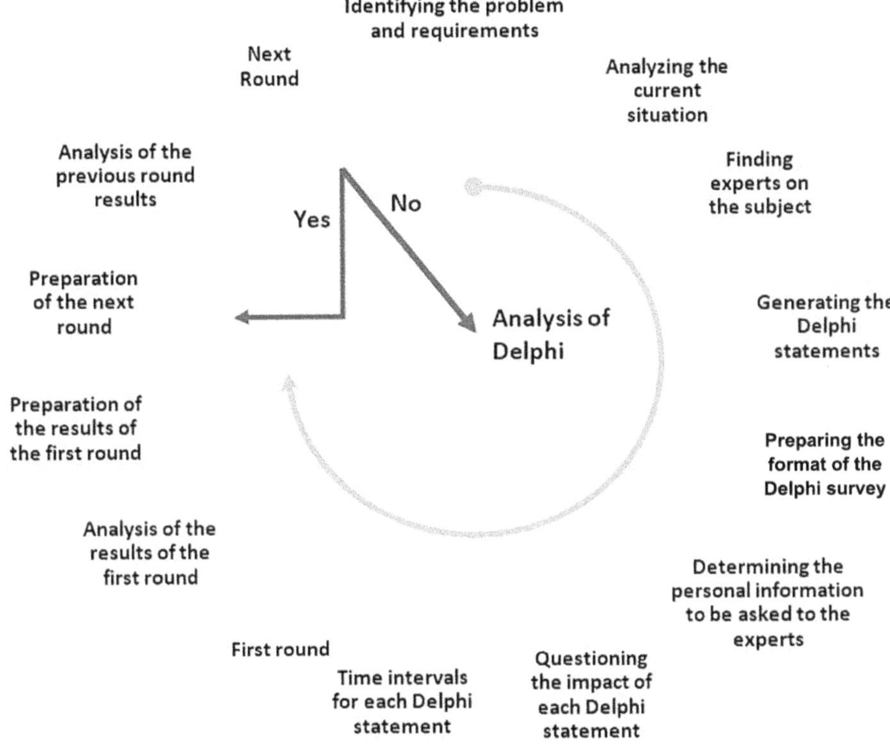

FIGURE 2.3   Steps of the Delphi survey.

participate in the study. The competence of the participants is essential in terms of the accuracy of the foresight result. The participant list should be able to represent the universe related to the subject. The number of experts participating in the study varies according to the issue and scope of foresight.

Creating Delphi statements is a process that requires expertise. To initiate this process, the project group prioritizes Delphi statement proposals. These suggestions are then evaluated by a narrower group of experts and take their final form. The number of Delphi statements can typically be between 20 and 50, although it depends on the subject of the study. It includes the format of the Delphi Inquiry and the questions to be asked to the participants in Steps 5 and 6 (whether there is an expert on the Delphi expression, the type of institution they work for, etc.).

The next step is to determine the variables to be used in the impact analysis of Delphi statements. These variables may be related to R&D studies, economic development, social life, competitiveness, or other issues. Technology foresight studies are usually done for 20 years or longer. Dividing the time into certain intervals in the Delphi interrogation may be a critical issue for the participants. For example, dividing 20 years into four will query the Delphi statement's probability for four periods for each of 5 years. Participants will be asked to choose whether or not to occur in the first 5 years or the other 5 years. After the preparation phases are over, the transition

TABLE 2.1
Sample Delphi Statement and Related Questions

Sample Delphi Statement: Aging and a natural reduction in the active population compel the national government to extend compulsory work time in terms of both hours (more than 40 hours/week) and years (beyond the age of 70).

Questions on Delphi Statement	Multiple Choice Answer	Questions on Delphi Statement	Multiple Choice Answer
Respondent's degree of expertise	• No knowledge • Familiar • Expert	Degree of impact on competitiveness of the country	High positive impact High negative impact High uncertain impact No significant impact
Probability to happen	• High • Medium • Low • Never	Degree of impact on healthcare	High positive impact High negative impact High uncertain impact No significant impact
Time of occurrence	Before 2030 Between 2031 and 2035 Between 2036 and 2040 Beyond 2040	Degree of impact on social welfare in the country	High positive impact High negative impact High uncertain impact No significant impact

to the application takes place with the first round. The experts are asked to evaluate the Delphi statements in the first round. Table 2.1 shows the sample Delphi statement and assessment questions for participants.

It would be appropriate to give the participants approximately 7–10 days to complete the first round. This period must be specified. However, it is helpful to encourage participants to complete the Delphi survey during this time. First-round results are analyzed. These results will be used for the second round. Therefore, it should be turned into both text and visual graphics.

The Delphi technique consists of at least two rounds. Sometimes, the number of rounds can be increased. Round 2 includes the same Delphi survey and the results of Round 1. The participant's responses for the first round and the reactions of all participants are given as a percentage. The participant is asked if their view has changed. If the change changes, the participant is asked to provide the new answer instead of the previous one. If their view has not changed, they move on to the following Delphi statement. The participants are notified of the start and end dates of the second round.

Delphi studies sometimes involve more than two rounds. This ensures that the Delphi statements that the experts have agreed upon come out more clearly. Various variables can be used to analyze Delphi results—for example, time of realization, importance, degree of impact, and distribution by specialization. At the end of this multidimensional analysis, Delphi statements suitable for the purpose can be specified and accepted as the primary strategic targets.

Delphi exercises related to healthcare: Technological change presents an excellent opportunity for countries that can identify new technologies early and predict their future development and impact. Priority technology investments are an essential problem for countries with limited resources. The adoption and implementation of new technologies by healthcare services is not easy. In particular, acquiring advanced technologies may require significant investments. Technology selection is one of the most challenging issues for decision-makers. The choice of technology involves many uncertainties. In Section 2.3, it is explained why technology foresight is so necessary in healthcare. This section will talk about the application of the Delphi technique in healthcare. There are many foresight techniques. Health services concern the whole of society and have a very complex structure. Therefore, it cannot be predicted with a simple method. Health services should be examined multi-dimensionally. In addition to short and medium-term health policies, long-term projections should be made.

The Delphi technique comes to the forefront compared to others in technology foresight studies in health policies. The Delphi technique provides significant input for strategy studies. This technique is not just based on information gathering. It also seeks to ensure consensus of experts' opinions by holding more than one round. It offers the opportunity to evaluate the issue in more dimensions than many other foresight techniques.

The advantages are as follows:

- The margin of error is very low. It includes multiple rounds aimed at reducing the biases of the participants.
- The individual opinions of the experts can be examined, and their contributions analyzed.
- The large number of participating experts enriches the data.
- The cost of Delphi work is less than many other methods.
- It can be applied very quickly after the preparations are completed.
- People who are not experts in Delphi work can also be consulted. Such data can be compared with expert data. This may reveal the general opinion.
- The process is repeated until the experts reach a consensus.
- The Delphi technique is not difficult to prepare and implement.
- No single person can change the view of the work or become the dominant person.
- Faster and less problematic feedback than most prioritization methods.

The major disadvantages are as follows:

- The Delphi technique does not produce a single solution.
- Expert consensus doesn't mean it's always right.
- Suggestions to come out of Delphi results are sometimes incompatible with the results of other techniques.
- Delphi does not have a single methodology in practice; it varies depending on the subject content scope.

2.4 SAMPLE DELPHI STUDY FOR HEALTHCARE

In this section, let's do an example of a Delphi study in healthcare. The first step is to determine on which subject the technology foresight will be made. For example, our restricted topic is how artificial intelligence and machine learning can be used in healthcare in the future.

It is suggested that a Delphi study would be helpful in this regard. Let's suppose it is done for the Ministry of Health of this country. First, the Ministry of Health must support this study—determination of the work project team after this support is provided. As can be understood, the subject is national and interdisciplinary. In this case, the project needs a steering committee. This committee's members, responsible for making strategic decisions, should consist of executives from the public, private sector, academia, and non-governmental organizations.

The responsibilities of the committee may be as follows:

- Approval of the work program, acceptance of the strategy, presentation of results, and selection of communication tools
- Defining/adjusting evaluation criteria and determining outputs
- Monitoring the project to maintain its quality
- Raising awareness

The next step should be to create the project group. The project group should include individuals from various disciplines. Besides the project manager, participants should consist of healthcare professionals, technology managers, computer programmers, statisticians, legal professionals, financial officers, and other relevant office workers. The responsibilities of the project team are summarized below:

- Continuous management of the project
- Keeping records of the project in terms of time, resources, and materials
- Following the technical objectives of the project
- Ensuring the compatibility of the project with other studies

The process continues by creating a core list of experts in healthcare, artificial intelligence, machine learning, and related topics. This limited group of experts and project workers prepares the draft Delphi statements. Delphi statements should be forward-looking statements on the subject, typically covering a future timeframe of 20–30 years. The number of Delphi expressions can vary by topic but should be around 30. The core expert group and project team determine the draft Delphi statement count. Draft Delphi statements are discussed in a limited focus group meeting of experts and finalized. On the other hand, the most extensive list of experts to be invited to participate in the Delphi study and their contact information is prepared. If the work is firm, regional, or sectoral, its scope and management mechanism should be changed accordingly. This section will provide the Delphi study for the relationship between artificial intelligence and cybersecurity and health services, broadly defined above. Let's take an example of Delphi expressions first. Table 2.2 shows four Delphi expressions for artificial intelligence and cybersecurity.

Broad definition of artificial intelligence (AI): Programming computers to perform tasks that mimic human abilities (such as understanding language, recognizing objects and sounds, learning, and problem-solving) using a variety of concepts.

Broad definition of machine learning (ML): The AI subset that gives computers the ability to learn without being explicitly programmed. It includes Supervised Learning (labeled data) and Unsupervised Learning (data not labeled).

TABLE 2.2

Artificial Intelligence and Cybersecurity Delphi Sentence Examples

Topic	Code	Delphi Statement
Artificial intelligence (AI)	AID-1	AI diagnostics is considered the international standard, replacing steps built into medical care standards.
	AID-2	Outside of traditional diagnostic and clinical settings, AI applications have revolutionized how people monitor their health.
	AID-3	Using personal datasets, AI applications suggest the best treatment based on people's health, life experiences, and genetic profiles.
	AID-4	Artificial intelligence applications have the potential to increase misinformation that can harm health.
Cybersecurity (CS)	SCD-1	Patient data is stored, shared, and analyzed electronically. This data is not secured and is vulnerable to attack.
	SCD-2	Cybersecurity applications provide a complete security strategy to prevent attacks on precious patient data.
	SCD-3	Creating strong, frequently changed, and unique passwords is insufficient. Instead, password-less authentication will be developed, which cannot be copied.
	SCD-4	Cybersecurity in healthcare is becoming a priority for the healthcare industry due to the massive digitization of data.

Deep Learning, a subset of ML, enables the computer to teach itself by exposing it to large amounts of data.

The statements prepared as a draft by the Delphi study project group are submitted for evaluation by the experts (restricted group) on this subject. Experts should consist of health professionals with a good knowledge of AI and cybersecurity. The number of Delphi statements depends on the topic, typically around 20–30. Statements approved by this expert group are made available for the Delphi survey. After that, the strategic areas that the Delphi expression will affect are determined. In this example, the first thing that naturally comes to mind will be the impact on healthcare. Following that, topics such as its impact on the country's economy, social security system, and human resources can be selected. Let's focus on just three issues: healthcare, the social security system, and R&D activities in healthcare. The design of the questionnaire should be different from other survey studies. First, some information about the participant is requested. For example, their education level, their sector of work, and how long they have been working.

The questions to be asked to the participants for each Delphi statement are usually in two groups. The first group of related Delphi statements is written, and questions such as the expertise of this statement, the probability of its occurrence, the years between which it will occur, etc., can be asked. Information from this group is evaluated separately for each variable. See Table 2.3.

The feedback from the first set of questions will be critical for this Delphi statement. Later, when the other rounds are finished, it will be possible to obtain a result, such as whether experts have reached a consensus about the statement. Once the first

TABLE 2.3

First Group Assessment of Experts for Delphi Statement

Delphi Statement: AID-2 Using personal datasets, AI applications suggest the best treatment based on people's health, life experiences, and genetic profiles.

Questions	Participant's Response
Degree of expertise related to the given Delphi statement	No knowledge
	Familiar
	Expert
Probability of the Delphi statement	High
	Medium
	Low
	Never
Time of occurrence of the Delphi statement	Before 2030
	Between 2031 and 2035
	Between 2036 and 2040
	Beyond 2040

TABLE 2.4

Second Group Assessment of Experts for Delphi Statement

Delphi Statement: AID-2 Using personal datasets, AI applications suggest the best treatment based on people's health, life experiences, and genetic profiles.

Impact on Healthcare	Impact on Social Security System	Impact on R&D Activities in Healthcare
• High positive impact	• High positive impact	• High positive impact
• High negative impact	• High negative impact	• High negative impact
• High uncertain impact	• High uncertain impact	• High uncertain impact
• No significant impact	• No significant impact	• No significant impact

round is completed, the overall results (averages) and the participants' responses will be used for the second and subsequent rounds. In Delphi studies, forms are generally prepared on a web basis. Therefore, the software designed for Delphi work should be able to store such data and then make it accessible for use. The second set of questions will be about the impact of each Delphi statement in predetermined areas. In this example, three fields were selected: healthcare, social security system, and R&D activities in healthcare. Table 2.4 shows the impact assessment process.

At the end of the first round, the results can be presented in Table 2.5. The numbers are randomly generated and do not represent accurate Delphi study results.

The participant, who sees the first-round results in Table 2.5 and their own answer, is asked if their mind has changed. If they change their mind, they are asked to add their new thoughts. In this way, a consensus is attempted to be achieved.

The participant, who sees the second-round results in Table 2.6 and their answer, is asked if their mind has changed. If they change their mind, they are asked to add their new thought. In this way, a consensus is attempted to be achieved. This completes the

TABLE 2.5

First-Round Results (1. Group Questions)

Delphi Statement: AID-2 Using personal datasets, AI applications suggest the best treatment based on people's health, life experiences, and genetic profiles.

Questions	Total Participant's Responses (%)	Your Response in the First Round
Degree of expertise related to the given Delphi statement	No knowledge: 15%	
	Familiar: 40%	X
	Expert: 45%	
Probability of the Delphi statement	High: 45%	X
	Medium: 30%	
	Low: 20%	
	Never: 5%	
Time of occurrence of the Delphi statement	Before 2030: 25%	
	Between 2031 and 2035: 50%	
	Between 2036 and 2040: 10%	X
	Beyond 2040: 15%	

TABLE 2.6

Second-Round Results (2. Group Questions)

Delphi Statement: AID-2 Using personal datasets, AI applications suggest the best treatment based on people's health, life experiences, and genetic profiles.

First-Round Results	Impact on Healthcare	Impact on Social Security System	Impact on R&D Activities in Healthcare
Total participants' responses (%)	High positive impact 60%	High positive impact 70%	High positive impact 80%
	High negative impact 5%	High negative impact 5%	High negative impact 2%
	High uncertain impact 15%	High uncertain impact 20%	High uncertain impact 8%
	No significant impact 20%	No significant impact 5%	No significant impact 10%
Your response in the first round	High positive impact	High positive impact	No significant impact

second round. After analyzing the results of the second round, a decision is made to continue the games or end the study.

2.5 EXPERT EVALUATION (PANEL) AND FOCUS GROUP METHODS

There are other methods used in foresight studies besides the Delphi technique. Among these, the panel and focus group methods stand out alongside the Delphi technique.

Expert panel method: The expert panel method is widely used in foresight studies. Panels typically consist of 10–30 participants [20]. Depending on the subject, study times can vary widely. For example, a foresight study on a national issue can sometimes take two years. Alternatively, for a business, similar work can be accomplished in less time with fewer people. Panels are formed to discuss the future of a particular subject area, whether it is a technology (e.g., biotechnology), a field of application (e.g., healthcare), or an economic sector. For example, the panel may consist of 15–20 experts for pharmaceuticals and may require a long-term study. Technology Foresight is, by definition, a participatory activity that must be based on the best available evidence and evaluation. Therefore, this method is used in foresight studies. Having a large number of participants and engaging in very detailed discussions provides a suitable environment for getting fruitful results. For these reasons, the panel method can be considered the center of parallel foresight methods.

Some of the reasons why the expert panel method is preferred are as follows:

I. At the heart of the foresight exercise is the availability of expert judgment, which can be mitigated, especially by uncertainties about the future.
II. The richness of interdisciplinary perspectives.
III. Concluding the results of other methods used in forecasting with panels.
IV. Panel members are essential foci for disseminating, communicating, and convincing others of panel findings.

Expert panels are involved in the following processes:

1. Gathering information on the relevant subject
2. Analyzing information
3. Disseminating prediction results to a much wider audience
4. Monitoring and evaluating foresight

Advantages and disadvantages of expert panel study: The main advantage of working with expert panels is gathering experts from various sectors that rarely meet. These may include sponsors, policymakers, researchers, users, and consumers, which enriches the work. Expert panels provide an environment where participants can freely express their different views. Some of the reasons that may make the work of the expert panel inefficient are as follows: one person is in charge of the study, and the other panel members are passive. Participants may hesitate to express their opinions on some issues. If there is a hierarchical structure (professor, assistant, etc.), some participants may feel uncomfortable with it. The lack of knowledge of the subject and process of the moderator or expert panel spokesperson prevents the study from being efficient enough.

Focus group method: Focus groups are a group consisting of a limited number of members related to foresight. The aim is to collect this group's information, comments, and suggestions.

Unfortunately, many people confuse focus groups with several other group methods used to gather information, such as public forums, nominal groups, advisory councils, and working groups. However, these are not defined as focus groups. Instead, a focus group consists of an average of ten experts. The purpose of a focus group is to reveal participants' knowledge. Groups rather than individuals are asked to answer the questions jointly. Therefore, an atmosphere of discussion arises spontaneously. Participants enrich the discussion by adding their comments to those of others.

Focus group studies can be conducted for many purposes.

Apart from foresight studies, some of them include:

- Identification of project needs
- Program/project design and development
- Pilot test creation process
- Organizational improvement
- Policy development
- Outcome evaluation.

Important: The purpose of focus group work is to gather information. It is not about making a decision or taking on a task. Focus group study results are used in decision-making, strategic goal-setting, or roadmap preparation.

Preparing questions for the Focus Group Study is the responsibility of the moderator who will lead the meeting. The questions should be designed in such a way that they can reveal the knowledge of the participants. Questions should be concise and clear, ensuring that participants can easily understand them. Unnecessary words can deflect the discussion. An open-ended question should address only one topic. Including more than one subject in the same question can make the answers complex and unanalyzable.

Focus group work generally consists of four steps:

- Introductory questions get participants to start thinking about the topic.
- Interim questions provide a link between the previous and next questions, encouraging participants to think in more detail.
- Specific questions focus on the subject and areas considered necessary. More time is needed to answer these types of questions.
- End-of-study questions close the discussion.

Focus group studies have some advantages and disadvantages. Among the essential benefits are:

- The study provides rich responses based on the profiles of the participants.
- Can test the relevance of results from other methodologies.
- This method is a cost-effective way of obtaining information.
- Results are obtained in a short time.
- An idea put forward during the discussion gets refined with the input of other participants.
- It is economical compared to many other methods.
- According to some perspectives, more diverse and rich data can be obtained.

On the other hand, focus group studies also have disadvantages. For example:

- Participants have less talk time compared to face-to-face meetings.
- Some participants may dominate the discussion, disregarding the views of others.
- The moderator may be biased.
- The cost of focus group work can sometimes be high.
- Some people find it challenging to participate in focus group work and may not feel comfortable expressing their opinions easily.

In conclusion, considering the advantages and disadvantages of this method, social interactions determine the quality and richness of the information received. The ability of the moderator affects the work outputs. A dominant participant negatively affects the results, which may prevent others from freely expressing their views. The questions to be prepared for the study are extremely important.

2.6 EXAMPLES OF SOME AREAS WHERE TECHNOLOGY FORESIGHT STUDIES FOR HEALTHCARE CAN BE DONE

Technology foresight plays a critical role in shaping the future of medical practices, patient care, and healthcare systems. Here are some areas where technology foresight can have a significant impact: Medical Diagnostics and Imaging: Anticipating advances in diagnostic technologies, such as AI-powered medical imaging, wearable devices for continuous monitoring, and point-of-care diagnostics, can lead to earlier and more accurate disease detection, improving patient outcomes.

Precision medicine: Predicting developments in genomics, biomarkers, and personalized treatment approaches can enable tailored therapies that are more effective and have fewer side effects.

Telemedicine and remote care: Identifying trends in telemedicine platforms, remote monitoring, and virtual care technologies can enhance accessibility to healthcare services, especially in rural or underserved areas.

Healthcare data and interoperability: Foresight can help anticipate advancements in healthcare data management, interoperability, and security, leading to better data-driven decision-making and improved patient care.

AI and ML: As AI and ML advance in areas such as drug development, disease prediction, and treatment planning, they can significantly improve the healthcare industry.

Robotics and automation: Using robotics and automation in healthcare leads to many innovative applications—for example, patient care, surgery, and significant improvement in hospital internal processes.

Nanotechnology and biomedical engineering: Nanotechnologies developed by physicists and innovations in biomedical engineering lead to significant improvements in health services in various areas, such as tissue development and wearable technology.

Health policy: We can accept technology foresight as an essential study that guides decision-makers about the future of health. These methods used in shaping the future are crucial tools for public health.

Health workforce training: Advances in technology require continuous health workforce training. Foresight studies provide essential input into the design and development of training programs.

Patient engagement and empowerment: Predicting trends in patient-centered technologies, healthcare applications, and wearable devices can enable individuals to be more active in managing their health and well-being.

Technology foresight studies are interdisciplinary, involving numerous stakeholders, such as representatives of the public and private sectors, healthcare professionals, technologists, policymakers, researchers, practitioners, and patients.

2.7 CONCLUSION AND POLICY RECOMMENDATIONS

Technology foresight is the study conducted to guide future technological developments, their potential impact, and innovation. It is known as an analytical and systematic way of shaping the future. Technology foresight aims to identify emerging trends, predict their future trajectory, and inform strategic decision-making so that organizations and societies are better prepared to capitalize on these advances. As in many other areas, advanced technologies are used in healthcare. The future of healthcare, a critical issue in terms of public health, is of interest to researchers. In healthcare, technology foresight plays a critical role in shaping the future of medical practice, patient care, and healthcare systems. Countries develop various health policies to create a healthy society for their citizens. National health policies are among the basic policies (including economic policies, education policies, security policies, science, and technology and innovation policies). We have reviewed some of the essential forecasting techniques. There are many techniques for predicting technology [21]. Besides the three techniques (Delphi, Expert Panel, Focus Group) we have examined in this section, some commonly used technology prediction techniques include:

- **Trend analysis**: It predicts by analyzing technological developments, market trends, and social changes.
- **Scenario preparation**: Various scenarios for the future can be prepared by considering different conditions. The number of scenarios is generally considered to be three: good, bad, and average scenario [22].
- **Technology roadmap**: A technology roadmap is part of the strategic plan to acquire future technologies.
- **Environmental scanning**: It is the study to capture and evaluate signals of possible advanced technologies and trends in the future.
- **Technology monitoring**: Technology monitoring involves systematically monitoring and analyzing technological developments in certain areas.
- **Horizon scanning**: These are studies aimed at the early detection of signals of future advanced technologies.

- **Big data**: Analyzing technology trends by examining big data.
- **Wild cards**: It is a technique to detect events that are not likely to happen but will negatively affect technological development using this method.

These techniques are not mutually exclusive and can be combined to increase the accuracy and depth of technology foresight efforts. They provide a structured and systematic approach to predicting future technological developments and informing decision-making processes. When comparing these techniques, it may not be correct to say that one is better than the other. The scope of the foresight study determines which technique will be used. Often, multiple methods are employed in parallel, as comparing the results of one method with others increases the depth of the study and provides more systematic input to the strategic approach to shaping the future. For example, a continuation of the Delphi and expert panel methods. Foresight studies on healthcare can have various dimensions: national, regional, local, or for a business. Foresight studies on health services can also encompass multiple dimensions: international (such as the European Union), national, regional, local, or for a business. Therefore, the first step is to decide on the subject and the study size. Then, the issue of choosing a method becomes one of the most critical considerations. After selecting the method, the other steps are applied as described in the chapter. Foresight research in healthcare is a current issue. It is understood that the establishment of a healthy society is one of the goals of countries. Health policy foresight studies should be carried out continuously for at least 20–30 years. National and local governments should establish separate units consisting of experts on the subject.

REFERENCES

1. Rees, A., & Morus, IR. (2019). Presenting futures past: science fiction and the history of science. *Osiris*, 34(1): 1–5.
2. Cainelli, A., & Janissek-Muniz, R., (2022). The roles of foresight in leveraging the innovativeness of organisations. *International Journal of Innovation Management*, 26(7).
3. Dalkey, N., & Helmer, O. (1963). An experimental application of the Delphi Technique to the use of experts. *Management Science*, 9(3), 458–467.
4. Georghiou, L., & Keenan, M. (2006). Evaluation of the 2002 foresight programme. *Technological Forecasting and Social Change*, 73(7), 737–755.
5. Glenn, J. C., & Gordon, T. J. (Eds.). (2009). *Futures Research Methodology*. The Millennium Project.
6. Hines, A., & Bishop, P. (Eds.). (2013). *Thinking about the Future: Guidelines for strategic foresight* (2nd ed.). Social Technologies.
7. Hsu, C. C., & Sandford, B. A. (2007). The Delphi technique: Making sense of consensus. *Practical Assessment, Research & Evaluation*, 12(10), 1–8.
8. Keenan, M., & Miles, I. (2001). Foresight in a network era. *Technological Forecasting and Social Change*, 68(2), 105–120.
9. Keenan, M., & Owens, S. (2017). Mobilizing collective intelligence for societal issues: New governance models. *Foresight*, 19(3), 274–294.
10. Linstone, H. A., & Turoff, M. (Eds.). (2002). *The Delphi Technique: Techniques and Applications*. Addison-Wesley.

11. Marinkovic, M., Al-Tabbaa, O., & Wu, J. (2022), Corporate foresight: A systematic literature review and future research trajectories. *Journal of Business Research, 144,* 289–311.
12. Marshall., H., Wilkins, K., & Bennett, L. (2023) Story thinking for technology foresight, *Futures,* 146, 103098
13. Martin, B. R. (2010). The origins of the concept of foresight in science and technology: An insider's perspective. *Technological Forecasting and Social Change, 77*(9), 1438–1447.
14. May, D., Delgado, J., & Denburg, A. (2016). Foresight in health: A systems approach to addressing complex problems. *Applied Systems Thinking Journal, 1*(1), 1–16.
15. Okoli, C., & Pawlowski, S. D. (2004). The Delphi technique as a research tool: An example, design considerations, and applications. *Information & Management, 42*(1), 15–29.
16. Roco, M. C., & Bainbridge, W. S. (Eds.). (2013). *Converging Technologies for Improving Human Performance*: *Nanotechnology, Biotechnology, Information Technology, and Cognitive Science.* Springer.
17. Rosenkötter, N., & Achterberg, P. (2018). Assessing potential futures: Experts, scenarios, and uncertainty in Germany's health sector. *Technological Forecasting and Social Change, 128,* 22–30.
18. Rowe, G., & Wright, G. (1999). The Delphi technique as a forecasting tool: Issues and analysis. *International Journal of Forecasting, 15*(4), 353–375.
19. Schuurman, D., Bakker, S., Bekkers, V., & Putters, K. (2018). The use of expert panels in foresight studies: Lessons from Dutch technology assessment. *Technological Forecasting and Social Change, 128,* 40–51.
20. Van Eeten, M. J., Van De Walle, B., & Van Den Hoven, J. (2004). Foresight in regulation and governance: Lessons from keeping up with ICT developments. *Technological Forecasting and Social Change, 71*(9), 875–887.
21. Vasseur, V., & Collins, B. (2016). Stakeholder-driven scenario planning for participatory foresight. *Technological Forecasting and Social Change, 111,* 74–85.
22. Weber, M., Vannoni, M., & Guarnera, U. (2014). A Delphi-based scenario analysis for the future of renewable energy in Europe. *Technological Forecasting and Social Change, 89,* 201–216.

3 Integration of Explainable Artificial Intelligence with IoT and Blockchain Technology in Industry 5.0

Meghna Chaudhary, M. Afshar Alam,
and Sherin Zafar

3.1 INTRODUCTION: BACKGROUND, OBJECTIVES AND SCOPE

Recently, the rise of the internet and the World Wide Web has experienced enormous expansion within a broad array of industries, including correlated cities, medical care, and automation in manufacturing, among others. Internet of Things (IoT) networks are expanding rapidly, incorporating a variety of gadgets that provide simple and approachable services online. The widespread use of IoT technology has made protection for connected objects a top priority, particularly given the dearth of inherent security methods as connected devices have limited functionality. As a result, several research groups are focused on enhancing IoT network security. A scalable, decentralized, and adaptable defense mechanism is required for IoT networks. Although the field of development offers cutting-edge security solutions that combine artificial intelligence (AI) and blockchain technology, there isn't a systematic, all-encompassing research discussing how AI and blockchain are combining to safeguard IoT networks. The review and comparison of current chapters that have been put out for identifying cybersecurity assaults in IoT contexts are the main topics of this chapter. To emphasize the limitations of findings as well as the potential for future paths, this study addresses three research concerns—to broaden the body of knowledge for improving IoT security, promote further research, and offer research paths. IoT, an up-and-coming technology, automates corporate and academic procedures in the form of straightforward operations.

The three main technologies advancing the next phase of the digital revolution are blockchain, IoT, and XAI. We contend that new business models will be made possible by the convergence of these technologies. In the future, autonomous agents—that is, sensors, vehicles, machinery, trucks, cameras, and other IoT devices—will function as independent profit centers that can (a) use IoT to create a digital twin; (b) send and receive money independently using blockchain technology; and (c) independently

DOI: 10.1201/9781032632223-3

make decisions as independent economic agents using AI and data analytics. We further contend that this convergence will propel the creation of these independent business models and, in turn, the industrial firms' digital transformation.

These days, blockchain, the IoTs, and XAI are acknowledged as having the power to upend whole sectors, enhance existing business processes, and develop new business models. For instance, by offering a shared and decentralized distributed ledger, blockchain can improve corporate processes' trust, transparency, security, and privacy. Similar to a register, a blockchain, or more generally a distributed ledger, can store a variety of assets, with data mostly pertaining to identities and finances. The automation of industries and the ease of use of business processes are being fueled by IoT and are critical to the European and German industrial sectors [1]. Finally, by identifying patterns and maximizing the results of various business processes, AI enhances processes.

Throughout the previous period, IoT applications have become more common in every aspect of life. IoT networks may link billions of objects worldwide at any time and from any location through either wireless or wired connections [2]. The number of components, retention, control, as well as functions of linked items vary from one another [3]. Personal computers, laptops, cell phones, smartphones, handheld devices, as well as various types of portable embedded devices can be part of the IoT network. Each of these sorts has a built-in sensor that gathers information about the area around it. The data that has been gathered can be used by the IoT to make wise choices [3].

IoT networks generate huge data with improved higher precision, performance, reliability, as well as variety compared to conventional networks, which produce much less data overall. IoT systems must thus be able to collect and analyze vast amounts of information having a specific purpose to accomplish several goals across many domains [4,5].

3.1.1 Objectives

Considering the nature of IoT, the following ambitious goals might be stated:

Connected description: The IoT links information from many sources to provide the community with low-cost self-services. Big data collection from many sources includes a variety of users and methods. Developing an IoT connection will therefore be challenging. Linked data has the power to detect fraud, which can increase customer trust. However, a lack of qualified workers, a lack of educational institutions, and structural problems are the biggest hazards associated with connected data.

Big feature: Big data analytics are critical to improving information communication since IoT networks produce a significant amount of data. The IoT may enhance the planning process and responses to unforeseen occurrences that boost industry performance. The IoT network is also utilized for monitoring tasks like checking the condition of industrial assets. In contrast, the primary privacy risk is a data breach.

Openness feature: IoT data may be made available for public usage. In order to provide transparency of corporate operations, the connected devices

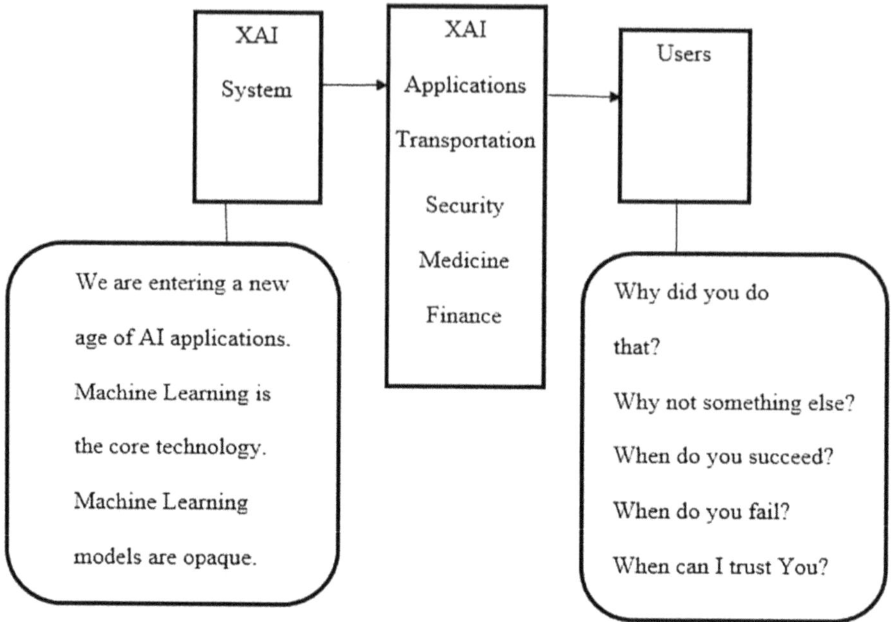

FIGURE 3.1 XAI model.

generate information accessible to the people. IoT enables other devices to use the network's open data by gaining access to it. Additionally, IoT enhances information accessibility to provide hands-on assistance customers.

3.1.2 SCOPE

The Industry 5.0 version provides great advantages to people. Additionally, firm has become more dynamic, which aids in luring top people [6]. Future visions of AI are personified by human robotics like Sophia [7]. This helps in manual judgments through technological advances to revolutionize a variety of industries (Figure 3.1).

3.2 EXPLAINABLE ARTIFICIAL INTELLIGENCE: OVERVIEW OF XAI, ITS ROLE IN VARIOUS SYSTEMS AND ITS BENEFITS AND CHALLENGES

Machine learning (ML) algorithms' output and results can be recognized and considered by users. A firm can opt for an accountable method for developing AI using ML and XAI [6].

3.2.1 OVERVIEW OF XAI

Users may find it difficult to understand all the phases of an algorithm. The complete mathematical steps are often reduced to a "black box" that is unintelligible and is sometimes referred to as such. A lot of information is required to create such models.

3.2.2　Role of XAI in Various Systems

The invention of ML innovations enabling the identification of various medical disorders and the creation of clinical decision support systems has shown outstanding progress during the past ten years. Particularly, the development of the new multidisciplinary subject of computational neuroscience has been made possible by the accessibility of enormous datasets and the rising complexity of hardware and software systems [8].

Due to their greater accuracy and efficiency, the use of deep learning frameworks has been adopted by scientific communities more frequently. Different kinds of methods for deep learning are used to create deep-layer artificial neural networks. Since they can be applied even when there are non-trivial correlations between the elements of a prediction job and their characteristics and the results, these models have demonstrated their usefulness in a variety of applications.

3.2.3　Benefits and Challenges of XAI

In the financial sector, the use of ML and AI solutions continues to have significant consequences due to their unmatched capacity to handle millions or even billions of transactions in a matter of seconds. However, given the enormous quantity of information analyzed, there are certain drawbacks, especially when making decisions for challenging jobs.

AI's capacity to explain things is reasonable, important, and exciting. However, XAI provides in-depth insights much beyond what conventional linear models could. Despite the advantages, XAI offers a unique set of difficulties.

The difficulties with XAI and how to overcome them are explained below:

Bias: Preventing the AI system from adopting biased or unbiased worldviews based on the discrepancies between the initial learning statistics, framework, and goal function, is a challenging issue.

Fairness: XAI faces difficulty in determining whether an AI system's judgment is fair as people's perceptions of fairness vary depending on context and the data used to train the ML Systems. Many ML algorithms are difficult to interpret, making it challenging for specialists to comprehend a logical justification for the algorithm's choices. Legal, moral, and practical difficulties may arise when using black-box tactics to reach illogical judgments.

Safety: Without considering the steps taken to arrive at a decision, it is challenging to determine whether AI is trustworthy. The statistical learning theory's generalization, which essentially demonstrates how organizations fill in the gaps in unobserved knowledge, makes this a difficulty.

3.3　INTERNET OF THINGS (IoT)

In this context, the term "interconnectedness" refers to the connection and connectivity-enabled communication of physical items, such as appliances and automobiles, that are connected to one another as well as transmit information (Figure 3.2).

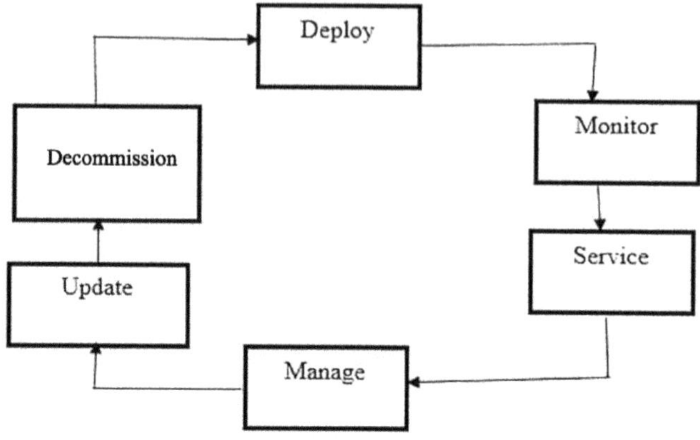

FIGURE 3.2   Lifecycle of IoT device.

This technique helps in gathering and sharing enormous information from the connected devices.

3.3.1   UNDERSTANDING IoT

The network of tangible objects, including firmware, hardware, intangible objects, and various types of capabilities, that share information among linked devices using the internet connection is generally termed the Internet of Things (Figure 3.3). Less expensive computers, massive schemas, cloud computing, statistical testing, and handheld devices help in distributing information by tangible objects with minimal

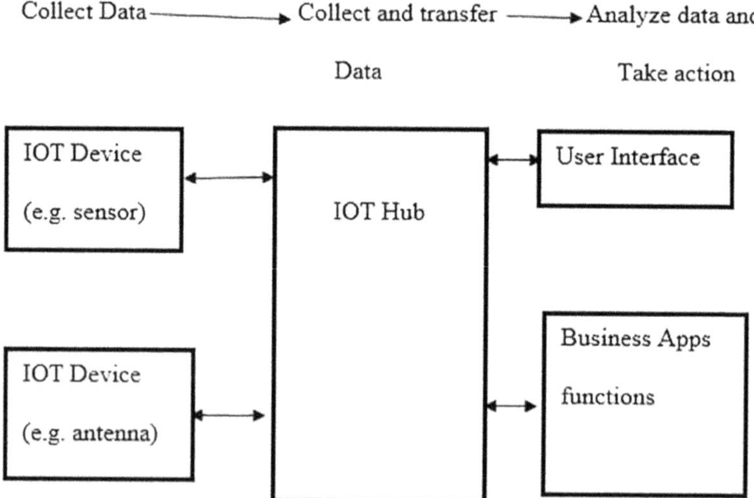

FIGURE 3.3   Example of an IoT device.

human interaction. Electronic devices can capture, observe, and modify every activity among connected devices [9].

3.3.2 ROLE OF AI IN IoT

IoT signals and analyzes real-world events to deliver appropriate answers. In this approach, AI is crucial to the IoTs and is present in any IoT application that uses software to respond to trigger events. The question of how extensively AI may be used should be asked by IoT users and developers, rather than whether AI should be used. That will depend on the complexity and variety of the real-world devices that IoT enables. Applying inferential AI techniques, algorithms for learning, and the use of adaptive AI require a supply of data and a set of rules. Feedback looping devices related to the internet are frequently handled using nothing more than ML for the simple reason that the time required to run more evaluations falls beyond the bounds of appropriate response speeds.

AI technologies that are quite simple help improve control loops. For example, if a truck carrying products arrives at a warehouse, rudimentary AI might provide a way to enable its operator to retrieve an identification number to navigate a security fence. By doing this, the expense of employing someone to visit the gate would be removed. Additionally, an embedded barcode or Radio Frequency Identification card (uses radio waves to identify people or objects) inside the vehicle may be scanned to grant access without the need for a code [10].

3.3.3 TRUSTWORTHINESS OF IoT SYSTEMS

The realization that neither reliability features can be successfully attained as a standalone technology, nor the system's trustworthiness can be realized by simply merging such technologies, is the first barrier to employing trustworthiness in an industry IoT system.

A simple combination of trustworthiness traits may not result in a really trustworthy system, as these qualities may either support or contradict one another. The solution is to shift the framework beyond the traits that make something trustworthy and toward techniques that are allocated to certain system components. Such techniques were widely employed in conventional systems but were not categorized according to the reliability criterion. Further characteristics can be added to this categorization.

Definition: A component, tool, technology, software program, operational method, or management directive is referred to as a "Trustworthiness Method" if it is linked with a minimum of one dependability trait.

3.3.4 OPPORTUNITIES AND CONSIDERATIONS IN IoT SYSTEMS

IoT will expand significantly in the upcoming years in a variety of ways, including:

> **Cloud computing and IoT**: Since cloud computing makes enabling IoT "Data Blending" less difficult, over 90% of the entire IoTs information will eventually be contained on service provider platforms within the next 5 years.

Security and IoT: 90% of all IT networks will experience connected device hacking attacks within two years, even though many of these incidents will be viewed as "inconveniences". The adoption of new IoT rules will be required of "Chief Information Security Officers (CISOs)".

Network capacity and IoT: Over three years, 50% of computing systems will shift from being able to manage more IoT devices than they can handle to becoming network-restricted, with roughly 10% of sites being overloaded. Through pervasive networking on the internet, IoT is transforming human existence by enhancing connection and functionality to the farthest degree. The real-life environment and the digital one will be combined to produce a more personalized and often predictive linked experience. Despite all its potential and promises, the IoTs still has three significant problems to address: uniform device standards, privacy, and security. IoT advancement would be hampered by legal disputes and societal opposition if good security at all IoT nodes and data protection are not taken into consideration.

3.4 BLOCKCHAIN TECHNOLOGY

A publicly accessible database that employs blockchain technology is safe, open, and unchangeable. The creation of a tamper-proof, decentralized database using this technique can completely change the way we interact with the internet.

3.4.1 INTRODUCTION TO BLOCKCHAIN

Over a distributed ledger such as blockchain, any information can be stored and shared, improving efficiency for all users [3]. Information plays an important role in business. It should be provided quickly and accurately. Blockchain technology is considered to be the best for providing such information (Figure 3.4). Since everybody can access a similar representation of the fact, we are able to view all functions related to the transaction from start to finish.

3.4.2 BLOCKCHAIN FOR VARIOUS DATA BASE MANAGEMENT SYSTEMS

Blockchain is an open record of operations that have occurred over a distributed network, serving as a distributed database of records. Imagine that Henry, George, Jim, and Smith, four business partners, are launching a network of stores. Each of them owns one store, totaling four establishments. The partners choose to keep track of each store's earnings and sales in a database (like MySQL, for example) (Figure 3.5).

The database is susceptible to a variety of possible errors, including but not restricted to the specific ones listed below:

- A malevolent actor might compromise the database.
- Because the database is centralized, a failure or crash would affect every record.
- A malevolent or negligent person might change database records.

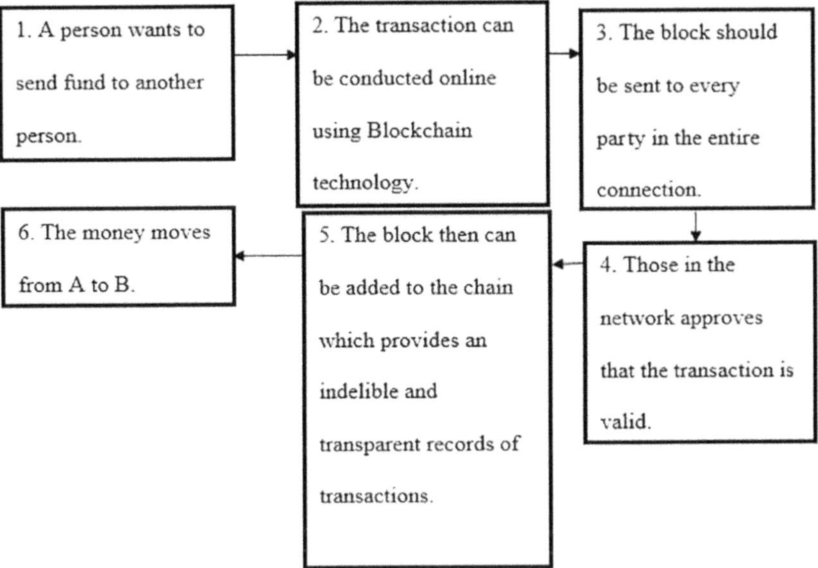

FIGURE 3.4   Working of blockchain technology.

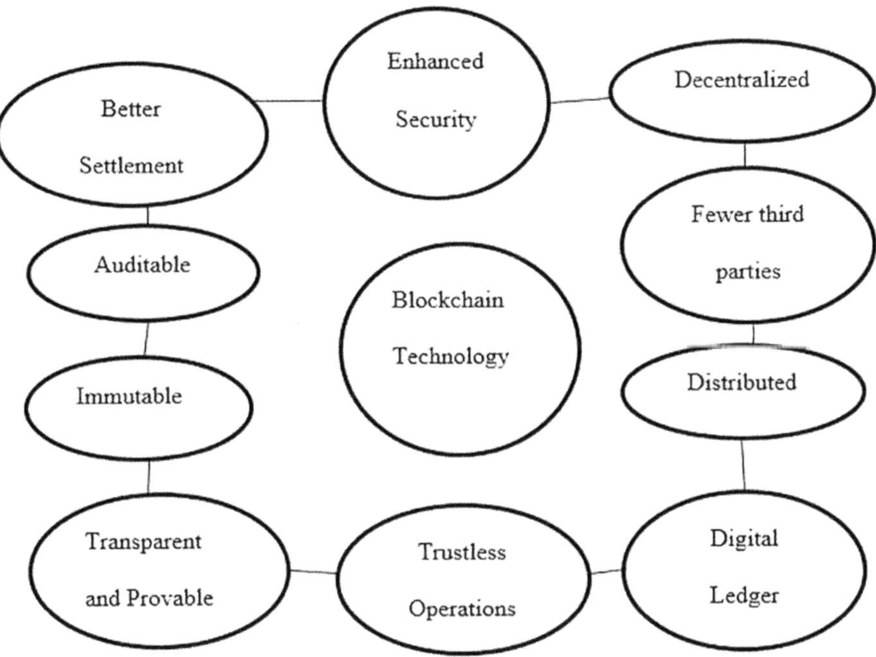

FIGURE 3.5   Blockchain technology features.

- Records might be added to the database by an authorized person without confirming their validity.
- Data entered by one partner may be mistakenly changed or removed by another partner.

3.5 THE ROLE OF ARTIFICIAL INTELLIGENCE, IoT AND BLOCKCHAIN TECHNOLOGY IN INDUSTRY 5.0

The next phase related to the digital transformation is being driven by important technologies including blockchain technology (Figure 3.6) and ML. We contend that convergence related to these technologies will give rise to fresh business strategies: Future autonomous profit centers will be self-learning entities (such as detectors, vehicles, devices, automobiles, recording devices, and several connected gadgets) that have a digital twin using IoT, independently send and receive money using blockchain technology, and independently make decisions using AI [11].

Every day, technological advancements are making life smarter and more comfortable. Examples of our rapidly changing way of life include Smart Society 5.0,

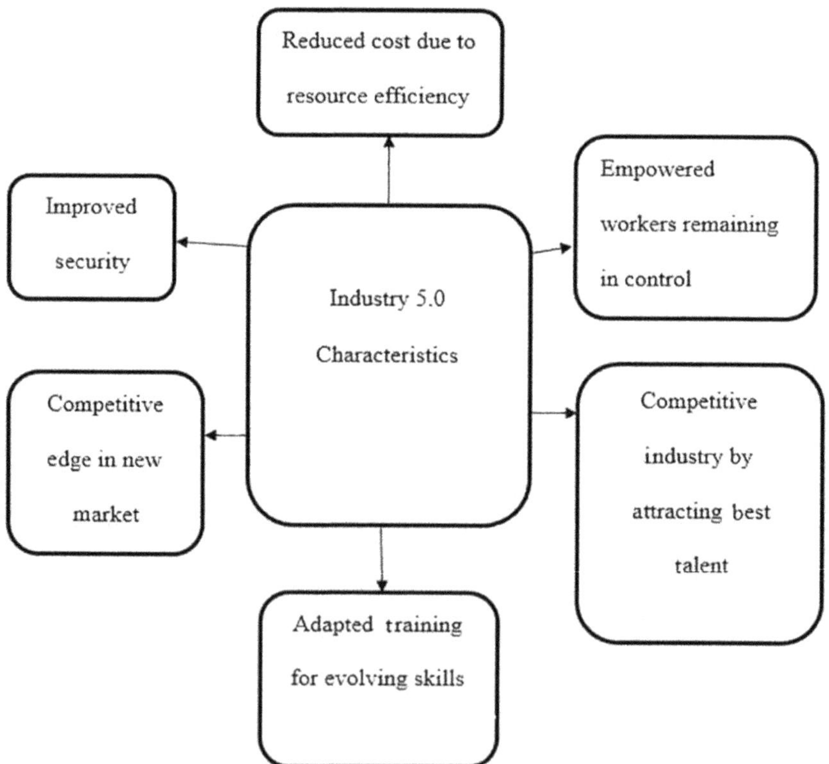

FIGURE 3.6   Industry 5.0 is a solution provider for the people.

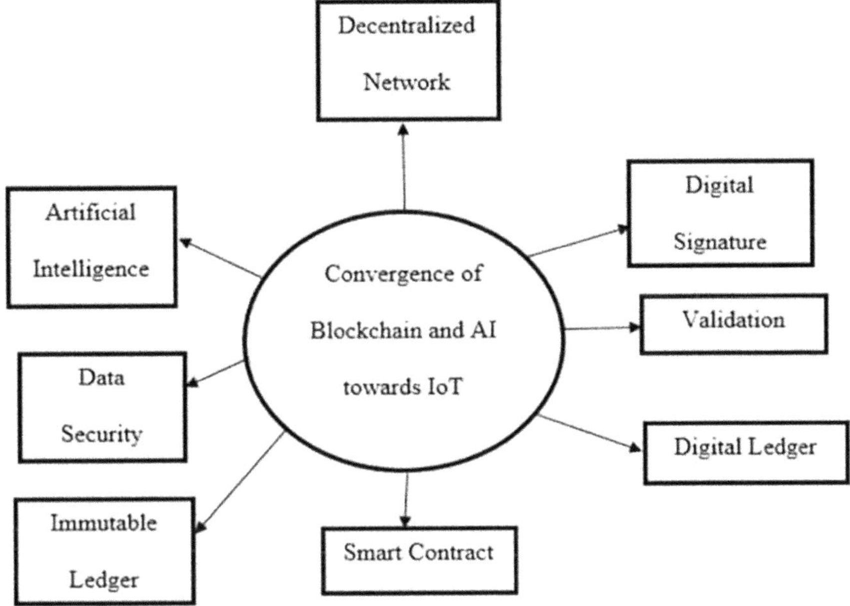

FIGURE 3.7 Convergence of blockchain and AI toward IoT.

Healthcare 5.0, and Agriculture 5.0. With the aid of cutting-edge technologies like XAI, the Industrial Revolution 5.0 (IR 5.0) integrates future industrial growth trends to reach prosperity beyond work by infusing more intelligence into our daily lives (Figure 3.7).

The enabling technologies for Industry 5.0 are reviewed, along with certain relevant research topics that need more attention. To pinpoint the gaps in completely achieving the revolution, the shift in manufacturing processes from mass production to mass customization, as well as the expected reliance on digital twins and Cyber-Physical Systems (CPS), are visualized in several research studies (Figure 3.8).

Combots is a multiplayer robot shooter set in fully procedurally generated maps with the physical environment. With features such as message editing, pinning, and deletion, Combot makes it easier for group administrators to manage their chats. Additionally, Combot includes community statistics and automatic moderation, making it a valuable tool for any networking group.

A collaborative robot, also known as a cobot, is an industrial robot that can safely operate alongside humans in a shared workspace. It includes the latest technology in robotics that has revolutionized the world of automation. Collaborative robots are equipped with various sensors, which makes them "sensitive robots", as it were. Therefore, they are extremely suitable for working with these kinds of products. Cobots can thus be used to automate a testing process or quality control.

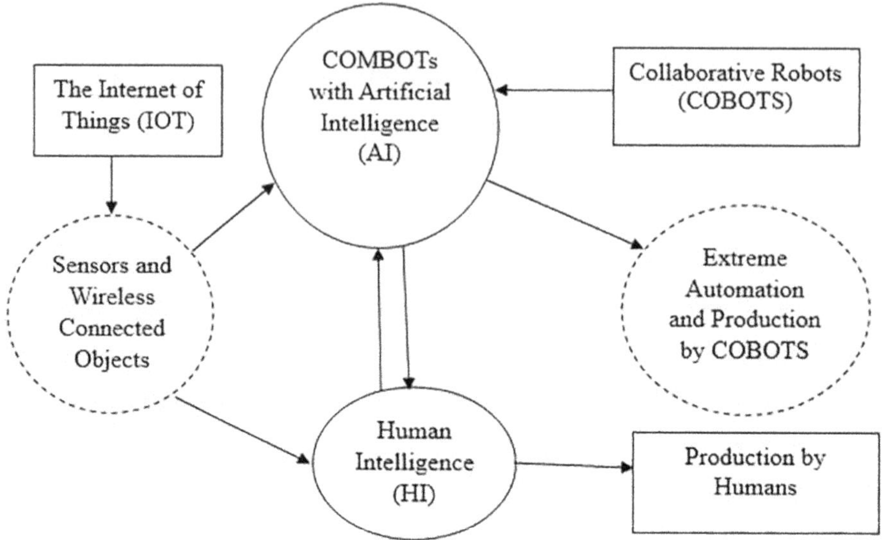

FIGURE 3.8   The emergence of Industry 5.0: using AI, the IoT, XAI, and extreme automation supporting big data analytics.

3.5.1 Integration of Technologies

Three concepts serve as the foundation for Industry 5.0.

1. **Focusing on people**: As part of Industry 5.0, a plan is in place to transform people from being viewed as resources to real assets. In practice, this implies that organizations will now serve individuals rather than the other way around. Therefore, the Industry's 5.0 edition reorients toward providing added value for workers to attract and retain the best personnel rather than only using talent to build a competitive edge and value for consumers.
2. **Endurance**: We have witnessed the sweeping effects of global issues like the COVID-19 outbreak and worldwide supply shortages as the globe has grown more interconnected over time. While many firms aim to increase productivity and maximize revenues, these elements do not necessarily enhance resilience. In contrast, some believe that emphasis on responsiveness and adaptability might actually reduce a company's resilience rather than increase it [12]. More resilient organizations would attempt to foresee and respond to any crises to maintain stability during trying times, rather than focusing on expansion, profit, and efficiency.
3. **Sector of sustainability**: By actively pursuing measures to bring about change, sustainability in Version 5.0 goes beyond merely minimizing or alleviating climate impact. This objective, often known as "Net Positive", strives to improve the planet by having businesses contribute to the issue rather than just being lip-service providers of sustainability initiatives [13].

3.5.2 Challenges and Opportunities in Industry 5.0

Issues (challenges) in Industry 5.0:

- Because of the automated industrial techniques, learning expertise is a massive effort that includes preparing the workforce for adopting cutting-edge technology and causing behavioral change to interact.
- Automation using collaborative robotics poses a significant risk to shop floor employees in addition to human coworkers [14].

Opportunities of Industry 5.0:

- Highly automated manufacturing processes provide clients with more customization options.
- It permits greater customization of individual items and freedom of design [15,16].

3.6 CONCLUSION AND FUTURE IMPLICATIONS

In this chapter, cutting-edge methods for protecting the IoT by fusing blockchain technology are systematically reviewed. The focus is on the architecture of the IoT, its security needs, difficulties, weaknesses, and cybersecurity threats. We also emphasize the types of blockchain and their properties. The findings demonstrate that combining AI with the IoT blockchain technique is a viable strategy that might produce new and potent technologies, improving IoT security in various ways and opening up new avenues for digitalization. Blockchain and AI complement each other and help overcome obstacles. A decentralized as well as disseminated technique framework, securely encrypted operations, safe data exchange, and an immutable IoT can all be created by integrating these technologies. As a result, it may trigger the next revolution in manufacturing and other fields. The Industry 5.0 version shows that both machines and human beings have collaborated in increasing the efficiency of industrial functions. The manufacturing industry is advancing rapidly, and company efficiency is rising, thanks to the development of intelligent systems and computational intelligence solutions [9]. The employees must properly engage with the machines and operators for businesses to implement Industry 5.0. Making judgments based on complex circumstances is the foundation of the corporate organization's function.

IoT technologies are all around us; they enable all the networked gadgets we use, such as virtual assistants and wearable technology. Therefore, Industrial Internet of Things (IIoT) is the application of the digital interconnectivity on which we have come to rely for large-scale manufacturing activities, where the risks are higher but the rewards are bigger. The technical definition of IIoT is "the application of interactive devices such as actuators and sensor technology for improving production and commercial processes." IIoT may be seen as a more human-centered approach to production as the manufacturing sector moves from the automated features and linked systems of Sector 4.0 to the improved personalization and computing capabilities in Industry 5.0's edition. The capacity of controllers to obtain superior choices for making better decisions, driven by big data insights obtained by IIoT solutions, is this strategy, also known as smart manufacturing.

REFERENCES

1. Aldhaheri, S., Alghazzawi, D., Cheng, L., Barnawi, A., Alzahrani, B.A. (2020). Artificial Immune Systems approaches to secure the internet of things: A systematic review of the literature and recommendations for future research. *J. Netw. Comput. Appl.*, 157, 102537.
2. Singh, S., Sharma, P.K., Yoon, B., Shojafar, M., Cho, G.H., Ra, I.H. (2020). Convergence of blockchain and artificial intelligence in IoT network for the sustainable smart city. *Sustain. Cities Soc.*, 63, 102364.
3. Atlam, H.F., Walters, R.J., Wills, G.B. (2018). Intelligence of things: Opportunities & challenges. In: *Proceedings of the 2018 3rd Cloudification of the Internet of Things (CIoT)*, Paris, France, 1–6.
4. Saxena, S., Bhushan, B., Ahad, M.A. (2021). Blockchain based solutions to secure IoT: Background, integration trends and a way forward. *J. Netw. Comput. Appl.*, 181, 103050.
5. Vishwakarma, R., Jain, A.K. (2020). A survey of DDoS attacking techniques and defence mechanisms in the IoT network. *Telecommun. Syst.*, 73, 3–25.
6. Liu, Y., Yu, F.R., Li, X., Ji, H., Leung, V.C. (2020). Blockchain and machine learning for communications and networking systems. *IEEE Commun. Surv. Tutor*, 22, 1392–1431.
7. Singh, S.K., Rathore, S., Park, J.H. (2020). Blockiotintelligence: A blockchain-enabled intelligent IoT architecture with artificial intelligence. *Future Gener. Comput. Syst.*, 110, 721–743.
8. Han, X., Zhang, R., Liu, X., Jiang, F. (2020). Biologically inspired smart contract: A blockchain-based DDoS detection system. In: *Proceedings of the 2020 IEEE International Conference on Networking, Sensing and Control (ICNSC)*, pp. 1–6.
9. Shen, M., Tang, X., Zhu, L., Du, X., Guizani, M. (2019). Privacy-preserving support vector machine training over blockchain-based encrypted IoT data in smart cities. *IEEE Internet Things J.*, 6, 7702–7712.
10. Qian, Y., Jiang, Y., Chen, J., Zhang, Y., Song, J., Zhou, M., Pustišek, M. (2018). Towards decentralized IoT security enhancement: A blockchain approach. *Comput. Electr. Eng.*, 72, 266–273.
11. Ahanger, T.A. (2018). Defense scheme to protect IoT from cyber-attacks using AI principles. *Int. J. Comput. Commun. Control*, 13, 915–926.
12. Ozyilmaz, K.R., Yurdakul, A. (2019). Designing a blockchain-based IoT with Ethereum, swarm, and LoRa: The software solution to create high availability with minimal security risks. *IEEE Consum. Electron. Mag.*, 8, 28–34.
13. Gupta, U., Javed, Z., Zafar, S. (2022) An analysis of blockchain-based IoT solutions to overcome current challenges. In: *Proceedings of the 4th International Conference on Information Management & Machine Intelligence*, Jaipur, India, 37.
14. Deebak, B.D., Fadi, A.T. (2021). Privacy-preserving in smart contracts using blockchain and artificial intelligence for cyber risk measurements. *J. Inf. Secur. Appl.*, 58, 102749.
15. Siddiqui, F., Tariq, A., Zafar, S. (2023) Performance evaluation of ensemble methods for predictive analysis: An experiment for smart cities, *AIP Conference Proceedings*, 2938(1), 020007.
16. Irfan, N., Zafar, S. (2023) A self diagnosis medical chatbot using Sklearn lecture notes in networks and systems. In *Proceedings of Fourth Doctoral Symposium on Computational Intelligence Lecture Notes in Networks and Systems*, pp. 197–208.

4 Use of Artificial Intelligence in Health Services

An Overview of Medical Education

Selin Göçen and Gülsün Kurubacak Cakir

4.1 INTRODUCTION

The use of technology in health services covers different purposes, such as facilitating educational goals and basic knowledge acquisition, improving decision-making, increasing perceptual diversity, ensuring the development of skills and competencies, and enabling practice in critical situations [1]. Different technologies such as simulation, virtual reality, augmented reality, and artificial intelligence (AI) are used in health services, directly affected by technological developments. However, it can be stated that AI technology has become prevalent in recent years. AI in healthcare services was first used as a medical diagnosis decision support system in the surgical field in 1976 by Gunn during the investigation of the possibility of diagnosing acute abdominal pain through computer analysis [2]. Today, it is known that it is used in various fields such as early diagnosis, accurate diagnosis, clinical decision-making, protecting and maintaining health, eliminating errors in health systems, and improving the effectiveness, efficiency, accuracy, and outcome of clinical practice [3]. However, despite its benefits, it is noted that AI cannot be utilized sufficiently due to existing policies and ethical rules [4].

Considering the developments in AI technology, professionals working in health services and learners who will be the health professionals of the future will encounter many new and different applications [5,6]. Since it is foreseen that current learners in the field of healthcare will use various AI techniques in clinical practice when they start their careers after completing their studies and education [7], it can be said that it will be useful to have sufficient knowledge and experience before graduation. In this book chapter, AI applications in the field of health services, AI ethics, and training of health professionals are included. However, since health services are very comprehensive, the chapter focuses especially on medical fields and medical education.

DOI: 10.1201/9781032632223-4

4.2   ARTIFICIAL INTELLIGENCE IN HEALTH SYSTEMS AND MEDICINE

The use of AI in the field of medicine can be divided into two different groups: virtual and physical aspects. The physical aspect consists of robotic surgery and wearable technologies, while the virtual aspect consists of electronic health records and artificial neural network-based decision support systems (diagnosis, treatment, and monitoring) for the treatment of diseases [8,9]. AI technologies improve the delivery of healthcare services in various ways, such as providing personalized health information, virtual consultation, remote monitoring, and providing recommendations based on historical data. The ability of AI to provide personalized health information is important for professionals as well as patients because this system helps patients better understand their health and make informed decisions about their care. It also assists healthcare professionals in monitoring their patients remotely and intervening early when necessary [10]. In this respect, the integration of AI into health services and different medical fields is important for patients in disadvantaged positions who cannot go to or access any health institution [11].

In medicine, AI is frequently used across different specialties. In the field of radiology, applications such as Imagen, CureMatrix, Icometrix, ZebraMed, Vuno, Optellum, HeartFlow, LiverMultiScan, Cleerly Labs, which contribute to improvement in imaging, diagnosis, and treatment planning, are used [9,12–14]. In surgical operation processes, different applications such as AlexNet, HoloLens, i-Knife, Da-Vinci, Gestonurse, ResNet-50, and Darknet-19 are utilized [9,14]. These sample applications contribute to the smooth execution of surgical operation processes by reducing the rate of overlooking or incorrect decision-making in the identification and diagnosis of abnormalities with the information processing capability of AI and increasing the speed of diagnosis verification.

In the field of cardiology, AI (Apple Watch, AliveCor, etc.) is used for personalized diagnosis, treatment, and monitoring in various ways such as analyzing data obtained from wearable devices, image analysis with ECG, voice-natural language analysis from the patient's voice, clinical risk determination, creation of hospital records, and precision medicine applications [15]. In predicting disease risks such as heart failure, it has been found that AI-supported decision systems are more successful than traditional decision support systems, although it varies depending on the sample [16]. Similarly, in a sample application in the field of dermatology for cancer diagnosis and treatment process, it was concluded that the performance of decision systems based on deep neural networks and dermatologists were the same [17]. An AI-based algorithm called Paige.ai is also reported to save pathologists time by predicting cancer with a high degree of accuracy [18].

In endocrinology, one of the areas where AI is integrated, the sensor called Guardian, developed for the follow-up of patients with diabetes and capable of measuring glucose levels, is used. To improve the results obtained from the sensor, cooperation was made with the Sugar.IQ system developed by IBM Watson Health. It was stated that continuous blood glucose monitoring enables patients to optimize their blood glucose control [19]. To monitor the seizures of epilepsy patients, wearable and mobile application-compatible technology called Embrace is used. With this technology, epilepsy seizures of patients can be detected, and their doctors and relatives can be informed about the location of the patient [20,21]. In the field of psychiatry, methods and applications such as MindLAMP (predicting the meaning and recovery process of mental disorders), BiAffect (staging bipolar disorders), Paro (managing the treatment process of dementia patients), and Siri (interacting in autism spectrum disorder) are used [22]. The World Health Organization and global health systems also recommend the use of AI technologies for equity, quality, standardization, improvement, and efficiency in health [23]. In addition, according to a study conducted in China, it is stated that AI will soon master clinical knowledge and will be able to make real clinical diagnoses more accurate and consistent than real medical experts [24,25]. However, despite all its potential, AI has not yet gained enough traction. This situation is attributed to reasons such as the insufficiency of conducted studies, reliance on the physician-patient physical relationship in traditional medical sciences, and the fact that the algorithm-dependent decisions of AI, referred to as "black box", are not sufficiently understood by professionals [15]. Concerns about medical ethics can be considered among these reasons.

4.3 MEDICAL ETHICS AND ARTIFICIAL INTELLIGENCE

Medical ethics, which is related to the professional regulation of the actions of health professionals, consists of rules regulating medical actions and values specific to medicine [26]. It deals with the definition, examination, and solution proposals of value problems in medical applications. Medical ethics consists of four basic principles: benefiting, not harming, respecting autonomy, and justice [27]. Along with these principles, it also includes four secondary principles: honesty, respect for private life, reliability, and loyalty [28]. Ethical problems that are thought to arise with AI technology are a very comprehensive issue that should be emphasized. They may occur in issues such as preventing misuse of AI; making erroneous, biased, or biased decisions and recommendations; protecting the confidentiality and security of sensitive data; ensuring social trust; and protecting human dignity. Apart from these problems, ethical problems such as transparency problems due to the inability to provide sufficient information about the process caused by algorithms and problems related to informed consent, patient autonomy problems arising from the designed AI system, restriction of patient rights, problems that may occur due to algorithm error (malpractice), may also be encountered [4, 29,30].

Possible ethical problems increase the responsibility of physicians, health professionals, and designers. In this case, skills and expertise requirements of physicians and all health professionals will change [28]. Physicians and healthcare professionals need to be sufficiently knowledgeable to better understand the benefits, limitations, and ethical dilemmas presented by AI that is used or recommended for use and to participate in discussions [31]. Therefore, it would be useful to design pre-service and in-service medical education to include knowledge, skills, and competencies related to AI ethics.

4.4 ARTIFICIAL INTELLIGENCE IN MEDICAL EDUCATION

Health systems are transforming and becoming more complex with health needs and technological developments. Medical education should include competencies in the use of modern technology and simulations, the basics of data collection, analysis skills, and AI applications [23,32]. Health professionals need to gain important competencies required by health informatics tools used at different levels such as planning, management, prevention, diagnosis, treatment, and monitoring. In addition, they are expected to show competence in ethical and effective use and contribute to the use of health informatics tools as useful technology [7,33]. It is important for physician candidates to grow up in a learning environment that will increase their knowledge on the subject, understand possible negativities, be competent about current practices, and have knowledge that will form the basis for future practices [5]. In support of this view, physician candidates also state that AI learning is important for their careers [34]. However, it is stated that there are obstacles such as not giving the necessary priority to AI in curriculum change in medical education, a lack of sufficient mathematics and computer science background for medical students, and insufficient financing [35].

Many health sciences higher education institutions abroad have announced that AI should be integrated into all levels of healthcare professional education. To utilize the great potential of AI in global health and improve the infrastructure, it has been proposed to create an AI ecosystem including learning processes [36–38]. Currently, AI in medical education is seen in simulations with virtual patients that allow practice for the profession and in individualized learning environments that allow learners to work at their own pace [39]. Apart from these, it is also used in measurement and evaluation processes for knowledge, skill, and competence assessment [40]. It is important for doctors to know enough design principles to help in the design of AI systems or to have an idea; to receive an education where they can gain competence in data mining in clinical settings and learn how to interact with AI [41]. Continuous research and regulation are needed to ensure that the benefits of AI are maximized, and potential risks are minimized; changes in the education of future health professionals may be observed due to developments in AI [10]. It is essential that medical education includes basic topics related to AI such as using and managing AI-supported systems, AI ethics, analyzing and transferring results to the patient, processing and analyzing data, and using patient records [25]. Although there is no general curriculum example, it is observed that there are universities and institutions (University of Toronto, Harvard Medical School, University of Texas, Duke Institute for Health Innovation, University of Florida, Carie Illinois Medical College, Sharon Lund Institute for Medical Intelligence and Innovation, Stanford University Center for Artificial Intelligence in Medicine and Imaging, University of Virginia Center for Engineering in Medicine, University of Ulsan, and Yonsei University) with pilot AI curricula [42,43]. Existing courses and lectures include different topics such as big data in health, fundamentals of AI, data processing, and AI ethics. However, sufficient arrangements have not yet been made in educational programs and learning environments for physician candidates to gain competence in the working principles of AI-supported decision systems and algorithms and AI ethics in medicine.

It is thought that it would be more beneficial for data scientists, health professionals, educators, designers, and institutions to work together in the design of learning environments and training programs that physician candidates need to gain AI competence in the training process.

4.5   CONCLUSION

Both patients and healthcare professionals will benefit from the integration of AI into healthcare and medical science. However, more research is needed to maximize the benefits of AI and minimize potential risks. The limited competence of doctors and healthcare professionals in AI may also bring ethical problems that may be encountered. Because any error or bias that may occur in the data set used in algorithm-based decision systems may cause problems in diagnosis and treatment processes. In medical education, AI is mostly used in skill acquisition and measurement and evaluation processes. For doctor candidates to gain AI competence, learning environments and training programs need to be redesigned in cooperation with different experts. It would be beneficial for health institutions and organizations to start reviewing the training program of doctor candidates in line with the changes and transformations that health informatics in general and AI in particular may create.

REFERENCES

1. Guze, P. A. (2015). Using technology to meet the challenges of medical education. *Transactions of the American Clinical and Climatological Association*, 126, 260–270.
2. Çilhoroz, Y., & Işık, O. (2021). Yapay zekâ: Sağlık hizmetlerinden uygulamalar. *Ankara Hacı Bayram Veli Üniversitesi İktisadi ve İdari Bilimler Fakültesi Dergisi*, 23(2), 573–588. https://dergipark.org.tr/tr/pub/ahbvuibfd/issue/64683/905614
3. Reddy, S., Fox, J., & Purohit, M. P. (2019). Artificial intelligence-enabled healthcare delivery. *Journal of the Royal Society of Medicine*, 112(1), 22–28.
4. Güvercin, C. H. (2020). Tıpta yapay zekâ ve etik. In: Ekmekci PE (ed). *Yapay Zekâ ve Tıp Etiği*. 1st edn. Ankara: Türkiye Klinikleri, pp. 7–13.
5. Öcal, E. E., Atay, E., Önsüz, M. F., Algın, F., Çokyiğit, F. K., Kılınç, S., Köse, Ö. S., & Yiğit, F. N. (2020). Tıp fakültesi öğrenenlerinin tıpta yapay zekâ ile ilgili düşünceleri. *Türk Tıp Öğrencileri Araştırma Dergisi*, 2(1), 9–16.
6. Yılmaz, Y., Uzelli Yılmaz, D., Yıldırım, D., Akın Korhan, E., & Özer Kaya, D. (2021). Yapay zeka ve sağlıkta yapay zekanın kullanımına yönelik sağlık bilimleri fakültesi öğrenenlerinin görüşleri. *Süleyman Demirel Üniversitesi Sağlık Bilimleri Dergisi*, 12(3), 297–308.
7. Park, S. H., Do, K. H., Kim, S., Park, J. H., & Lim, Y. S. (2019). What should medical students know about artificial intelligence in medicine? *Journal of Educational Evaluation for Health Professions*, 16.
8. Amisha, P. M., Pathania, M., & Rathaur, V. K. (2019). Overview of artificial intelligence in medicine. *Journal of Family Medicine and Primary Care*, 8(7), 2328–2331.
9. Yılmaz, F., Mete, A. H., Fidan Türkön, B., & İnce, Ö. (2022). Sağlık hizmetlerinin geleceğinde metaverse ekosistemi ve teknolojileri: Uygulamalar, fırsatlar ve zorluklar. *Eurasian Journal of Health Technology Assessment*, 6(1), 12–34. https://doi.org/10.52148/ehta.1082705
10. Dave, M., & Patel, N. (2023). Artificial intelligence in healthcare and education. *British Dental Journal*, 234(10), 761–764. https://doi.org/10.1038/s41415-023-5845-2

11. Ahuja, A. S., Polascik, B. W., Doddapaneni, D., Byrnes, E. S., & Sridhar, J. (2023). The digital metaverse: Applications in artificial intelligence, medical education, and integrative health. *Integrative Medicine Research*, 12(1), 100917.
12. European Society of Radiology (ESR). (2019). What the radiologist should know about artificial intelligence: An ESR white paper. *Insights Imaging*, 10, 44. https://doi.org/10.1186/s13244-019-0738-2
13. Lobig, F., Subramanian, D., Blankenburg, M. et al. (2023). To pay or not to pay for artificial intelligence applications in radiology. *NPJ Digital Medicine*, 6, 117. https://doi.org/10.1038/s41746-023-00861-4
14. Zhou, L. Q., Wang, J. Y., Yu, S. Y., Wu, G. G., Wei, Q., Deng, Y. B., & Dietrich, C. F. (2019). Artificial intelligence in medical imaging of the liver. *World Journal of Gastroenterology*, 25(6), 672.
15. Kaya, C. (2022). Kardiyolojide yapay zeka uygulamaları. *Ankara Üniversitesi Tıp Fakültesi Mecmuası*, 75(1), 41–45. https://doi.org/10.4274/atfm.galenos.2022.36449
16. Briganti, G., & Le Moine, O. (2020). Artificial intelligence in medicine: Today and tomorrow. *Frontiers in Medicine*, 7, 27. https://doi.org/10.3389/fmed.2020.00027
17. Esteva, A., Kuprel, B., Novoa, R. A., Ko, J., Swetter, S. M., Blau, H. M., & Thrun, S. (2017). Dermatologist-level classification of skin cancer with deep neural networks. *Nature*, 542(7639), 115–118. https://doi.org/10.1038/nature21056
18. Campanella, G., Hanna, M. G., Geneslaw, L., Miraflor, A., Werneck Krauss Silva, V., Busam, K. J., ..., & Fuchs, T. J. (2019). Clinical-grade computational pathology using weakly supervised deep learning on whole slide images. *Nature Medicine*, 25(8), 1301–1309.
19. Lawton, J., Blackburn, M., Allen, J., Campbell, F., Elleri, D., Leelarathna, L., ..., & Hovorka, R. (2018). Patients' and caregivers' experiences of using continuous glucose monitoring to support diabetes self-management: Qualitative study. *BMC Endocrine Disorders*, 18(1), 1–10.
20. Bruno, E., Simblett, S., Lang, A., Biondi, A., Odoi, C., Schulze-Bonhage, A., ..., & RADAR-CNS Consortium. (2018). Wearable technology in epilepsy: The views of patients, caregivers, and healthcare professionals. *Epilepsy & Behavior*, 85, 141–149.
21. Regalia, G., Onorati, F., Lai, M., Caborni, C., & Picard, R. W. (2019). Multimodal wrist-worn devices for seizure detection and advancing research: Focus on the Empatica wristbands. *Epilepsy Research*, 153, 79–82.
22. Ediboğlu, G. O. (2023). Yapay zekanın insan zekasına psikoterapötik yaklaşımı. *Çukurova Tıp Öğrenci Dergisi*, 3(1), 12–18.
23. Orhan, M., & ve Bülez, A. (2022). Sağlık personellerinin yapay zekâ ile ilgili düşüncelerinin değerlendirilmesi. *Kesit Akademi Dergisi*, 8(33), 52–69.
24. Hoşgör, H., & Bozkurt, Ş. A. (2023). Sağlıkta yapay zekâ ve robotlar hakkında kimler ne düşünüyor? Kuşaklar üzerine bir araştırma. *Social Sciences Research Journal*, 12(1), 13–25.
25. McCoy, L. G., Nagaraj, S., Morgado, F., Harish, V., Das, S., & Celi, L. A. (2020). What do medical students actually need to know about artificial intelligence? *NPJ Digital Medicine*, 3(1), 86.
26. Yıldırım, G., & Kadıoğlu, S. (2007). Etik ve tıp etiği temel kavramları. *Cumhuriyet Üniversitesi Tıp Fakültesi Dergisi*, 29(2), 7–12.
27. Kırılmaz, H., & Ulusinan, E. (2021). Tıp Etiği Çerçevesinde Sezaryen. *Türkiye Biyoetik Dergisi*, 8(2), 114–125.
28. Güvercin, C. H. (2022). Yapay zekâ ve tıp etiği. In: Mülazımoğlu Durmuşoğlu L, Altıkardeş ZA (eds), *Tıpta ve Enfeksiyon Hastalıklarında Yapay Zekâ*, 1st edn. Ankara: Türkiye klinikleri, pp. 24–9.

29. Nuffield Council on Bioethics (2018). *Artificial intelligence (AI) in healthcare and research* (Briefing). https://healthcare.report/Resources/Whitepapers/31b40935-fca9-4018-b44b-1c08034d11c4_Artificial-Intelligence-AI-in-healthcare-and-research.pdf

30. Rigby, M. J. (2019). Ethical dimensions of using artificial intelligence in health care. *AMA Journal of Ethics*, 21(2), 121–124. https://doi.org/10.1001/amajethics.2019.121

31. Blease, C., Kharko, A., Bernstein, M., Bradley, C., Houston, M., Walsh, I., Hägglund, M., DesRoches, C., & Mandl, K. D. (2022). Machine learning in medical education: A survey of the experiences and opinions of medical students in Ireland. *BMJ Health & Care Informatics*, 29(1), e100480. https://doi.org/10.1136/bmjhci-2021-100480

32. Wartman, S. A., & Combs, C. D. (2018). Medical education must move from the information age to the age of artificial intelligence. *Journal of the Association of American Medical Colleges*, 93(8), 1107–1109. https://doi.org/10.1097/ACM.0000000000002044

33. Sezer, B., Onan, A., & Elçin, M. (2016). Sürekli tıp eğitiminde bilişim teknolojileri. *Türkiye Klinikleri Journal of Medical Educationl-Special Topics*, 1(3), 1–6.

34. Yun, D., Xiang, Y., Liu, Z., Lin, D., Zhao, L., Guo, C. et al. (2020). Attitudes towards medical artificial intelligence talent cultivation: An online survey study. *Annals of Translational Medicine*, 8, 11.

35. Krive, J., Isola, M., Chang, L., Patel, T., Anderson, M., & Sreedhar, R. (2023). Grounded in reality: Artificial intelligence in medical education. *JAMIA Open*, 6(2), ooad037. https://doi.org/10.1093/jamiaopen/ooad037

36. Topol, E. (2019). The topol review: Preparing the healthcare workforce to deliver the digital future. *National Health Service*. https://topol.hee.nhs.uk/wp-content/uploads/HEE-Topol-Review-2019.pdf

37. Fan, K. Y., Hu, R., & Singla, R. (2020). Introductory machine learning for medical students: A pilot. *Medical Education,* 54(11), 1042–3.

38. Reznick, R., Harris, K., Horsley, T., & Sheikh Hassani, M. (2020). *Task Force Report on Artificial Intelligence and Emerging Digital Technologies.* Royal College of Physicians and Surgeons of Canada. https://www.royalcollege.ca/content/dam/documents/about/health-policy/rc-ai-task-force-e.pdf

39. Han, E. R., Yeo, S., Kim, M. J., Lee, Y. H., Park, K. H., & Roh, H. (2019). Medical education trends for future physicians in the era of advanced technology and artificial intelligence: An integrative review. *BMC Medical Education*, 19(1), 1–15.

40. Chan, K. S., & Zary, N. (2019). Applications and challenges of implementing artificial intelligence in medical education: Integrative review. *JMIR Medical Education*, 5(1), e13930.

41. Masters, K. (2019). Artificial intelligence in medical education, *Medical Teacher*, 41(9), 976–980. https://doi.org/10.1080/0142159X.2019.1595557

42. Carin, L. (2020). On artificial intelligence and deep learning within medical education. *Academic Medicine*, 95(11S), S10–S11.

43. Lee, J., Wu, A. S., Li, D., & Kulasegaram, K. M. (2021). Artificial intelligence in undergraduate medical education: A scoping review. *Academic Medicine*, 96(11S), S62–S70.

5 Predictive Analytics and Early Intervention of Diseases Using Industry 5.0

Samia Khan, Farheen Siddiqui, and Mohd. Abdul Ahad

5.1 INTRODUCTION

Industry 5.0, commonly referred to as the Fifth Industrial Revolution, uses big data, ICT tools, smart sensors, artificial intelligence (AI), robotics, and other technologies to fulfill the individualized demands of clients [1]. Nowadays, mass customization is less popular than mass personalization. The Industrial Revolution has made it possible to cater to individual customer preferences. Millions of IoT sensors will be connected, sharing data across a 5G network to enable smart healthcare, according to Industry 5.0. Through the provision of individualized components like medical implants, artificial organs, body fluids, etc., Industry 5.0 makes mass personalization a reality. Healthcare is patient-centered and required medical procedures are handled with minimal doctor involvement. According to their needs, it provides its consumers with particular products. The Industrial Revolution put humans and machines together to work. This chapter is composed as follows: Section 5.1 discusses the introduction and background of Industry 5.0, Section 5.2 discusses the evolution and some important features of Industry 5.0, Section 5.3 deals with the substantial technologies of Industry 5.0, Section 5.4 offers a discussion about the early intervention of disease using Industry 5.0, Section 5.5 contrasts and compares the opportunities and challenges faced in Industry 5.0, and finally, Section 5.6 explores the future aspects of the research.

5.2 EVOLUTION AND IMPORTANT FEATURES OF INDUSTRY 5.0

The industry has evolved from Industry 1.0, which began in 1780, to Industry 5.0 at the present time, as shown in Figure 5.1. Since 1780, the industry has experienced tremendous growth, and it continues to expand rapidly. Industry 1.0, commonly referred to as the First Industrial Revolution, primarily focused on machines driven by steam and water. The electrification-based Second Industrial Revolution, often known as Industry 2.0, began around 1870 and contributed to mass production.

DOI: 10.1201/9781032632223-5

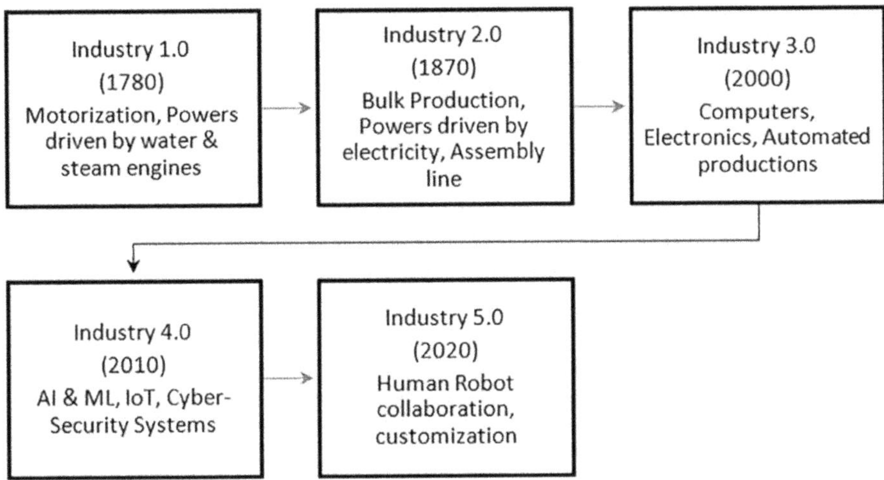

FIGURE 5.1 Evolution of Industry 1.0 to Industry 5.0.

Industry 3.0, influenced by technological advancements, emphasized the use of computers and electronics, facilitating globalization and the distribution of mass production around the globe. We are currently in the era of Industry 4.0 and heading toward Industry 5.0, which focuses on digitalization, cybersecurity systems, automation and robotics, AI and machine learning, and big data [1].

5.3 SUBSTANTIAL TECHNOLOGIES FOR INDUSTRY 5.0 IN HEALTHCARE

The expanding network enables the linking healthcare systems and medical equipment to the internet, allowing doctors to share patient information. In hospitals, various smart sensors are connected to oxygen pumps, monitoring devices, and tracking systems, enabling doctors to anticipate a patient's illness [2]. Since the patient's health is continuously monitored in real time to provide prompt assistance, Industry 5.0 is better equipped to meet each person's unique needs. Below is a discussion of some of the technologies propelling Industry 5.0:

- **4-D CT**: Four-Dimensional Computed Tomography is a type of CT scanning that collects multiple images over time. The fourth dimension, time, is added to the 3D scan to capture real-time images of internal organs such as the lungs, kidneys, heart, and other tissues.
- **4D MRI**: A cutting-edge imaging technique called four-dimensional magnetic resonance imaging (MRI) allows clinicians to see the blood flow through the cardiovascular system while also providing more accurate and thorough images of the heart and aorta.
- **IoT**: Anything or gadget linked to the internet and can transport data over a network without any human or machine interaction is considered a part of the IoT.

- **Holography**: It is a photographic method that produces 3D images devoid of the need for a lens in a way that no straightforward shot can. The interference pattern in the film captures the image by combining the coherent laser light reflected off an object and merged in the film as light from a reference beam.
- **Smart sensor**: It is a device that gathers information from the environment to carry out a preset function on a specific piece of information and transmits the data via a networked connection.
- **Big data**: It alludes to enormous databases that are too complicated for data processing software to handle to extract usable information from them; predictive analytics is required.
- **Artificial intelligence**: AI refers to the impersonation of human-like intelligence processes by computers. It encompasses speech recognition, machine vision, and natural language processing, among other things.
- **Collaborative robots**: Industrial robots that can work safely alongside people in a shared environment are also referred to as cobots. Due to their isolation from human contact, these industrial robots differ from more typical ones in this regard.

As depicted in Figure 5.2, substantial technologies for Industry 5.0 include smart sensors, 4D CT, 4D MRI, 4D printing, the IoT, big data, smart sensors, and AI. They produce results quickly and accurately. The Industrial Revolution caused the healthcare industry to advance from Healthcare 1.0 to Healthcare 5.0. Healthcare 5.0 connects people, services, and organizations using technology to share health information and immediately aid patients in need of medical care.

Table 5.1 discusses the practical applications of the substantial technologies in healthcare and provides an overview of their usage by doctors and healthcare providers. The primary substantial technologies of Industry 5.0 were already covered in the previous section, and their real-world applications have now been reviewed in the literature, as shown in Table 5.2.

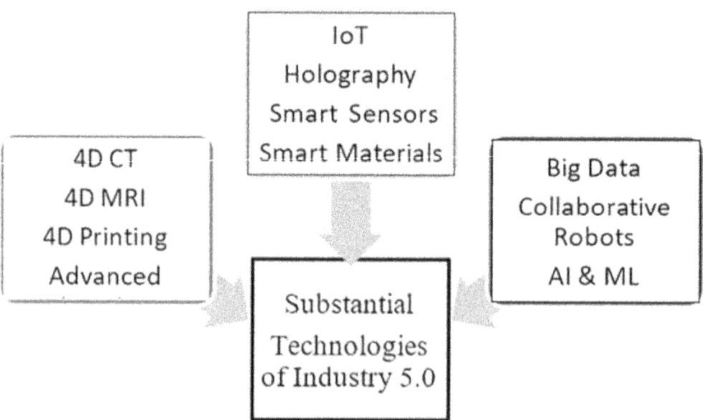

FIGURE 5.2 Substantial technologies of Industry 5.0.

TABLE 5.1

Substantial Technologies and Their Applications in Industry 5.0

S. No.	Type of Technology	Applications
1.	4D CT	4D printing opens up interesting potential for the development of tissue engineering and intelligent medical implants that can change their structure inside the body. It creates intelligent cardiac tubes, which are useful in cardiology and can be utilized to build a variety of environment-adaptive objects and structures. Using 4D CT, a cardiologist can quickly develop a 3D model of the heart that resembles an exact heart model depending on the information gathered about a damaged heart. Product design software is used, and after that, 4D printing technology might create a 3D heart model using the appropriate smart materials. 4D printing can quickly produce stents for use in the heart valve that can then be expanded to the desired shape using heat produced by the patient's body [3].
2.	4D MRI	Using 4D-MRI techniques, it is possible to increase patient imaging quality. With increased accuracy, 4D printing can handle complex medical printing procedures including skin grafting, advanced surgery, developing smart implants, and printing organs. These scanning techniques produce a video playback of the scanned pictures. With the use of intelligent material and CAD data, 4D printing builds 3D physical items and implants layer by layer. This method enables smart materials to adapt their shape over time in response to changes in pressure, temperature, and humidity. In orthopedics, the joint issue of the patient can be extremely effectively analyzed while observing their physical mobility [4].
3.	IoT	IoT is increasingly used in healthcare, dentistry, and orthopedics. It employs sensors that provide real-time data on assessment of bone and fracture. This technology provides reliable information on blood pressure, bone pain, and brain function, guiding injured patients in the direction of suitable exercises for quick recovery. IoT advances orthopedic care, surgery, information, training, research, and development. It collects data about patients' daily activities and exercise routines, assisting them in monitoring their post-surgery recuperation [5].
4.	Holography	Imaging for pathology, urology, dentistry, ophthalmology, otology, bone, and tissue is facilitated by holographic technology. A hologram provides a three-dimensional (3D) image that may be observed without physical contact. These incredibly detailed 3D images of human anatomy also demonstrate how each body part works. Holography includes creating a 3D representation of the complete object, allowing the viewer to examine it from various angles. This technology enables exciting new developments in medical diagnosis, imaging quality, therapy, and information dissemination [6].

(Continued)

TABLE 5.1 (*Continued*)
Substantial Technologies and Their Applications in Industry 5.0

S. No.	Type of Technology	Applications
5.	Smart sensors	Smart sensors are low-cost and serve as non-invasive health and activity monitoring devices, enabling healthcare professionals to monitor significant physiological indicators of their patients in real time, assess health problems, and provide feedback from remote locations. In place of costly healthcare facilities, remote health monitoring, based on non-invasive and wearable sensors, actuators, and modern communication and information technologies, offers an effective and affordable alternative that enables seniors to remain in their own homes [7].
6.	Big data	The term "big data" in the context of healthcare refers to digitalized versions of health information that are so large and complicated that they are difficult to manage using traditional software and/or hardware, as well as typical data management tools and procedures. The adoption of Big Data Analytics (BDA) in the healthcare industry enables the application of cutting-edge technologies in patient care and health administration. Big Data analytics involves methods and devices used to examine and glean information from large amounts of data, with outcomes that can be utilized to make future predictions. It enables the analysis of massive datasets from thousands of patients in the healthcare industry, revealing clusters and correlations between datasets [8].
7.	Artificial intelligence	Methods from Computational Intelligence (CI) and Artificial Intelligence (AI) can be used to solve real-world problems. Because these algorithms display human-like intelligence, they can be used to build intelligent systems. CI, which is developing as a viable area for the development of intelligent systems, is made up of Swarm Intelligence, Neural Networks, Genetic Algorithms, and other biologically inspired algorithms to create intelligent systems [9].
8.	Collaborative robots	The use of collaborative robots has been crucial in overcoming obstacles and improving healthcare facilities. Nurses are trained to work with robots to provide services like muscle massage and the mending of shattered bones. The use of medical COBOTS in repairing broken limbs has assured higher precision in returning mobility to people who have suffered multiple limb fractures. Collaborative robots are a major advancement in orthopedic medical facilities as a result. Through the use of collaborating robots, surgeons can carry out delicate and complicated procedures like organ implantation that could otherwise be impossible or very difficult [10].

TABLE 5.2

Early Intervention of Disease Using Industry 5.0

S. No.	Authors	Outcome of Research
1.	Amine Rghioui et al. [11]	This paper offers a machine learning–based intelligent architecture for monitoring diabetes patients. To collect real-time data/measurements, the architecture components use smart tools, smart sensors, and smartphones. This intelligent architecture collects data as provided by patients and applies machine learning for data classification, resulting in a diagnosis for the patients. Analysis of the results showed that the Sequential Minimal Optimization (SMO) approach provides accurate classification, improved sensitivity, and better precision compared to other existing algorithms.
2.	Reyazur Rashid et al. [12]	This paper proposes a revolutionary healthcare monitoring system that analyzes illness processes and predicts diseases based on data collected from patients in remote regions. IoT sensor devices are used to collect data. The Homomorphic Encryption (HE) approach is then employed for safe data storage. Finally, the illness identification framework is created using the Centered Convolutional Restricted Boltzmann Machines-based whale optimization (CCRBM-WO) algorithm.
3.	Ahsan Shahzad et al. [13]	Uterine Fibroids are a typically benign tumor that affects fertile women. Treatment for Uterine Fibroids (UF) is beneficial when it is detected and diagnosed early. Deep learning-based algorithms have shown promising results in their automated diagnosis from medical imagery. In this study, the authors assessed cutting-edge Deep Learning (DL) architectures, such as InceptionV3, VGG16, and ResNet50, and they also proposed a novel Dual-Path Convolutional Neural Network (DPCNN) architecture for Uterine Fibroids detection. Their proposed DPCNN architecture outperformed existing DL models with the greatest accuracy of 99.8%.
4.	Riccardo Rescinito et al. [14]	Global public health issues such as Intra-Uterine Growth Restriction (IUGR) have significant effects on infant health. For the newborn to have a successful prognosis, the issue must be diagnosed early. In recent years, risk variables have been identified and early IUGR predictions have been made using AI & ML approaches. To assess the effectiveness of AI and ML models in identifying the risk of IUGR in fetuses, the authors have done a systematic review (SR) and meta-analysis (MA).
5.	Theyazn H. H. et al. [15]	By easing the integration of smart technology with traditional medical procedures, Computational Intelligence (CI) and Artificial Intelligence (AI) have shown significant roles in the enhancement of smart and viable healthcare systems. Serving as the cornerstone and paradigm shift for sustainable healthcare, the IoT and CI healthcare systems significantly rely on data collection and machine learning tools. This study uses Gated Recurrent Units (GRU), a more advanced type, to demonstrate the effectiveness of a secure IoMT in the early prediction and detection of breast cancer.

TABLE 5.3

Opportunities and Challenges Faced in Industry 5.0

Opportunities	Challenges
• Highly automated systems can help in mass customization and mass personalization of their customers by providing immediate services with real-time data monitoring.	• Data Security is one of the important challenges. With the 4G/5G networks, continuous monitoring of the health conditions of patients is done, posing a threat to their privacy.
• It helps in the optimization of human efficiency, the amount of time is reduced with the use of machines and gives greater throughput.	• In developing countries like India, it's not possible to train every individual with the latest technologies, this creates work polarization where trained and qualified are highly paid, and untrained and low-qualified are underpaid.
• Blockchain technology can be implemented to provide security and privacy.	• Cyber security threat is increased due to the increased connectivity.
• Entrepreneurs can come up with innovative ideas with new products and services provided by the government.	• Installation of machines needs huge investments and infrastructure which is not possible to adopt by the entrepreneurs.
• Quality service can be provided remotely with the help of robots.	• A high degree of precision and accuracy is needed for medical equipment.
• Increased connectivity with 5G networks.	• A fast and effective network should be established to provide fast and accurate services.

Even though the healthcare sector has significantly improved as a result of the Industrial Revolution, some concerns should also be taken into consideration [16]. The issues that need to be overcome include data security, individual privacy, cybersecurity concerns, training of unskilled workers in new technologies, growing work polarization, and significant investments (Table 5.3).

5.4 CONCLUSION AND FUTURE ASPECTS

To support patient-centric healthcare and achieve mass personalization, we have attempted to investigate several aspects of Industry 5.0 through this research. It has enabled medical experts to provide quick and effective therapy according to user needs. Robots will soon be proficient at performing complex surgeries, and cutting-edge techniques will meet customers' individualized demands, creating a virtual world using ICT technologies. Digital twins will be created to replicate objects or processes in making predictions. In conclusion, Industry 5.0 will prove to be beneficial for both present and future aspects [17]. Future work can implement Industry 5.0 techniques to optimize healthcare through early intervention in diseases. By collecting data from individuals and applying necessary techniques for predictive analytics, we can enhance our healthcare sector and meet the needs of the hour.

REFERENCES

1. Haleem, A., Javaid, M. (2019). Industry 5.0 and its expected applications in medical field. *Current Medicine Research and Practice*, 9(4), 167–169.
2. Prabha, C., Singh, J., Agarwal, S., Verma, A., Sharma, N. (2023). Introduction to computational intelligence in healthcare. In: *Computational Intelligence in Healthcare.* CRC Press, 15 pages. ISBN 9781003305347.
3. Haleem, A., Javaid, M. (2018). 4D printing applications in cardiology. *Current Medicine Research and Practice*, 8(6), 201–246.
4. Haleem, A., Javaid, M. (2019). Expected role of four-dimensional (4D) CT and four-dimensional (4D) MRI for the manufacturing of smart orthopaedics implants using 4D printing. *Journal of Clinical Orthopaedics and Trauma*, 10(s1), S1–S264.
5. Haleem, A., Javaid, M., Khan, I.H.(2019). Internet of things (IoT) applications in orthopaedics. *Journal of Clinical Orthopaedics and Trauma*, 11(Supplement 1), S1–S186.
6. Haleem, A., Javaid, M., Vaishya, R. (2019). Holography applications for orthopaedics. *Indian Journal of Radiology and Imaging*, 29:477–479.
7. Majumder, S., Mondal, T., Deen, J.M. (2017). Wearable sensors for remote health monitoring, *Journal Sensors*, Special issue of sensors 'State-of-the-Art Sensors Technologies', 17(1). doi:10.3390/s17010130, https://www.mdpi.com/journal/sensors.
8. Batko, K., Ślęzak, A. (2022). The use of big data analytics in healthcare. *Journal of Big Data*, 9:3. doi:10.1186/s40537-021-00553-4.
9. Amin, S.U., Hossain, M.S., Muhammad, G., Alhussein, M., Rahman, M.A. (2019). *Cognitive Smart Healthcare for Pathology Detection and Monitoring*, Vol. 7. IEEE.
10. Taesi, C., Aggogeri, F., Pellegrini, N. (2023). COBOT applications: Recent advances and challenges, *Journal Robotics*, Special Issue 'The State-of-the-Art of Robotics' in Europe,. 12(3):79. doi:10.3390/robotics12030079.
11. Rghioui, A., Lloret, J., Sendra, S., Oumnad, A. (2020). A smart architecture for diabetic patient monitoring using machine learning algorithms. *Journal of Healthcare.* 8(3):348. doi:10.3390/healthcare8030348.
12. Irshad, R.R., Alattab, A.A., Alsaiari, O.A.S., Sohail, S.S., Aziz, A., Madsen, D.O., Alalayah, K.M. (2023). An optimization-linked intelligent security algorithm for smart healthcare organizations. *Journal of Healthcare.* 11(4):580. doi:10.3390/healthcare11040580.
13. Shahzad, A., Mushtaq, A., Sabeeh, A.Q., Ghadi, Y., Mushtaq, Z., Arif, S., Zia ur Rehman, M., Quresh, M.F., Jamil, F.(2023). Automated uterine fibroids detection in ultrasound images using deep convolutional neural networks. *Journal of Healthcare,* Special Issue Digital Transformation in Healthcare: Second Edition.. 11(10):1493. doi:10.3390/healthcare11101493.
14. Rescinito, R., Ratti, M., Payedimarri, A.B., Panella, M. (2023). Prediction models for intrauterine growth restriction using artificial intelligence and machine learning: A systematic review and meta-analysis. *Healthcare*, 11(11), 1617, Special Issue Artificial Intelligence Applications in Medicine.
15. Theyazn, H.H., Aldhyani Khan, M.A., Almaiah, M.A., Alnazzawi, N., Al Hwaitat, A.K., Elhag, A.,Shehab, R.T., Ali Saleh, A. (2023) A secure internet of medical things framework for breast cancer detection in sustainable smart cities. *Journal of Electronics*, 12(4), 858, Special Issue IoT-Enabled Smart Applications for Post-COVID-19.
16. Natarajan, R., Lokesh, G.H., Flammini, F., Premkumar, A., Venkatesan, V.K., Gupta, S. (2023). A novel framework on security and energy enhancement based on internet of medical things for healthcare 5.0. *Journal of Infrastructures*, 8(2), 22, Special Issue Data Infrastructures.
17. Bourechak, A., Zedadra, O., Kouahla, M.N., Guerrier, A., Seridi, H., Fortino, G. (2023). At the confluence of artificial intelligence and edge computing in IoT-based applications: A review and new perspective. *Journal of Sensors*, 23(3), 1639, Section Internet of Things.

6 The Impact of Industry 5.0

The Artificial Intelligence, IoT and Blockchain Revolution in Home Healthcare

Yasemin Demir Avcı and Sebahat Gozum

6.1 INTRODUCTION

As in other fields, the unabated advance of technological developments in today's world is leading to revolutionary changes in healthcare services as well. Home healthcare services and home care are important areas that are affected by these changes. A wide perspective is needed to fully grasp the significance of the transformation that artificial intelligence (AI), the Internet of Things (IoT), Blockchain, and other technologies are bringing about.

This section aims to describe in detail the transformation introduced by modern technologies in the area of home healthcare services and home care. Innovative technologies such as AI, IoT, and Blockchain (Figure 6.1) are creating changes that are vital to older adults and individuals with chronic diseases who need constant

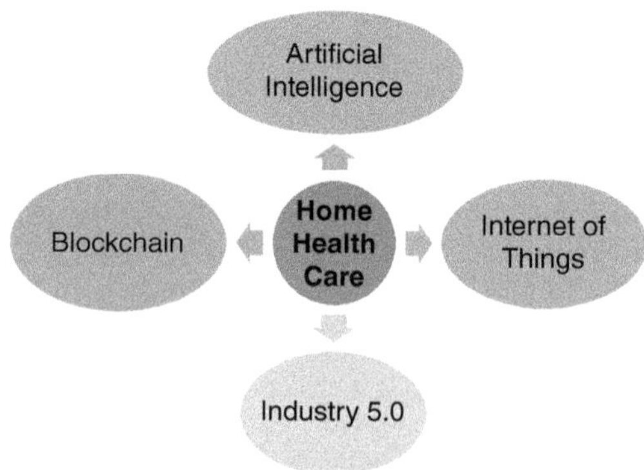

FIGURE 6.1 The impact of home healthcare.

  DOI: 10.1201/9781032632223-6

treatment and care. Some of these changes that have the potential to raise the quality of life include counseling services dispatched remotely, providing an opportunity for early intervention [1], detection systems for falls at home that require immediate emergency aid [2], blockchain technology that secures patient data at the highest level [3], and systems that provide reminders to ensure that medications are taken [4]. The transformative effect of these technologies in healthcare not only involves reshaping existing healthcare practices but also creates a new vision for the future in the context of home healthcare services.

The opportunities and technological innovations arising from Industry 5.0 have opened the door to a new era in the field of healthcare services. This new period is not only affecting professional and formal care processes but also making a radical impact on transforming informal care practices and the way individuals manage their own health. This comprehensive study presents the reader with information on how technological developments are steering home healthcare and home care services, while also providing enlightening knowledge on what the potential future of the field looks like.

Advances in information technologies, especially their inclusion in Turkey's healthcare regulations [5], introduce new opportunities for home healthcare services [6]. In particular, the definitive methodology introduced to the health sector regarding the management of medical data creates the advantage of improving the quality of medical services provided at home. The IoT and AI form the foundation of effective and sustainable treatment options for patients receiving home healthcare [7]. The IoT is an innovative information technology that unites the physical and digital worlds, facilitating communications between technological "things" or devices and human beings. IoT enables remote communication between doctors and patients, particularly in healthcare. However, this may create problems for patient privacy. Today's popular blockchain technology was invented as a solution to such problems. Blockchain's properties of centralization, unchangeability, and transparency not only increase the functionality of the healthcare system but, when joined together with IoT, offer a significant advantage [8,9].

6.2 THE IMPORTANCE OF HOME HEALTHCARE SERVICES AND HOME CARE, AND THE ADVANTAGES AND CHALLENGES OF TECHNOLOGICAL ADVANCEMENT

One of the fundamental goals of home healthcare services is to provide medical services in the comfort of an individual's own home, in familiar surroundings where they can feel safe. This is particularly critical for older adults, individuals with chronic diseases, and those in need of long-term care [10]. In recent years, the innovations technology introduced into the health sector have raised the quality of home healthcare services, made accessibility to services easier, and lowered costs [11]. Artificial intelligence, wearable devices, and technologies such as telehealth have contributed to raising the satisfaction levels of patients and health professionals. These developments have especially led to significant improvements in the rendering of home healthcare services in the absence of needed resources [12]. The technological transformation in-home healthcare services and home care offers the health sector many advantages, but to ensure an effective change in the system, certain challenges must be addressed. The Advantages and Challenges of Technological Transformation are summarized below. The advantages of technological change are as follows:

Access to care: Telemedicine and mobile health applications have facilitated patients' access to doctors and other health professionals [13]. Telehealth is a useful tool for patients in remote areas who lack access to healthcare facilities. This may contribute to reducing inequities in healthcare, providing everyone quality care [11].

Cost-effectiveness: Reducing the need for hospital stays or long-term care can lower healthcare expenses [14].

Real-time monitoring: Thanks to smart devices' and sensors' ability to track patients' vital signs in real time, emergencies can be identified early on [15].

Personalized care: According to Guk et al. [15], personalized treatment regimens can be developed using data analysis and AI to cater to the needs of specific patients.

Reducing the carbon footprint: Telemedicine and mobile health applications can cut down on the number of visits patients make for routine checkups to the doctor's office or hospital. This will lessen the transportation sector's carbon footprint. Telemedicine can aid in lowering greenhouse gas emissions and air pollution by fewer vehicles on the road [11].

Challenges with technological changes are as follows:

Privacy and security: In the context of preventing data breaches and averting cybersecurity threats, concerns about the safety of health data are justified [16].

Technology adaptation: It could take some time for patients and healthcare personnel to get used to new technology [16].

Costs: For organizations and individuals with low resources in particular, the high costs of utilizing new technology may initially be a barrier [14].

The effect of human touch: The human touch and feelings of empathy cannot be replaced by technology. This is a crucial point to take into account, especially for older folks or people who find using technology uncomfortable [13].

6.3 EXAMPLES OF TECHNOLOGIES THAT CAN BE APPLIED TO HOME HEALTHCARE

In the field of home healthcare services, AI holds significant promise for defining individual needs and objectives. For instance, speech recognition technology enables the use of home automation systems to check on elderly or disabled residents who live alone [17]. To remind patients to take their medications or update them on their daily activities, AI-supported chatbots and virtual assistants can be helpful [18]. Additionally, AI-based sensors can notify family members or caretakers anytime anomalous behavior deviating from the norm is discovered [19]. The Internet of Things plays an important role in providing and effectively maintaining continuous home care. Smart devices and wearable technologies are able to monitor patient health in real time. For example, wearable devices can sound an alert when an abnormality is detected in an individual's heart rate, blood pressure, or blood glucose level [20]. Smart bed sensors monitor an individual's quality of sleep and pinpoint changes in sleep patterns [21].

Data about the medical condition of an individual being cared for is sensitive information that must be shared by various health professionals. Blockchain technology makes it possible for this information to be shared safely, transparently, and unalterably. Each data block is cryptographically connected to the previous block, making it more difficult to tamper with or corrupt data [3]. This ensures that the individual's data is correct and updated, while at the same time allowing only authorized persons access to private information [22]. The effect of technology on home care becomes even more potent when the technologies are used in an integrated system. The integration of AI, IoT, and blockchain technologies can improve patient care in completely new and unexpected ways [23]. When these technologies are coupled with smart home systems, this provides patients with the opportunity to live more independently and comfortably and gives health professionals the chance to monitor their patients more effectively and productively [24].

Technological progress also brings about the capability of collecting and evaluating home healthcare processes and patients' physiological data instantaneously. Working with deep learning algorithms and wide data sets makes it possible to predict potential health risks ahead of time [25]. This gives caregivers and health professionals the chance to intervene before the risks become a reality [26,27]. As an example, data about a patient's movements can be used to assess their risk of falling. If the algorithm identifies a risk, the device alerts the caregiver and the family members so that preventive measures can be taken [2]. Also, digital health platforms can provide patients and caregivers with information and support without their having to consult a medical professional. Such platforms can analyze symptom entries, medicine follow-ups, and other health data and give patient-specific advice [23]. When these are used in conjunction with video conferences or other virtual technologies, medical visits can be reduced. Thus, telemedicine allows both the patient and the healthcare provider the opportunity to save on time and treatment costs [24]. This type of integrated approach not only increases the quality of home care but also the quality of life of the patient [27,28].

Another example of homecare technology is the Connected Care operating model [29]. Digitalization is one of the main driving forces of innovation and may be the solution to the problem of achieving sustainability in the healthcare sector [30]. Connected Care is rapidly gaining a strategic position in digital health services in Italy, and to empower patients, organizational models that integrate hospital and local services are being created with the aim of placing the individual/patient at the focal point of the system. The system of Connected Care allows clinical data to be shared between all actors (e.g., hospital staff, doctors, and nurses, local and home healthcare workers, patients, insurance companies, institutional representatives) in the treatment process by means of organizational models and technological solutions. The goal of the system is to meet emerging needs and to maintain the balance in the healthcare system through an operating system in which almost all institutions (for example, Ministry of Health, private hospitals, and primary care health services) are joined together on a central platform [29].

The purpose of the Connected Care model is to place the individual and the patient at the center of the system, and to empower the patient through organizational models that support integrated healthcare provided by hospitals and other health institutions.

New technologies are of fundamental importance not only in terms of the access and use of health data and services but also in monitoring the medical course and general development (or stabilization) of a patient's condition, offering tools to improve services and relationships between patients and health professionals. At the same time, the analysis of statistical models can aid in determining how these types of technologies can encourage preventive behaviors [29].

6.4 A GENERAL DESCRIPTION OF INDUSTRY 5.0 AND HOW IT AFFECTS HOME CARE AND HEALTHCARE SERVICES FROM AN OFFICIAL, INFORMAL, AND SELF-CARE PERSPECTIVE

Industry 5.0 is a concept seeking to join the technological innovations introduced by the fourth industrial revolution with human creativity and sensitivity [4]. The concept is thus part of a new era in which not only AI, robots, big data, or IoT, but also the human being's problem-solving capabilities and ethical values are brought into the equation. The goal is to seamlessly combine technology and human talents to create a more personal, ethical, and sustainable society [31]. This approach has the potential to play an important role in home healthcare services. For example, AI-supported diagnostic tools can monitor a patient's medical condition in real time. This helps health professionals to make more accurate and conscious decisions. In short, caregivers can draw up more effective treatment plans specifically for each patient. This would not only improve healthcare services but also render them in a more personalized and ethical manner [11].

The impact of Industry 5.0 on home healthcare services offers informal caregivers and those with a perspective on self-care various advantages. Informal caregivers are usually family members or close relatives and in this context, Industry 5.0 brings in technological tools such as wearable devices and home automation systems that can greatly facilitate the caregiving process [32]. These types of technologies enable caregivers and health professionals to monitor patients more closely and effectively. At the same time, in terms of patients' self-care needs, Industry 5.0 introduces tools such as personal health assistants and interactive health applications to allow individuals to take a more active and effective role in their own health and welfare [33].

An example of how Industry 5.0 can have an impact on home healthcare services is the CAREUP project, an integrated healthcare platform designed to monitor the "Intrinsic Capacity" (the composite of all the physical and mental capacities of an individual) of older adults. This platform simplifies and converts complex data into a more comprehensible form to facilitate users' understanding of their medical situation. The system brings together a series of devices, sensors, and functions to provide care and monitoring fashioned around an individual's specific living conditions. The CAREUP platform compares individuals' current medical conditions with their health goals, presenting a visualization of any change that has been detected. This helps users and health professionals to make more informed decisions about their health. The platform is of benefit to three main groups:

Older adults (primary users): CAREUP can regularly monitor the health of older adults and accordingly detect any changes over time, helping to take precautions when necessary.

Caregivers: The platform contributes to more effectively conducting the caregiving process since care plans can be better organized with this system, thus reducing the workload.

Health professionals: The data picked up by CAREUP can be helpful to doctors and other health professionals in better understanding the medical condition of older adults so that appropriate treatment plans can be drawn up [32,33].

Industry 5.0 is the product of technology and human beings working together [34]. In home healthcare services, this means generating technological solutions that are more sensitive to the needs of patients and caregivers, making caregiving processes more effective, productive and compassionate. With technology playing an active role, home healthcare services become not only more accessible but also more personalized and more focused on the individual. For example, AI-supported diagnostic tools and remote monitoring systems enable health professionals to monitor their patients' conditions in detail and in real time. This renders treatment plans more effectual and represents a substantial potential for rapid intervention. Also, these types of technologies allow patients themselves to monitor and manage their own health, facilitating the adaptation to self-care and informal care processes. In short, the technological innovations brought about by Industry 5.0 can not only modernize home healthcare services but also transform healthcare into a more compassionate, fair, and sustainable endeavor [35,36].

6.5 A GENERAL DESCRIPTION OF ARTIFICIAL INTELLIGENCE AND HOW IT AFFECTS HOME CARE AND HEALTHCARE SERVICES

Artificial intelligence, machine learning, and software have the capability to mimic the human aspects of intelligence such as reasoning, problem-solving, perception, and natural language processing. This technology, based on algorithms and data analysis, has the capacity to automate and optimize complex tasks [37]. The opportunities emerging from digitalization, AI, robotics, and other innovative technologies make home healthcare services more effective and productive, while at the same time providing leverage for improving patient monitoring. Telemedicine devices present amazing potential for the telemonitoring and telerehabilitation of individuals with chronic diseases. AI systems, in particular, can now provide quite beneficial support in management and decision-making processes in many clinical areas. Digitalization combined with AI can make possible the remote monitoring of patients' medical conditions [29]. Especially concerning diagnostic and treatment recommendations, AI-supported systems can issue advice to match the individual needs of each patient, thus facilitating the delivery of more personalized and goal-oriented care [38].

The different kinds of artificial intelligence can be used for different purposes in-home healthcare services. Artificial intelligence is not composed of a single technology but rather comprises a collection of technologies. Most of these technologies are directly related to healthcare, varying greatly according to the processes and tasks they support [38]. Some specific AI technologies that have large potential in the context of home healthcare services are defined and described below.

Machine learning and its more complex version of deep learning provide many benefits in the field of medicine, particularly in home healthcare services [39]. Personalized medicine, an approach that aims to find the best treatment appropriate for each patient, has become much more effective thanks to AI technologies. For example, the treatment or medicines an individual needs at home can be more accurately ascertained through a personalized analysis of the individual's data. In the same way, AI-supported monitoring systems can send a patient's doctor information about his/her medical condition at home in real time, making it possible to make faster and more accurate treatment plans [38]. In technical areas such as radiology, simple medical imaging taken at home can be subjected to complex analysis using deep learning processes. For example, a home X-ray of the individual can facilitate the quick evaluation of any potential signs of cancer. Furthermore, these technologies provide healthcare professionals the opportunity to improve communication with their patients by means of voice commands or voice recognition [40].

Natural Language Processing (NLP) offers effective solutions in areas such as speech recognition, text analysis, and translation. In particular, important steps have been taken in recent years through the capacity of NLP to use machine learning techniques such as deep learning. Inhome healthcare applications, the NLP system allows doctors and caregivers to rapidly analyze unstructured clinical notes to obtain detailed information on the patient's condition and the treatment plan. This can make it possible for them to make more effective decisions according to their patient's needs in real time. For example, the personal health system e-Nabız (e-Pulse) used in Turkey is a platform that provides access to an individual's health records (subject to authorization, time limits, and specified boundaries) online or through mobile devices (Figure 6.2). This platform collects all data incoming from Turkey's healthcare institutions and is accessible on the website https://enabiz.gov.tr/. Several applications are providing a series of different services within the E-Nabız system. The first of these is the "Central Doctor's Appointment System" (Merkezi Hekim

FIGURE 6.2   E-nabız personal health system [41].

Randevu Sistemi-MHRS) from which appointments can be obtained from public medical facilities via the website https://mhrs.gov.tr/. Another useful feature is the "Neyim Var" (What Do I Have?) application, where users can have their symptoms evaluated and be referred to the appropriate facility via https://neyimvar.gov.tr/website [41]. Also, through its speech recognition capabilities, NLP can make interactions between doctors/caregivers easier, thus increasing the effectiveness of home healthcare. In short, NLP home healthcare applications not only lighten the workload of healthcare professionals but also achieve the personalization of services for patients, offering a more effectual homecare experience [42].

Clinical decision-supporting systems provide data and analyses to help healthcare professionals with diagnostics and treatment plans. The importance of these types of systems is steadily growing, especially in the area of home healthcare. Home healthcare encompasses managing the different needs of patients as well as their multiple chronic conditions, a task that requires a care environment containing many variables. Clinical decision support systems help healthcare personnel providing care at home with the means of evaluation in real time, allowing them to predict possible complications and ascertain appropriate treatment options. For example, machine learning algorithms can foresee future health risks by analyzing the current health data of an individual. This gives home healthcare providers the chance to intervene in time and create a proactive care plan. However, when considering the personalized and variable nature of home healthcare, continuous updates and adaptations need to be made for these systems to integrate successfully [43].

Physical robots are being used to carry out a range of tasks–from industry to hospitals–and the increasing capabilities of AI make it possible to handle a steadily increasing host of complex processes. These developments carry enormous potential for home healthcare services. For example, robots that carry out home care can be of help to individuals with physical limitations; they can remind them to take their medicines or monitor vital signs. Used in combination with technologies such as telemedicine, robots can make it possible for doctors to monitor their patients remotely and in real time. In particular, robots can increase the quality of life of older adults and those with chronic conditions, allowing healthcare professionals to manage the homecare process more effectively [44].

AI has brought about a startling transformation in care planning and automation. By analyzing patients' genetic data, lifestyle information, and past medical records, AI has the capacity to facilitate the drawing up of patient-specific care plans, a concept that has revolutionized the health sector. When personalized plans are integrated with home automation systems, patients can live more independently and comfortably in their daily lives [40]. AI-supported chatbots and virtual assistants also facilitate these processes. For example, medicine dosage reminders, appointment prompters, or advice concerning general health are all applications that can be managed by AI. This encourages individuals to make more conscious decisions regarding their health while also raising general health awareness. Such integrated systems lead to an increase in quality of life while at the same time lightening the load of healthcare professionals [34].

6.6 A GENERAL DESCRIPTION OF THE INTERNET OF THINGS AND HOW IT AFFECTS HOME CARE AND HEALTHCARE SERVICES

The IoT signifies the ability to tie everything together via the internet. "Everything" means connecting all electronic systems, software, actuators, and other technologies, gathering and exchanging data between systems by means of embedded devices and household appliances [45]. The Internet of Things (IoT) is made up of four key parts: sensors/devices, connectivity, data processing, and a user interface. The sensors/devices component gathers crucial data from the IoT platform using a variety of sensors and devices, including GPS, QR codes, and RFID. Through communication technologies like Bluetooth, Zigbee, and WLAN, the acquired data is advanced, processed, stored, and transmitted to users and/or cloud servers. The collected data is processed via a combination of cloud and end-to-end data processing. Users can access the IoT interface with smartphones, smartwatches, microphones, cameras, monitors, and other devices (Figure 6.3) [45,46].

The IoT promises many benefits in terms of predicting health issues proactively, making diagnoses both in and outside the hospital, and facilitating and improving the health services needed for treatment and monitoring patients. All over the world, government leaders and decision-makers have been using technology and applying new policies in response to a possible new epidemic of the coronavirus. The "Hayat Eve Sığar" or HES Code mobile application, initiated during the COVID-19 pandemic in Turkey, is one example of how new technologies are being used successfully in healthcare. The application, activated with a QR code, informs users of their infection risk while they are in crowded locations such as public transportation vehicles [47]. It is becoming more and more important to learn how healthcare systems can be supported safely and effectively using present and potential IoT technologies [48]. In [49], the authors put forward an IoT-based system for the compression of medical images for telehealth applications. At the same time, recognition of the potential problems that can emerge from IoT-based health services and the barriers standing in the way of the adoption of IoT technologies by health professionals and patients have brought to light the significance of related ethical issues involving matters such as security, privacy, anonymity, freedom to withdraw, informed consent, integration, accessibility, authorization, access control, standardization, pricing, data storage and control/ownership, censorship and electronic eavesdropping [50]. The importance of expandable AI was put forward in [51] by evaluating 410 research articles.

The IoT is a technology that connects physical devices, instruments, buildings, and other "things" to each other over the internet, allowing access to data centers. This technology has had a revolutionary impact on home healthcare services and home care. For example, IoT devices allow the constant collection of medical data from older adults and chronic patients living at home, also providing the opportunity to monitor these individuals from remote locations. Smart bracelets, bed sensors, or medical devices for home use can be employed to collect and relay the patient's body temperature, heart rate, sleep quality, and other critical health parameters to health professionals in real time [52]. This enables a rapid and effective intervention when needed at any moment. At the same time, the technology facilitates communication

FIGURE 6.3   Components of IoT technology. Drawn by OpenAI's DALL-E model.

between the patient and health professionals, possibly helping the individual at home to live a more independent life. On the other hand, because of the key role IoT plays in preventing disease, telemonitoring patient functions in real time, testing treatments, as well as in healthcare and healthcare management research, the risks involved in providing health services and access to patient data should never be overlooked [50].

6.7   A GENERAL DESCRIPTION OF BLOCKCHAIN AND HOW IT AFFECTS HOME CARE AND HEALTHCARE SERVICES

Blockchain technology can be summarized as a shared, immutable structure of data containing blocks of information that are cryptographically interconnected. Each block in the structure is connected with the previous block, meaning that the data is preserved in a secure system in which unauthorized changes cannot be made and data cannot be corrupted [22]. These capabilities are especially important in areas where sensitive data is stored, such as in the health sector. Blockchain technology makes treatment processes more easily and effectively adaptable to monitoring. All steps in the treatment plan of a patient can be monitored and recorded. This helps doctors, nurses, and other health professionals to more closely follow up on and manage their patients' treatment plans, also enabling them to follow up on the patient's response to treatment. Additionally, automatic or smart contracts stored on blockchains make the automation and improvement of homecare services possible. This enables the more effective provision of healthcare, including a range of useful services such as medication and appointment reminders [53].

Health data contain private and sensitive information, and safeguarding such data is a major source of concern. Blockchain technology offers a powerful framework of security aimed at preventing the access of unauthorized persons. Especially in-home healthcare services, in situations where an individual is being cared for by more than one caregiver or health professional, blockchain technology plays a critical role in maintaining security and access control. The integration and transparency Blockchain provides increase the quality of securely storing patient data. This technology enables the continuous and immutable storage of all records, thus improving the quality of home healthcare services and ensuring that health professionals receive accurate information [27,54].

6.8 HOW THE INTERNET OF THINGS, BLOCKCHAIN, AND ARTIFICIAL INTELLIGENCE WILL AFFECT HOME HEALTHCARE IN THE FUTURE

The future of home healthcare and home care foresees that nurses and care providers will be able to work more effectively with the conveniences that artificial intelligence, the Internet of Things, and blockchain technologies provide. Artificial intelligence can evaluate the medical condition of patients in real time, even predicting potential problems in advance and making continuous assessments to provide nurses with feedback [51]. This enables the drawing up of a more personalized care plan and provides the opportunity to monitor a patient more closely. Devices connected to the Internet of Things can instantaneously follow up on vital signs, activity levels, and other important metrics. This makes it easier for homecare personnel and nurses to immediately intervene and inform the doctor as soon as an abnormality is detected. Smart pillows, smart assistants, chatbots, wearable health monitors, smart medicine cases, and many more devices make home healthcare more proactive and effective.

Blockchain technology allows for the secure storage of a patient's health records, medicine information, and treatment history, making it possible for different health professionals to safely access the same data. This integrated technological structure lessens the workload of nurses and caregivers, providing the potential for more effective and safer delivery of care while also offering patients a higher quality of care. All of these technologies merge with the security and transparency of blockchain to achieve data privacy and establish a framework of ethics. Health records, treatment plans, medicine prescriptions, and other sensitive data are safely stored in the blockchain. Different healthcare professionals and caregivers are allowed access to the data, but making changes or additions to the information is subject to authorization. This means that data integrity is safeguarded, and patients' privacy is secured. Such integration of technology allows individuals, especially the elderly and those with chronic diseases, to live a safer and more independent life at home. In short, the combination of AI, IoT, and blockchain technologies not only makes home healthcare more effective and accessible but also provides the means of serving individuals safely and with a personalized approach that respects their dignity.

6.9 CONCLUSION

The era of Industry 5.0 is shaping the future of home healthcare services and home care, while also highlighting the harmony of technology interacting with human beings. The spread of new technologies such as AI, IoT, and blockchain suggests a transformation in home healthcare and home care services. While artificial intelligence carries notable potential in areas such as personalized care and early diagnosis, IoT offers extensive opportunities for the automation and improvement of homecare services. Similarly, blockchain technology can maintain the integrity, security, and transparency of home healthcare data and help ensure its appropriate use, giving health professionals the chance to treat their patients with more effective tools. All of these technological developments have the potential to raise the quality of home healthcare and increase the quality of life of individuals at home, signifying an exciting transformation for the home healthcare and home care sectors.

REFERENCES

1. Beatty, A. L., Beckie, T. M., Dodson, J., Goldstein, C. M., Hughes, J. W., Kraus, W. E., Martin, S. S., Olson, T. P., Pack, Q. R., Stolp, H., Thomas, R. J., Wu, W. C., & Franklin, B. A. (2023). A new era in cardiac rehabilitation delivery: Research gaps, questions, strategies, and priorities. *Circulation*, 147(3), 254–266. doi:10.1161/CIRCULATIONAHA. 122.061046
2. Torres-Guzman, R. A., Paulson, M. R., Avila, F. R., Maita, K., Garcia, J. P., Forte, A. J., & Maniaci, M. J. (2023). Smartphones and threshold-based monitoring methods effectively detect falls remotely: A systematic review. *Sensors (Basel, Switzerland)*, 23(3), 1323. doi:10.3390/s23031323
3. Mustaçoğlu, A. F. (2018). Blockchain-based data sharing and managing sensitive data. *European Journal of Science and Technology*, 14, 235–240.
4. Xu, L., Sanders, L., Li, K., & Chow, J. C. L. (2021). Chatbot for health care and oncology applications using artificial intelligence and machine learning: Systematic review. *JMIR Cancer*, 7(4), e27850. doi:10.2196/27850
5. Rebuclic of Turkey Ministry of Health. (2023). Regulation on home health service provision. Official Gazette No. 32209. https://www.resmigazete.gov.tr/eskiler/2023/06/20230602-1.htm. Retrieved November 3, 2023
6. Rebuclic of Turkey. Ministry of Health. (2023). Remote healthcare services regulations. Republic of Turkey Official Gazette No 32209. https://www.resmigazete.gov.tr/eskiler/2023/06/20230602-1.htm. Retrieved September 7, 2023
7. Alzubi, O. A., Alzubi, J. A., Shankar, K., & Gupta, D. (2021). Blockchain and artificial intelligence enabled privacy-preserving medical data transmission in Internet of Things. *Transactions on Emerging Telecommunications Technologies*, 32, e4360.

8. M Bublitz, F., Oetomo, A., S Sahu, K., Kuang, A., X Fadrique, L., E Velmovitsky, P., M Nobrega, R., & P Morita, P. (2019). Disruptive technologies for environment and health research: An overview of artificial intelligence, blockchain, and internet of things. *International Journal of Environmental Research and Public Health*, 16(20), 3847. doi:10.3390/ijerph16203847

9. Ratta, P., Kaur, A., Kaur, A., Sharma, S., & Dhiman, G. (2021). Application of blockchain and internet of things in healthcare and medical sector: Applications, challenges, and future perspectives. *Journal of Food Quality*, 2021(1), 1–20. doi:10.1155/2021/7608296

10. Gilmour H. (2018). Unmet home care needs in Canada. *Health Reports*, 29(11), 3–11.

11. Amjad, A., Kordel, P., & Fernandes, G. (2023). A review on innovation in healthcare sector (telehealth) through artificial intelligence. *Sustainability*, 15(8), 6655. doi:10.3390/su15086655

12. Merih, Y. D., Ertürk, N., Yemenici, M., & Satman, İ. (2021). Technology use in home health service. *Journal of Health Institutes of Turkey*, 4(3), 76–89.

13. Gonçalves-Bradley, D. C., Maria, A. R. J., Ricci-Cabello, I., Villanueva, G., Fønhus, M. S., Glenton, C., Lewin, S., Henschke, N., Buckley, B. S., Mehl, G. L., Tamrat, T., & Shepperd, S. (2020). Mobile technologies to support healthcare provider to healthcare provider communication and management of care. *The Cochrane Database of Systematic Reviews*, 8(8), CD012927. doi:10.1002/14651858.CD012927.pub2

14. Galavi, Z., Montazeri, M., & Ahmadian, L. (2022). Barriers and challenges of using health information technology in home care: A systematic review. *The International Journal of Health Planning and Management*, 37(5), 2542–2568. doi:10.1002/hpm.3492

15. Guk, K., Han, G., Lim, J., Jeong, K., Kang, T., Lim, E. K., & Jung, J. (2019). Evolution of wearable devices with real-time disease monitoring for personalized healthcare. *Nanomaterials (Basel, Switzerland)*, 9(6), 813. doi:10.3390/nano9060813

16. Steindal, S. A., Nes, A. A. G., Godskesen, T. E., Dihle, A., Lind, S., Winger, A., & Klarare, A. (2020). Patients' experiences of telehealth in palliative home care: Scoping review. *Journal of Medical Internet Research*, 22(5), e16218. doi:10.2196/16218

17. Fahn, C. S., Chen, S. C., Wu, P. Y., Chu, T. L., Li, C. H., Hsu, D. Q., Wang, H. H., & Tsai, H. M. (2022). Image and speech recognition technology in the development of an elderly care robot: Practical issues review and improvement strategies. *Healthcare (Basel, Switzerland)*, 10(11), 2252. doi:10.3390/healthcare10112252

18. Roca, S., Lozano, M. L., García, J., & Alesanco, Á. (2021). Validation of a virtual assistant for improving medication adherence in patients with comorbid type 2 diabetes mellitus and depressive disorder. *International Journal of Environmental Research and Public Health*, 18(22), 12056. doi:10.3390/ijerph182212056

19. Grgurić, A., Mošmondor, M., & Huljenić, D. (2019). The smart habits: An intelligent privacy-aware home care assistance system. *Sensors (Basel, Switzerland)*, 19(4), 907. doi:10.3390/s19040907

20. Huhn, S., Axt, M., Gunga, H. C., Maggioni, M. A., Munga, S., Obor, D., Sié, A., Boudo, V., Bunker, A., Sauerborn, R., Bärnighausen, T., & Barteit, S. (2022). The impact of wearable technologies in health research: Scoping review. *JMIR mHealth and uHealth*, 10(1), e34384. doi:10.2196/34384

21. Laurino, M., Arcarisi, L., Carbonaro, N., Gemignani, A., Menicucci, D., & Tognetti, A. (2020). A smart bed for non-obtrusive sleep analysis in real world context. *IEEE Access*. 1–1. doi:10.1109/ACCESS.2020.2976194.

22. Mustafa, M., Alshare, M., Bhargava, D., Neware, R., Singh, B., & Ngulube, P. (2022). Perceived security risk based on moderating factors for blockchain technology applications in cloud storage to achieve secure healthcare systems. *Computational and Mathematical Methods in Medicine*, 2022, 6112815. doi:10.1155/2022/6112815

23. Sharma, H. K., Kumar, A., Pant, S., & Ram, M. (2022). Role of artificial intelligence, IoT and blockchain in smart healthcare. In: *Artificial Intelligence, Blockchain and IoT for Smart Healthcare*, 1st edn., New York: River Publishers. doi:10.1201/9781003333050

24. Haleem, A., Javaid, M., Singh, R. P., & Suman, R. (2021). Telemedicine for healthcare: Capabilities, features, barriers, and applications. *Sensors International*, 2, 100117. doi:10.1016/j.sintl.2021.100117

25. Kumar, S. N., Lenin Fred, A., Padmanabhan, P., Gulyas, B., Ajay Kumar, H., & Jonisha Miriam, L. R. (2021). Deep learning algorithms in medical image processing for cancer diagnosis: Overview, challenges and future. *Deep Learning for Cancer Diagnosis*, 908, 37–66

26. Kim, K., & Lee, W. G. (2023). Portable, automated and deep-learning-enabled microscopy for smartphone-tethered optical platform towards remote homecare diagnostics: A review. *Small Methods*, 7(1), 2200979.

27. Kumar, N. M., & Mallick, P. K. (2018). Blockchain technology for security issues and challenges in IoT. *Procedia Computer Science*, 132, 1815–1823.

28. Angelopoulou, E., Papachristou, N., Bougea, A., Stanitsa, E., Kontaxopoulou, D., Fragkiadaki, S., Pavlou, D., Koros, C., Değirmenci, Y., Papatriantafyllou, J., Thireos, E., Politis, A., Tsouros, A., Bamidis, P., Stefanis, L., & Papageorgiou, S. (2022). How telemedicine can improve the quality of care for patients with alzheimer's disease and related dementias? A narrative review. *Medicina (Kaunas, Lithuania), 58*(12), 1705. doi:10.3390/medicina58121705

29. Cingolani, M., Scendoni, R., Fedeli, P., & Cembrani, F. (2023). Artificial intelligence and digital medicine for integrated home care services in Italy: Opportunities and limits. *Frontiers in Public Health*, 10, 1095001. doi:10.3389/fpubh.2022.109500

30. Stoumpos, A. I., Kitsios, F., & Talias, M. A. (2023). Digital transformation in healthcare: Technology acceptance and its applications. *International Journal of Environmental Research and Public Health*, 20(4), 3407. doi:10.3390/ijerph20043407

31. Maddikunta, P. K. R., Pham, Q. V., Prabadevi, B., Deepa, N., Dev, K., Gadekallu, T. R., ..., & Liyanage, M. (2022). Industry 5.0: A survey on enabling technologies and potential applications. *Journal of Industrial Information Integration*, 26, 100257

32. Velciu, M., Spiru, L., Dan Marzan, M., Reithner, E., Geli, S., Borgogni, B., Cramariuc, O., et al. (2023). How technology-based interventions can sustain ageing well in the new decade through the user-driven approach. *Sustainability*, 15(13), 10330. doi:10.3390/su151310330

33. Mbunge, E., Muchemwa, B., & Batani, J. (2021). Sensors and healthcare 5.0: Transformative shift in virtual care through emerging digital health technologies. *Global Health Journal*, 5(4), 169–177.

34. Xu, X., Lu, Y., Vogel-Heuser, B., & Wang, L. (2021). Industry 4.0 and Industry 5.0-Inception, conception and perception. *Journal of Manufacturing Systems*, 61, 530–535.

35. Adel, A. (2022). Future of industry 5.0 in society: Human-centric solutions, challenges and prospective research areas. *Journal of Cloud Computing*, 11, 40 doi:10.1186/s13677-022-00314-5

36. Alojaiman, B. (2023). Technological modernizations in the industry 5.0 Era: A descriptive analysis and future research directions. *Processes*, 11(5), 1318. doi:10.3390/pr11051318

37. Howard J. (2019). Artificial intelligence: Implications for the future of work. *American Journal of Industrial Medicine*, 62(11), 917–926. doi:10.1002/ajim.23037

38. Davenport, T., & Kalakota, R. (2019). The potential for artificial intelligence in healthcare. *Future Healthcare Journal*, 6(2), 94–98. doi:10.7861/futurehosp.6-2-94

39. Hobensack, M., Song, J., Scharp, D., Bowles, K. H., & Topaz, M. (2023). Machine learning applied to electronic health record data in home healthcare: A scoping review. *International Journal of Medical Informatics*, 170, 104978.

40. Hosny, A., Parmar, C., Quackenbush, J., Schwartz, L. H., & Aerts, H. J. W. L. (2018). Artificial intelligence in radiology. *Nature Reviews: Cancer*, 18(8), 500–510. doi:10.1038/s41568-018-0016-5

41. Republic of Turkey Ministry of Health. (2023). About e-Nabız. https://enabiz.gov.tr/Yardim/Index?page=a1&detail=b13. Retrieved September 7, 2023

42. Woo, K., Song, J., Adams, V., Block, L. J., Currie, L. M., Shang, J., & Topaz, M. (2022). Exploring prevalence of wound infections and related patient characteristics in homecare using natural language processing. *International Wound Journal*, 19(1), 211–221.

43. Nibbelink, C. W., & Brewer, B. B. (2018). Decision-making in nursing practice: An integrative literature review. *Journal of Clinical Nursing*, 27(5–6), 917–928. doi:10.1111/jocn.14151

44. Yang, G., Pang, Z., Jamal Deen, M., Dong, M., Zhang, Y. T., Lovell, N., & Rahmani, A. M. (2020). Homecare robotic systems for healthcare 4.0: Visions and enabling technologies. *IEEE Journal of Biomedical and Health Informatics*, 24(9), 2535–2549. doi:10.1109/JBHI.2020.2990529

45. Madakam, S., Ramaswamy, R. and Tripathi, S. (2015) Internet of Things (IoT): A literature review. *Journal of Computer and Communications*, 3, 164–173. doi:10.4236/jcc.2015.35021.

46. Alizadehsani, R., Roshanzamir, M., Izadi, N. H., Gravina, R., Kabir, H. M. D., Nahavandi, D., Alinejad-Rokny, H., Khosravi, A., Acharya, U. R., Nahavandi, S., & Fortino, G. (2023). Swarm intelligence in internet of medical things: A review. *Sensors (Basel, Switzerland)*, 23(3), 1466. doi:10.3390/s23031466

47. Rebuclic of Turkey Ministry of Health. (2023). *What is the HES Codu?* https://hayatevesigar.saglik.gov.tr/. Retrieved September 7, 2023

48. Kelly, J. T., Campbell, K. L., Gong, E., & Scuffham, P. (2020). The internet of things: Impact and implications for health care delivery. *Journal of Medical Internet Research*, 22(11), e20135. doi:10.2196/20135.

49. Zafar, S., Iftekhar, N., Yadav, A., Ahilan, A., Kumar, S. N., & Jeyam, A. (2022). An IoT method for telemedicine: Lossless medical image compression using local adaptive blocks. *IEEE Sensors Journal*, 22(15), 15345–15352. doi:10.1109/JSEN.2022.3184423.

50. Zakerabasali, S., & Ayyoubzadeh, S. M. (2022). Internet of things and healthcare system: A systematic review of ethical issues. *Health Science Reports*, 5(6), e863. doi:10.1002/hsr2.863.

51. Nizam, T., & Zafar, S. (2023). Explainable artificial intelligence (XAI): Conception, visualization and assessment approaches towards amenable XAI. In: Hassanien, A. E., Gupta, D., Singh, A. K., Garg, A. (eds) *Explainable Edge AI: A Futuristic Computing Perspective. Studies in Computational Intelligence*, vol 1072, Cham: Springer. doi:10.1007/978-3-031-18292-1_3

52. de Zambotti, M., Cellini, N., Goldstone, A., Colrain, I. M., & Baker, F. C. (2019). Wearable sleep technology in clinical and research settings. *Medicine and Science in Sports and Exercise*, 51(7), 1538–1557. doi:10.1249/MSS.0000000000001947

53. Wylde, V., Rawindaran, N., Lawrence, J., Balasubramanian, R., Prakash, E., Jayal, A., Khan, I., Hewage, C., & Platts, J. (2022). Cybersecurity, data privacy and blockchain: A review. *SN Computer Science*, 3(2), 127. doi:10.1007/s42979-022-01020-4

54. Wang, J., Chen, W., Wang, L., Ren, Y., & Sherratt, R. S. (2020). Blockchain-based data storage mechanism for industrial internet of things. *Intelligent Automation and Soft Computing*, 26(5), 1157–1172.

7 Blockchain Technology for Healthcare

Revolutionizing the Future of Medicine

S. Srividhya and K. Pradeepa

7.1 INTRODUCTION

Blockchain has proven a tried-and-true method of storing transactions in a distributed database within a decentralized, peer-to-peer network. It addresses the confidence in a single entity problem by employing a distributed computing model. Consequently, a distributed ledger of all previous transactions is consistently and securely maintained by a number of nodes cooperating in a blockchain network. While blockchain technology gained prominence with the introduction of cryptocurrencies like Bitcoin by Satoshi Nakamoto in 2008 [1], its applications extend far beyond digital currencies. It serves as a distributed, decentralized ledger system that enables multiple parties to record and verify transactions securely and transparently. A blockchain comprises a chain of blocks, with each block containing a list of transactions. These blocks are cryptographically linked together, forming a chronological and immutable record of all transactions across the network. Unlike traditional centralized systems, blockchains are decentralized, with multiple nodes (computers) participating in the validation and maintenance of the blockchain. This decentralization enhances security, as there is no central point of failure or control. Blockchain technology is particularly groundbreaking and promising as it helps eradicate fraud, address security concerns, and increase transparency to unprecedented levels. While initially associated with cryptocurrencies and non fungible tokens (NFTs) in the 2010s, blockchain technology has since evolved into a management tool used by a wide range of international businesses. It has the potential to transform data handling and ownership in various domains, including gaming innovation, healthcare data security, and food supply chain transparency. Distributed ledger technology (DLT), often referred to as blockchain technology, facilitates the transfer of digital information, such as Bitcoin, between parties without the need for a middleman. Transactions are simultaneously verified by several nodes in the network, thanks to blockchain technology [2]. The term "cryptocurrency" is now widely used in both business and academia, with Bitcoin, one of the most popular cryptocurrencies, experiencing significant growth, with its market capitalization reaching $10 billion in 2016 [3]. Transactions on the Bitcoin network could occur without the involvement of a third party with the use

DOI: 10.1201/9781032632223-7

of a specifically created data storage structure. The blockchain, which was first proposed in 2008 and put into use in 2009, is the fundamental technology behind Bitcoin [4]. Blockchain technology manages sensitive data in healthcare, medical research, etc. [5]. Blockchain has been proposed as a solution to address some of the major issues facing the healthcare industry, including compliance with data protection laws and safe medical record exchange [6]. In the healthcare industry, interoperability often focuses on data sharing between corporate entities, such as multiple hospital systems via a state-wide Health Information Exchange (HIE). One significant development that may create new opportunities for data exchange in healthcare is the move toward patient-centered interoperability. However, for this kind of data sharing to be successful at scale, patient-centered interoperability introduces new requirements and challenges around security and privacy, technology, incentives, and governance. Many of these issues remain unresolved for traditional interoperability. Therefore, it makes sense to explore cutting-edge or unconventional interventions that might be useful in moving toward patient-centered interoperability. The benefits of data liquidity—clinical, scientific, and operational—could be reconciled with the significant interoperability obstacles that characterize the health data-sharing environment with the help of such measures [7].

7.2   OVERVIEW OF BLOCKCHAIN TECHNOLOGY

In 2008, blockchain—a peer-to-peer network atop the internet—was presented as a component of a proposal for Bitcoin. The blockchain is a publicly accessible ledger consisting of a series of blocks that contain the complete history of all network-wide transaction records. A block is mostly made up of a header and a body. Every block has a header that includes the hash of the block before it. As a result, each block structure is predicated on the one before it, forming a chain or linked list. Blockchain is a specific kind of database that may be controlled by a network of verified users, or nodes. It holds blocks of unchangeable data that can be strongly traded without the intervention of outside parties. Data is maintained and recorded through the use of consensus techniques and cryptographic signatures, which are employed as key enablers in their application. One of the main goals of adopting Block Chain Technology is data preservation, especially in the healthcare industry, where a large amount of data is shared and disseminated. The advancement of blockchain technology and its implementation in diverse settings have reached various phases of realization [8,9]. The peer network, smart contract, membership, events, ledger, system integration, wallet, and system management are some of the components that make up the blockchain architecture. A blockchain that offers a solution to a blockchain-based business network involves a number of actors, including developers, users, architects, regulators, operators, membership services, etc. Every participant and element in a blockchain contributes significantly to the network's increased dependability and security [10].

Here's an overview of how blockchain operates and its essential elements:

Blocks: A blockchain is a chain of blocks, with each block containing a collection of transactions. Transactions can represent various types of data, not just financial transactions like in cryptocurrencies. For example, a blockchain for supply chain management could contain transactions representing the movement of goods along the supply chain.

Transactions: Transactions are the fundamental units of data that are recorded on the blockchain. Each transaction contains information about the sender, receiver, timestamp, and any relevant data specific to the type of transaction. Once a transaction is validated and included in a block, it becomes a permanent part of the blockchain.

Cryptographic Hashing: Each block contains a unique cryptographic hash, a fixed-size string of characters, generated based on the data in the block. This hash serves as a digital fingerprint of the block. Any change in the data within the block will result in a completely different hash, providing a tamper-resistant mechanism. Additionally, each block includes the hash of the previous block, forming a link that creates the blockchain's chronological sequence.

Consensus Mechanisms: To ensure agreement among network participants on the state of the blockchain, consensus mechanisms are used. They define the rules for validating and adding new blocks to the chain. Common consensus mechanisms include Proof of Work (PoW), where nodes compete to solve complex mathematical puzzles to add a block, and Proof of Stake (PoS), where validators are chosen to add blocks based on the amount of cryptocurrency they hold as "stake."

Peer-to-Peer Network: A blockchain operates on a peer-to-peer network of computers or nodes. Each node maintains a copy of the entire blockchain, and they communicate and share information to reach a consensus on the validity of transactions and the order of blocks. This decentralized network structure ensures that there is no single point of failure and enhances security and resilience.

By combining these key components, blockchain technology enables secure, transparent, and trustless transactions and data management across a variety of applications and industries. Blockchain components are shown in Figure 7.1.

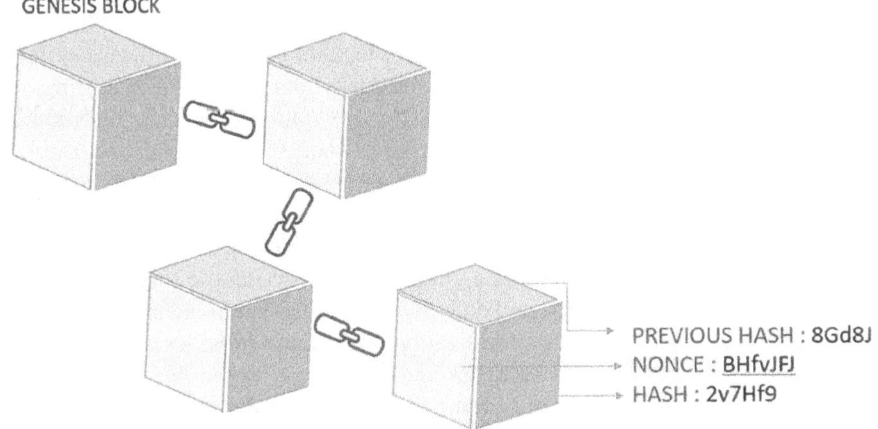

FIGURE 7.1 Blockchain components.

7.3 ROLE OF BLOCKCHAIN IN SECURING HEALTH RECORDS AND SENSITIVE DATA

Blockchain plays a crucial role in securing health records and sensitive data by leveraging its core features, such as immutability, encryption, decentralization, and transparency. Blockchain enhances security in managing health records.

Once health data is recorded on the blockchain, it becomes immutable, meaning it cannot be altered or deleted. This feature ensures the integrity of the data and prevents unauthorized modifications or tampering [11]. Blockchain can store encrypted health records, ensuring that only authorized users with the appropriate keys can access and decrypt the data. This protects sensitive patient information from unauthorized access. Blockchain operates on a decentralized network of nodes, reducing the risk of a single point of failure or data breach. Health records are distributed across multiple nodes, making it more challenging for hackers to compromise the entire system. The consensus mechanism used in blockchain ensures that only valid transactions are added to the blockchain. This prevents fraudulent or unauthorized changes to health records. With blockchain, patients can have more control over their health records and grant specific permissions to healthcare providers or researchers. This empowers patients to decide who can access their sensitive data. Blockchain's transparent nature allows for easy auditing of health records. Any access or changes made to the data are recorded on the blockchain, creating an audit trail that enhances accountability and transparency. Blockchain can facilitate interoperability between different healthcare systems, enabling secure and seamless data sharing between healthcare providers while maintaining data privacy. Smart contracts can be used to define access control rules for health records. These self-executing contracts can automate permission management, ensuring that only authorized entities can view or modify specific data. Blockchain can be employed to secure and authenticate data from medical Internet of Things (IoT) devices, preventing unauthorized access and data manipulation. The decentralized nature of blockchain makes it more resilient to distributed denial-of-service (DDoS) attacks and other cyber threats, as there is no central point of vulnerability. Blockchain's immutability ensures that health records remain secure and unchanged over time, making it suitable for long-term data preservation. By incorporating blockchain technology into healthcare systems, organizations can significantly enhance the security and privacy of health records and sensitive data. It empowers patients with more control over their information, improves data integrity, and reduces the risk of data breaches and unauthorized access, ultimately fostering trust between patients, healthcare providers, and other stakeholders. However, successful implementation requires careful planning, adherence to data privacy regulations, and continuous monitoring to address emerging security challenges. Blockchain plays a vital role in bolstering the security and safeguarding sensitive health records and data. By leveraging its unique features, such as immutability, encryption, and decentralization, blockchain provides an unparalleled level of protection against data breaches and tampering. When health records are recorded on the blockchain, they become immutable, rendering any unauthorized alterations practically impossible. Moreover, the utilization of encryption ensures that only authorized individuals with the appropriate cryptographic keys can access

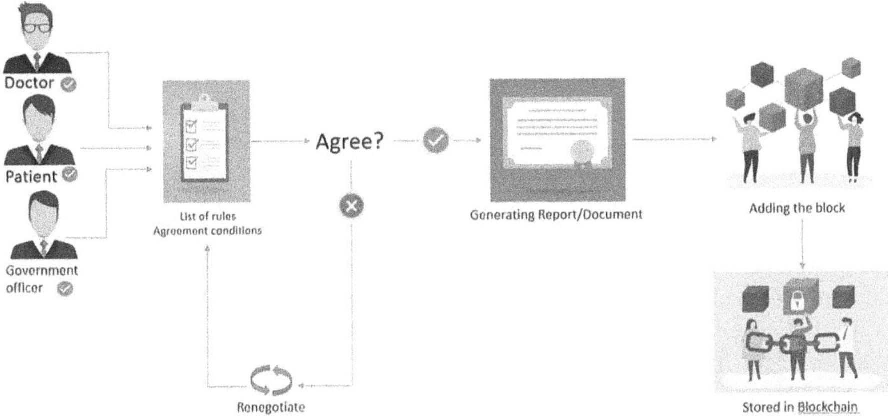

FIGURE 7.2   Securing and storing health records.

and decipher the data, shielding it from unauthorized eyes. The decentralized nature of the blockchain network further enhances security by eliminating single points of failure and reducing the risk of data breaches. Additionally, the consensus mechanism guarantees that only valid and verified transactions are added to the blockchain, preventing fraudulent or unauthorized changes to sensitive data. Patients, empowered with control over their data, can grant specific permissions to healthcare providers or researchers, thereby dictating who can access their private information. Transparency and auditability are also facilitated, enabling easy monitoring and accountability of any interactions with health records. Ultimately, blockchain technology instills trust in the healthcare ecosystem, ensuring the confidentiality and integrity of health data while fostering a secure and patient-centric approach to data management. Securing and storing health records in blockchain is shown in Figure 7.2.

7.4   ENSURING PATIENT PRIVACY AND CONSENT MANAGEMENT

Ensuring patient privacy and effective consent management are paramount considerations in the implementation of blockchain technology in healthcare. With blockchain's capability to securely store and share health data, maintaining patient privacy becomes a top priority. Through encryption and cryptographic keys, sensitive information can be safeguarded, ensuring that only authorized parties can access patient records. Patient consent plays a pivotal role in this context, as blockchain allows for granular control over data-sharing permissions. Patients can grant specific access rights to healthcare providers, researchers, or other entities, ensuring that their data is used in line with their preferences. This patient-centric approach empowers individuals to actively participate in their healthcare decisions and control the flow of their personal information. Transparent and auditable smart contracts can be employed to enforce consent agreements automatically, ensuring data access adheres to patients' explicit instructions. By incorporating robust privacy measures and empowering patients to manage their consent, blockchain in healthcare can foster a foundation of trust, strengthening the patient-provider relationship and facilitating responsible data sharing for research and treatment purposes.

7.5 ELECTRONIC HEALTH RECORDS ON THE BLOCKCHAIN

Electronic Health Records (EHRs) on blockchain technology offer a transformative solution to healthcare data management. By leveraging the blockchain's inherent security and decentralization, EHRs can be stored in a tamper-resistant and transparent manner. Each patient's medical information is recorded as a series of transactions in blocks, linked cryptographically, ensuring data integrity and immutability [12]. This not only reduces the risk of unauthorized access and data breaches but also enhances trust among patients, healthcare providers, and other stakeholders. Encryption and private keys protect sensitive patient data, ensuring that only authorized parties can access and view the records. Moreover, patients can exercise granular control over their EHRs, granting consent to specific individuals or institutions, and streamlining data sharing for medical treatment and research while preserving patient privacy. Interoperability is also improved, enabling seamless data exchange between different healthcare systems and promoting better care coordination and patient outcomes. By adopting blockchain for EHRs, healthcare organizations can lay the foundation for a secure, patient-centric, and efficient healthcare ecosystem, empowering patients and healthcare providers alike with access to accurate, complete, and trustworthy medical information.

7.6 SUPPLY CHAIN MANAGEMENT IN HEALTHCARE

Supply chain management in healthcare is a crucial function that ensures the smooth and efficient flow of medical products, equipment, and services from manufacturers to healthcare providers and patients. It plays a vital role in maintaining adequate inventory levels, managing costs, and delivering quality care. Healthcare supply chains face unique challenges, such as regulatory compliance, perishable and time-sensitive products, and demand variability. To address these challenges, healthcare organizations employ various strategies, including inventory management, traceability, and visibility through advanced technologies like RFID and barcode scanning, and supplier management. Compliance with strict regulations is essential to ensure the safety and authenticity of medical products throughout the supply chain. Moreover, embracing technological advancements like blockchain and IoT can enhance supply chain transparency and efficiency. Ultimately, an effective supply chain management system in healthcare contributes to improved patient care, reduces risks, and enhances the overall healthcare delivery process.

7.7 UTILIZING BLOCKCHAIN TO OPTIMIZE DRUG AND MEDICAL DEVICE SUPPLY CHAINS

Blockchain technology holds significant potential for optimizing drug and medical device supply chains. By enhancing transparency, traceability, and security, blockchain can address various challenges in the healthcare supply chain. Here are key ways in which blockchain can be applied to improve efficiency and reliability in the pharmaceutical and medical device sectors:

Traceability and transparency: Blockchain enables a secure and immutable record of the entire supply chain journey for each drug or medical device, from manufacturing to distribution and retail. This ensures transparency and traceability, reducing the risk of counterfeit products entering the supply chain.

Supply chain efficiency: Automated smart contracts on the blockchain can streamline and automate processes such as order processing, invoicing, and payments. This reduces delays and errors associated with manual processes, improving overall supply chain efficiency.

Inventory management: Real-time monitoring of inventory levels at each point in the supply chain is possible with blockchain. This helps prevent stockouts or overstock situations and allows for better demand forecasting.

Authentication and anti-counterfeiting: Each drug or medical device can be assigned a unique digital identity recorded on the blockchain. This makes it difficult for counterfeit products to enter the supply chain, as any deviation from the authorized product's identity can be easily detected.

Data security and privacy: Blockchain's decentralized nature enhances the security of sensitive data related to pharmaceuticals and medical devices. The distributed ledger reduces the risk of a single point of failure, making it more resistant to hacking.

Regulatory compliance: The immutability of blockchain records ensures compliance with regulatory requirements by providing a tamper-proof record of activities within the supply chain.

Collaboration and information sharing: Through permissioned access, blockchain facilitates better collaboration, communication, and information sharing among manufacturers, distributors, regulatory authorities, and other participants in the supply chain.

Recall management: In the event of a product recall, blockchain enables quick and accurate identification of affected products, minimizing the impact on public health. Timely action can prevent widespread harm.

Payment and financial transactions: Blockchain can facilitate secure and efficient financial transactions within the supply chain. Cryptocurrencies or blockchain-based tokens can be used for faster and more transparent payment processes. Implementing blockchain in the healthcare supply chain requires collaboration among stakeholders, adherence to industry standards, and consideration of regulatory requirements. While challenges exist, the potential benefits in terms of increased efficiency, transparency, and security make blockchain an attractive technology for optimizing drug and medical device supply chains.

7.8 TELEMEDICINE AND PATIENT ENGAGEMENT

Telemedicine has emerged as a transformative healthcare practice, leveraging technology to provide remote medical services and consultations. It allows patients to access healthcare professionals and services from the comfort of their homes, overcoming geographical barriers and improving healthcare accessibility.

However, as telemedicine becomes more widespread, ensuring patient engagement and data security becomes increasingly critical. Blockchain technology offers a promising solution to address these challenges, enhancing patient engagement in telemedicine while safeguarding sensitive healthcare data. Telemedicine, the practice of delivering healthcare services remotely through telecommunication technology, has gained immense popularity due to its convenience and accessibility [13]. However, one of the challenges faced by telemedicine is maintaining patient engagement and ensuring the security and privacy of sensitive medical data. Blockchain technology presents a compelling solution to address these issues and enhance patient engagement in telemedicine. Blockchain's decentralized and immutable nature provides a secure and transparent platform for storing and managing patient data. Medical records and other sensitive information can be securely recorded on the blockchain, ensuring that data remains tamper-proof and protected from unauthorized access. Patients can have greater confidence in sharing their medical information as they retain control over who can access their data, thus fostering trust and engagement.

Blockchain's ability to create a comprehensive and interoperable health data ecosystem enhances patient engagement in telemedicine. Patients can have a single source of truth for their medical history, facilitating seamless sharing of records among healthcare providers. This streamlined data exchange leads to more informed medical decisions, improved continuity of care, and ultimately, a higher level of patient engagement in their health management. Incorporating smart contracts in telemedicine can further incentivize patient engagement. Patients can receive tokens or rewards for actively participating in their health management, adhering to treatment plans, and achieving health goals. These incentives motivate patients to take a more proactive role in their well-being and healthcare journey. Patient engagement in telemedicine can also be enhanced through decentralized telehealth platforms built on blockchain. These platforms connect patients with healthcare professionals and allow for transparent and direct interactions. Patients can access their medical data, schedule appointments, and securely communicate with their providers, promoting continuous engagement and involvement in their healthcare decisions. Blockchain's ability to provide transparent tracking of medical supply chains and pharmaceutical data enhances patient safety and trust in telemedicine. Patients can be assured of the authenticity and quality of medications and medical devices used in telemedicine practices, further strengthening patient engagement and confidence in remote healthcare services.

7.9 ENHANCING TELEMEDICINE PLATFORMS WITH BLOCKCHAIN TECHNOLOGY

Medical kits and equipment for home use can aid patients in self-diagnosis outside clinical settings. Utilizing readily available test kits and equipment to measure specific biochemical reactions for self-examination and early illness diagnosis can reduce overall healthcare expenses. However, the lack of transparency, traceability, and data provenance about medical kits in traditional centralized telehealth-based systems poses challenges for doctors and patients to obtain reliable medical kits from reputable suppliers [14,15]. Enhancing telemedicine platforms with blockchain technology can yield several benefits, improving data security, patient privacy, and overall efficiency. Blockchain's decentralized and tamper-resistant nature ensures that patient data is securely stored and cannot be altered or deleted without authorization. Medical records, treatment plans, and other sensitive information can be recorded on the blockchain, providing a reliable and auditable source of truth. This technology can enable robust patient identity verification, reducing the risk of fraud and ensuring that healthcare services are delivered to the right individuals. Patients can have control over their digital identities, allowing them to share only the necessary information with healthcare providers. Blockchain-based smart contracts can facilitate consent management, ensuring that patients explicitly authorize the use and sharing of their medical data. This provides patients with greater control over their data and builds trust in the telemedicine platform. Blockchain enables seamless and secure data exchange between different healthcare providers and systems. This interoperability streamlines communication and coordination, leading to more comprehensive and efficient patient care. Blockchain-based cryptocurrencies or tokens can be used for secure and transparent telehealth payments. Patients can be incentivized to participate in telemedicine services through token rewards, encouraging greater engagement and adherence to treatment plans.

The advantages of blockchain technology in telemedicine platforms are as follows:

Medical Supply Chain Management: Blockchain can be utilized to track and verify the authenticity of medical supplies, medications, and devices used in telemedicine. This ensures patient safety and reduces the risk of counterfeit products.

Teleconsultation and Telemonitoring: Blockchain can facilitate encrypted and secure teleconsultation sessions between patients and healthcare providers. Additionally, it can securely store data from remote patient monitoring devices, enabling real-time tracking of health metrics.

Research and Data Sharing: Blockchain's transparency and data integrity can be leveraged to facilitate research collaborations and data sharing among different healthcare institutions. Researchers can access anonymized patient data while maintaining patient privacy and data security.

Regulatory Compliance: Blockchain's immutable audit trail can simplify regulatory compliance in telemedicine platforms. The platform can provide transparent records of data access, sharing, and usage, making it easier to demonstrate compliance with data protection regulations.

Disaster Recovery: Blockchain's distributed nature ensures that data is redundantly stored across multiple nodes, reducing the risk of data loss in case of system failures or cyberattacks.

By incorporating blockchain technology into telemedicine platforms, healthcare providers can offer enhanced security, privacy, and trust to patients, leading to more widespread adoption of telemedicine services. As the technology continues to evolve, the integration of blockchain with telemedicine holds the potential to revolutionize healthcare delivery and improve patient outcomes in the digital age.

7.10   SMART CONTRACTS IN HEALTHCARE

Smart contracts have emerged as a transformative technology in the healthcare industry, revolutionizing various aspects of patient care, data management, and administrative processes. These self-executing contracts, operating on blockchain platforms, offer unparalleled transparency, security, and automation. While the wording of agreements between two or more parties is incorporated into blockchain technology, smart contracts allow agreements to be executed automatically in a distributed environment when certain circumstances are satisfied, surpassing the capabilities of traditional contracts. Executable scripts known as "smart contracts" operate on top of the blockchain to enable, carry out, and uphold agreements between unreliable parties without the need for a third party to be trusted [16]. Network automation and the conversion of paper contracts into digital contracts were made possible by smart contracts. Smart contracts, as opposed to regular contracts, allow users to automate transactions under the supervision of a central authority, thereby codifying agreements and trust relationships [17]. One of the primary applications of smart contracts in healthcare is automated consent management for patients participating in clinical trials and research studies. By recording patients' consent on the blockchain, smart contracts ensure that data usage adheres strictly to the agreed-upon terms, enhancing patient privacy and data protection. Moreover, these contracts streamline insurance claims and payment processes, reducing administrative burdens and improving efficiency for both patients and insurance providers. Additionally, smart contracts facilitate supply chain management, tracking the authenticity and provenance of medications and medical devices, thereby enhancing patient safety. With the ability to establish patient-provider agreements, standardize data formats, and support telemedicine consultations and remote patient monitoring, smart contracts promote interoperability, personalized care, and improved patient outcomes. Furthermore, in research collaborations, these contracts govern data sharing and intellectual property rights, fostering a more trustworthy and collaborative research ecosystem. As the adoption of blockchain and smart contracts continues to grow, their role in healthcare is poised to transform the industry, creating a patient-centric, secure, and efficient healthcare system.

7.11   UNDERSTANDING SMART CONTRACTS AND THEIR APPLICATIONS IN MEDICINE

Smart contracts are automated, self-executing agreements coded on blockchain networks that find valuable applications in the medical field. These digital contracts offer increased transparency, tamper-proof security, and trust among the parties involved. In medicine, smart contracts can revolutionize various aspects of healthcare. They can securely manage electronic health records, allowing patients to control access while ensuring data integrity. Prescription and medication management can be automated, enabling timely reminders and refill execution. Smart contracts streamline clinical trials, automating data collection and participant consent while maintaining transparency. In healthcare payments and insurance, smart contracts facilitate secure and automated transactions, reducing administrative burdens and fraud.

Furthermore, they can ensure the authenticity and safety of pharmaceuticals throughout the supply chain. By enabling controlled data sharing and research collaboration, smart contracts also foster advancements in medical research. While promising, challenges such as regulatory compliance and data privacy must be addressed to fully unleash the transformative potential of smart contracts in medicine.

7.12   TRANSFORMING HEALTHCARE THROUGH BLOCKCHAIN

By using blockchain innovation to comprehend completed features, issues in healthcare facilities may be avoided. Blockchain-based medical policy processes have been found to be beneficial. Blockchain technology has the potential to transform healthcare by revolutionizing data management, security, and patient-centric services. Through its decentralized and immutable nature, blockchain can provide a secure and transparent platform for storing electronic health records (EHRs) [18]. This enables patients to have greater control over their data, while healthcare providers can access accurate and up-to-date information. Interoperability between different healthcare systems can be enhanced, leading to more efficient and coordinated care. Additionally, blockchain can facilitate the secure sharing of medical research data, promoting collaboration among researchers while preserving data privacy. Supply chain management in the pharmaceutical industry can be improved, ensuring the authenticity and traceability of medicines. Smart contracts, running on blockchain, automate various healthcare processes, such as insurance claims, prescription management, and clinical trial operations, reducing administrative burdens and enhancing efficiency. Moreover, blockchain's immutability and tamper-resistant nature help in combating healthcare fraud and ensuring the integrity of health-related data. While challenges like regulatory compliance and scalability remain, the potential benefits of blockchain in healthcare are vast, promising to reshape the industry to prioritize patient outcomes and data security. Blockchain technology won't be a cure-all for database issues, while occasionally upsetting the healthcare sector with its arrival. Alternatively, it might be a fantastic journey with the phased implementation of Blockchain. In essence, Blockchain is a safe transaction database that is accessible to all participants in the network of computers. By documenting all transactions that take place in the computer network and distributing copies of every transaction to every node, the Blockchain now eliminates the need for a reliable third-party transaction analyzer. Because the Blockchain reduces or does away with the need for a third-party payment processor, it has the potential to revolutionize the industry and save costs for companies. In addition, it offers non-trusted entities a reliable and transparent channel to interact with, eliminating the need for outside verification [19].

7.13   EMPOWERING PATIENTS WITH GREATER
CONTROL OVER THEIR HEALTH DATA

Empowering patients with greater control over their health data through blockchain technology can revolutionize the healthcare landscape, fostering patient-centered care and promoting transparency, privacy, and data ownership. Here's how blockchain can achieve this empowerment: Blockchain enables patients to become the sole owners of their health data. Using private keys, patients can grant consent for specific data sharing or revoke access when needed. This puts patients in charge of their data and ensures that their information is only accessed with explicit permission. Patients can have a transparent view of who has accessed their health data and for what purposes. The decentralized and immutable nature of blockchain ensures an audit trail of data access, providing patients with a complete record of data usage, promoting accountability, and reinforcing trust [20]. With blockchain's interoperability, patients can access their complete and up-to-date health records across various healthcare providers and institutions. This comprehensive view enables better decision-making, improves care continuity, and reduces the risk of medical errors. Blockchain enables encrypted and secure data sharing between patients and healthcare providers. Patients can selectively share relevant portions of their health data with different providers, ensuring the right information reaches the right hands without compromising the entire record. Patients can securely share their health data from remote monitoring devices with healthcare professionals through blockchain. This promotes remote care, better chronic disease management, and timely interventions without compromising data security. Blockchain-based tokens or cryptocurrencies can be used to reward patients for sharing their health data or participating in research initiatives. This incentivizes patients to actively engage in their health management and contributes to the advancement of medical science. Patients can securely and transparently participate in medical research studies through blockchain. They can grant researchers access to specific data while retaining control over its usage, ensuring privacy, and contributing to scientific progress. Blockchain can support the creation of smart contracts that execute personalized treatment plans based on patients' health data and conditions. These contracts can trigger reminders for medication adherence or suggest lifestyle modifications, improving patient outcomes. Patients can choose to monetize their health data by sharing it with researchers, institutions, or pharmaceutical companies. Blockchain enables a fair and transparent data marketplace, where patients are compensated for their contributions. The decentralized architecture of blockchain reduces the risk of large-scale data breaches, safeguarding sensitive health information from unauthorized access and protecting patient privacy. Through blockchain technology, patients gain greater control over their health data, leading to more patient-centric and personalized healthcare. Empowered patients are more likely to actively participate in their own health management, leading to improved health outcomes, better research opportunities, and a stronger partnership between patients and healthcare providers. Blockchain technology holds great promise for the healthcare industry, offering several advantages and potential benefits. However, it also faces certain limitations and challenges.

The advantages of blockchain in the healthcare sector are as follows:

- Database security procedures can cost a lot of money and take a long time to complete. Since each Blockchain transaction has its own proof of authenticity and authorization to impose restrictions, using the technology can be avoided. Additionally, it implies that the transactions can be independently validated and processed [21].

- Blockchain's decentralized and cryptographic nature enhances data security, making it challenging for unauthorized access and tampering. Patients' sensitive medical information can be stored securely and accessed only by authorized parties with the necessary keys or permissions.
- Blockchain can facilitate interoperability between different healthcare systems and institutions by providing a standardized and secure way to share patient data. This can improve care coordination, reduce duplication of tests, and enhance overall healthcare efficiency.
- Blockchain enables patients to have more control over their health data. Patients can grant specific permissions to providers, researchers, or other entities, ensuring that they have a say in how their information is used and shared.
- The immutability and transparency of blockchain enable easy auditing of healthcare transactions and data access. This can enhance accountability among healthcare providers and ensure compliance with regulatory standards.
- Blockchain can streamline the clinical trial process by securely storing and sharing trial data among stakeholders. It can also provide transparency in research results and prevent data manipulation or fraud. Blockchain can improve the tracking and traceability of medical supplies and pharmaceuticals throughout the supply chain, reducing the risk of counterfeit products and ensuring the authenticity of medications.

The challenges of blockchain in healthcare are as follows:

- Blockchain technology faces challenges with scalability, especially for public blockchains. As the number of transactions and data size increases, the network can experience slower processing times and higher transaction fees [22].
- Integrating blockchain in healthcare requires navigating complex regulatory frameworks concerning data privacy, consent, and security. Compliance with existing regulations can be challenging, especially if they vary between different jurisdictions.
- To fully realize the interoperability benefits of blockchain, there needs to be a standardized format for healthcare data. Currently, different healthcare systems use various data formats, making data integration more complicated.
- The security of blockchain relies on cryptographic keys. If patients or providers lose access to their private keys, it may result in the permanent loss of access to encrypted data.
- While blockchain enhances data security, it does not eliminate the risk of human error or malicious actors gaining access to the system. Phishing attacks and other social engineering techniques can still compromise blockchain users.

Implementing blockchain solutions requires specialized technical expertise and resources. Integrating blockchain with existing healthcare systems may be costly and time-consuming.

7.14 CONCLUSION

Blockchain technology provides a secure, transparent, and decentralized way of recording and verifying transactions, with applications extending beyond cryptocurrencies to various industries such as finance, supply chain, healthcare, and more. Blockchain technology offers the promise of increased security, transparency, and efficiency in various industries, potentially transforming how we conduct transactions and manage data in the future. However, it's important to acknowledge that it is still a developing technology, and its widespread adoption and implementation face both technical and regulatory challenges. Blockchain technology offers several potential benefits for the healthcare industry, such as increased data security, interoperability, and patient control over data. However, it is essential to address the limitations and challenges to fully harness its capabilities and ensure its successful integration into healthcare systems. Collaboration among stakeholders, adherence to regulatory requirements, and continuous advancements in blockchain technology are key to unlocking its full potential in healthcare. Blockchain technology significantly enhances data integrity, accessibility, and availability in healthcare by providing a secure, transparent, and decentralized platform for health data management. Through interoperable EHRs, healthcare stakeholders can access accurate and timely information, leading to more efficient care delivery and improved patient outcomes. By prioritizing data security and privacy, blockchain strengthens the foundation of trust and collaboration between patients and healthcare providers, fostering a patient-centric healthcare ecosystem. Blockchain technology holds immense potential to revolutionize telemedicine and patient engagement. By ensuring the security, privacy, and interoperability of medical data, blockchain enhances patient trust in telemedicine practices. Incentivization through smart contracts and the creation of decentralized telehealth platforms further encourage patients to actively participate in their health management, ultimately leading to better healthcare outcomes and a more engaged and empowered patient population.

REFERENCES

1. Haleem, A., Javaid, M., Pratap Singh, R., Suman, R., Rab, S. (2021). Blockchain technology applications in healthcare: An overview. *International Journal of Intelligent Networks*, 2, 130–139.
2. Ghosh, P.K, Chakraborty, A., Hasan, M., Rashid, K., Siddique, A.H. (2023). Blockchain application in healthcare systems: A review. *Systems*, 11(1), 38. doi:10.3390/systems11010038.
3. Griggs, K. N., Ossipova, O., Kohlios, C. P., Baccarini, A. N., Howson, E. A., Hayajneh, T. (2018). Healthcare blockchain system using smart contracts for secure automated remote patient monitoring. *Journal of Medical Systems,* 42, 130.
4. Gupta, R., Tanwar, S., Tyagi, S., Kumar, N., Obaidat, M. S., Sadoun, B. (2019). HaBiTs: Blockchain-based telesurgery framework for healthcare 4.0. In: *Proceedings of the International Conference on Computer, Information and Telecommunication Systems,* CITS, Beijing, China, 28–31 pp. 1–5.
5. Plotnikov, V., Kuznetsova, V. (2018). The prospects for the use of digital technology "blockchain" in the pharmaceutical market. In: *MATEC Web of Conferences, EDP Sciences,* Ho Chi Minh, Vietnam, vol. 193, p. 02029.

6. Khezr, S., Moniruzzaman, M., Yassine, A., Benlamri, R. (2019). Blockchain technology in healthcare: A comprehensive review and directions for future research. *Applied Sciences*, 9, 1736, doi:10.3390/app9091736.

7. Zheng, Z., Xie, S., Dai, H., Chen, X., Wang, H.(2018), Blockchain challenges and opportunities: A survey. *International Journal of Web and Grid Services*, 14, 352.

8. Mendling J., Weber I., Aalst W. V. D., Brocke J. V., Cabanillas C., Daniel, F. et al. (2018). Blockchains for business process management-challenges and opportunities. *ACM Transactions on Management Information Systems (TMIS)*, 9(1), 1–16.

9. Kuo, T. T., Gabriel, R. A., Ohno-Machado, L. (2019). Fair compute loads enabled by blockchain: Sharing models by alternating client and server roles. *Journal of the American Medical Informatics Association*, 26(5), 392–403. doi: 10.1093/jamia/ocy180.

10. Aggarwal, S., Kumar, N. (2021), Blockchain components and concepts. *Advances in Computers*, 121, 387–398.

11. Taherdoost, H. (2023). Smart contracts in blockchain technology: A critical review, *Emerging Industrial Applications: Orchestration of Machine Learning, the IoT, and Blockchain*, 14(2), 117–136.

12. Habib, G., Sharma, S., Ibrahim, S., Ahmad, I., Qureshi, S., Ishfaq, M. (2022). Blockchain technology: Benefits, challenges, applications, and integration of blockchain technology with cloud computing. *Future Internet,* 14(11), 341.

13. Meinert, E., Alturkistani, A., Foley, K. A., Osama, T., Car, J., Majeed, A., Van Velthoven, M., Wells, G., Brindley, D. (2019). Blockchain implementation in health care: protocol for a systematic review. *JMIR Research Protocols*, 8(2), e10994.

14. Li, R. (2005). Multifunctional self-diagnostic device for in-home health-checkup, US Patent App. 10/904,818, June.

15. Weissman, S. M., Zellmer, K., Gill, N., Wham, D. (2018). Implementing a virtual health telemedicine program in a community setting. *Journal of Genetic Counseling*, 27(2), 323–325.

16. Buterin, V. et al (2014) A next-generation smart contract and decentralized application platform. White paper.

17. Singh, A., Parizi, R. M., Zhang, Q., Choo, K. K. R., Dehghantanha, A. (2020) Blockchain smart contracts formalization: Approaches and challenges to address vulnerabilities. *Computers & Security,* 88, 101654.

18. Pandey, R., Khatri, A., Premalatha, G., Verma, L. N. M. D., Shingadiya, C. J. (2023) Integration of blockchain technology in health care system: an intensive review. In: *2023 3rd International Conference on Advance Computing and Innovative Technologies in Engineering (ICACITE)*, Greater Noida, India, 2023, pp. 968–972, doi:10.1109/ICACITE57410.2023.10182960.

19. Huang, G., Foysal, A. A. (2021). Blockchain in healthcare. *Technology and Investment* 12(3), 168–181.

20. Rupasinghe, T., Burstein, F., Rudolph, C., Strange, S. (2019). Towards a blockchain based fall prediction model for aged care. In: *Proceedings of the Australasian Computer Science Week Multiconference*, pp. 1–10, doi:10.1145/ 3290688.3290736.

21. Fauvel, W. (August 2017). Blockchain advantages and disadvantages. https://medium.com/nudjed/blockchainadvantage-and-disadvantages-e76dfde3bbc0

22. Adler-Milstein, J. (2018). Moving past the EHR interoperability blame game. *The New England Journal of Medicine*, n.d. https://catalyst.nejm.org/ehr-interoperability-blame-game/. Accessed March 28, 2018.

8 Internet of Things (IoT) in the Indian Healthcare Sector

A Comparative Study during Pre- and Post-Pandemic Period

Gaikar Vilas, Sawant Mitali, and Tedla Berhane

8.1 INTRODUCTION

The incorporation of the Internet of Things (IoT) into the healthcare industry represents a significant milestone, offering potential breakthroughs in patient care and operational effectiveness [1]. "Internet of Things (IoT) in healthcare" pertains to the networked infrastructure of medical equipment and software applications that engage in communication and data sharing [2]. This network enables real-time monitoring, data collection, and analysis, fostering informed decision-making and timely interventions. It opens up avenues for remote patient monitoring, medication adherence systems, and innovative diagnostic and treatment solutions, improving accessibility and quality of healthcare [3,4]. However, while offering numerous benefits, it also poses challenges, particularly regarding data security and privacy [5,6]. Balancing the promises and concerns, IoT continues to redefine the paradigms of healthcare delivery [7].

According to the results of the Digital Health Report published by Statista, the digital health industry is projected to experience a compound annual growth rate of 21.12%, reaching a market size of $30.73 billion by 2028. These findings are based on the Digital Health Report released by Statista. The Global Smart Healthcare Market Report forecasts that the market for smart healthcare products in India will grow at a compound annual growth rate of 15.37% from 2023 to 2030. This projection is derived from an analysis of the global market.

IoT is defined as the interconnection of smart devices capable of communicating with each other, analyzing the data they collect, and taking action based on their findings [2]. It encompasses a wide variety of applications, from wearable devices for patients to networked medical equipment that enhances diagnostic capabilities and optimizes patient care [8,9]. One example of an application falling under this category

DOI: 10.1201/9781032632223-8

is a smartwatch. Given the significant revolutionary potential of these technologies, it is essential to understand how they will be accepted and their consequences, particularly in a culture characterized by persistent healthcare disparities [9].

In India's medical industry, the use of IoT technology has expanded over the past few years. The integration of IoT devices in the healthcare industry has led to significant changes, fundamentally transforming the industry by enabling live tracking, enhancing systematic care, and facilitating operational performance [10]. These changes have occurred due to the assimilation of IoT applications into the healthcare industry.

The need for remote patient monitoring and telemedicine, particularly in rural areas [11] with limited availability of healthcare services, is a primary driver for the development of the IoT in the Indian healthcare industry. This need is especially pronounced in areas where healthcare facilities are scarce. According to research conducted by Dr. Rajashekhar Karjagi, an expert in Analytics Solutions at Wipro, the use of IoT devices, such as wearables and remote monitoring equipment [12], enables healthcare professionals to effectively monitor the vital signs of patients and take prompt action when necessary. This technology has the potential to alleviate the workload of hospitals and clinics.

Additionally, IoT has made significant contributions to the improvement of healthcare supply chain management, facilitating the efficient distribution of medications and medical supplies [13]. Given the widespread distribution of COVID-19, the significance of this has increased [14].

IoT's impact on India's healthcare industry is also driven by its ability to optimize healthcare operations, improve patient experiences, and reduce costs [15]. The growth of IoT in Indian healthcare is expected to continue, offering new opportunities for innovation [16] and better healthcare services [17].

McKinsey & Company (2022) defines IoT as *"The Internet of Things (IoT) describes physical objects embedded with sensors and actuators that communicate with computing systems via wired or wireless networks—allowing the physical world to be digitally monitored or even controlled."*

Analytics Solutions at Wipro highlights the benefit of IoT as *"Internet of Things (IoT)-enabled devices have made remote monitoring in the healthcare sector possible, unleashing the potential to keep patients safe and healthy, and empowering physicians to deliver superlative care."*

8.1.1 Objectives of this Study

1. Assessing the extent of IoT adoption within the Indian healthcare industry prior to the global pandemic, with a focus on identifying primary areas of application and integration.
2. Analyzing the shifts and expansion of IoT within healthcare institutions post-pandemic, emphasizing new areas of utilization and innovations driven by pandemic needs.
3. Evaluating the tangible and intangible impacts of IoT integrations on patient care, healthcare operations, and overall medical outcomes during the comparative periods.

8.2 REVIEW OF LITERATURE

IoT technology has significantly impacted the healthcare sector, streamlining processes, improving patient care, and enhancing the overall healthcare ecosystem. Researchers [1] have explored several facets of IoT in healthcare, including its applications, benefits, and challenges [18]. IoT plays a pivotal role in controlling and enhancing healthcare operations [19] across different departments. Its presence has simplified tasks and made healthcare services more accessible [20]. IoT has imposed its control on various departments within healthcare, making it easier to monitor patients, manage medical equipment, and improve data collection and analysis. IoT has the potential to transform healthcare by delivering both niche and mass-market services [21]. It enables remote monitoring, telemedicine, and real-time health data tracking [22]. IoT-based smart healthcare monitoring systems have gained prominence [7]. These systems utilize IoT to monitor patients' health remotely and provide real-time data to healthcare professionals for better decision-making [23]. The benefits of IoT include enhanced accuracy and reliability of medical data, improved patient outcomes, and increased productivity in healthcare services [24]. IoT has the capacity to fundamentally transform the healthcare sector through the provision of fast and precise information. Nevertheless, the healthcare sector encounters many hurdles in employing the Internet of Medical Things (IoMT), which encompasses apprehensions over the safety and confidentiality of data, complications related to interoperability, and the necessity for regulatory frameworks [25,26]. While IoT offers immense potential in healthcare, security remains a critical concern [27]. Researchers have delved into ensuring the security of IoT-based healthcare systems. Literature reviews also discuss the importance of security in IoT healthcare systems [28]. Comprehensive analysis is provided to ensure the security of patient data and connected devices [21]. IoT is revolutionizing healthcare by changing how data is collected, processed, and utilized. It is discussed in various research papers as a technology that functions and revolutionizes healthcare processes [19]. IoT in healthcare is an evolving field. Researchers are exploring future directions and addressing challenges to harness its full potential [29].

Knowledge Gaps: Literature reviews have identified knowledge gaps in IoT research in healthcare, paving the way for further exploration and innovation [30]. Researchers [20] highlighted the potential of IoT in augmenting healthcare services. Their study emphasized that IoT-enabled devices and applications, such as live tracking and monitoring and smart healthcare infrastructure, contributed to more efficient healthcare services [31,32]. The ability to collect and transmit real-time data improved diagnosis accuracy, streamlined workflows, and reduced healthcare costs, ultimately benefiting both providers and patients [33]. IoT devices in healthcare, such as wearable monitors and sensors, continuously collect data [34]. Artificial intelligence (AI) systems analyze this data to provide actionable insights and support medical decision-making, contributing to personalized medicine [35].

Hypothesis 1

H_{01}: Prior to the global pandemic, there was no significant difference in the adoption of the IoT within the Indian healthcare sector compared to the post-pandemic period.

Hypothesis 2

H_{02}: The onset of the pandemic did not significantly impact the expansion and diversification of IoT applications in healthcare institutions. This led to the advent of new areas of utilization, such as telemedicine support and real-time pandemic analytics.

The primary aim of this research endeavor is to perform a comparative examination relating to the implementation and consequences of IoT within the healthcare sector of India, encompassing periods preceding and following the occurrence of the pandemic [14,36]. This study utilizes both primary and secondary data sources. The researchers employed a survey methodology to gather primary data from a representative sample of 399 individuals who use smart healthcare devices in the Mumbai Metropolitan Region, located in India [37]. The subjects were selected by purposive sampling [38]. The process of gathering secondary data involved examining publicly accessible sources, including academic papers and journals.

8.3 FINDINGS AND INTERPRETATION

A dichotomous variable, often referred to as a binary or dummy variable, takes on two possible outcomes or values. In the context of our analysis, the dichotomous variable 'Pre_Post' serves as an indicator of two different periods: the pre-pandemic and post-pandemic periods. Specifically, when 'Pre_Post' is 0, it represents the pre-pandemic period. When 'Pre_Post' is 1, it represents the post-pandemic period. Using such a variable allows us to quantify and understand the shift or difference in IoT adoption and its overall impact between these two distinct periods. The overall summary statistics are represented in Table 8.1.

Model 1 (IoT Adoption):

- $\text{IOT\_Adoption} = \beta_0 + \beta_1 \times \text{Pre\_Post} + \varepsilon$

Model 2 (Overall Impact of IoT):

- $\text{Overall\_Impact} = \alpha_0 + \alpha_1 \times \text{Pre\_Post} + \varepsilon$

Model 1 (IoT Adoption): In Table 8.2, the transition to the post-pandemic period is associated with a significant increase in the adoption level of IoT. Specifically, the

---

TABLE 8.1

Overall Summary Statistics

Statistic	Count	Mean	Std. Dev.	Min	25%	Median	75%	Max
IOT_Adoption	399	2.335	1.791	0.000	1.000	1.000	4.000	5.000
Overall_Impact	399	3.971	0.905	1.000	3.000	4.000	5.000	5.000
Pre_Post	399	0.500	0.500	0.000	0.000	0.500	1.000	1.000

Source: Primary Data Collection.

TABLE 8.2
Model 1: IOT_Adoption~Pre_Post

Variable	Coefficient	*t*-Statistic	*p*-Value
Const	0.810	17.223	0.00000
Pre_Post	3.050	45.886	0.00000

Source: Primary data collection.

TABLE 8.3
Model 2: Overall_Impact~Pre_Post

Variable	Coefficient	*t*-Statistic	*p*-Value
Const	3.366	99.976	0.00000
Pre_Post	1.211	25.425	0.00000

Source: Primary data collection.

adoption level of IoT post-pandemic has increased by about 3.05 units, on average, compared to the pre-pandemic period.

Model 2 (Overall Impact of IoT): In Table 8.3, the overall impact or rating of IoT adoption has experienced a significant boost in the post-pandemic period. On average, the overall impact has risen by about 1.21 units in the post-pandemic period compared to the pre-pandemic times.

8.4 INTERPRETATION

The significance value in Tables 8.2 and 8.3 is 0.00 (<0.05), which indicates that the independent variable(s) under consideration do contribute meaningfully to explaining variations in the dependent variable. It implies that deviations in the independent variable have a statistically significant effect on the dependent variable. Thus, the null hypotheses H_{01} and H_{02} are rejected. It can be witnessed from Table 8.2 that patient engagement and remote monitoring due to IoT have changed considerably as the adoption level has increased by 3.05 units during the post-pandemic period. The adoption of IoT in the Indian healthcare sector likely saw a substantial difference before and after the global pandemic, primarily due to the pandemic's influence on accelerating digital transformation in healthcare worldwide driven by the need for remote healthcare solutions and data-driven decision-making.

The pandemic did have a substantial effect on the expansion and diversification of IoT applications in healthcare institutions, leading to the advent of novel areas of operation, such as telemedicine support and real-time pandemic analytics. The pandemic acted as a catalyst for the modernization of healthcare systems, making them more reliant on digital technologies like IoT for improved patient care and disease management. Health monitoring devices, virtual health consultations, teletherapy, and mHealth apps were the major noticeable benefits of using IoT among healthcare users.

8.5   LIMITATIONS AND FUTURE SCOPE OF STUDY

In the present study, consideration was given to the preferences of users in the Mumbai Metropolitan Region regarding the influence that the Internet of Things would have in the healthcare sector. Given that respondents will be asked about practices and outcomes before the pandemic, there's potential for recall bias. IoT's definition and the technologies encompassed within it can vary. Hence, what one individual considers IoT might differ from another. Additionally, this work has considered samples from a specific geographical location which can be further studied by taking into account other areas and segments. Future research can be extended by incorporating new variables or dimensions related to IoT.

8.6   SUGGESTIONS AND CONCLUSION

Developing robust healthcare infrastructure that includes seamless connectivity between urban and remote areas is essential to ensure that even patients in the most remote locations can access and benefit from remote healthcare monitoring systems. To accommodate the constraints in rural areas, an architectural model for connectivity should focus on being self-sustained, minimizing costs, and supporting local processing due to the lack of reliable internet connectivity. Creating user-friendly mobile applications for remote healthcare monitoring is crucial. Patients should have access to their health data and the ability to communicate with their healthcare professionals through these applications, which should also be secure and easy to use. Establishing a regulatory framework that promotes innovation in remote healthcare monitoring while protecting the patient's right to privacy and providing a secure environment for their data is paramount. Developing remote healthcare monitoring in India requires a holistic approach, combining technology, infrastructure development, and regulatory support to ensure the well-being of patients across the country.

The advent of IoT in India's healthcare sector might lead to significant advancements in patient care. This is because IoT has the potential to vastly enhance the standard of care delivered and the experience enjoyed by patients. The widespread use of this phenomenon has resulted in several advantages and significant shifts. The aforementioned factors contribute to improved chronic disease management, enhanced patient care, fitness tracking, and more precise measurement of health outcomes. Moreover, it has revolutionized the delivery of healthcare by making huge strides in improving the safety and security of healthcare services. When it comes to IoT, market forecasts from the 2023 Nasscom Future of Work Survey indicate promising prospects for growth in the Indian healthcare industry. IoT has had a major influence on India's healthcare system, leading to widespread change and improvement. Businesses in an extensive array of industries have benefited from the widespread use of this technology, and it has helped them solve a number of problems they've been facing.

REFERENCES

1. Kashani, M. H., Madanipour, M., Nikravan, M., Asghari, P., Mahdipour, E. (2021). A systematic review of IoT in healthcare: Applications, techniques, and trends. *Journal of Network and Computer Applications*, 192, 103164.
2. Bhatt, C., Dey, N., Ashour, A. S. (Eds.). (2017). Internet of things and big data technologies for next-generation healthcare. *Internet of Things and Big Data Technologies for Next Generation Healthcare,* 23, 3–12.
3. Jeong, J. S., Han, O., You, Y. Y. (2016). A design characteristics of smart healthcare system as the IoT application. *Indian Journal of Science and Technology*, 9(37), 1–8.
4. Yuehong, Y.I.N., Zeng, Y., Chen, X., Fan, Y. (2016). The internet of things in healthcare: An overview. *Journal of Industrial Information Integration*, 1, 3–13.
5. Bommareddy, S., Khan, J. A., Pandey, D. (2022). IoT implementation and challenges in healthcare industries. In: Pooja Singh, Omprakash Kaiwartya, Nidhi Sindhwani, Vishal Jain, and Rohit Anand (eds.) *Networking Technologies in Smart Healthcare*, pp. 211–230. CRC Press.
6. Thibaud, M., Chi, H., Zhou, W., Piramuthu, S. (2018). Internet of Things (IoT) in high-risk Environment, Health and Safety (EHS) industries: A comprehensive review. *Decision Support Systems*, 108, 79–95.
7. Birje, M. N., Hanji, S. S. (2020). Internet of things based distributed healthcare systems: A review. *Journal of Data, Information and Management,* 2, 149–165.
8. Chakraborty, S., Palodhi, K. (2021). IoT in the healthcare industry: Medical internet of things: Techniques. *Practices and Applications*, 21, 22.
9. Tyagi, S., Agarwal, A., Maheshwari, P. (2016, January). A conceptual framework for IoT-based healthcare system using cloud computing. In: *2016 6th International Conference-Cloud System and Big Data Engineering (Confluence)*, pp. 503–507. IEEE.
10. Onasanya, A., Elshakankiri, M. (2021). Smart integrated IoT healthcare system for cancer care. *Wireless Networks*, 27, 4297–4312.
11. Dimitrievski, A., Filiposka, S., Melero, F. J., Zdravevski, E., Lameski, P., Pires, I. M., Trajkovik, V. (2021). Rural healthcare IoT architecture based on low-energy LoRa. *International Journal of Environmental Research and Public Health*, 18(14), 7660.
12. Gaikar, V.B., Gautamkumar Deshmukh, R., Rajasanthosh kumar, T., Chowdhury, S., Sesharao, Y., Abilmazhinov, Y. (2023). IoT based solar energy monitoring system. *Materials Today: Proceedings*, 80(3), 3697–3701. doi:10.1016/j.matpr.2021.07.364.
13. Pace, P., Aloi, G., Gravina, R., Caliciuri, G., Fortino, G., Liotta, A. (2018). An edge-based architecture to support efficient applications for healthcare industry 4.0. *IEEE Transactions on Industrial Informatics*, 15(1), 481–489.
14. Redda, E.H., Gaikar, V., Tedla, B.A. (2021). E-commerce companies, online shopping and customer's satisfaction: A comparative study of Covid-19 lockdown in India. *Journal of Management Information and Decision Sciences*, 24(6), 1–17.
15. Mani, N., Singh, A., Nimmagadda, S. L. (2020). An IoT guided healthcare monitoring system for managing real-time notifications by fog computing services. *Procedia Computer Science*, 167, 850–859.
16. Cherian, J., Jacob, J., Qureshi, R., Gaikar, V. (2020). Relationship between entry grades and attrition trends in the context of higher education: Implication for open innovation of education policy. *Journal of Open Innovation: Technology, Market, and Complexity*, 6(4), 199. doi:10.3390/joitmc6040199.
17. Mathew, P. S., Pillai, A. S., Palade, V. (2018). Applications of IoT in healthcare. In: Sangaiah, A., Thangavelu, A., and Meenakshi Sundaram, V. (eds) *Cognitive Computing for Big Data Systems Over IoT: Frameworks, Tools and Applications*, Springer, Cham, 14, pp. 263–288.

18. Khan, M. A. (2021). Challenges facing the application of IoT in medicine and healthcare. *International Journal of Computations, Information and Manufacturing (IJCIM)*, 1(1), 39–55.19.   Mohamad Jawad, H. H., Bin Hassan, Z., Zaidan, B. B., Mohammed Jawad, F. H., Mohamed Jawad, D. H., Alredany, W. H. D. (2022). A systematic literature review of enabling IoT in healthcare: Motivations, challenges, and recommendations. *Electronics*, 11(19), 3223.

20. Kelly, J. T., Campbell, K. L., Gong, E., Scuffham, P. (2020). The Internet of Things: Impact and implications for health care delivery. *Journal of Medical Internet Research*, 22(11), e20135.

21. Quraishi, S. J., Yusuf, H. (2021). Internet of things in healthcare: A literature review. In: *2021 International Conference on Technological Advancements and Innovations (ICTAI)*, Tashkent, Uzbekistan, pp. 198–202, doi:10.1109/ICTAI53825.2021.9673369.

22. Maddahi, Y., Chen, S. (2022, September). Applications of digital twins in the health-care industry: Case review of an IoT-enabled remote technology in dentistry. *Virtual Worlds*, 1(1), 20–41.

23. Alkeya, B., Devi Boddeti, N., Salomi Monica, K., Ramadoss, P., Ramani, V. (2020). IoT-based smart healthcare monitoring systems: A literature review. *European Journal of Molecular & Clinical Medicine* 7(11), 2761–2769.

24. Hassan, A., Prasad, D., Khurana, M., Lilhore, U. K., Simaiya, S. (2021). Integration of internet of things (IoT) in health care industry: An overview of benefits, challenges, and applications. *Data Science and Innovations for Intelligent Systems*, 1, 165–180.

25. Gaikar, V. B., Tedla, B.A., Rane, C. (2023). Trust chain for managing trust in block-chain-associated IoT-enabled supply-chains. In: Goar V., Kuri M., Kumar R., Senjyu T. (eds) *Advances in Information Communication Technology and Computing. Lecture Notes in Networks and Systems*, vol. 628. Springer. doi:10.1007/978-981-19-9888-1_14

26. Joyia, G. J., Liaqat, R. M., Farooq, A., Rehman, S. (2017). Internet of medical things (IoMT): Applications, benefits and future challenges in healthcare domain. *Journal of Communication*, 12(4), 240–247.

27. Tongkachok, K., Alolo Abdul-Rasheed Akeji, A., Mohammed Wumbei, B., Ibn Musah, A.A., Sunil Kumar Domathoti, H., Vilas Bhau, G. (2023). Optimization of the enter-prise HR management by using iot. *Materials Today: Proceedings*, 80(3), 3444–3450, doi:10.1016/j.matpr.2021.07.268.

28. Chacko, A., Hayajneh, T. (2018). Security and privacy issues with IoT in healthcare. *EAI Endorsed Transactions on Pervasive Health and Technology*, 4(14), 1–7.

29. Bovenizer, W., Chetthamrongchai, P. (2023). A comprehensive systematic and biblio-metric review of the IoT-based healthcare systems. *Cluster Computing*, 26, 1–27.

30. Rejeb, A., Rejeb, K., Treiblmaier, H., Appolloni, A., Alghamdi, S., Alhasawi, Y., Iranmanesh, M. (2023). The Internet of Things (IoT) in healthcare: Taking stock and moving forward. *Internet of Things*, 22, 100721.

31. Rajput, D.S., Gour, R. (2016). An IoT framework for healthcare monitoring systems. *International Journal of Computer Science and Information Security*, 14(5), 451–455.

32. V.N, V.V, Ulle, R.S. (2023). Challenges and opportunities for IoT deployment in India's healthcare sector. In: *Computational Intelligence for Clinical Diagnosis*, 2023, 561–571.

33. Gaikar, V.B. (2021). An evaluation of public health schemes in India: A case study of Maharashtra state. *Journal of Management Information and Decision Sciences*, 24, 1–10.

34. Dang, L. M., Piran, M. J., Han, D., Min, K., Moon, H. (2019). A survey on the internet of Things and cloud computing for healthcare. *Electronics*, 8(7), 768.

35. Shah, R., Chircu, A. (2018). IoT and AI in healthcare: A systematic literature review. *Issues in Information Systems*, 19(3), 33–41.

36. Gaikar, V.B., Joshi Bharat, M., Jaywant, B.P., Mhatre, N., Chitra, K.C., Cheriyan, S., Rane Caroleena, G. (2021). An impact of covid-19 on virtual learning: The innovative study on undergraduate students of mumbai metropolitan region. *Academy of Strategic Management Journal,* 20, 1–19.

37. Cherian, J., Gaikar, V., Paul, R., Pech, R. (2021). Corporate culture and its impact on employees' attitude, performance, productivity, and behavior: An investigative analysis from selected organizations of the United Arab Emirates (UAE). *Journal of Open Innovation: Technology, Market, and Complexity,* 7(1), 45, doi:10.3390/joitmc7010045.

38. Gaikar, V.B., Lakhani, S. A. (2020). Demographic variables influencing financial investment of urban individuals: A case study of selected districts of maharashtra state. *International Journal of Advanced Science and Technology,* 29(5), 962–974. https://sersc.org/journals/index.php/IJAST/article/view/9749.

9 Edge AI and Blockchain for Smart Sustainability Healthcare Systems

Swabra Yahya Umutoni and
Seval Kardeş Selimoğlu

9.1 INTRODUCTION

As the first child is most of the time forgotten, especially upon the arrival of the second one, so does Industry 5.0 seem to have emerged to address what Industry 4.0 has not accomplished. Literature mentions that the main focus of Industry 4.0 has only been on digitalization and AI, neglecting social fairness and sustainability. Industry 5.0 reportedly is embraced for introducing new ideas aimed at maintaining the significance of both Research and Innovation while ensuring sustainable humanity service. Even though it is considered a new notion, existing studies describe the attributes of Industry 5.0 based on their study that could not predict its capable outcomes for various firms and how it can converge both real and virtual reality [1]. Industry 5.0 is largely regarded as a value paradigm that propels the evolution of technology with a specific objective in mind. Consequently, it revolves around three key interconnected fundamental principles:

Human-centricity: The major focus of human-centricity as a feature of Industry 5.0 lies in prioritizing human needs during the production process. Instead of pondering about the potential applications of new technology, it dwells on understanding what the new technology has to offer and the opportunities gained. Industry 5.0 helps foster skills and empowerment of man; its primary aim is to combine human expertise with that of machines since machines do not have the capacity to perform all tasks independently. It empowers humans to work hand in hand with machines in various fields, such as healthcare, production, and others [2,3]. For example, the Motion Analysis research laboratory staff of the Islamic University in Uganda introduced a fresh innovation using a tool called "the utility model application", a system for country-wide reporting of hospital-managed infectious diseases such as Ebola and Covid [4].

Resilience: The resilience component suggests that it is very important for businesses to establish a robust and supportive framework that can help during a crisis like the devastating earthquake that struck on 6 February 2023, which claimed a lot of lives and loss of property in Turkiye, for example, Ophy care (20 March 2023), an Artificial Intelligence (AI) powered telemedicine agency that mainly caters for

DOI: 10.1201/9781032632223-9

patients whose native language is not English, wrote about a telehealth technology, one of the AI technology, that is reported to have been launched during this time to respond swiftly to the affected people of the two affected countries, Turkiye and Syria during the aftermath of the earthquake. This was widely helpful because medical personnel, with their knowledge, managed to interact with people at a distance in real-time by video conferencing and provided the necessary comfort to traumatized victims. To ensure long-term viability, businesses must focus on effectively utilizing and conserving natural resources with the effort to reduce waste. This entails the development of new resources, their purposeful utilization, and the implementation of recycling processes. By adopting these measures, a company can actively reduce pollution and minimize the negative impact on the environment.

Sustainability: Sustainability is one of the three vital principles of Industry 5.0 as reported by previous research; the application of the term sustainability was first coined in 1715 in which both French and English foresters praised the method of tree planting in a bid to have sustained-yield forestry. More could be found in the book of Hans Carl Von Carlowitz, a German forester, and scientist; it describes actions that seem to be better than other opponents' practices [5].

9.2 SMART HEALTHCARE

As the name suggests, the term smart healthcare promotes human well-being and has step by step transformed through the application of emerging technologies like AI, The Internet of Things (IoT), Big Data, cloud computing, and others. It was found that IBM started the planet with IoT, whereby information is processed by smart computers and wearable devices, transforming the old medical system into a sophisticated system to ensure the efficiency of medical workers, good patient services, and other institutional stakeholders [6]. According to [7], sustainability can have a positive influence on hospital laboratories, enhancing proper resource allocation and utilization. The sustainability model explains the fact that hospitals not only work to support human health improvement but also enhance the natural environment for the entire economy through the application of emerging technologies under Industry 5.0. AI consists of two words, "artificial" and "intelligence", indicating man-made intelligence or knowledge. It means that machines attempt to process and analyze human reasoning and simplify complex tasks; this form of knowledge is popularly known as machine learning [8]. However, while AI is a technologically advanced system with sophisticated networks and mechanisms, it does not guarantee the ability to perform all tasks like humans; in other words, it is man-made and monitored by man [9,10].

The application of AI has led to significant changes and improvements, prompting the invention of large multisource datasets frequently through the use of automated devices. Intelligent healthcare services ensure communication among diverse healthcare providers, boosting resource allocation, individual task management, and well-informed decision-making within that circle [11]. Blockchain refers to datasets supporting the dissemination of data within domains that may not trust or be familiar with each other. The introduction of blockchain has advanced businesses in various sectors, especially in the supply chain and healthcare, by facilitating mutual decision-making processes [12]. In the past, financial transactions used to take time, but with the presence of blockchain technology, which is known to be monitored, such loopholes has been minimized. For example, in some developing countries like Uganda, telecommunication companies offer mobile money services that expedite money transactions at any time. The sender initiates the transaction to send money to someone else, supported by the existing details of the receiver in the system. With blockchain, this process has been simplified because it clarifies correct information about the two parties involved in the transaction, eliminating the need for a third party. For example, MTN mobile services, a South African-based telecommunication company, offers such services.

9.3 BLOCKCHAIN AND ARTIFICIAL INTELLIGENCE IMPACT ON HEALTHCARE SYSTEMS

Without a doubt, the two advanced technologies, namely AI and blockchain, can have a positive impact on health systems in terms of equipment and services provided, which aids in the proper care of both inpatients and outpatients, as depicted in Figure 9.1. As previously explored in prior research, advanced technologies can enhance healthcare systems by respecting the elements of privacy, data management, and accuracy, and providing many other benefits [13]. Just like any other field, health systems ought to yield better results since these technologies can create a clear and accurate connection between medical personnel and their patients. It is commonly known that in any business function, a customer is the boss, regardless of the circumstances. This is one of the hidden reasons why companies carefully consider

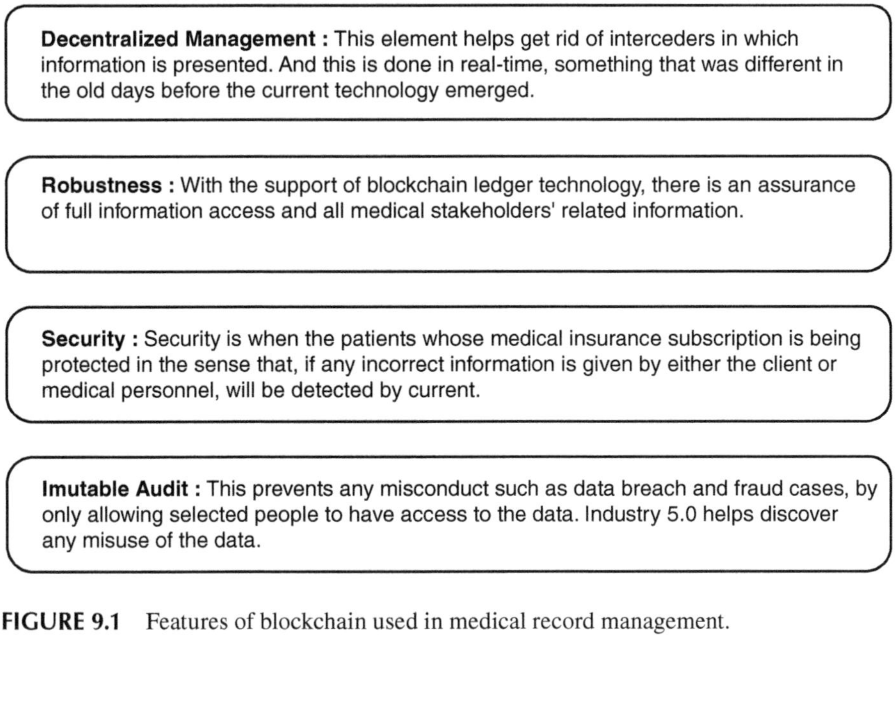

FIGURE 9.1 Features of blockchain used in medical record management.

various factors during the process of new worker recruitment, such as a receptionist. Factors such as who has receptive behavior, someone with a friendly demeanor, and someone who communicates nicely with clients, are all taken into consideration. The same applies to the health system when applying AI technologies because they help in improving medical research by learning more about the needs or complaints of their clients. A case in point is for those patients who really need special attention, as far as their medical history is concerned; AI would be helpful if applied correctly to determine what kind of drugs need to be produced to suit the level/type of these patients. These are reported to limit cases of patients' complaints regarding drug side effects, and generally, all drug shops will now have an idea of what exactly to sell or not to sell in terms of medicine [14]. Previously, illnesses such as cancer took some time to be detected, but with the presence and assistance of AI networks, such as IBM computerized systems, good treatment suggestions were created, aiding in the rapid detection of such illnesses [15]. The features of blockchain used in medical record management are represented in Figure 9.1.

9.4 SMART HEALTHCARE SYSTEMS AND THEIR APPLICATION

The smart healthcare system has considerably improved due to advanced technologies that have made it possible for different medical departments to ensure the necessary information is shared among themselves. The internal control systems in most cases, such as the health sector, have been under attack by privacy invasion, data theft, and so on. Blockchain, in this regard, has been a solution by applying its extraordinary features such as a decentralized storage system, security, etc. For example, previous research points out that blockchain's HashID can help find out a patient's identity even without them revealing it; in this regard, patients' confidentiality is maintained even without pulling out all the data about them. Moreover, blockchain has assumed complete ownership of data, resolving data ownership conflicts that have been occurring among medical organizations for some time. For individuals who may attempt to misuse medical facilities, such as manufacturing drugs, stealing them, and creating an outer market for them, this can be discovered by the use of blockchain traceable technology. Therefore, the stakeholders involved in the system are being saved or monitored with this transparency element, unlike in the pre-Industry 5.0 revolution where improper calculations of produced drugs were a challenge [16,17]. Also, [18–20], in their paper titled " Healthcare data gateways: Found Healthcare Intelligence on Blockchain with Novel Privacy Risk Control", on supporting the provision of patients' control and protecting their own data, suggested a useful application called 'healthcare data gateways', which improved the smart healthcare system for patients and protected their private information from access by other parties [21,22]. In conclusion, the two advanced technologies have highly contributed to great healthcare services and products since information sharing has been facilitated among stakeholders including manufacturers, supply chain crew, patients, and health personnel, and individual-patient information has been protected through the application of extraordinary tools of both AI and Blockchain.

REFERENCES

1. Attili, S., Ladwa, S. K., Sharma, U., & Trenkle, A. F. (August 2016). Blockchain: The chain of trust and its potential to transform healthcare-our point of view. In: *ONC/NIST Use of Blockchain for Healthcare and Research Workshop, ONC/NIST*, Gaithersburg, MD.
2. Culver, K. (2016). Blockchain technologies: A whitepaper discussing how the claims process can be improved. In: *ONC/NIST Use of Blockchain for Healthcare and Research Workshop*, ONC/NIST, Gaithersburg, MD.
3. Huang, G., Huang, G. Bin, Song, S., & You, K. (2015). Trends in extreme learning machines: A review. *Neural Networks*, 61, 32–48. https://doi.org/10.1016/j. neunet.2014.10.001
4. Islam, S. M. R., Kwak, D., Kabir, M. H., Hossain, M., & Kwak, K. S. (2015). The internet of things for health care: A comprehensive survey. *IEEE Access*, 3, 678–708. https:// doi.org/10.1109/ACCESS.2015.2437951
5. uiu.ac.ug (26 September 2023). Innovation By IUIU staff Granted a Utility Model. https:\\iuiu.ac.ug\news-page.php?!=359&a=iuiu
6. Komalavalli, C., Saxena, D., & Laroiya, C. (2020). Overview of blockchain technology concepts. In: *Handbook of Research on Blockchain Technology*. INC. https://doi. org/10.1016/B978-0-12-819816-2.00014-9
7. Li, W., Si, J., Xing, J., Zhang, Y., Liu, D., & Sui, Z. (2021). Unified attribute-based encryption scheme for industrial internet of things. In: *2021 IEEE 5th International Conference on Cryptography, Security and Privacy, CSP 2021*, 12–16. https://doi. org/10.1109/CSP51677.2021.9357493
8. Maciaszczyk, M., Makieła, Z., & Miśkiewicz, R. (2023). Industry 5.0. In: *Innovation in the Digital Economy*. https://doi.org/10.4324/9781003384311-5
9. Molero, A., Calabrò, M., Vignes, M., Gouget, B., & Gruson, D. (2020). Sustainability in healthcare: Perspectives and reflections regarding laboratory medicine. *Annals of Laboratory Medicine*, 41(2), 139–144. https://doi.org/10.3343/alm.2021.41.2.139
10. Nofer, M., Gomber, P., Hinz, O., & Schiereck, D. (2017). Blockchain. *Business and Information Systems Engineering*, 59(3), 183–187. https://doi.org/10.1007/s12599-017-0467-3
11. Ophy Care (20 March 2023). How are telehealth technologies helping in the aftermath of the recent Turkiye-Syria earthquake? https://ophycare.com/2023/03
12. Paul, D., Sanap, G., Shenoy, S., Kalyane, D., Kalia, K., & Tekade, R. K. (2021). Artificial intelligence in drug discovery and development. *Drug Discovery Today*, 26(1), 80–93. https://doi.org/10.1016/j.drudis.2020.10.010
13. Paul, D., Sanap, G., Shenoy, S., Kalyane, D., Kalia, K., & Tekade, R. K. (2021). Artificial intelligence in drug discovery and development. *Drug Discovery Today*, 26(1), 80–93. https://doi.org/10.1016/j.drudis.2020.10.010
14. Petiwala, F. F., Shukla, V. K., & Vyas, S. (2021). IBM Watson: Redefining Artificial Intelligence Through Cognitive Computing. 173–185. https://doi.org/10.1007/978-981-33-4087-9_15.
15. Shruti, Rani, S., & Srivastava, G. (2024). Secure hierarchical fog computing-based architecture for industry 5.0 using an attribute-based encryption scheme. *Expert Systems with Applications*, 235, 121180. https://doi.org/10.1016/j.eswa.2023.121180
16. Siau, K. (2018). A qualitative research on marketing and sales in the artificial intelligence age supply chain management view project. In: *Information Systems Conference*, May 18, 2018. https://aisel.aisnet.org/mwais2018/41
17. Tripathi, G., Ahad, M. A., & Paiva, S. (2020). S2HS: A blockchain based approach for smart healthcare system. *Healthcare*, 8(1), 100391. https://doi.org/10.1016/j. hjdsi.2019.100391

18. Xu, X., Lu, Y., Vogel-Heuser, B., & Wang, L. (2021). Industry 4.0 and Industry 5.0-Inception, conception and perception. *Journal of Manufacturing Systems*, 61, 530–535. https://doi.org/10.1016/j.jmsy.2021.10.006

19. Tagde, P., Tagde, S., Bhattacharya, T., Tagde, P., Chopra, H., Akter, R., Kaushik, D., & Rahman, M. H. (2021). Blockchain and artificial intelligence technology in e-Health. *Environmental Science and Pollution Research*, 28(38), 52810–52831. https://doi.org/10.1007/s11356-021-16223-0

20. Tian, S., Yang, W., Grange, J. M. Le, Wang, P., Huang, W., & Ye, Z. (2019). Smart healthcare: Making medical care more intelligent. *Journal of Global Health*, 3(3), 62–65. https://doi.org/10.1016/j.glohj.2019.07.001

21. Wirtz, B. W., Weyerer, J. C., & Geyer, C. (2019). Artificial intelligence and the public sector-applications and challenges. *International Journal of Public Administration*, 42(7), 596–615. https://doi.org/10.1080/01900692.2018.1498103

22. Yue, X., Wang, H., Jin, D., Li, M., & Jiang, W. (2016). Healthcare data gateways: Found healthcare intelligence on blockchain with novel privacy risk control. *Journal of Medical Systems*, 40(10). https://doi.org/10.1007/s10916-016-0574-6

10 A Comprehensive Review on the Cognitive Radio for the Implementation in 5G Wireless Communication for the Development of Healthcare

Rogina Sultana, Jayanta Kumar Ray,
Quazi Mohmmad Alfred, and Imtiaj Ahmed

10.1 INTRODUCTION

To address the shortage of medical staff and hospital space, multidisciplinary researchers from the fields of computer science, sophisticated communications technologies, and medical science are collaborating to develop a smart e-healthcare system. The use of wireless body area networks (WBANs) in healthcare applications is showing promise. WBANs enable continuous patient monitoring in the patient's preferred environment. The industrial, scientific, and medical band (ISM) is utilised by these equipment for interaction. According to the World Health Organisation (WHO), approximately 246 million people worldwide have diabetes each year, and 17.5 million people die from heart attacks. By 2025, it is predicted that 20 million more people will die from cardiovascular illnesses. The WBAN-based e-healthcare system offers a way to prevent these fatalities. Various electronic health applications can communicate medical data using wireless communication technology. Additionally, this technology enhances service mobility and flexibility for many telemedicine applications. The human body's key physiological characteristics, such as temperature, heart rate, blood vessel pressure, rate of respiration, oxygen saturation (SpO_2), as well as the degree of consciousness, are now being monitored by WBANs [1].

Yet, there are two significant obstacles to employing wireless technology for communication in a hospital setting. Firstly, the electromagnetic interference that wireless devices generate to biomedical devices might seriously impair their functionality.

DOI: 10.1201/9781032632223-10

Secondly, since various types of electronic medical records apps have varied priorities, connectivity over the wireless channel through devices that are linked needs to be ordered [2]. In order to provide healthcare services, electronic health (e-health) merges information processing and communications technology. For a variety of e-health applications, including telemedicine, mobile hospital information systems, and remote patient monitoring, in order to improve mobility and service flexibility, wireless communication is an essential technology [3].Nevertheless, electromagnetic interference (EMI) brought on by wireless communications is a concern for many medical devices. The interference may cause medical equipment to malfunction, which might be dangerous for patients utilizing healthcare services (such as autobreakdown, auto reset, signal distortion, and screaming). To minimize this EMI issue, wireless communication networks for e-health applications must be appropriately built, especially in healthcare institutions like hospitals or clinics. In order to avoid this EMI problem, it is crucial that wireless communication networks used for applications related to e-health, especially in medical establishments such as hospitals or clinics, are appropriately developed. A cognitive smart radio transceiver may assess the state of the operational environment through observation and learning, make a choice, and modify the wireless transmission settings as necessary. By taking into consideration the strict restrictions on EMI to medical equipment and the varying quality of service needs in various e-health software, the cognitive radio concept may be used for wireless communications for applications in e-health. It was proposed that a medical institution employ an illuminating network to decrease the EMI problem. This network operates on a radio frequency and uses high-brightness light-emitting diodes (LEDs) as its carrier signal. The use of light as the carrier signal, which can be frequently obscured by items in the surrounding environment, limits the utility of this technology. The healthcare industry is a perfect illustration of how cognitive radio (CR) and cognitive networking (CNF) approaches may be used to improve the reliability, scalability, and utility of medical equipment and systems that rely on wireless networks for communication. The use of technology for wireless communication in healthcare facilities has grown in popularity because they may considerably improve patients' accessibility, which is essential for quick recuperation from operations and other treatments. Electrocardiograms, dosimeters, motion alerts, and pulse oximeters are a few examples of these uses. Furthermore, the application of portable biomedical sensors enables telemedicine systems to remotely monitor patients with chronic illnesses and the elderly at residence [4].

10.2 SPECIFICATIONS FOR WIRELESS COMMUNICATION SYSTEMS USED IN E-HEALTHCARE WITH CR

- In a healthcare setup, many medical instruments are susceptible to Electromagnetic Interference (EMI). Consequently, any wireless communication systems implemented in applications related to e-health must meet electromagnetic compatibility (EMC) criteria. For instance, the wireless equipment utilised in e-health systems must restrict power transfer to prevent damaging interference to nearby medical equipment. In this scenario, the IEC 60601-1-2 standard, which specifies the EMI immunity levels of medical equipment, may be used to estimate the transmission characteristics of wireless gadgets [5–7].

- According to their communication needs, e-health apps may be divided into four categories: real-time critical and non-critical programming, remote control software, and office/support services [8]. Two important communication qualities of service performance metrics for these applications are loss and latency. A real-time patient monitoring programme, for instance, may be used to continually monitor a cardiac patient. If vital physiological information is transmitted slowly, the patient could not get help right away if an aberrant situation develops. With QoS support, IEEE 802.11e wireless technology that is being utilised in e-health applications. This feature grants various classes of applications distinct permissions for accessing channels by establishing various reduced window sizes [9].
- In hospitals, several wireless technologies are employed together. IEEE 802.11-based wireless LAN (WLAN) and IEEE 802.15.4a/ultra-wideband (UWB)-based wireless personal area network (WPAN) technologies may both be used for e-health applications with high bandwidth requirements, such as telehealth and information systems for hospitals applications. Applications for Bluetooth and ZigBee can be used in human body sensor networks, such as healthcare monitoring and physical rehabilitation. Due to the use of several of the same or nearby frequency bands by various technologies, interference as well as spectrum access management presents significant difficulties. As an illustration, the 2.4 GHz commercial, scientific, and medical (ISM) band is used by IEEE 802.11b/g, Bluetooth, and ZigBee [10].
- The mobility of e-health applications may be significantly increased through mobile communications. When the patient is moving around, the biosignal data may be continually observed. The various medical wellness and patient monitoring software should be accessible online for the mobile medical personnel. Mobility management, such as roaming and handoff, is required to offer uninterrupted service and achieve greater effectiveness for e-health applications.
- Medical information must be secure, and thus there should be absolutely no opportunity for infiltration or unauthorised listening. Consequently, effective techniques for authentication as well as encryption are necessary for e-health applications, using, for instance, 802.1x-based authentication and IEEE 802.11i-based key transmission over a WLAN [11].

10.3 ACCESSIBILITY OF COGNITIVE RADIO (CR) IN E-HEALTHCARE

The first draft of a document describing the medium access control layer and the physical features of the radio interfaces for WBAN applications has been prepared by the wireless body area network (WBAN) standardization committee (IEEE 802.15.6) [5]. Numerous sensor nodes, each having the ability to sample, interpret, and transmit one or more critical signals, make up a healthcare BAN (also known as a WBAN for medical purposes). The body network controller (BNC), which receives this biological data, is informed of it [6]. The initial tier of a telemedicine system, known as intra-WBAN interactions, is made up of the MBAN. MBANs have numerous advantages for the healthcare industry, but as they become more widely adopted, there will undoubtedly be additional situations where they interact with various combined digital systems. The CR framework, which can offer resolutions for such overlapping situations and also improve scalability, allows for the opportunistic access of unlicensed (secondary) users to licensed (primary) portions of the electromagnetic spectrum. A CR user (CRU) is able to take advantage of geographic database access, spectrum sensing, as well as dynamic transceiver parameter reconfiguration to prevent interfering affecting primary users (PUs) and assess occupancy [4].

10.4 CR INTRODUCING A BIG OPPORTUNITY FOR ULTRA WIDEBAND IN E-HEALTHCARE

Besides its ability to provide high-rate communications with a broad bandwidth of a minimum of 500 MHz, UWB technology has additional appealing features for MBANs. Due to their exceptionally low maximum effective isotropically radiated power (EIRP) spectral density of −41.3 dBm/MHz, ultra-wideband signals naturally exhibit noise-like behaviour. This improves UWB's resilience against jamming and makes it harder to detect, thus negating the need for advanced encryption techniques in tiny, affordable transceivers. Additionally, with MB-OFDM, symbols are interleaved throughout a number of sub-bands throughout both time and frequency, as opposed to single-band OFDM, where symbols are continuously delivered on one frequency band. Multiband UWB can retain the signal strength level involved with the single-band OFDM transmission while greatly increasing the data throughput by integrating the OFDM signals across sub bands in this way. MB-OFDM can cover up to 10 m with UWB technology at speeds that vary between 53.3 and 480 Mb/s. Also, UWB transmissions do not pose a risk to the security of patients and do not significantly interact with other medical equipment. The construction of impulse radio transceivers is straightforward, and they exhibit very low energy consumption traits. These characteristics make it easier to miniaturize them for wearable biological sensors [12].

10.5 ADVANTAGES OF CR FOR E-HEALTHCARE

10.5.1 SENSING TECHNOLOGY

For such Impulse Radio-Ultra Wideband (IR-UWB) systems, the capacity to detect other narrowband or wideband systems is crucial. Impulse radio UWB technology has been proposed as a remedy in the IEEE 802.15.6 standard and is currently under development by the IEEE 802.15 Task Group 6 [13]. There are wearable systems in place for the medical industry. The goals include developing body-area wireless devices that are low-power, low-complexity, low-cost, and capable of highly dependable transmissions. Due to the UWB front-end filter's large bandwidth, it might be difficult to determine which particular frequencies are truly impacted by interference. Therefore, utilising power spectral density (PSD) data for each subband obtained from the FFT step in an MB-OFDM receiver, MB-OFDM UWB systems clearly outperform IR-UWB with respect to sensing capabilities. Through a wavelength resolution not less than comparable to the subcarrier separation in the UWB signal, UWB devices may use this method to detect the existence of coexisting systems. Combining the two approaches might result in a subband or network ranking methodology. The first approach involves identifying available channels using the subband PSD data. Yet this does not always imply that the observed bit error rate [BER] represents the channel quality. In order to remedy this, the second technique employs the BER data collected from active channels to provide channel quality estimate data for more detailed ranking data in a way similar to the usage of received strength signals [14]. The lookup table (LUT) within transceivers can be used to store and retrieve the information on channel ranking.

10.5.2 Avoidance of Interference

Subband ranking for selective subband picking offers energy and cost benefits, in addition to a decrease in implementation complexity, when compared with OFDM spectral sculpting and the construction of spectral holes in the waveform to prevent interference. Since the receiver signal processing loop already provides the PSD information, this strategy may be seen as having minimal processing overhead. To keep the channel ranking LUT accurate, BER-based channel ranking needs extra logic. Unlike the PSD approach, which only identifies the availability of subbands, this method can provide information on the level of quality of the dynamic subbands. Both strategies allow us to use the spectrum selectively, maneuver around subbands where interference could be present, and trade-off cost for subband selection precision. If a subband is considered to be occupied or subject to interference, its rank is decreased; otherwise, it is raised. Using the UWB MB-OFDM system, the top-ranked subbands are able to be employed for data transmission. Consequently, a multi-band methodology employing OFDM in the framework of WBANs provides for a decrease in design complexity, greater versatility regarding how spectrum is allocated, and greater conformity to regulations and bandwidth plans used globally. By leveraging various spectrum regulatory laws, we may exchange data throughput for flexibility, resistance to interference, and effortless operation across national borders.

10.5.3 Energy Consumption

For MBANs and their components, energy usage is a crucial concern, especially for interactions at the first level of activity. Energy efficiency simplifies operation for the individual using it by minimizing the need for battery recharges; however, the user may struggle to complete such duties given his or her present health. By lowering the likelihood that the network or its sensors would become inoperable owing to energy exhaustion, it also increases dependability. MBANs use a variety of techniques to cut back on communications energy use [6]. Through a minimum of two important channels, CR is also extremely relevant to energy conservation in MBANs. The first is superior dynamic spectrum selection, which avoids interference and hence lowers the required received power and, in turn, broadcast power. As was covered before in this article, MB-OFDM-based UWB allows for customisation of broadcasts to the interference band with the least amount of noise. The use of cognition to improve knowledge of context, such as need for higher-layer communication, and the shifting overall environment, including the battery energy level, is the second energy-saving benefit of employing CR [4].

Given the present and expected interference circumstances, fluctuations in needed data rates, and restrictions, this understanding may be leveraged to enhance the duration of transfers and dynamic media access control (MAC) as well as physical (PHY) placement. If a subband has interference, its rank is decreased; if it does not, its rank is enhanced. According to the patient's state and the time of day, MBAN readings from sensors like heart rate, saturation level of oxygen, and blood sugar levels may be collected at varying intervals and rates due to fluctuations overall channel circumstances and sensor energy availability. Learning and cognition can play an important role in predicting the future in terms of necessities such as these measurements and battery levels likely to vary to enable the constant preservation of a suitable setup of the MBAN interaction with minimized interruption resulting from battery energy depletion and scheduled for interaction every information with appropriate delay constraints. Depending on the battery's state, this may be matched to the schedule, rate, and MAC/PHY properties of the sensor gearbox. Furthermore, the patient's motions may be used to capture energy for kinetic purposes to drive battery conditions. Another important use of cognition is gaining knowledge and forecasting of such increases [4].

10.6 A COGNITIVE RADIO NETWORK FOR E-HEALTHCARE APPLICATION

The objectives of this cognitive radio system are to distinguish the QoS for diverse e-health applications and to shield medical equipment from harmful electromagnetic interference (EMI). Two e-health technologies are present here, including a real-time non-critical telemedicine system and a hospital data system. Telemedicine applications include the transfer of patient information, remote diagnostics, and delay- and loss-sensitive remote consultation, whereas hospital information system software gathers medical data, including patient, technical, and facility data, which is then processed, displayed to healthcare workers, and stored within an information system.

Cognitive radio approaches may be utilised for effective coexistence of the many users/applications during horizontal sharing of spectrum situations, such as radio access within the unlicensed band, and therefore increase the utilisation for the radio spectrum as a whole. In a vertical spectrum sharing scenario, such as radio access in the licenced band, cognitive radio technology can be used by secondary users to impulsively access the radio spectrum licenced during the primary users and thereby achieve better utilisation of existing wireless communications networks [15]. Emergency networks created for crisis scenarios can employ cognitive radio-based wireless communication [16]. The process for the transmission of information in multiple formats is adjusted in accordance with the identification of under utilised spectrum channels by the cognitive radio system. Medical gadgets, which are susceptible to interference from wireless transmission, are the users who are protected. There are medical gadgets that are both passive and active. Passive medical equipment includes incubators, infusion pumps, anaesthetic machines, and defibrillators. Although these gadgets don't send out any wireless signals, their electrical parts are EMI-sensitive. Incubators, infusion pumps, anaesthesia machines, and defibrillators are examples of passive medical devices. Although these gadgets don't send out any wireless signals, their electrical parts are EMI-sensitive.

Wireless transmissions from other non-medical devices may obstruct the data transfer of these functional medical devices. Two wireless services have been designated by the Federal Communications Commission (FCC) for use in medical applications: The usage of wireless medical telemetry service (WMTS) allows for the remote monitoring of a patient's vital indicators, such as blood pressure and body temperature. There should be no room for intrusion or unauthorised listening in the system. As a result, secure authentications as well as encryption methods are essential for e-Health applications. For licensed healthcare workers, 14 MHz of frequency bands, including 608–614, 1,395–1,400, and 1,427–1,432, were assigned by the FCC. Using the Medical Implant Communications Service (MICS), it is possible to remotely monitor the body's vital signs. For instance, pacemakers for cardiac function and implanted defibrillators can convey a patient's heart status. The frequency ranges 402–405 MHz are set aside for this cellular service. An e-health cognitive radio system can run on either licensed or unlicensed bands.

10.7 COGNITIVE RADIO ON BOTH LICENSED AND UNLICENSED BANDS FOR E-HEALTH APPLICATIONS

- **For unlicensed band**: A secondary user is not obligated to be conscious of the existence of primary users since every user in this situation possesses the identical ability to utilise the radio spectrum. The protected users' and apps' EMI restrictions do still apply. In order to create service differentiation, channel access would also need to prioritise among various users and applications. Due to its ability to monitor, learn, and access spectrum dynamically, a cognitive radio network may permit spectrum accessibility with QoS differentiation across diverse healthcare applications while safeguarding medical equipment. For channel access, the use of spectrum overlay or a spectrum underlay technique may be utilized [15]. The usage of a base station to gather data on spectrum occupancy and choose the best spectrum accessibility policy in order to cut down on electromagnetic radiation is one scenario taken into consideration in this study. However, this system did not provide QoS distinction. For the purpose of providing QoS in cognitive radio networks, a collaborative medium access control (MAC) algorithm was devised. In order to ensure that each group's bandwidth needs are met in a dynamic environment, secondary users are organised and each group actively distributes spectrum.
- **For licensed bands**: To allow a cognitive radio network to function in the licensed spectrum bands such as the WMTS and MICS bands, secondary users have to maintain track of the primary users and deliberately transmit

the spectrum in a non-interfering fashion. A cognitive radio operator in the healthcare setting must keep track of the status for both active and passive medical equipment. It is possible to install a cognitive radio network that supports e-health applications in a variety of settings, including hospital critical care units (ICUs). Patient monitoring devices, telemedicine for doctor-patient consultations via the internet, and hospital technology solutions for discovering patient information, along with remote healthcare asset monitoring systems for identifying healthcare equipment, are among the few e-health applications. Every service makes use of a particular wireless technology, such as WLAN for telehealthcare and healthcare information systems or Bluetooth connectivity wireless sensors that are used in patient monitoring systems. Additionally, there are several types of digital medical devices working in ICUs for various patients, including infusion pumps, ECG analyser, and electromyography monitors. Therefore, it is important to carefully select the wireless transmission characteristics in order to prevent interference with medical equipment in ICUs [2].

10.8 LIMITATION OF CR IN E-HEALTH CARE

This article addressed security flaws and workarounds that may be used to secure5G-based intelligent healthcare networks to prevent and resolve issues. However, there are still a number of security gaps in 5G-based networks, which include the following security issues:

Evidence and confidentiality: Due to the absence of universal communication or sensor design standards, it is challenging to guarantee whether the network is receiving and sending data through an authorised sensor since sensors are available in a variety of configurations, each requiring its own hardware and software. The specialised technology employed by sensors and the weak areas in wireless networks make it difficult to maintain the secrecy of health information [17]. Reducing authentication and secrecy constraints might thereby jeopardise patient health.

Accessibility: Access to both historical and current data should always be available to examiners and patients. In addition, data has to remain in the correct format and systems and sensors can never malfunction. These operating parameters are perhaps beyond the capabilities of current scientific and technological advancements. However, developments in other fields, like superconductors or quantum computing, might alter the source of this difficulty.

Computational and memory limitations: Smart healthcare sensors have limited memory capacity and processing power due to their frequent small size. These sensors require security algorithms that function with the least amount of memory possible without compromising the sensor's functionality. Because the majority of security algorithms in use today are too complex to reliably execute with minimal resources, novel computational methodologies are required.

Fault tolerance and data progressiveness: In the event that a system component fails or goes down, intelligent healthcare components should still be able to function. While backup sensors are one possibility, intelligent healthcare sensors also need to continuously provide medical professionals access to the most recent data.

Non-repudiation: Two entities with contracts in place and the necessary authorization should have no trouble obtaining data or proving their identity. While the contemporary method of ensuring data integrity is through digital signatures, some sensor types may not have the computational capacity or expertise to compute signatures.

Self-healing: Eventually, it should be possible for smart healthcare sensors to identify hardware problems, outages, and connectivity problems. They should also be able to automatically identify and fix these problems. Because there is such a wide range of technology for sensors and needs, this remains an open topic.

Adaptability: Networks for smart healthcare must be able to grow or shrink in response to the needs of patients. It should not be necessary to make changes that compromise the reliability of the present system in order for new sensors to be seamlessly integrated into an already-existing one.

Algorithms: The most important open problem is definitely designing security techniques for systems and gadgets that are resilient and light enough to operate on very little CPU resources [18].

10.9 FUTURE RESEARCH DIRECTIONS

Several interesting directions for future 5G-based intelligent healthcare research were identified by the analysis of the reviewed publications. These suggestions aim to improve privacy and security in smart healthcare, but they could also benefit other developing applications.

Machine learning: In a 5G-based intelligent healthcare network, unstructured, noisy, and overlapping sensor data are common. Additionally, sensors produce vast amounts of data very fast, thus before decoding the data, it is essential to filter the information from the noise. It is possible to train machine learning algorithms to interpret sensor data and distinguish between important information and noise. They could also lessen the quantity of data that needs to be manually sorted by medical personnel and the number of devices needed for data collection.

Blockchain: The ability of blockchain systems to link records through encryption may alter security and privacy in 5G-based smart healthcare, enabling patients and medical professionals to share data in a secure and transparent manner. It could be necessary to integrate smart contracts and decentralised apps, as well as build blockchain-based access and identity management systems, in order to automate and simplify healthcare procedures. However, incorporating blockchain into 5G-based smart healthcare necessitates greater processing power, which can be difficult for devices with limited resources.

Energy optimization: There is a temporal restriction on how long sensors can analyse and calculate data since they have only a certain amount of computing capacity. Energy generation and consumption in smart healthcare are far from optimal. Thus, creating hardware and algorithms that are both effective and lightweight is a difficult but crucial endeavour.

Smart gateways: By offering an encrypted data entry point, smart gateways enhance authorization and verification processes. These gateways can withstand denial-of-service assaults and other cyberattacks that rely on user-supplied data that is prohibited. They can also withstand routing attacks. Smart gateways have the potential to handle many aspects of network routing, improve security, and combine data from several devices [19].

10.10 CONCLUSION

We have proposed the use of cognitive radio technology in e-health applications. The system's cognitive capacity results from its knowledge of EMI, which enables it to regulate the wireless access settings and accomplish the appropriate QoS distinction between various users and applications. This cognitive radio system has taken into account two e-health applications: healthcare and a hospital information system. In comparison to the Interference Mitigating Factor (IMF), the cognitive radio technique performs better. To lessen routing challenges involving bandwidth, efficiency, and power consumption, CR networks employ the clustering method. The network's lifespan is increased while using less energy thanks to this clustering approach. This fact, along with the expanding usage of radio communication technologies in healthcare, motivates further investigation into interference reduction strategies over medical communication environments. Scalability and coexistence concerns may both be addressed with the help of cognitive radio, and the implementation difficulties that come with it bring fresh and intriguing research prospects.

REFERENCES

1. Vivekanand, C. V., Inbamalar, T. M., Nadar, K. P., Kannagi, V., & Arthi Devarani, P. (2023). Energy-efficient compressed sensing in cognitive radio network for telemedicine services. *Wireless Communications and Mobile Computing*, 1–12. doi:10.1155/2023/5415616
2. Phunchongharn, P., Hossain, E., Niyato, D., & Camorlinga, S. (2010). A cognitive radio system for e-health applications in a hospital environment. *IEEE Wireless Communications*, 17(1), 20–28. doi:10.1109/mwc.2010.5416346
3. Varshney, U. (2007). Pervasive healthcare and wireless health monitoring. *Mobile Networks and Applications*, 12(2–3), 113–127. doi:10.1007/s11036-007-0017-1
4. Chavez-Santiago, R., Nolan, K. E., Holland, O., De Nardis, L., Ferro, J. M., Barroca, N., ... Balasingham, I. (2012). Cognitive radio for medical body area networks using ultra wideband. *IEEE Wireless Communications*, 19(4), 74–81. doi:10.1109/mwc.2012.6272426
5. (N.d.). https://ieee802.org/15/pub/TG6. Retrieved from 1 February 2024.
6. Chen, M., Gonzalez, S., Vasilakos, A., Cao, H., & Leung, V. C. M. (2011). Body aream networks: A survey. *Mobile Networks and Applications*, 16(2), 171–193. doi:10.1007/s11036-010-0260-8
7. Medical electrical equipment-Part 1-2: General Requirements for Safety-Collateral Standard: Electromagnetic Compatibility– Requirements and Test, National Standard of Canada CAN/CSA-C22.2 No. 60601-1-2:03 (Adopted IEC 60601-1-2:2001), 2003.
8. Soomro, A., & Cavalcanti, D. (2007). Opportunities and challenges in using WPAN and WLAN technologies in medical environments. *IEEE Communications Magazine*, 45(2), 114–122. doi:10.1109/mcom.2007.313404
9. Baker, S. D., & Hoglund, D. H. (2008). Medical-grade mission critical wireless networks. *IEEE Engineering in Medicine and Biology Magazine*, 27(2), 86–95.

10. Di Benedetto, M.-G., & Giancola, G. (2004). *Understanding Ultra Wide Band Radio Fundamentals*. Prentice Hall.

11. Lee, C., Kim, J., Lee, H. S., & Kim, J. (September 2009). Physical layer designs for WBAN systems in IEEE802.15.6 proposals. In: *2009 9th International Symposium on Communications and Information Technology. Presented at the 2009 9th International Symposium on Communications and Information Technology (ISCIT), Icheon, South Korea*.doi:10.1109/iscit.2009.5341123

12. Hossian, M. M. A., Mahmood, A., & Jantti, R. (2009, September). Channel ranking algorithms for cognitive coexistence of IEEE802.15.4. In: *2009 IEEE 20th International Symposium on Personal, Indoor and Mobile Radio Communications. Presented at the 2009 IEEE20th International Symposium on Personal, Indoor and Mobile Radio*. Producer: Communications (PIMRC), Tokyo. doi:10.1109/pimrc.2009.5449986

13. Lee, C., Kim, J., Lee, H. S., & Kim, J. (September 2009). Physical layer designs for WBAN systems in IEEE802.15.6 proposals. In: *2009 9th International Symposium on Communications and Information Technology. Presented at the 2009 9th International Symposium on Communications and Information Technology (ISCIT). Icheon, South Korea*.doi:10.1109/iscit.2009.5341123

14. Hossian, M. M. A., Mahmood, A., & Jantti, R. (2009, September). Channel ranking algorithms for cognitive coexistence of IEEE802.15.4. In: *2009 IEEE 20th International Symposium on Personal, Indoor and Mobile Radio Communications. Presented at the 2009 IEEE20th International Symposium on Personal, Indoor and Mobile Radio Communications (PIMRC 2009)*, Tokyo. doi:10.1109/pimrc.2009.5449986.

15. Hossain, E., & Bhargava, V. K. (Eds.). (2007). *Cognitive Wireless Communication Networks*. Springer.

16. Zhang, Q., Kokkeler, A. B. J., & Smit, G. J.M. (2006)."Cognitive Radio for Emergency Networks," *Proceedings Global Mobile Congress, Delson Group*, Volume 2006, Oct. 2006, pp. 32–37, ISSN (Print):1557-0622.

17. Azzaoui, A. E., & Park, J. H. (2020). Post-quantum blockchain for a scalable smart city. *Journal of Internet Technology*, 21(4), 1171–1178.

18. Abdul Ahad, Zakir Ullah, Bahrul Amin, Atiq Ahmad. (2017). Comparison of Energy Efficient Routing Protocols in Wireless Sensor Network. *American Journal of Networks and Communications*, 6(4), 67–73. https://doi.org/10.11648/j.ajnc.20170604.12

19. Ahad, A., & Tahir, M. (2022). Perspective-6G and IoT for intelligent healthcare: Challenges and future research directions. *ECS Sensors Plus*. doi:10.1149/2754-2726/acabd4

11 Quantum Immortality

Simber Atay

11.1 INTRODUCTION

"He lives, he wakes—'tis Death is dead, not he;
Mourn not for Adonais"
Percy Bysshe Shelley, Adonais:
An Elegy on the Death of John Keats (1821, 361–362)

Immortality is a mythological, theological, mnemonic, philosophical, literary, artistic, scientific, technological, and of course medical phenomenon. Therefore, it is a genetic and memetic design. These disciplines discuss, define, and work to produce solutions to the problem of immortality in their ways, independently or interdisciplinarily. Life, death, and immortality are intertwined circles of existence. Immortality is a challenge against Kronos. It is an alternative life model. In romantic terms, immortality is a universal utopia. In this context, medical science has a privileged position among the disciplines mentioned above. The key to a long and quality life is in the hands of medicine. *Mens sana in corpore sano!* While working toward a healthy body and soul, medical science has also developed medical categories that include the concept of immortality. Therefore, medical science is constantly evolving. For example, the practice of in vitro fertilization, with its various applications, fulfills the genetic desire of prospective parents to exist in future generations. Organ transplantation extends life. Bionic prostheses complete the body's missing physical and neurological functions. Robocop, a cinema saga, tells about this subject. In the 2014 version of the saga directed by José Padilha, the film's protagonist, Detroit P.D. Alex Murphy (Joel Kinnaman) is seriously injured, but OmniCorp, a global corporation, in a transhumanist way recreates him as a bionic man to use as a security instrument. Plastic surgery, along with trauma treatments, gives people beauty and youth, at least in appearance. Because ironically, the ideal model of immortality is eternal youth. It is possible to call this situation the *Dr. Faust Syndrome*. For example, the movie Death Becomes Her (1992, Robert Zemeckis) is a love triangle comedy. The protagonist of the film, Madeline Ashton (Meryl Streep), wants to be younger and more beautiful due to love and jealousy and becomes immortal by drinking an elixir. But this does not solve their struggle for survival, and these rival women become the living dead in a burlesque way. Immortality is not always an advantage, sometimes it is a condemnation or curse. What is important is a young, beautiful, healthy, energetic, active, and free immortal life. However, there is no 100% perfect immortality. Various immortality designs can be predicted from a medical perspective, but they all depend on the circumstances, so immortality is an existential problem. In addition, mythology and art and literature inspired by mythology are environments where this problem in question is discussed in detail [3].

DOI: 10.1201/9781032632223-11

In this context, Prometheus, his fate, and his adventures are subjects that are frequently interpreted. As it is known, Prometheus stole fire from the gods and gave it to humans, for which he was punished by Zeus. Hesiod describes this punishment in Theogony as follows:

"And he bound Prometheus with ineluctable fetters,
Painful bonds, and drove a shaft through his middle,
And set a long-winged eagle on him that kept gnawing
His undying liver, but whatever the long-winged bird
Ate the whole day through, would all grow back by night" [18].

Beyond fire, Prometheus gifted civilization to humanity, meaning he gave people knowledge spanning everything from architecture to agriculture, prophecy to animal anatomy, mathematics to language and grammar, and maritime skills to understanding the rhythm of nature and natural resources. He saved them from their blind ignorance with the light of science and art: "very art of mankind comes from Prometheus". Therefore, Prometheus' fire has both literal and metaphorical meanings. Prometheus is considered the founder of medical science. In Aeschylus' tragedy *Prometheus Bound*, Prometheus himself describes this as follows:

"If you hear the rest, you will marvel even more
at what crafts and what resources I contrived.
Greatest was this: when one of mankind was sick,
there was no defense for him-neither healing food
nor drink nor unguent; for lack of drugs they wasted,
until I showed them blendings of mild simples
with which they drive away all kinds of sickness" [1].

The immortality of the soul is provided by mythology, philosophy, literature, works of art, and belief systems, but the immortality of the body is a direct responsibility of medical science. Knowledge of anatomy and anatomical functions is also one of the major components of robotics. Medical science works for health as well as disease. Eventually, it plays a very active role in ensuring and increasing the health, strength, and endurance of the human soul and body at every stage of daily life practice, from sports to military service, from space exploration to body art. Of course, this situation has made doctors in modern times, from a Foucaultian perspective, representatives of an Übermensch power in terms of medicine, surgery, pharmaceuticals, and biotechnology. Sometimes they are depicted culturally and artistically as the protagonists of several conspiracy theories. However, from time to time, this privileged position causes these people who know life and death to become targets of the primitive instinct of violence, especially in totalitarian mediocrity societies. Again, medical science has a primary position in the field of forensic science. Therefore, it has a mission to ensure current and historical justice by discovering the truth about death events and crimes. At this point, the subject includes criminology as well as archaeology and anthropology from time to time. Relatedly, in the context of euthanasia, medicine performs the role of Atropos. Besides, cryogenics is another medical promise of immortality. It is also a science-fictional design. On the other hand, its related mythological sample is Endymion. Upon the request of Selene, who was in love with Endymion, Zeus gave this young and extraordinarily handsome shepherd eternal youth and eternal sleep.

Another archetypal model is the Snow-White tale; between eating the poisoned apple and the prince's kiss, Snow White is in cryogenic sleep.

11.2 TECHNOLOGIES OF IMMORTALITY BY MOVIES

In the movie The Minority Report (2002, directed by Steven Spielberg), adapted from Philip K. Dick's story (1956), the police use a special warning system, half metaphysical and half technological, that detects the near future, and criminals are caught before the crime is committed and punished by being imprisoned in cryo tanks. Police Chief John Anderton (Tom Cruise), the protagonist of the film, realizes over time that the system he serves is a repressive simulation of the justice system and begins to fight. In the movie Oxygène (2021, directed by Alexandre Aja), the protagonist, Elizabeth Hansen (Mélanie Laurent), wakes up from a deep sleep in a cryogenic tube connected to a life unit managed by an artificial intelligence named Milo. On one hand, she tries to get out, and on the other hand, with Milo's help, she slowly begins to remember who she is. However, the situation does not change, and she voluntarily returns to her eternal cryogenic sleep. She is a clone created in her image by a genetic engineer named Elizabeth Hansen, and what she remembers are appropriate memory records belonging to Elisabeth uploaded to the system [4,5].

Mummification, an extremely sophisticated medical practice performed in Egypt during the time of the Pharaohs to preserve the body perfectly, represents the hope of resurrection. According to André Bazin: "If the plastic arts were put under psychoanalysis, the practice of embalming the dead might turn out to be a fundamental factor in their creation" and this includes photography [6].

The mass-produced humanoids in Aldous Huxley's Brave New World (1932) are a cloning design realized with a Jules Verne-like futurist vision. Thus, the fusion of artistic imagination specific to science-fiction literature and scientific/technological imagination is proven once again. Furthermore: "It is extremely hopeful that some human cell lines can be grown on a medium of precisely known chemical composition. Perhaps the first step will be the production of a clone from a single fertilized egg, as in Brave New World. But this would be of little social value. The production of a clone from cells of persons of attested ability would be a very different matter, and might raise the possibilities of human achievement dramatically" [23].

In the movie Blade Runner 2049 (2017, directed by Denis Villeneuve), which is also a Philip K. Dick (1968, adaptation 1968) adaptation, police officer K., who is also a replicant, is on a mission to catch replicants that do not comply with system standards. But over time, he begins to question the system and investigate his own identity. How much of a replicant and how much of a human being? On the other hand, the mass replicant producer Wallace Corporation, which has monumental clone laboratories, is seeking to clone replicants that can reproduce like humans. By the way, K. is a name loaded with literary connotations. Joseph K. of Franz Kafka's The Trial (1925), K. of Franz Kafka's The Castle (1926), Ka of Orhan Pamuk's Snow (2004). These people are immortal figures who represent individuals persecuted, destroyed, and alienated by deep organizations in conservative, authoritarian, and naturally repressive social systems. Cloning is eventually a genetic engineering work, but for now, it is popularly perceived as a science-fictional human reproduction design [7].

The movie Oblivion (2013, directed by Joseph Kosinski) is another example in this regard. Jack Harper (Tom Cruise) is an officer who performs surveillance duty at a base in the post-apocalyptic world and receives orders from the artificial intelligence space station called Tet. While Tet controls the world, it also provides energy from the ocean for people who are supposed to take shelter in a satellite called Titan in the depths of space. However, this is a simulation. There are no humans; Tet is exploiting the world's resources, and Jack Harper himself is one of countless Jack Harper clones being used and then destroyed. However, Jack Harper sometimes has dreams about his life in pre-apocalyptic times. One day, during his mission, he discovers an oasis and starts having happy times there, and then he encounters real human people living underground. Ultimately, he joins their resistance movement, together they destroy Tet and save the world. Then Jack Harper—yet another clone of him—returns one day to his happy oasis on Earth. Throughout Art History, the stories of mortals and the stories of immortal heroes have been intertwined. For example, vampires suck the blood of their victims; it's a transgressive blood transfusion metaphor. In this case, being a vampire is a cursed immortality, and vampires ironically continue to be bloodsucking nocturnal animals to survive [8,9].

The figure of the legendary vampire Dracula is an enduringly popular and often-interpreted character. Bram Stoker's Dracula (1992, directed by Francis Ford Coppola) movie is one such interpretation, adapted from Bram Stoker's novel of the same name. However, this time, Dracula (Gary Oldman) is slightly different. He is the representative of a globally organized evil that migrated from Transylvania to England in search of blood. He is not confined to the night alone; in addition, he can transform into a young and handsome man to lure women. The story of a vampire, together with his vampire partners, physically exploiting people in this way acquires socially realistic meanings far beyond fantasy, considering today's international organ trafficking and pharmacological experiments [18].

11.3 IMMORTALITY CULTURE

Immortality is a desire; it is an environment of existence. In this environment, life and death are merely thresholds. There are immortality environments with different qualities. An immortality environment can be real, virtual, visible, invisible, natural, artificial, simulative, as lieu de mémoire or afterlife. From a mnemonic perspective, immortality is to be remembered forever. However, in this context, Themis sometimes intervenes in the situation and can ensure that the criminal is forgotten forever – damnatio memoriae.

According to Richard Dawkins: "Cultural transmission is analogous to genetic transmission". Based on the characteristics of the gene and genetic science, Dawkins defined the phenomenon of meme (cultural gene) and developed the science of memetics. Similar to genetic engineering's work with genes, social engineering develops mnemonic strategies by examining the nature, transformations, and modification of collective memory by investigating memes. In this context, being civilized means being aware of the difference between political history and art history. Despite historical or current ideological anger, grudge, conflict, and often vandalistic desire for revenge, the vitality and preservation of artistic and cultural values in all circumstances are the universal condition of civilization. Because works of art, museums, libraries, architectural works, archaeological sites, monuments, sculptures, related cultural elements, rituals, and environments that have the quality of lieu de mémoire, represent immortality despite Kronos. Therefore, immortality is a civilization's ideal and historical consciousness. The immortality indicators of different civilizations, political systems, and relevant cultural structures are the material and spiritual foundations of a harmonious future [12].

For an immortal, immortality is an endless path through which the intellectual adventures of comrade immortals are articulated among themselves. In this context, Nikos Kazantzakis' (1883–1957) autobiographical novel titled Report to Greco is a notable source. This book was first published in English in 1961 by Simon and Schuster, in Greek in 1964 by Eleni N. Kazantzakis Publications, and in Turkish in 1975 by E Publications with the title El Greco'ya Mektuplar. The text in question is a homage to El Greco, as both the Painter and the Writer were born in Crete. Kazantzakis writes the following in the Author's note section of his book: "Report to Greco is not a biography. My life has relative value only to me and no one else. The only value I accept is that a person reaches the highest point that his determination and strength allow, as a result of his efforts to climb from one step to the next. What I arbitrarily call the "Cretan view"… "Everyone who deserves to be called a human being shoulders his cross and begins to climb his own Golgotha… In my upward ascent, there have been four decisive steps, and each has a sacred name: Jesus, Buddha, Lenin, Odysseus" [19].

Immortality is a metaphysical problem, but at the same time, concrete data is required to achieve immortality. Moreover, the data in question should always be available for the objective definition of new global paradigms, even if historical conditions change. For this very reason, it is one of the primary subjects of philosophy. Relatively speaking, from a historical perspective and sometimes from a collective memory perspective, immortality is beyond good and evil. However, there is a problem at this point; Federico Garcia Lorca is immortal, but is it possible to use the same adjective for General Franco, although for a while (1975–2019), he dialectically shared the immortality of the republican martyrs in Valle de los Caídos-? Primo Levi is immortal, but is it possible to use the same adjective for Dr. Mengele? Robert J. Oppenheimer is immortal, but is it possible to use the same adjective for Senator McCarthy? Because intuitively, immortality is a special level. On this subject, Kurt Gray and seven of his colleagues have joint research in the field of psychology, conducted in six studies using Amazon Mechanical Turk, with approximately 100 subjects for each study. Accordingly, they explain the research topic as follows: "We suggest that immortality is tied to morality…Good people may have transcendent immortality, with their souls escaping the Earth to enjoy spiritual liberty. On the contrary, evil people may have trapped immortality, with their souls bound to a particular location; Then, as results of Study 1: Immortality and (Im)morality Across Historical Figures, "people are generally motivated for good people to become immortal, but have an independent tendency to perceive both good and evil individuals as living on after death" [15].

Immortality is an extremely rich source of inspiration, both in terms of subject and creative strategies. The essence of literary and artistic intertextuality lies in immortality. Roland Barthes, who declared The Death of the Author, justifies this passionate claim through immortals such as Balzac, Baudelaire, Van Gogh, Tchaikovsky, Mallarmé, Proust, Brecht (1977:142–148). With this mythological action, he grants us, the readers, an active position in the immortality symposium of literature, yet he himself is already an immortal figure [14].

Immortality means not being forgotten.

Dr. Grigoris Lambrakis (1912–1963), a partisan of the Greek resistance that fought against the Nazi occupation in World War II and deputy of the socialist EDA Party, was the victim of a political assassination. "At the funeral, people chant 'Z!' (zei) meaning 'He is alive!' or 'Lambrakis is alive' slogans" (Koçak, 2015:367). Historically, Lambrakis/Z is an immortal symbol representing political victims like himself, and in the same context, Z is a common cultural code of the family of man. Besides, the Lambrakis tragedy was written as a novel (1967) by Vassilis Vassilikos with the title Z. Costa-Gavras then adapted this novel to the cinema with the same title (1969). Yves Montand interprets the role of Z and this film is one of the classic masterpieces of political cinema. Vassilis Vassilikos, Costa-Gavras, and Yves Montand fulfilled the mission of immortalizing Grigoris Lambrakis. As artists, humanist intellectuals, and political activists who share similar ideals with Lambrakis, they are also immortal figures themselves. The novel Z and the movie Z form the intersection point of this immortality process [20].

The following line from Virgil's Aeneid is written on the wall of the 9/11 Memorial & Museum: No day shall erase you from the memory of time (nulla dies umquam memori vos eximet aevo, Aeneid, Book IX, 447). Naturally, there are many translations of the Aeneid. But this quote is, in Seider's definition, an "elegant translation" (2017: 173). Regarding this, Nisus and Euryalus, whose story Virgil tells, are two Trojan soldiers who were comrades of Aeneas. They were martyred while fighting against the Rutulians. In the face of their memory full of courage and loyalty, Virgil writes as follows:

> *"Fortunati ambo! si quid mea carmina possunt,*
> *nulla dies umquam memori vos eximet aevo,*
> *dum domus Aeneae Capitoli immobile saxum*
> *accolet imperiumque pater Romanus habebit" [31].*

An English translation of these verses is as follows: *"Happy pair! if my verse is aught of avail, no length of days shall ever blot you from the memory of time, while the house of Aeneas shall dwell by the Capitoline's steadfast stone, and the lord of Rome hold sovereignty" (Virgil, BOOK NINTH THE SIEGE OF THE TROJAN CAMP, 1885:206, 446–449).* However, regarding this section, we quote Türkân Uzel's Turkish translation here, for the sake of immortality, with your permission. We think that Uzel's translation represents also perfectly the spirit of Virgil, just like the translation on the wall of the 9/11 Memorial & Museum.

> *"Ne mutlu ikinize ki gücü varsa şiirimin,*
> *durdukça Aeneaslar soyu Capitolium'un*
> *sarsılmaz kayasında, Romalı Ata orada*
> *egemen olduğu sürece, silinip gitmeyecek*
> *yeni kuşakların belleğinden sizin hatıranız!" [30]*

11.4 POSTHUMANISM AND IMMORTALITY

Immortality is a posthumanism phenomenon. Ihab Hassan makes the following determination in his creative essay titled Prometheus as Performer: Toward a Posthumanist Culture?: "The cosmos is performance, posthumanist culture is a performance in progress, and their symbolic nexus is Prometheus" (Hassan, 1977:838). However, Prometheus's power, creativity, and tragic fate are the active elements of a design that defines the future of humanity as well as the development of civilization. Ihab Hassan draws attention to the following popular developments: "Artificial intelligences, from the humblest calculator to the most transcendent computer, help to transform the image of man, the concept of the human…Technology and the pharmaceutical industry have already altered most performances in the Olympic Games… or the TV series The Six Million Dollar Man". Thus, in his own words, he paints an "optimistic but kitsch" picture. Again, Ihab Hassan points out the possibility of situations such as hunger and global war, as well as technological and medical developments and applications in the futuristic and cybernetic sense (p.848), and ultimately describes Prometheus' identification with the family of man with this following poetic expression: "We are ourselves that performance; we perform and are performed every moment. We are changing the form of Desire. Everything changes, and nothing, not even Death, can tire" (p.850) [17].

Rosi Braidotti has a cautious discourse against the euphoria of immortality developed by medicine and digital technologies from a posthumanist perspective. According to Braidotti: "Each of us is always already a 'has been', as we are mortal beings. Desire as the ontological drive to become (*potentia*) seduces us into going on living"(Braidotti, 2013:134). Potentia is a concept developed by Braidotti. It also represents individual free will regarding life and death in posthuman conditions. However: "It connects us trans-individually, trans-generationally, and eco-philosophically", and it can be claimed that this explanation is a definition of immortality. Again, according to Braidotti: "The posthuman nomadic subject is materialist and vitalist, embodied and embedded" [10].

Nomadism is a very attractive context, indicating spontaneous mobility, cosmopolitanism, polyglotism, and unlimited intercultural geographies. Looking at Braidotti's biography, she is also a nomad. However, there is a contradiction at this point. Mobilistically, how can the state of being embodied and being embedded be compatible with nomadity? On the other hand, her book *Posthuman* is almost a eulogy of Amor Fati, as the Author herself points out: "We need to be 'worthy of the present' (p.189). But, posthumanist critique is a reality but not a submission discourse. Furthermore, what about nostalgia? What about utopia? What will happen to metaphor, especially in this age of simulation and metaverse? Whereas: "We live with metaphors. We communicate with metaphors, more and more intense; interestingly, as the transparency increases, the production of metaphors is proportionally increasing. Because metaphor is not just a literary figure of speech or a rhetorical performance but a cultural phenomenon that exists in all our lives". Because "The world is a metaphor" [2,24]

Transhumanism and Posthumanism are the evolutionary stages of humanism. Renaissance Humanism continues to enlighten, energize, and inspire humanity as a universal cultural heritage. However, modern technologies have harmed people as much as they have been beneficial to them in the production and consumption stages. In addition to alienation and industrial discrimination, the war industry, use of chemical weapons, exploitation of Earth and underground resources, atomic bombs, nuclear disasters, and synthetic drugs have caused irreversible apocalyptic consequences. During World War II, the death industry in Nazi Concentration Camps turned humans into a commodity; the human body was transformed into recycled material and used like experimental animals for medical and pharmaceutical procedures and experiments. Consequently, humanism has been critically redefined at every stage according to the current human condition. In our era, intense emancipation processes are experienced. Additionally, conventional identity qualities have begun to blur. Moreover, in the context of the existence of cyborgs, human vanitas as creator has little meaning. Transhumanism, one of the contemporary humanism paradigms, is based on the principle of improving human physical and mental qualities and providing bionic endurance and perfection through medical methods, genetic engineering, and digital technologies as a biopolitical strategy. Artificial organs, prostheses, genetic interventions, and smartphones that have become extensions of the body – such as Ihab Hassan's calculator and computer – are transhumanist elements. However, there is still a problem. Ideologically, biological structure and bionic structure are equated, but can everyone have social and economic transhumanist advantages under equal conditions? According to Fukuyama, some transhumanist practices already exist in contemporary medical practice: However, "the first victim of transhumanism might be equality" (2009:1). On the other hand, according to Bostrom: "Transhumanists view technological progress as a joint human effort to invent new tools that we can use to reshape the human condition and overcome our biological limitations, making it possible for those who so want to become 'post-humans'." (1998:1). Posthumanism represents an advanced stage of transhumanism. The scientific and cultural conditions that prepared and represented transhumanism also apply to posthumanism. However, from time to time, posthumanism diverges and surprisingly tries to build distinctive ethics by displaying a futuristic example of schizophrenia. According to Merzlyakov: "We may not like the idea of human exceptionalism for some ethical reasons, but from a purely scientific point of view, this is not grounds to deny human exceptionalism…Thus, posthumanism with its vector to expand the presence of consciousness in the world—up to the animation of inanimate objects—turns out to be a form of animism and contradicts science" (2022:1). Therefore, posthumanism is not an environment of cyber-metaphysics; It is a valid paradigm to the extent that it is a criterion of criticism identified not only with technology but also with aesthetics and mythology [15].

11.5 FEATURES OF QUANTUM IMMORTALITY

According to Ce Han: "Quantum Immortality usually refers to, in a classical sense, a person who is 'lucky' enough to survive in any incident in the world. To accomplish this evaluation, the concepts of the main two interpretations of quantum physics: 1) Copenhagen Interpretation and 2) Many Worlds Interpretation (or MWI) will be necessarily involved. Therefore, it is necessary to briefly describe the above-mentioned scientific components of quantum immortality here, albeit modestly. "Toward the end of 1927, the differences of opinion converged to a consensus based on Niels Bohr's principle of complementarity, which holds that a physical phenomenon is observed in two different 'complementary' ways depending on the experimental setup. For example, light could sometimes behave like waves and other times like particles. Both images were necessary to obtain a complete description of the phenomenon, even though they excluded each other" (n.a., 2012:1). At the beginning of Christopher Nolan's film Oppenheimer (2023), Oppenheimer states that quantum thought is the ability to see things differently, and three artistic elements accompany this statement, each of which has revolutionized its field and represents a different perception: *Le Sacre du Printemps* (1913) by Igor Stravinsky, *The Waste Land* (1922) by T. S. Eliot, and *Femme assise aux bras croisés* (1937) by Pablo Picasso. Thus, modern scientific paradigms and modern/avant-garde paradigms constantly synthesize each other [11].

Besides, "Complementarity is first and foremost a semantic and epistemological reading of quantum mechanics that carries certain ontological implications". The Copenhagen interpretation is also related to Schrödinger's cat thought experiment (1935): "In this experiment, there is a cat in a closed box and a mechanism that is half as likely to kill the cat. Schrödinger predicts that the cat is in a superposition (that is, both dead and alive) until this box is opened, but when the box is opened, the cat's wave function collapses and only one of these possibilities is real" [13,29].

In Chapter 39 of his book titled Camera Lucida, Roland Barthes analyzes the portrait of Lewis Payne (1865) taken by Alexander Gardner in the context of punctum/stigmatum. The nature of the punctum in question is Time. Payne, in the photo, was sentenced to death after an assassination attempt and is handcuffed in his cell, waiting to be hanged. Barthes explains this photo in this way: "I read at the same time: This will be and this has been" (1981:96). The young and handsome man in the photograph is dead in the context of *this will be*, but alive in the context of *this has been*. In the auratic medium of photography, death, and life are equally superposed. However, everyone mentioned here is immortal. Gardner immortalized Payne by taking his photograph. But at the same time, Gardner is an immortal hero in the History of Photography with his performance as a photographer. With this comment, Barthes confirms the immortality of both and shares this immortality with everyone concerned. One of the most famous photos in the History of Photography is The Falling Soldier (September 5, 1936), taken by Robert Capa at Cerro Muriano, Córdoba Front, during the Spanish Civil War. This is a photo of the moment of death. The Falling Soldier's name is Federico "El Taino" Borrell García. He is a militia member of la Confederación Nacional del Trabajo (CNT, the National Confederation of Labor), and he was martyred while fighting against the fascists on the side of the Republicans.

The time of photography is Kairos, and "In the indefinite and amorphous flow, time finally presents a unique and unrepeatable 'now', in which eternity and time, identity and otherness, converge in an absolute unity… Kairos reveals the quality of time". Iconographically, a weighing scale balanced on a razor's sharp edge device in Kairos' hand, ready to slide at any time, represents "erèmia: the 'pregnant pause' between two successive moments" (Baert, 2020:1). The moment of life, the moment of death, but the Loyalist Soldier is not on the ground; he exists in a crystallized falling instant, forever. What remains is Capa's immortality and the collective memory records of the Republicans who fought in the Spanish Civil War [33].

On the other hand, according to Hugh Everett (1957), who developed the theory of The Many Worlds Interpretation: "Since the universal validity of the state function description is asserted, one can regard the state functions themselves as the fundamental entities, and one can even consider the state function of the whole universe. In this sense, this theory can be called the theory of the 'universal wave function,' since all of physics is presumed to follow from this function alone" (Everett, 1957, as cited in Gribbin, 2020:1). In this context, Bryce DeWitt's (1960) comment is as follows: "every quantum transition taking place in every star, in every galaxy, in every remote corner of the universe is splitting our local world on Earth into myriad copies of itself." [16]

The Many Worlds, parallel universes, or multiverse...such a wonderful plot design!

In the movie Spider-Man: Across the Spider-Verse (2023, directed by Joaquim Dos Santos, Kemp Powers, Justin K. Thompson), Miles Morales is the protagonist of this animated version of the Spider-Man Saga. But he is also one element of the spider-people multitude; Spider-Verse is a real heteroglossia and therefore it can be said that this multiverse is a social-realist metaphor representing an ideal pluralistic and humanist society.

11.6 TRANSMIGRATION AND IMMORTALITY

Transmigration is a mode of cyber-immortality. In this context, Plato's dialogues are probably one of the basic principles of academic and intellectual studies for generations. Regardless of the period in which it takes place, these dialogues guide in defining contemporary paradigms. The subject of the Phaedo dialogue is immortality. In this dialogue, Phaedo, one of the witnesses of Socrates' last moments, narrates what happened there and what was said between them. One of these speeches is as follows:

Socrates: 'Well then, what do we call whatever doesn't admit death?'
Cebes: 'Im-mortal.'
Socrates: 'But soul doesn't admit death?'
Cebes: 'No.'
Socrates: 'Then soul is immortal.'
Cebes: 'It's immortal'.

(Plato, 2002:59–60, 105-e; Plato, 1997:108, 105-e) (Figure 11.1)

Eventually, the transmigration of the soul is also mentioned; Cebes to Simmias says: "Every soul wears out many bodies". Jorge Luis Borges defines this subject as follows in his hypertext titled "Immortality": "Transmigration gives us the possibility of a soul that travels from body to body, in human bodies, and animals". However, the cyber incarnation is a little more comprehensive. Will Caster (Johnny Depp), the protagonist of the movie Transcendence (2014, directed by Wally Pfister), is a

FIGURE 11.1 Socrates, Ephesus Archaeological Museum. S. Atay © 2023.

scientist working in the field of artificial intelligence. However, one day, he is seriously injured by an anti-AI radical attack, and when he is about to die, he uploads himself to the system, becomes AI itself, and continues his cyber existence by preserving his virtual image. Beyond fiction, dead people continue to communicate with this world through cyberspace migrants, AI chatbots, and specialized companies such as HereAfter AI. Or, with deepfake technology, dead people are resurrected kinetically and photographically in any desired context. On the other hand, transmigration is a transformation process. Metamorphosis stories in classical mythology have transformed immortality into a dazzling environment and an endless source of inspiration. At this point, the roads again lead to Plato. In Plato's Theaetetus dialogue, which seeks and discusses the answer to the question of what knowledge is, Socrates quotes the following famous sentence from Protagoras: "Of all things, the measure is man, of the things that are, the existence of things that are and the non-existence of things that are not". Therefore, the structure and functioning of the neural architecture of the human brain are the main models in the Deep Learning Network's computational design. Deep Learning Networks have multiple and diverse functionalities from medicine to pedagogy multidisciplinary monitoring research to generating artistic works, from biological and virtual resurrection research to hyper-realistic aesthetics of the uncanny valley phenomenon in digital games [25–27].

In this context, Malhotra and Jindal studied the possibilities of several deep learning techniques within related research studies for the detection of psychiatric problems like depression, auto-destruction, or suicide inclination linked to social network content. "This systematic review has shown that deep learning techniques have wide applications for mental health diagnosis using social media content" [21].

Artificial Intelligence is the creation of human intelligence. As a science-fiction prediction, these two intelligences will continue to develop in parallel for now, but may eventually come face-to-face in the future. In this context, digital immortality can become a concrete design by recording and preserving the personal brain data of an individual or individuals to perfect natural or artificial human machines according to the logic of Generative Adversarial Networks. However, will the subject of this digital immortality be able to have a biological body? By what criteria will this individual or individuals be selected as candidates for immortality? Is digital immortality a technology vanity? Is animation/regeneration/resurrection of historical figures or ordinary people by Artificial Intelligence software using conventional records and removing them from their chronological and real context a kitsch intervention? Or will the human struggle for existence turn into an ironic living people-zombie people dilemma like in the movie World War Z (2013, directed by Marc Forster)? What does such a definition of immortality mean? Or is digital immortality the final stage of alienation? Life and death are two basic components and variables of being. Interdisciplinary science and technology will continue to process informative and psychological human data for humans and post-humans. On the other hand, the subject of brain data in question is also a cultural and mnemonic issue, and for thousands of years, libraries, museums, archives, cinemathéques, monuments, archaeological sites, les lieux de mémoire, collections, books, and encyclopedias are the places where the utopia of immortality has been realized and reigned [22–28,32].

11.7 CONCLUSION

Asclepius, the god of medicine, not only treats patients as a physician but also sometimes grants them immortality. Zeus, jealous of this, kills him with a lightning bolt, and he transforms into the constellation Ophiuchus. The snake, which is the symbol of medicine and pharmacy today, is his sacred animal. In Greece and Western Anatolia, there are sacred places dedicated to Asclepius called Asclepions, which are medical centers and temples (Figure 11.2).

Therefore, immortality has been defined as a function and possibility of medicine from the beginning. This is the ultimate goal of contemporary medical technologies. Furthermore, the metaphor of immortality is needed to define life and death ontologically. Immortality is a source of creativity and a criterion of criticism. It is a romantic challenge (Figure 11.3).

Immortality is an evolving concept according to contemporary paradigms: quantum, cyberculture, and posthumanism. It is a subject of formalist research and is a humanist privilege that only some people throughout history have truly possessed

FIGURE 11.2   (a) Asclepios, İzmir Archeological Museum. S. Atay © 2023. (b) Grave steel with snake motif, İzmir Archeological Museum. S. Atay © 2023. (c) Column with snake motif, Asclepion, Pergamon. S. Atay © 2023.

(Continued)

FIGURE 11.2 (*Continued*)   (a) Asclepios, İzmir Archeological Museum. S. Atay © 2023. (b) Grave steel with snake motif, İzmir Archeological Museum. S. Atay © 2023. (c) Column with snake motif, Asclepion, Pergamon. S. Atay © 2023.

FIGURE 11.3 (a) Tiberius, Bronz Snake, Livia, Ephesus Archaeological Museum. S. Atay © 2023. (b) Asclepion, Pergamon. S. Atay © 2023. (c) Asclepion Temple, Pergamon. S. Atay © 2023.

and shared with the generations that followed them. As Borges underlines ironically in his story *The Immortal* (1947): "To be immortal is commonplace; except for man, all creatures are immortal, for they are ignorant of death" [8].

EPILOGUE

This article was written during a very special period, on the centenary of the founding of the Republic of Turkey (October 29, 1923–October 29, 2023). Mustafa Kemal Atatürk, the founder of the Republic of Turkey, made the following determination about the Republic of Turkey: "Benim naçiz vücudum bir gün elbet toprak olacaktır fakat Türkiye Cumhuriyeti ilelebet payidar kalacaktır" – "My humble body will surely turn to dust one day, but the Republic of Turkey will be everlasting".This is also a perfect definition of quantum immortality. Accordingly, quantum immortality is the energetic vitality of the basic humanistic principles and classical ideas wherever and whenever.

REFERENCES

1. Aeschylus (1953). Prometheus bound. In: *The Complete Greek Tragedies II*, 2nd edn (D. Grene and R. Lattimore, Eds., D. Grene, Trans.) Chicago, IL: The University of Chicago Press, pp. 131–180.
2. Atay, S. (2019). Killing commendatore in-between. *European Journal of Literary Studies*, 2(1). https://oapub.org/lit/index.php/EJLS/article/view/112. Date accessed 14 September 2023.
3. Baert, B. (2020). Kairos: The Right Moment or Occasion. https://www.ias.edu/ideas/baert-kairos.
4. Barthes, R. (1981). *Camera Lucida: Reflections on Photography* (R. Howard, Trans.) New York: Hill and Wang.
5. Barthes, R. (1977). The death of the author. In: *Image, Music, Text* (S. Heath, Trans.) London: Fontana, pp. 142–148.
6. Bazin, A. (1960). *The Ontology of the Photographic Image* (H.Gray, Trans.). *Film Quarterly*, 13(4), 4–9.
7. Borges, J. L. (2014). *The Immortal in Jorge Luis Borges Labyrinths Selected Stories and Other Writings* (D. A. Yates and J. E. Irby, Eds.), New York: New Directions, pp. 105–118.
8. Borges, J. L. (1999). Immortality (E.Weinberger, Trans.). *NER New England Review*, 20(3), 11–16. www.jstor.org/stable/40243722.
9. Bostrom, N. What Is Transhumanism? (Original Version Appeared in 1998, Here Slightly Revised and with a Postscript Added in 2001). https://nickbostrom.com/old/transhumanism.
10. Braidotti, R. (2013). *The Posthuman*. Cambridge, Malden: Polity Press. https://ageing-companions.constantvzw.org/books/The_Posthuman_-_Rosi_Braidotti.pdf.
11. Ce, H. (2021). Theoretical quantum immortality and its mathematical authority. *Journal of Physics: Conference Series*, vol. 1936. In: 2021 *11th International Conference on Applied Physics and Mathematics (ICAPM 2021) 1–3* February 2021, Shanghai, China, Conf. Ser. 1936012015. https://iopscience.iop.org/article/10.1088/1742-6596/1936/1/012015/pdf.
12. Dawkins, R. (2006). *The Selfish Gene*. Oxford: Oxford University Press.

13. Faye, J. (2019). Copenhagen interpretation of quantum mechanics. In: E. N. Zalta (Ed.), *The Stanford Encyclopedia of Philosophy*, Winter 2019 edn. https://plato.stanford.edu/archives/win2019/entries/qm-copenhagen/

14. Fukuyama, F. (23 October 2009). Transhumanism. https://foreignpolicy.com/2009/10/23/transhumanism/

15. Gray, K. et al. (2018). To be immortal, do good or evil. *Personality and Social Psychology Bulletin*, 44(6), 868–880.

16. Gribbin, J. (20 May 2020). The many-worlds theory, explained. *The MIT Press Reader*. https://thereader.mitpress.mit.edu/the-many-worlds-theory/.

17. Hassan, I. (Winter, 1977). Prometheus as performer: Toward a posthumanist culture? *The Georgia Review*, 31(4), 830–850. https://www.jstor.org/stable/41397536.

18. Hesiod (2016). Hesiod. In: *Anthology of Classical Myth: Primary Sources in Translation* (S. M. Trzaskoma, R. Scott Smith, S. Brunet, Eds. and Trans.), Indianapolis, IN: Hackett Publishing Company Inc, pp. 129–167.

19. Kazancakis, N. (2003). *El Greco'ya Mektuplar* (A. Angın, Trans.) İstanbul: Can.

20. Koçak, F. (2015). Çevirmenin Notu. In: *Z* (Vasili Vasilikos, Author, F. Koçak Trans.) İstanbul: Sel, p. 367.

21. Malhotra, A&Jindal, R. (2022). Deep learning techniques for suicide and depression detection from online social media: A scoping review, *Applied Soft Computing*, 130(109713), 1–37.

22. Merzlyakov, S.S. (29 September 2022). Posthumanism vs. transhumanism: from the "end of exceptionalism" to "technological humanism". *Global Trends*, 92, S475–S482. doi:10.1134/S10193331622120073.

23. Mittwoch, U. (2002). "Clone": The history of a euphonious scientific term. *Medical History*, 46, 381–402. https://pubmed.ncbi.nlm.nih.gov/12194426/.

24. Murakami, H. (2005). *Kafka on the Shore* (P. Gabriel, Trans) London: Vintage Books. https://nbi.ku.dk/english/www/niels/bohr/koebenhavnerfortolkningen/

25. Plato (Eflatun) (1990). *Theaitetos* (M. Gökberk, Trans.), İstanbul: M.E.B.

26. Plato (Eflatun) (1997). *Phaidon* (S. K.Yetkin and H. R. Atademir, Trans.) İstanbul: M.E.B.

27. Plato (2002). *Phaedo* (D. Gallop, Trans.) Oxford: Clarendon Press. https://www.faculty.umb.edu/gary_zabel/Phil_100/Plato_files/310585462-Plato-Phaedo.pdf.

28. Seider, A. (2017). Crossing borders: Appropriations and collaborations allure without allusion: Quoting a Virgilian Epitaph in a 9/11 Memorial. *INTERFACES Image Texte Language*, 38, 173–194, https://journals.openedition.org/interfaces/321.

29. Telimenli, C. C. & Bakırcı, Ç. M. (2018, January 21). Kopenhag Yorumu Nedir? Kuantum Mekaniği ile İlgili Ne Söyler? *Evrim Ağacı*. https://evrimagaci.org/s/3198.

30. Vergilius (2019). *Aeneis* (T. Uzel, Trans.) İstanbul: Jaguar.

31. Virgilio (2007). *Eneide* (M. Scaffidi Abbate, Trans.) Roma: Newton.

32. Virgil (1885). *The Aeneid* (J. W. Mackail, MA fellow of Balliol College, Oxford, Trans.) London: Macmillan. https://www.gutenberg.org/files/22456/22456-h/22456-h.htm#BOOK_NINTH. Accessed 6 September 2021.

33. Zaccaria Ruggiu, A. (1998). Appendice: Aion Chronos Kairos. L'immagine del tempo nel mondo greco e romano. In: *Filosofia del Tempo* (L. Ruggiu, Ed.) Milano: Bruno Mondadori, pp. 293–318.

*Prabu Selvam, M. Sumathi, P. Saravanan,
and M. Marimuthu*

12 TransADD
Transformer-Based Network for Alzheimer's Disease Detection Using Brain MRI Images

12.1 INTRODUCTION

Due to demographic changes, age-related diseases like Alzheimer's have reached a high prevalence, with more than 47 million cases worldwide. AD is a neurodegenerative disease affecting brain memory tissues, leading to cognitive impairments, disorientation, and a progressive decline in conversational abilities. Today, AD poses numerous challenging issues for healthcare organizations and the global health system, with significant economic implications for each country. In many countries, the elderly population accounts for over 30% of the total. More than 16 million caregivers in the United States dedicate over 18 million hours to AD care. By 2050, an estimated one in 85 individuals will be affected by AD. As a result, identifying AD early on is crucial for caregivers and society [1–3].

Predicting the early stages of AD is paramount, as finding a cure or halting disease progression in its later stages remains an elusive goal. To date, no effective treatment for AD exists. Thus, early detection becomes the primary means of taking preventive measures, raising patient awareness, implementing treatment plans, evaluating treatment effectiveness, and promoting lifestyle changes [3].

AD prediction can be broadly categorized into Region Of Interest (ROI), voxel-based, and patch-based techniques. Voxel techniques involve extracting features through statistical or voxel selection processes, often leading to noisy information. In ROI techniques, MRI images are segmented, and features are extracted from each segment, resulting in high-dimensional data. Patch techniques analyze multiple ROIs to extract features for each patch [4]. Constructing an effective prediction model requires analyzing the relationship between various predictive factors, such as clinical diagnosis, cognitive scores, ventricular volume, and MRI image analysis. Machine learning and Deep Learning (DL) models are employed for accurate predictions. Compared to traditional machine learning models, DL models enhance AD diagnosis performance [5]. Despite the challenge of generalization during

DOI: 10.1201/9781032632223-12

testing due to complex neural network layers, DL remains preferable in healthcare applications.

DL techniques, including 2D and 3D patch and brain image analysis, are pivotal in medical image analysis. However, in existing models, directly feeding whole brain images to DL models has led to unsatisfactory diagnoses and irrelevant results. Thus, current DL analyses focus on ROI-based approaches [6]. Given the immense complexity of raw MRI image analysis, feature extraction and classification techniques are vital to reduce processing complexity while improving accuracy. The widely used method of partitioning images into distinct regions—ROI—facilitates discriminative multi-task feature selection [7]. To enhance DL performance, 3D convolutional images integrate local and global features, often combined with 3D-patch and 2D-slicing techniques. Despite addressing data scarcity, training DL models with multiple classifiers increases parameter count [8]. The Siamese CNN, utilizing triple ResNet-34 for structural MRI analysis, employs two CNN groups, ReLU activations, convolution sequences, and accumulation procedures to concurrently train multiple images and segments [9].

ROI analysis is used when there is a prior hypothesis about specific brain regions associated with AD, and the goal is to assess the health or abnormality of these regions. Voxel-based analysis is data-driven and can reveal spatial patterns of abnormalities that might not be evident with ROI-based approaches. It's used when the exact locations of AD-related changes are not known in advance. Patch-based approaches are used when there is an interest in capturing both global and local spatial patterns of AD-related changes.

The remainder of this chapter is structured as follows. Section 12.2 presents a literature review of existing works, discussing their strengths and weaknesses. In Section 12.3, we delve into the proposed transformer-based network for AD detection using brain MRI images, outlining its architecture and relevant equations. Section 12.4 showcases experimental results from the proposed approach, comparing them with existing methodologies. Finally, Section 12.5 concludes the proposed work.

Prabu et al. [10] proposed a multi-scale deep neural network for early AD detection, capturing brain metabolic activity through DL-based fluorodeoxyglucose positron emission tomography. This technique analyzed MRI in different discriminative ways, achieving improved results compared to single-scale classification methods. Hett et al. [11] introduced the adaptive fusion of texture-based grading for AD classification. Compared to a patch-based framework, this texture-based approach yielded improved classification accuracy. To enhance patch-based performance, the technique integrated multi-directional texture maps with 3D Gabor filters, achieving an accuracy of 91.3%.

Li et al. [12] explored multiple cluster-dense convolutional networks for AD diagnosis, combining local feature analysis of MRI brain images with AD classification. Brain images were partitioned into local regions to enhance accuracy, and 3D patches were extracted from each region. K-means clustering formed region groups, and DenseNet learned patch features. Features from discriminative clusters were then ensembled, yielding the final result. This technique was tested on a small dataset, excluding multi-modal brain images and positron emission tomography images.

Spasov et al. [13] proposed parameter-efficient DL for predicting conversion from Mild Cognitive Impairment (MCI) to AD. This technique simultaneously predicted AD vs. healthy control classification and MCI to AD conversion, employing limited parameters to counter data overfitting. Separate input streams were used to extract additional information from MRI, effectively addressing various templates and irrelevant features. Ge et al. [14] employed a multi-stream, multi-scale deep CNN for AD detection in MRI. Utilizing a 3D multi-stage CNN, they integrated multi-resolution features, processing each tissue region through parallel 3D multi-scale CNN. A two-level fusion detection approach was applied, enhancing classification performance through dimension reduction and feature boosting.

Jain et al. [15] employed CNN for AD classification, utilizing a VGG-16-trained dataset for FE to reduce computational complexity. 3D MRI scan images were sliced into 2D images for informative slice selection, mitigating computational load. CNN eliminated manual processes, and transfer learning aided in reducing computational complexity. Basheera and Ram [16] proposed a CNN-based AD classification technique using a hybrid approach, combining binary and multi-class classification for T1 and T2 MRI images. The images underwent segmentation and preprocessing, followed by adaptive fusion of geometric distortion and Gaussian filters. Skull-stripping removed non-brain tissues, with the MCI-CN classification achieving an accuracy rate of 98%. Mendoza-Leon et al. [17] introduced the single-slice AD classification and analysis using Supervised Switching Autoencoders (SSA). SSA combines supervised and unsupervised models, effectively analyzing disease semantics and complex visual neurodegeneration patterns. Patch-level analysis was employed for classifying AD-infected and healthy images, with a majority rule applied for result prediction. SSA achieved a high sensitivity of 95% for sagittal and coronal planes, performing well on single-class datasets but not on multi-class datasets.

Feng et al. [18] utilized FE for AD classification through Nonsubsampled Contourlet Subband-Based Individual Networks (NCSIN). NCSIN captured correlations in abnormal energy distribution patterns for AD prediction. Directional subbands were obtained from 2D MRI images via nonsubsampled contourlet transformation. Edge weights were assigned through connection strength, and AD classification was achieved through node and edge feature concatenation. NCSIN outperformed conventional methods in accuracy, although it was not directly correlated with brain atrophy regions. Chen and Xia [19] employed iterative sparse and DL techniques for AD diagnosis. They combined Feature Extraction (FE) and critical cortical region identification to diagnose AD. FE extracted features from 62 cortical regions using local and global structural information. Critical cortical regions were identified through sparse regression, and the FE and sparse regression processes were iteratively updated to enhance accuracy. This technique offered rapid computational time for complex classification and performed effectively across various datasets, albeit focusing on single-modality images rather than multi-modality images.

Liang et al. [20] employed a deep recurrent neural network model for AD progression analysis, predicting imputed missing values and future progression based on historical measurements. Progression was assessed using MRI volumetric measurements, clinical status, and cognitive scores, enabling clinical diagnosis at each time point. This multi-task learning process enhanced end-to-end performance analysis for accurate prediction. The prediction accuracy remained consistent across different aspects, highlighting its robustness. Liu et al. [21] discussed AD detection using depthwise separable convolutional neural networks (CNN). While integrating this technique with mobile phones presented computational challenges due to parameter volume, depthwise separable convolution required fewer parameters and lower computational complexity, making it suitable for mobile devices without sacrificing accuracy.

Sathiyamoorthi et al. [22] proposed deep CNN-based AD diagnosis for MRI images, overcoming the challenge of noisy data through the 2D adaptive bilateral filter (2D-ABF) algorithm. Adaptive histogram adjustment (AHA) improved image quality, and adaptive mean-shift modified expectation maximization aided AD segmentation. A DL feature selection technique facilitated classification. Hedayati et al. [23] proposed FE-based convolutional autoencoders for AD diagnosis, generating a 3D input image through an autoencoder-based FE module before employing CNN. The technique analyzed AD vs. Normal Condition (NC), AD vs. Mild Cognitive Impairment (MCI), and MCI vs. NC. It achieved high diagnostic accuracy and lower error rates in NC detection.

12.2 PROPOSED SYSTEM

Figure 12.1 depicts the overall architecture of our proposed framework. This framework comprises four important modules: Image Serialization, Feature Extraction, Encode and Decoder.

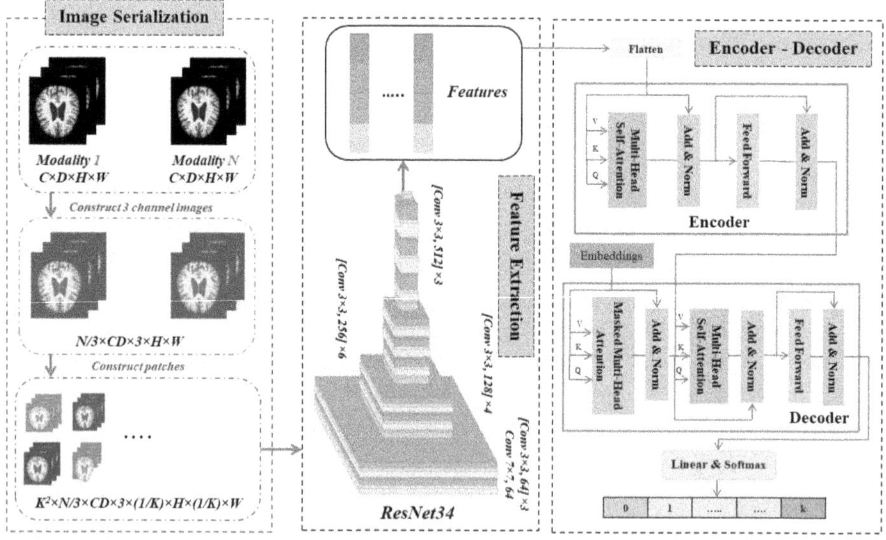

FIGURE 12.1 Overall architecture of the proposed system.

12.2.1 IMAGE SERIALIZATION

In the context of a multi-modal image, denoted as $\left(I \in \mathbb{R}^{C \times D \times H \times W \times B \times M}\right)$, where C represents the number of channels, D stands for depth, B signifies batch size. At the same time, H and W denote spatial resolution, and M indicates the number of modalities. A sequence conversion becomes necessary before the input image can be sent to the feature extraction module.

Initially, we overlay three adjacent 2D slices of the multi-modal image, resulting in the creation of three-channel images denoted as I'. This process follows the approach outlined in [24]. Subsequently, each of these resulting images is divided into size patches $(M \times M)$, where a larger M value corresponds to smaller patch sizes. Finally, the superimposed image is encoded into a patch, represented as $\left(I'' \in \mathbb{R}^{K^2 \times N/3 \times CD \times 3 \times (1/K) \times H \times (1/K) \times W}\right)$.

Once the image sequence has been constructed, it becomes suitable for input to a CNN, as detailed in [25]. In this context, the final fully connected layer of the CNN is replaced with a linear projection layer, which is responsible for mapping the features of the vector patch into the potential embedding space.

12.2.2 EMBEDDINGS AND TOKENS

The input layer comprises five embeddings: position embedding, patch embedding, class embedding, class token, and patch token. Position and patch embeddings capture and encode spatial and location information for each patch, resulting in patch tokens. The term "patch embedding" refers to the representation of the output of each patch from the CNN. The class token and class embedding are present but not the same because class embedding excludes patch embedding. The class embedding is a trainable vector. Expressions for class token x_{CT} and patch token x_{PT} can be found in Equations (12.1) and (12.2).

$$x_{CT} = W^c \tag{12.1}$$

$$x_{PT} = Conv(x) + x_{PE} \tag{12.2}$$

where x, x_{PE} and W^c represent input, positional embedding and trainable vectors. The class token is affixed to the patch tokens before they are directed to the Transformer's input layer. These tokens then proceed through the intermediate layers of the Transformer. The ultimate output from the fully connected layer is the basis for predicting the class.

12.2.3 FEATURE EXTRACTION USING RESNET

We utilize ResNet-34 as a CNN backbone to extract low-level features in this research work. The main reasons for choosing ResNet as our backbone are that skip connections in the residual blocks resolve the vanishing/exploding gradient problem, and it allows us to construct a more flexible CNN structure that helps to increase recognition accuracy [26]. The network configuration of ResNet-34 is shown in Table 12.1.

TABLE 12.1

The ResNet-34 Configuration

Network Layer	Configuration		Output Feature Map Dimension
conv1	7×7, 64, stride 2		112×112
	3×3 max pool, stride 2		
conv2_x	$\begin{bmatrix} \text{Channel}:64 & \text{Kernel}:3\times 3 \\ \text{Channel}:64 & \text{Kernel}:3\times 3 \end{bmatrix}\times 3$		56×56
conv3_x	$\begin{bmatrix} \text{Channel}:128 & \text{Kernel}:3\times 3 \\ \text{Channel}:128 & \text{Kernel}:3\times 3 \end{bmatrix}\times 4$		28×28
conv4_x	$\begin{bmatrix} \text{Channel}:256 & \text{Kernel}:3\times 3 \\ \text{Channel}:256 & \text{Kernel}:3\times 3 \end{bmatrix}\times 6$		14×14
conv5_x	$\begin{bmatrix} \text{Channel}:512 & \text{Kernel}:3\times 3 \\ \text{Channel}:512 & \text{Kernel}:3\times 3 \end{bmatrix}\times 3$		7×7

The standard ResNet-34 architecture comprises 34 convolutional layers, a max-pooling layer with a 3×3 size, an average pooling layer, and a fully connected layer. In our approach, we eliminate the fully connected layer, using the extracted feature maps as input for the encoder-decoder module, which handles the classification task. Rectified Linear Unit (ReLU) activation and batch normalization are applied after all convolution layers within the "BasicBlock" block. The ReLU activation function, a modified linear unit, is commonly used in artificial neural networks. In mathematics, the ramp function is sometimes referred to as the ReLU function (see Equation 12.3).

$$\text{Activation function} = \text{ReLU}(\text{input}) = \max\{0, \text{input}\} = \begin{cases} \max, & \text{if input} > 0 \\ 0, & \text{else} \end{cases} \tag{12.3}$$

12.2.4 Transformers Aggregate Multi-Modal Features

We endeavour to adhere as precisely as possible to the original Transformer implementation in this approach. This deliberately straightforward arrangement has the advantage of reducing the effect of other techniques on the model's performance and demonstrating the advantages of Transformers. Multi-Head Self-Attention (MHSA), Self-Attention (SA), and Multi-Layer Perceptron (MLP) are the crucial components of the Transformer. It takes a variety of embeddings and tokens as its input. Unlike the classical Transformer, we remove the distillation token to perform this classification. In this section, we will describe each of these components.

12.2.5 Self-Attention (SA)

As shown in Figure 12.2, Attention is used in three different contexts in the Transformer: SA in the encoder, SA in the decoder, and encoder-decoder Attention

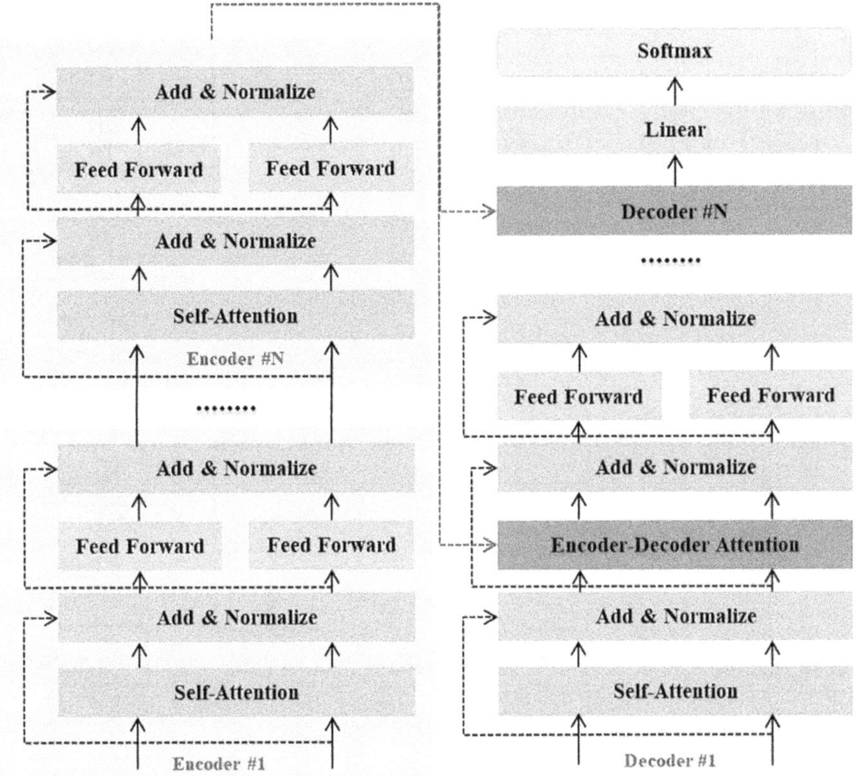

FIGURE 12.2   Visualization of various blocks in encoder and decoder.

in the decoder. The query, key, and value are the parameters used as the input for the attention layer. SA in the first encoder produces an encoded representation and attention scores for the input image. Similarly, the SA in the first decoder produces an encoded representation and attention scores for the target image. Furthermore, the encoder-decoder attention receives representations from both the input and the target. As a result, it generates a representation that includes the attention scores for each element in the target image and influences the input image's attention scores. In the decoder self-attention, masking aims to prevent the decoder from "peeking" ahead at the rest of the target class while predicting the subsequent class.

12.2.6   MULTI-LEVEL REPRESENTATIONS IN SA

Initially, a CNN-based network is employed to extract feature vectors $V = v_1, v_2,...,$ v_k from medical images, where k is the number of feature vectors in V, and v_i is a vector which indicates a dominant subject location. Here, instead of feeding feature vectors directly into the encoder-decoder module, we constructed a new Multi-Level Semantic Representation Network (MLSRE), which includes both low-level and high-level features to enhance their representations, as depicted in Figure 12.3.

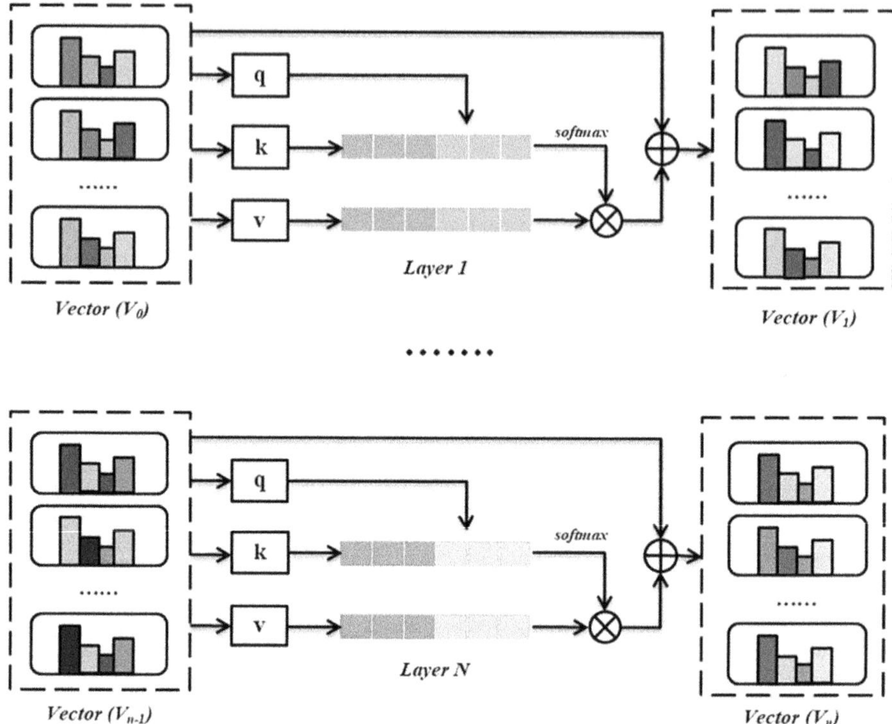

FIGURE 12.3 Illustration of multi-level semantic representation network.

Discriminant region feature vectors are crucial for cancer identification. The feature vector $V = \mathbb{R}^{k \times d}$ is fed into the attention module. Equations (4) to (7) illustrate the overall operation of MLSRE:

$$V_{i+1} = \text{Attention}\left(V_i,\ WT_q,\ \text{Key},\ \text{Value}\right) \tag{12.4}$$

$$\text{Key} = \left(V_i, WT_k, MY_k\right) \tag{12.5}$$

$$\text{Value} = \left(V_i, WT_v, MY_v\right) \tag{12.6}$$

$$\text{Attention}\left(Q, K, V\right) = \text{softmax}\left(\frac{QK^T}{\sqrt{d_k}}\right) . V \tag{12.7}$$

where WT_q, WT_k, WT_v are the weights of the query, key, and value. MY_k and MY_k are the memory vectors of key and value. The scaling factor $\sqrt{d_k}$ denotes the dimension of the key vector, which is used to control the gradient value of the softmax function. It's evident that the attentive weights exclusively rely on the pairwise similarity between the linear projections of input feature vectors [27]. Consequently, the self-attention function can be characterized as a mechanism for encoding the relationships between pairs of regions. We treat this self-attention function as a single layer and aggregate specific layers to construct multi-level representations. In this scheme, the initial layers generate low-level feature representations in vector form, while the final layers produce high-level feature representations. It's reasonable to expect that multiple layers may influence the final image features differently. Unlike the conventional self-attention technique, we augment the key and value with additional vectors to establish a persistent memory system [28]. These memory vectors are designed to capture generic knowledge rather than context-dependent information, as they are shared among all attention heads. They are essentially trainable weights that function as an enduring memory. These supplementary vectors are established as learnable weights and do not depend on the input image feature vectors. Our experiments have demonstrated the substantial impact of these additional vectors.

12.2.7 MULTI-HEAD SELF-ATTENTION (MHSA)

The Transformer's Attention module carries out its computations concurrently and regularly. Each of these computations is referred to as an Attention Head. The Attention module divides its Query, Key, and Value components into N partitions, and each partition is processed separately by a different Head (see Figure 12.4). These separate computations culminate in a final attention score, known as "Multi-Head Self-Attention." This approach significantly enhances the Transformer's ability to capture each pixel's diverse relationships and intricate details. The MHSA can be represented using Equations (8) and (9):

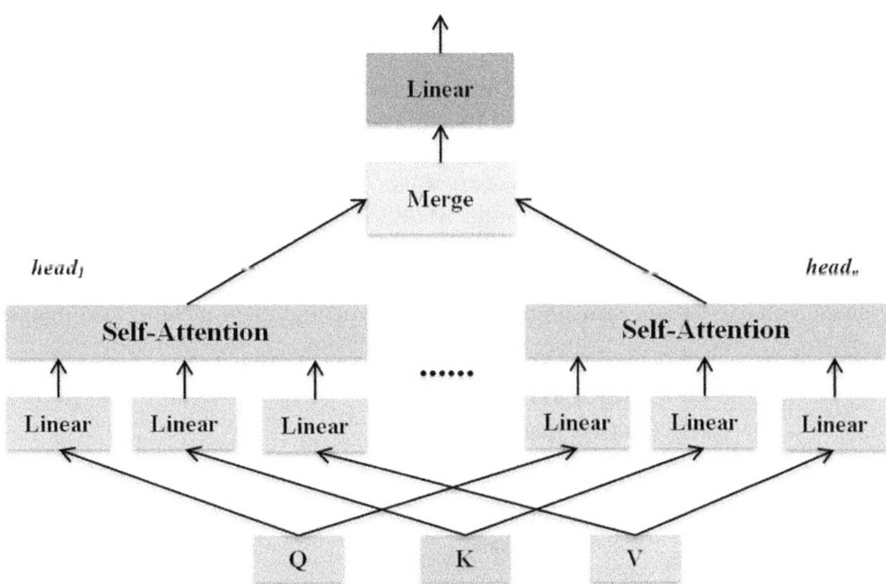

FIGURE 12.4 Illustration of multi-head self-attention mechanism.

$$\text{Head}_i = \text{Attention}\left(QWT_q, \, KWT_k, MY_k, \, VWT_v, MY_v\right) \tag{12.8}$$

$$\text{MHSA}\left(Q,K,V\right) = \text{Merge}\left(\text{head}_1,\ldots,\text{head}_i\right)WT_O \tag{12.9}$$

where the variables WT_q, WT_k, WT_v and WT_o are the trainable parameters, and head$_i$ denotes the ith attention head. MHSA has the advantage of enabling the model to learn sequence and position information across several representation subspaces.

12.2.8 Feed Forward Network Layer (FFNL)

Initially, the encoder sends its input to an MHSA block. Then, MHSA processes the input and passes its output to the Feed Forward Network (FFN). Finally, FFN passes the processed input to the next encoder. Here, both the SA and FFN sublayers have a residual skip connection around them, followed by a Layer-Normalization. The output of the final encoder is sent into each decoder in the decoder block. Consequently, it is assumed that x_{t-1} is the representation of $t-1$th layer, LN denotes layer normalization, the output of tth layer can be expressed using Equations (12.10) and (12.11).

$$\overrightarrow{x_t} = \text{FFN}\left(LN\left(x_t'\right)\right) + x_t' \tag{12.10}$$

$$x_t = \text{MHSA}\left(LN\left(\overrightarrow{x_t}\right)\right) + \overrightarrow{x_t} \tag{12.11}$$

12.3   EXPERIMENT

12.3.1 Dataset Details

In this section, the effectiveness of our proposed framework is thoroughly evaluated using the Open Access Series of Imaging Studies (OASIS) [29]. Table 12.2 and Figure 12.5 show the OASIS benchmark dataset details and sample dataset images, respectively. https://www.oasis-brains.org/#data

The OASIS dataset contains a total of 382 images. Among these, 167 images belong to the "No Dementia" class, indicating individuals without any signs of dementia. The "Very Mild Dementia" class comprises 87 images representing individuals with early-stage dementia. The "Mild Dementia" class includes 105 images,

TABLE 12.2

OASIS Dataset Details

Class Type	No. of Images
No dementia	167
Very mild dementia	87
Mild dementia	105
Moderate AD	23
Total	382

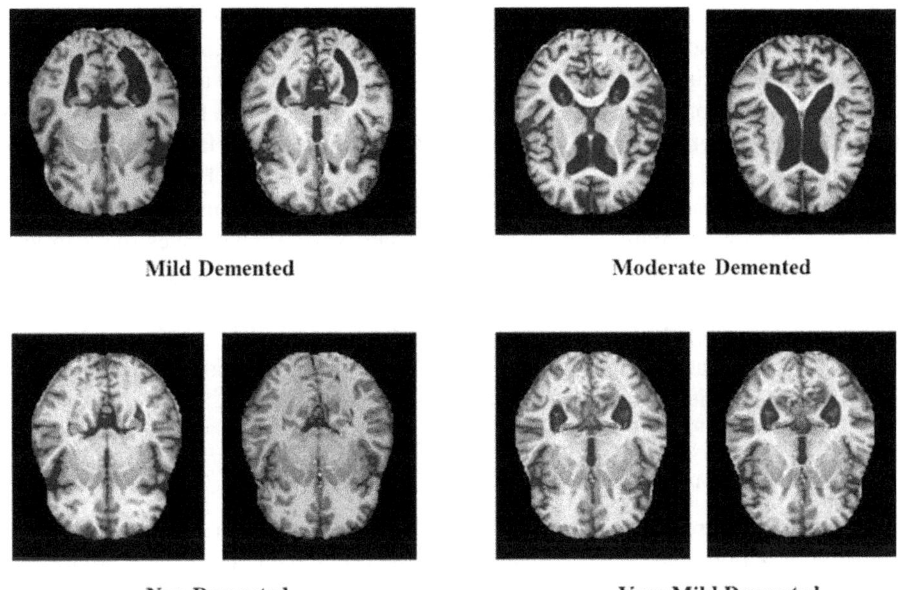

FIGURE 12.5   Illustration of sample OASIS dataset images.

indicating individuals with a slightly more advanced stage of dementia. Finally, the "Moderate AD" class consists of 23 images representing individuals with moderate Alzheimer's Disease. We increased the dataset size by applying data augmentation techniques, including rotation, flipping, cropping, and introducing noise [10,30]. These techniques helped address the lack of training data during the development of the Alzheimer's disease detection model.

12.3.2   IMPLEMENTATION DETAILS

The TransADD network proposed in this study was implemented using the PyTorch framework. All experiments were conducted on a 4-core PC, specifically the i7-6700 3.4GHz model, with 8 GB of RAM. To train the network over 20,000 iterations, a fixed margin of 0.2 was applied, employing random sampling techniques. The dataset used in our experiments consisted of 382 images sourced from the OASIS database, and these images were categorized into four classes: Non-Dementia, Very Mild Dementia, Mild Dementia, and Moderate Dementia. The age range of Alzheimer's disease patients in the dataset spanned from 20 to 88 years. The data distribution involved allocating 70% for training and 30% for testing. The proposed model underwent training for 100 epochs with a batch size of 4.

12.3.3   ABLATION STUDY

Ablation experiments were performed to showcase the impact of transformers in the TransADD framework. Specifically, altering the backbone from VGG to ResNet led to a notable enhancement of 2.1% in the average accuracy within the TransADD model. The influence of varying patch sizes on image serialization performance was additionally investigated. This was achieved by altering the K values while keeping other conditions constant [31]. The experimental findings reveal that larger K values lead to inferior performance. This could be attributed to the fact that tiny image patches disrupt the inherent semantic information of the image. Existing deep learning models for analyzing whole brain images, such as those used in Alzheimer's disease detection or brain segmentation, may face several challenges that can lead to irrelevant or inaccurate results. Typical limitations include the preprocessing of brain images, such as skull stripping, noise reduction, and normalization, which can significantly impact the performance of deep learning models. Inadequate preprocessing can introduce irrelevant noise or artifacts into the data, affecting the model's results. This limitation can be overcome by image serialization.

12.3.4 PERFORMANCE COMPARISON

Table 12.3 compares the proposed TransADD model with current state-of-the-art approaches. Upon analyzing the demerits of the previous methods, it becomes evident that the variations in their accuracies can be attributed to certain limitations inherent in their designs. While Basheera et al. [16] achieved an accuracy of 78.66%, the lack of consideration for multi-modal brain images and positron emission tomography likely impacted the overall accuracy. Liang et al. [20] presented an accuracy of 81.97%, but the method's performance was confined to a narrow scope, excluding a comprehensive assessment of multi-modality images. Similarly, Feng et al. [18] achieved an accuracy of 83.34%, but the method's limitations in directly correlating with brain atrophy regions may have contributed to this accuracy level.

Liu et al. [21] demonstrated an accuracy of 82.58%, but the trade-off between computational challenges and parameter volume may have hindered further accuracy improvements, particularly when integrated with mobile devices. Sathiyamoorthi et al. [22] addressed noisy data with an accuracy of 87.82%, yet the emphasis on classification and less focus on feature selection potentially limited its performance. Hedayati et al. [23] achieved an accuracy of 90.11%, but their focus on FE-based

TABLE 12.3

Performance Comparison of the Proposed TransADD with Existing Approaches

Methods	Accuracy (%)
Basheera et al. [16]	78.66
Liang et al. [20]	81.97
Feng et al. [18]	83.34
Liu et al. [21]	82.58
Sathiyamoorthi et al. [22]	87.82
Hedayati et al. [23]	90.11
TransADD	96.07

convolutional autoencoders might not have fully exploited the potential of feature extraction and classification.

Comparatively, the proposed TransADD network outperforms these methods with a remarkable accuracy of 97.36% (as shown in Table 12.3). By addressing the limitations present in the previous approaches, TransADD demonstrates the potential to advance the accuracy of AD detection and diagnosis significantly, thus proving its efficacy as an innovative solution in the field.

12.3.5 Experimental Results

As shown in Figure 12.6, the confusion matrix provides an insightful breakdown of the model's classification performance for each class. Across the classes, the diagonal elements represent the True Positives (TP), indicating the instances that were correctly predicted. Off-diagonal elements represent the False Positives (FP) and False Negatives (FN), indicating misclassified instances [32]. The matrix reflects how well the model has distinguished the different classes.

No Dementia: The model correctly predicted the absence of dementia in 160 instances, while it incorrectly classified three instances as Mild Dementia and one instance as Moderate AD. The low misclassification rate suggests strong performance

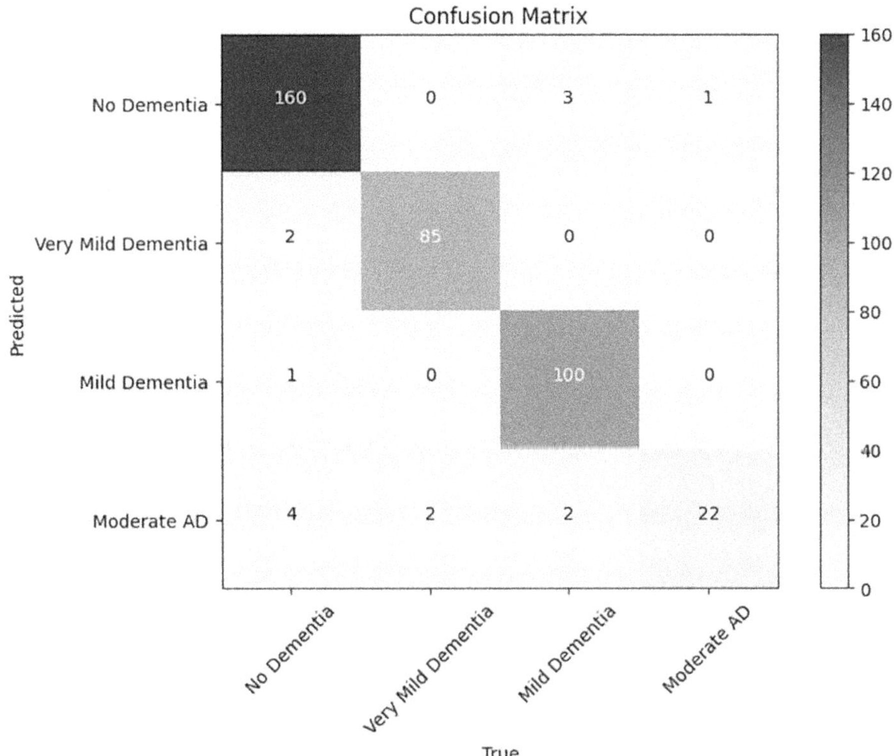

FIGURE 12.6 Confusion matrix of the proposed transADD network.

in recognizing cases without dementia. Very Mild Dementia: The model correctly identified 85 instances of very mild dementia. There were two instances incorrectly classified as No Dementia. Mild Dementia: The model accurately identified 100 instances of mild dementia. One instance was misclassified as No Dementia, and one instance was misclassified as Very Mild Dementia. Moderate AD: The model correctly predicted 22 instances of moderate Alzheimer's Disease (AD). However, there were four instances misclassified as No Dementia, and two instances misclassified as Very Mild Dementia and Mild Dementia. This class appears to be the most challenging for the model. The accuracy and loss graphs of the TransADD network are presented in Figures 12.7 and 12.8.

Figures 12.7 and 12.8 show the proposed network's accuracy and loss graphs. The overall accuracy of the model is approximately 96.07%. This measure indicates the percentage of correctly classified instances out of the total instances. With a high accuracy, the model demonstrates a strong ability to make accurate predictions across the four classes.

Figure 12.9 shows the sample result obtained by the TransADD network. The high overall accuracy suggests that the model performs well across the various classes. It's particularly effective in identifying instances without dementia and cases of very mild dementia. However, some misclassifications, especially in the Moderate AD class, suggest that there may be room for improvement. This performance summary provides valuable insights into the model's strengths and areas that may require further attention, potentially guiding adjustments to enhance the classification accuracy for all classes.

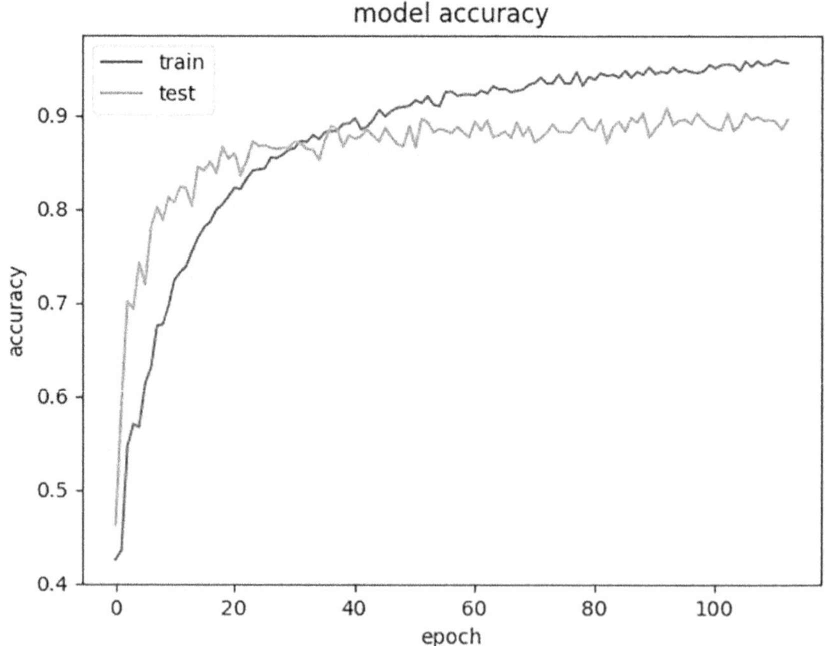

FIGURE 12.7   Accuracy graph of the proposed transADD network.

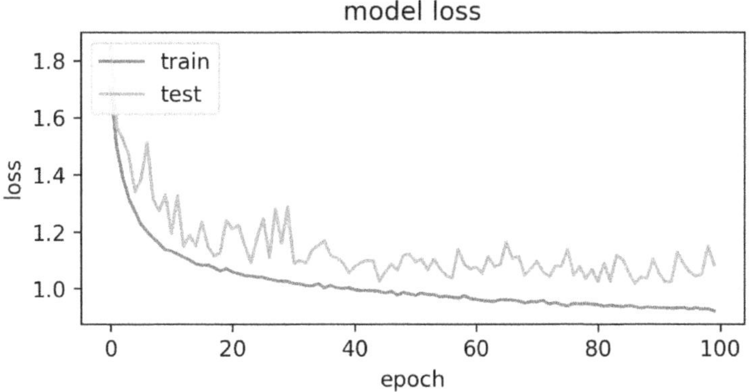

FIGURE 12.8   Loss graph of the proposed transADD network.

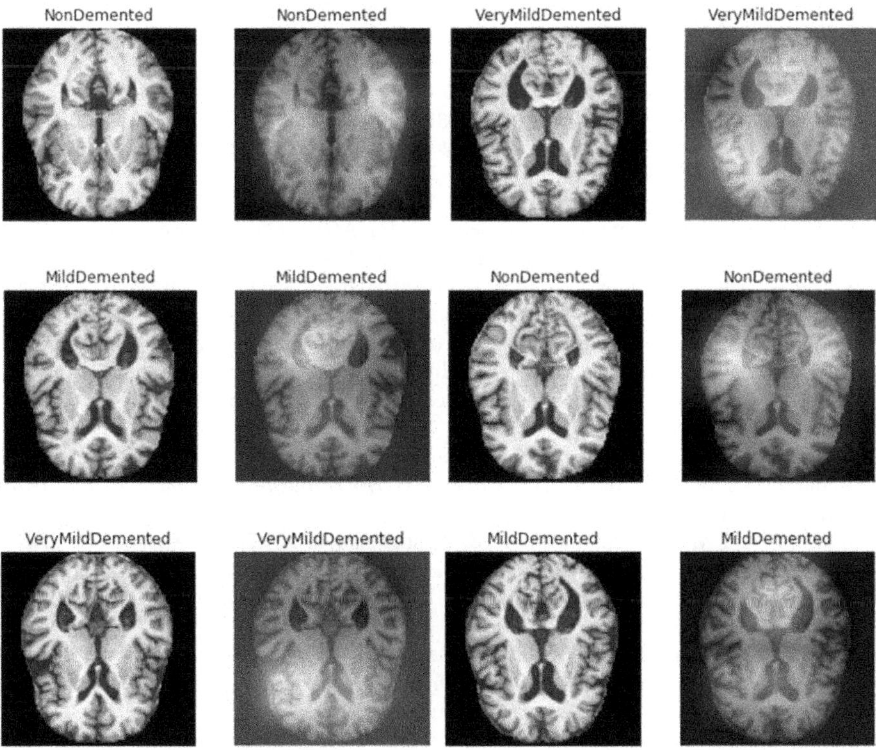

FIGURE 12.9   Illustration of input images and classified images.

12.4   CONCLUSION

The prevalence of Alzheimer's Disease as a leading cause of death and disability among the elderly remains a global concern. Despite the lack of a definitive treatment, current therapies offer limited relief. Thus, early AD detection is crucial.

Medical image analysis has seen advancements in deep learning, yet AD classification remains unexplored. This research introduces a novel approach, employing a Transformer-based Network (TransADD) for multi-class AD classification via MRI images. TransADD integrates CNN and Transformers, capturing image features and dependencies. The addition of a Multi-Level Semantic Representation Network enhances feature representation. Evaluation of the OASIS dataset showcases TransADD's superiority over existing models, attested by its remarkable accuracy of 96.07%.

REFERENCES

1. Prince, M., Comas-Herrera, A., Knapp, M., Guerchet, M., & Karagiannidou, M. (2016). World Alzheimer report 2016: Improving healthcare for people living with dementia: Coverage, quality and costs now and in the future. *LSE Research Online* (pp. 1–141).
2. Carrillo, M. C., Bain, L. J., Frisoni, G. B., & Weiner, M. W. (2012). Worldwide Alzheimer's disease neuroimaging initiative. *Alzheimer's & Dementia*, 8(4), 337–342.
3. Baumgart, M., Snyder, H. M., Carrillo, M. C., Fazio, S., Kim, H., & Johns, H. (2015). Summary of the evidence on modifiable risk factors for cognitive decline and dementia: A population-based perspective. *Alzheimer's & Dementia*, 11(6), 718–726.
4. Ju, R., Hu, C., & Li, Q. (2017). Early diagnosis of Alzheimer's disease based on resting-state brain networks and deep learning. *IEEE/ACM Transactions on Computational Biology and Bioinformatics*, 16(1), 244–257.
5. Liu, M., Zhang, J., Adeli, E., & Shen, D. (2018). Joint classification and regression via deep multi-task multi-channel learning for Alzheimer's disease diagnosis. *IEEE Transactions on Biomedical Engineering*, 66(5), 1195–1206.
6. Lian, C., Liu, M., Zhang, J., & Shen, D. (2018). Hierarchical fully convolutional network for joint atrophy localization and Alzheimer's disease diagnosis using structural MRI. *IEEE Transactions on Pattern Analysis and Machine Intelligence*, 42(4), 880–893.
7. Suk, H. I., Lee, S. W., Shen, D., & Alzheimer's Disease Neuroimaging Initiative. (2015). Latent feature representation with stacked auto-encoder for AD/MCI diagnosis. *Brain Structure and Function*, 220, 841–859.
8. Cui, R., & Liu, M. (2018). Hippocampus analysis by combination of 3-D DenseNet and shapes for Alzheimer's disease diagnosis. *IEEE Journal of Biomedical and Health Informatics*, 23(5), 2099–2107.
9. Amin-Naji, M., Mahdavinataj, H., & Aghagolzadeh, A. (2019). Alzheimer's disease diagnosis from structural MRI using Siamese convolutional neural network. In: *2019 4th International Conference on Pattern Recognition and Image Analysis (IPRIA)*, Tehran, Iran (pp. 75–79). IEEE.
10. Selvam, P. (2023). A deep learning framework for surgery action detection. In: Harish Garg and Jyotir Moy Chatterjee (eds.) *Deep Learning in Personalized Healthcare and Decision Support* (pp. 315–328). Academic Press.
11. Hett, K., Ta, V. T., Manjón, J. V., Coupé, P., & Alzheimer's Disease Neuroimaging Initiative. (2018). Adaptive fusion of texture-based grading for Alzheimer's disease classification. *Computerized Medical Imaging and Graphics*, 70, 8–16.
12. Li, F., Liu, M., & Alzheimer's Disease Neuroimaging Initiative. (2018). Alzheimer's disease diagnosis based on multiple cluster dense convolutional networks. *Computerized Medical Imaging and Graphics*, 70, 101–110.
13. Spasov, S., Passamonti, L., Duggento, A., Lio, P., Toschi, N., & Alzheimer's Disease Neuroimaging Initiative. (2019). A parameter-efficient deep learning approach to predict conversion from mild cognitive impairment to Alzheimer's disease. *Neuroimage*, 189, 276–287.

14. Ge, C., Qu, Q., Gu, I. Y. H., & Jakola, A. S. (2019). Multi-stream multi-scale deep convolutional networks for Alzheimer's disease detection using MR images. *Neurocomputing*, 350, 60–69.

15. Jain, R., Jain, N., Aggarwal, A., & Hemanth, D. J. (2019). Convolutional neural network based Alzheimer's disease classification from magnetic resonance brain images. *Cognitive Systems Research*, 57, 147–159.

16. Basheera, S., & Ram, M. S. S. (2020). A novel CNN based Alzheimer's disease classification using hybrid enhanced ICA segmented gray matter of MRI. *Computerized Medical Imaging and Graphics*, 81, 101713.

17. Mendoza-Léon, R., Puentes, J., Uriza, L. F., & Hoyos, M. H. (2020). Single-slice Alzheimer's disease classification and disease regional analysis with Supervised Switching Autoencoders. *Computers in Biology and Medicine*, 116, 103527.

18. Feng, J., Zhang, S. W., Chen, L., Xia, J., & Alzheimer's Disease Neuroimaging Initiative. (2021). Alzheimer's disease classification using features extracted from nonsubsampled contourlet subband-based individual networks. *Neurocomputing*, 421, 260–272.

19. Chen, Y., & Xia, Y. (2021). Iterative sparse and deep learning for accurate diagnosis of Alzheimer's disease. *Pattern Recognition*, 116, 107944.

20. Liang, W., Zhang, K., Cao, P., Liu, X., Yang, J., & Zaiane, O. (2021). Rethinking modeling Alzheimer's disease progression from a multi-task learning perspective with deep recurrent neural network. *Computers in Biology and Medicine*, 138, 104935.

21. Liu, J., Li, M., Luo, Y., Yang, S., Li, W., & Bi, Y. (2022). Alzheimer's disease detection using depthwise separable convolutional neural networks. *Computer Methods and Programs in Biomedicine*, 203, 106032.

22. Sathiyamoorthi, V., Ilavarasi, A. K., Murugeswari, K., Ahmed, S. T., Devi, B. A., & Kalipindi, M. (2023). A deep convolutional neural network based computer aided diagnosis system for the prediction of Alzheimer's disease in MRI images. *Measurement*, 171, 108838.

23. Hedayati, R., Khedmati, M., & Taghipour-Gorjikolaie, M. (2023). Deep feature extraction method based on ensemble of convolutional auto encoders: Application to Alzheimer's disease diagnosis. *Biomedical Signal Processing and Control*, 66, 102397.

24. Dosovitskiy, A., Beyer, L., Kolesnikov, A., Weissenborn, D., Zhai, X., Unterthiner, T., & Houlsby, N. (2021). An image is worth 16x16 words: Transformers for image recognition at scale. In *Proceedings of the 9th International Conference on Learning Representations, Austria* (pp. 1–22).

25. Selvam, P., Koilraj, J. A. S., Romero, C. A. T., Alharbi, M., Mehbodniya, A., Webber, J. L., & Sengan, S. (2022). A transformer-based framework for scene text recognition. *IEEE Access*, 10, 100895–100910.

26. Prabu, S., & Koilraj, J. A. S. (2022). A deep learning framework for grocery product detection and recognition. *Food Analytical Methods*, 15(12), 3498–3522.

27. Prabu, S., Sundar, K. J. A., & Abraham, J. (2023). Enhanced attention-based encoder-decoder framework for text recognition. *Intelligent Automation & Soft Computing*, 35(2), 2071–2086.

28. Prabu, S. (2022). Object segmentation based on the integration of adaptive K-means and GrabCut algorithm. In: *2022 International Conference on Wireless Communications Signal Processing and Networking (WiSPNET)*, Chennai, India (pp. 213–216). IEEE.

29. Chen, W., Qian, S., Fan, D., Kojima, N., Hamilton, M., & Deng, J. (2020). Oasis: A large-scale dataset for single image 3d in the wild. In: *Proceedings of the IEEE/CVF Conference on Computer Vision and Pattern Recognition*, Seattle, Washington (pp. 679–688).

30. Prabu, S., Jawali, N., Sundar, K. J. A., Sharvani, K., Shanmukhanjali, G., & Nirmala, V. (2022, December). Indian coin detection and recognition using deep learning algorithm. In: *2022 6th Asian Conference on Artificial Intelligence Technology (ACAIT)*, Changzhou, China (pp. 1–6). IEEE.

31. Prabu, S., & Sundar, K. J. A. (2023). DocPresRec: Doctor's handwritten prescription recognition using deep learning algorithm. In: S. N. Kumar, Sherin Zafar, Eduard Babulak, M. Afshar Alam and Farheen Siddiqui (eds.) *Artificial Intelligence in Telemedicine*, (pp. 33–48). CRC Press.
32. Swaminathan, B., Selvam, P., Joseph, A. S. K., & Vairavasundaram, S. (n.d.). (2023). Improved YOLOv5 with attention mechanism for real-time weed detection in the paddy field: a deep learning approach. In: Bashir Alam and Mansaf Alam (eds.) *Intelligent Data Analytics, IoT, and Blockchain* (pp. 326–341). Auerbach Publications.

13 On-Body Sensing Solutions for Automatic Health Monitoring Systems Using IoT

A. Dhanamathi and C. Gunasundari

13.1 INTRODUCTION

Aging-related diseases commonly occur at all stages, impacting people's mental well-being. Models or technologies for clinical and healthcare are needed [1]. Health monitoring is facilitated through Radio Frequency Identification (RFID) technology, which collects real-time data, observes, tracks, and detects objects by using radio waves to transport data from an electronic tag [2]. RFID tags collect sensitive personal information according to different types of application scenarios. Only authorized groups can access the sensitive information, ensuring secure access. Cloud-based RFID mutual authentication schemes with efficient privacy methods ensure the safety and reliability of information flow in the system [3]. The revolutionary technology in embedded systems, the Internet of Things (IoT), helps to integrate the physical world with smart devices. Security and privacy of communication between devices must be ensured in IoT-based systems [4].

Smart pills are specialized capsules equipped with electronic or mechanical components designed to navigate the gastrointestinal (GI) tract, serving various functions such as diagnostic, therapeutic, sampling, or surgical purposes. Over time, several smart pill concepts have been suggested to enhance the diagnosis of GI diseases and gain a better understanding of their origins. These diagnostic smart pills are categorized into two groups: those that incorporate imaging technologies like optical and autofluorescent imaging, and those that employ sensors to identify physical alterations in the GI environment, including pressure, pH, or chemical substances. The endoscope in the smart pill depends on the surface of the mucosal image. The image can be obtained from smart pills equipped with batteries and cameras [5].

A variety of smart pills have been created based on various sensing mechanisms, including pressure sensing, temperature sensing, biological sensing to identify biological processes, examination of hemoglobin and other soluble biomarkers, pH sensing, and gaseous biomarkers which identify gas-related biomarkers linked to the metabolic actions of the microbiome. Biological sensing is also utilized to detect bacterial growth. Engaging these intelligent capsules in drug formulation investigations allows for the collection of comprehensive and authentic data regarding the

DOI: 10.1201/9781032632223-13

absorption of a particular drug formulation from critical regions within the intestinal tract. The use of drug delivery capsules equipped with integrated sensors or cameras provides a possible opportunity for simultaneously identifying and treating unhealthy intestinal tissue. This approach aids in patient treatments and reduces side effects for them [5].

A wireless sensor network (WSN) is a network of independent devices spread out in space, using sensors to collaboratively oversee various physical or environmental conditions at different locations. These conditions include factors like temperature, sound, vibration, pressure, motion, or pollutants. Initially, the creation of WSNs was driven by military needs, such as monitoring battlefields. However, these networks are now widely employed in non-military sectors, such as environmental and habitat monitoring, healthcare applications, home automation, and traffic management. Limitations in the size and cost of sensor nodes lead to restrictions on resources like energy, memory, processing capability, and bandwidth. In the field of information and communication, WSNs are important research areas integrated with IoT. WSNs often find application in the monitoring of specific areas. This involves deploying the WSN across a designated region where a particular phenomenon is under surveillance. The chosen data-propagation strategies for diverse applications will vary based on factors like the necessity for real-time responses, data redundancy (addressed through data aggregation techniques), security requirements, and more [6].

Sensor nodes are envisioned as compact computing devices, characterized by their minimalistic interfaces and apparatuses. The nodes typically comprise a processing unit with limited computing capabilities and storage, sensors (such as specialized circuitry), a communication apparatus (commonly wireless transceivers or optical mechanisms), and are powered by an energy supply, usually provided through a battery. Additional potential components include energy harvesting modules, secondary application-specific integrated circuits (ASICs), and potentially secondary communication devices (such as RS232 or USB interfaces). On the other hand, base stations are distinct elements within the WSN that possess significantly greater computational power, energy resources, and communication capabilities. These stations serve as intermediaries between the sensor nodes and the end user. Many elderly people suffer from at least one chronic disease, and those affected by such conditions face difficulties in taking care of themselves. In the existing system, patient monitoring utilizes GSM technology to transmit information.

In the event of an emergency situation, the device sends details about the patient to predefined contacts such as relatives, personal doctors, etc. Upon receiving the alert message, the client-side application alerts nearby emergency contacts about the patient's condition.

The patient monitoring system involves storing and transmitting sensor data to physicians through ZigBee communication. A WSN is implemented to continuously monitor a patient's physiological state using ZigBee technology. Sensors observe the patient's anatomical conditions, and the ZigBee network facilitates data transmission from these sensors. This data is then relayed to a remote monitor to capture the patient's anatomical signals. The infusion pump is a widely used apparatus in medical healthcare settings, both within hospitals and homes. It administers fluids, including medications and nutrients, such as pain relievers, chemotherapy drugs, hormones, insulin, and antibiotics, into a person's body in various quantities [7]. Several types of pumps exist, such as insulin pumps, syringe pumps, large-volume pumps, elastomeric pumps, patient-controlled analgesia (PCA) pumps, and enteral pumps. The enteral pump delivers medications and liquid nourishment to the patient's digestive system, while the PCA pump provides pain medication [7]. These devices are essential for nurses as they provide information about the status of fluids administered to patients, making them popular in hospital settings for monitoring medication administration.

The limitations of the existing system are as follows

- It requires more time and cost to track GSM technology, which cannot be used for continuous monitoring to transmit the information.
- The existing technology only alerts the client when their patient is in an emergency condition.
- The client can monitor patients' health only at the present time.

13.2 PROPOSED METHODOLOGY

In the proposed system, ingestible miniature electromechanical devices, known as "digital pills," serve as a convergence point for the biomedical, medicinal, and pharmaceutical industries. Cutting-edge technologies such as electronics, sensors, and miniature robotics enable access, analysis, and manipulation of internal bodily aspects. A hardware prototype has been developed to gather data from food intake sensors, utilizing a high-quality microphone positioned on the person's neck to accurately capture sound signals during meals in a non-intrusive manner. The sound information, along with data from the valiberate sensor, is pre-processed and then transmitted to a smartphone using ZigBee communication. The smartphone is responsible for identifying the types of food being consumed. A high-precision throat microphone is engaged to detect sound signals while eating, placed near the user's jaw on their neck, enabling medical treatments that were previously impractical using conventional methods. The vibration sensor is employed within a system for monitoring patient tablet intake and interacts with IoT. Through IoT technology, medical information regarding the patient is transmitted over the internet continuously. This approach boasts excellent patient acceptance and affordability. Changes occurring within the human body are continuously monitored and transmitted wirelessly to a nearby monitor, allowing doctors to monitor these changes in real time.

A wearable device that monitors eating behavior to identify different food types is an outcome of IoT. The system primarily consists of two components: a smartphone application and embedded hardware. The embedded hardware is created to gather and pre-process food consumption information and tablet intake. Acoustic sensors non-intrusively gather high-quality sound signals of eating activities. The information is sent to a smartphone using a wireless network, providing details such as types of food and tablet intake. The use of IoT in conjunction with a global mobile communication system makes doctors and patients more comfortable in the contemporary healthcare setting. One of the key IoT innovations in the healthcare industry is body sensor networks. The IoT Ethernet Kit, powered by AWS IoT, employs an

Ethernet LAN8740A facilitated by a 32-bit microcontroller featuring 2 MB of Flash memory (PIC32MZ EF). This microcontroller offers ample memory space for applications. On the sensor aspect, a wide array of diverse sensors can be inserted into the MikroElektronika mikroBUS™ interface, enabling the creation of prototypes for various IoT proof-of-principle. This IoT kit capitalizes on the AWS IoT service, ensuring a seamless user experience with preloaded firmware. It is an accomplished cloud area designed for simple and secure communication between linked devices, cloud services, and other devices.

ZigBee is an IEEE 802.15.4 compliant RF ZigBee transceiver that connects sensors without additional overhead, such as designing antennas or RF, since it is mounted with the facility needed to transmit data [8]. A baseband microcontroller communicates through a 4-wire SPI port. The different layers in ZigBee perform various functionalities such as signal identification, encryption, communication between devices, channel assessment, and authentication [8]. This module is an application-ready solution for fast-to-market, offering the development engineer an extensive array of options for a host controller and stack firmware provider without any limitations [8].

ZigBee serves as a wireless protocol designed for monitoring and controlling sensors within a personal area network (PAN). Sea Solve, an Alliance Partner of National Instruments, has crafted a comprehensive test suite encompassing transmit (TX), receive (Rx), and compliance tests specifically for ZigBee. The criteria for assessing a ZigBee receiver were broadly divided into two categories: simulating the media access control (MAC) layer and conducting impairments testing at the physical layer (PHY) [8]. The initial category, MAC layer simulation, is employed to verify the ZigBee receiver's correct response to generated commands. In the second category, impairment testing involves deliberately degrading the variation in the quality of the test inducement to evaluate the receiver's performance. The provided illustrations utilize Sea Solve's solution for generating signals within the WiPAN LVSG (Low Voltage Sensor and Actuator Network) context in conjunction with a PXI vector signal generator [7]. Figure 13.1 depicts the ZigBee layer.

The IEEE 802.15.4 standard outlines four fundamental frame configurations suitable for receiver testing. The receiver testing also involves the selection of specific sub-frames, listed by type, as follows [9]:

- Association request is a request for association with a PAN coordinator [9].
- Association response is a reply from the coordinator with association status (possibilities include: Association Successful, PAN at capacity, and Access denied) [9].
- Disassociation notification is employed by either a device or a coordinator to notify other nodes regarding disconnection [9].
- Data request is used to request data from a coordinator.
- PAN ID conflict notification is transmitted when a PAN identifier conflict is detected.
- Orphan notification is used by an associated device that has lost synchronization with its coordinator.
- Beacon request is used for synchronization, to transmit superframe information [9].

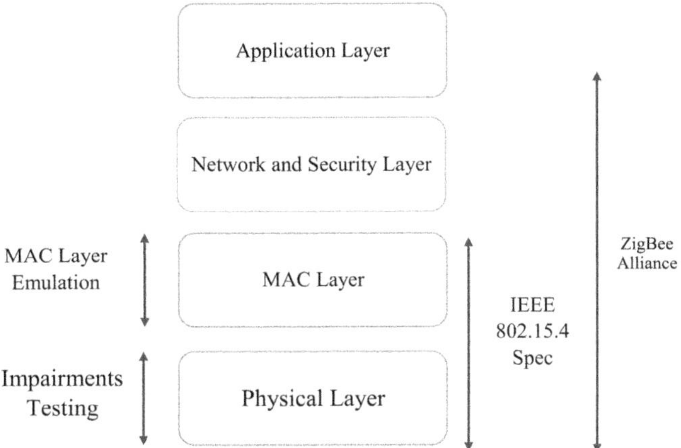

FIGURE 13.1 ZigBee layer.

- Coordinator realignment serves as a response from the coordinator to an orphan notification command. It is also utilized when modifications occur in PAN attributes alongside logical channel details. This communication can be directed either to the entire PAN or to a single orphaned device.
- GTS request is employed by an associated device to ask for the assignment of a fresh guaranteed time slot (GTS) or to seek the removal of an already allocated GTS from the PAN coordinator. This request also outlines the specifics of the GTS, including attributes like length, direction, and type [9].

A 16×2 LCD denotes that it has the capacity to exhibit 16 characters across each line, with a total of two lines used to display the output. Within this LCD, every character is showcased within a 5×7 pixel grid. This LCD is equipped with a duo of registers: the Command register and the Data register. The Command register is responsible for retaining the instructions that guide the actions carried out by the LCD. A command serves as a directive provided to the LCD for executing a predetermined action, such as initializing, erasing the displayed content, determining the marker's location, or managing the display. Within the LCD, the data register holds the information meant to be exhibited. This data corresponds to the ASCII value of the character slated for presentation on the LCD screen. For further insights into the inner workings of an LCD, you can click to discover more about its internal structure. The Arduino Uno R3 is a microcontroller board that centers around the ATmega328 chip and is used in this work for IoT implementation [10].

13.3 SYSTEM ARCHITECTURE

The patient's health condition is continuously monitored using acoustic and valibrate sensors, and the information can be accessed by the patient's relatives and doctor, and controlled by the admin. The measured medical data is analyzed and uploaded to the web page, where it is monitored and controlled by the admin. In case of an

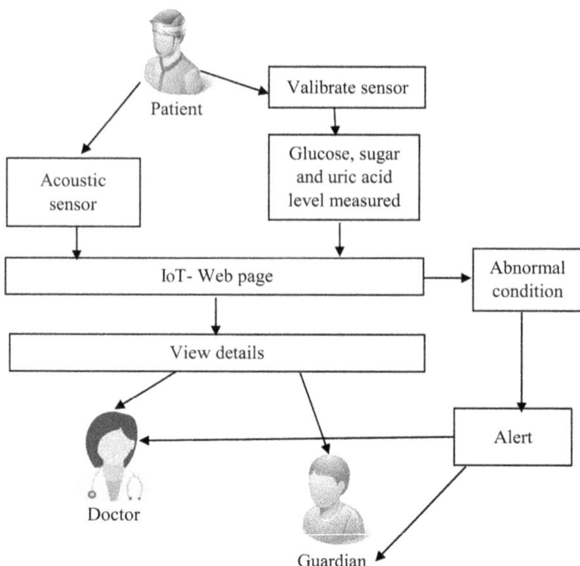

FIGURE 13.2 System architecture.

abnormal situation, an automatic alert is sent to the doctor and guardian. Once an alert is received, rescue medicine will be made available for the patient. The patient's intake, including food and tablets, and intake time are monitored. If the patient swallows the pill at the incorrect time, an alert will be sent via Short Message Service (SMS). This allows verification if the tablet was taken at the right time or not. The Arduino takes analog input from the sensor and processes it to produce digital output, which is then stored in the cloud for future use [5] (Figure 13.2).

The registration module serves as an all-inclusive patient management system, capturing thorough and appropriate patient details. It is employed for generating new users who are enabled to access the webUI. The Login module, on the other hand, addresses security concerns, user logins, and the process of authentication. This hardware module is used to interface the web UI with the sensors. In the IoT workflow, the data acquisition phase entails the choice of sensor readings and the subsequent transmission of this data to the web user interface linked to the respective patient.

13.4 SIMULATION OF THE IOT CIRCUIT USING PROTEUS

The ISIS Intelligent Schematic Input System, also referred to as the Intelligent Switching Input System, serves as the platform for creating and simulating electronic circuit designs. ISIS incorporates a foundational Virtual System Modeling (VSM) engine that offers assistance for the following capabilities:

- DC/AC voltmeter and ammeter, along with oscilloscopes and logic analyzers.

- Analog signal generators and a digital pattern generator.
- Timer functionalities, as well as protocol analyzers encompassing RS232, I²C, and SPI.

VSM is integrated within the ISIS environment, enabling graphical SPICE circuit simulation and animatronics. The SPICE simulator at the core is built upon the Berkeley SPICE3F5 model, capable of simulating microprocessor-based systems. Through the VSM engine, direct interaction with the circuit is achievable during simulation. Real-time monitoring of changes in buttons, switches, or potentiometers, as well as the display of LED indicators and LCD screens, and the visualization of "Hot/Cold" wires, are supported. Proteus 7.0 incorporates VSM, merging the simulation, dynamic apparatuses, and microprocessor prototypes to collectively mimic intricate designs focused on microcontrollers. It serves as an essential tool for engineers, facilitating the testing of their microcontroller designs before embarking on the creation of a physical prototype. The software empowers consumers to collaborate with their designs through on-screen indicators, LED and LCD, as well as switches and buttons when connected to a PC. The core of Proteus 7.0 features its circuit simulation element, which utilizes a fusion of the SPICE3f5 analog simulator kernel with a digital simulator driven by events. This amalgamation allows users to employ SPICE models from any company. Proteus VSM is replete with wide-ranging debugging functionalities such as breakpoints, single-step execution, and variable display, ensuring a refined design process prior to hardware prototyping. Proteus 7.0 is an optimal solution for simulating the interplay between microcontroller-operated software and any connected analog or digital electronic components.

A digital pill is a pharmaceutical dosage form that is collected from the valibrate sensor. The sensor begins to transmit the data. In this module, transmitted data from the valibrate sensor is stored and examined for the drugs; it contains information about the drugs, the intake time, and the causes of the drugs. Depending on the user's permission, this information may then be sent to a list of up to four carefully chosen recipients. An alert system has been implemented to send reminders to the guardian regarding the patient's medication schedule. Users have the option to specify the date and time using the date picker and time picker functionalities. Additionally, patients can send SMS to their doctor when they require medical guidance. Figure 13.3 represents the simulation output.

13.5 CONCLUSION

The valiberate sensor was used to monitor patient intake (food, tablets). The intake is analyzed and communicated using ZigBee. The alarm system immediately warns the doctor, when the threshold value is reached, allowing him to take action more swiftly. By decreasing doctor visits, hospital stays, and diagnostic testing procedures, monitoring systems help to lower healthcare expenditures. In an abnormal situation, the alert message will be sent to a list of four carefully chosen recipients. In the future, it will be possible to discover and control more parameters, which will greatly improve the efficiency of the wireless monitoring system in the field of biomedicine.

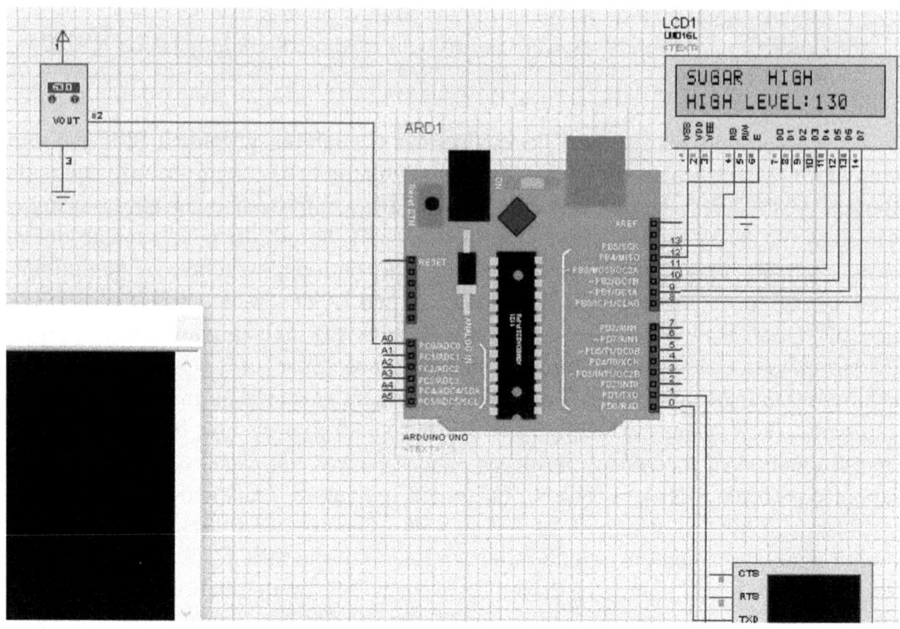

FIGURE 13.3   Simulation output.

REFERENCES

1. Jaul E & Barron J. (2017). Age-related diseases and clinical and public health implications for the 85 years old and over population. *Frontiers in Public Health*, 5:335. doi:10.3389/fpubh.2017.00335
2. Weinstein R. (2005). RFID: A technical overview and its application to the enterprise. *IEEE IT Professional*, 7(3):27–33.
3. Gope P & Hwang T. (2015). A realistic lightweight authentication protocol preserving strong anonymity for securing RFID system. *Computers & Security*, 55:271–280.
4. Gope P & Hwang T. (2015). Untraceable sensor movement in distributed IoT infrastructure. *IEEE Sensors Journal*, 15(9):5340–5348.
5. Cummins G (2021). Smart pills for gastrointestinal diagnostics and therapy. *Advanced Drug Delivery Reviews*, 177:113931.
6. Kumar P & Lee H. (2012). Security issues in healthcare applications using wireless medical sensor networks: A survey. *Sensors (Basel, Switzerland)*, 12(1):55–91. doi:10.3390/s120100055
7. FDA. (2018). Infusion Pumps. Retrieved from www.fda.gov: https://www.fda.gov/medical-devices/general-hospital-devices-and-supplies/infusion-pumps
8. Abacom. (nd). EasyBeeTM. Retrieved from www.abacom-tech.com: https://www.abacom-tech.com/wp-content/uploads/easybee%20ds480.pdf
9. Zen K, Habibi D, Rassau A, & Ahmad I. (2008). *Performance Evaluation of IEEE 802.15.4 for Mobile Sensor Networks*. ECU Publications. doi:10.1109/WOCN.2008.4542536.
10. Arduino. (nd). Arduino UNO R3. Retrieved from UNO R3 Docs: https://docs.arduino.cc/static/861930f95a43ffd6525223ce75c762fe/A000066- datasheet.pdf

14 Deep Learning and Fuzzy Logic System Implementation in Smart Health Care

S. Menaga, R. Rathna, A. Anandkumar, and R. Swaranambigai

14.1 INTRODUCTION

The number of people is increasing in cities and metropolises nowadays, and migration or numerous journeys are common. The issue of healthcare has to receive special consideration in order to create better policies and administrations. The healthcare sector has seen substantial pressure in the last few years, leading to a constant increase in the number of patients with chronic diseases and the long-term medical care they require. To lessen the burden of chronic hospital patients, several therapeutic apps have been developed. Because it is concerned with bettering lifestyle development, the topic of intelligent medical care has drawn a lot of interest and having a clear scientific and technological vision. Much recent advancement has occurred in information technology, and gadgets have been utilized according to the distinctive characteristics of users. Fuzzy and neural networks were used to govern and process the collected data. Several sensors sense health data from individual persons, and these sensor devices can be as simple as a smartwatch or as complex as some kind of gadget used by the individual. One of the most fundamental philosophical foundations fuzzy logic (FL) has up to this point is the application involving fuzzy sets in healthcare enterprises and different aspects of medicine. The data is protected by the fuzzy method of analysis in the intelligent healthcare system, which also ensures the confidentiality of individual health records [1,2]. Meanwhile, as artificial intelligence technology continues to develop, the basics of intelligent medical decision-making. Deep learning is widely used in many fields because of its powerful expression abilities and ability to perform complex feature-fitting functions. There has been success with deep learning models in the medical field. In contrast, traditional deep learning is almost measured and developed by crisp values, whereas medical diagnosis and treatment are often based on imprecise, uncertain, and vague data. A medical dataset usually has high-dimensional, unstructured information and is subjected to artifacts and noise. It is fortunate that fuzzy deep learning, derived from fuzzy sets, is capable of handling uncertainty and inaccuracy with great success.

DOI: 10.1201/9781032632223-14

Fuzzy deep learning offers new perspectives on solving these problems. Recent contributions to uncertain medical data have been made by fuzzy deep learning [3,4].

Lotfi Zadeh introduced the fuzzy logic concept in 1965. Items that are ambiguous or confusing are referred to as fuzzy. Since it is often challenging to determine when a scenario is true or not in reality, their fuzzier reasoning provides extremely valuable flexibility for thought. In fuzzy logic, truth values fall between 0 and 1 for any real number. Partially true values can range from completely false to completely true when fuzzy logic is used. There is an algebraic approach that addresses partial or ambiguous data by describing confusion and unpredictability in decision-making. The grouping function, which determines the extent to which an input value belongs to a certain set or category, is the essential idea behind fuzzy logic. A mapping from an input value to a membership degree between 0 and 1, where 0 denotes not being a member of the group and 1 denotes full membership in the group. In fuzzy logic, the inputs and outputs are evaluated by using fuzzy rules, which represent the relationship between them in fuzzy terms. The fuzzy model, however, fails to endorse the logic of absolute truth and absolute untrue value. Fuzzy reasoning, however, produces an intermediate answer that is partly true and partially wrong [5,6]. As Figure 14.1 shows, an approach to fuzzy logic includes the following steps: Rule base, Fuzzification, Inference, and Defuzzification.

Rule base: It provides the set of rules or guidelines including IF-THEN conditions, needed to manage the system that makes decisions based on data related to languages.

Fuzzification: Numerical inputs are transformed into fuzzy sets. For example, temperature, blood pressure, heart rate, rpm, etc., are crisp inputs, which are measurements taken by the sensors and then entered into the control system.

Inference: Based on the input box and the degree to which the present fuzzy input meets each rule, it determines the rules that should be triggered. The fired rules are then concatenated to generate the control actions

Defuzzification: The inferring set of fuzzy numbers is transformed into crisp values using it. There are various techniques for defuzzification, but the most effective one is usually used in conjunction with a certain trained system to reduce the error probability.

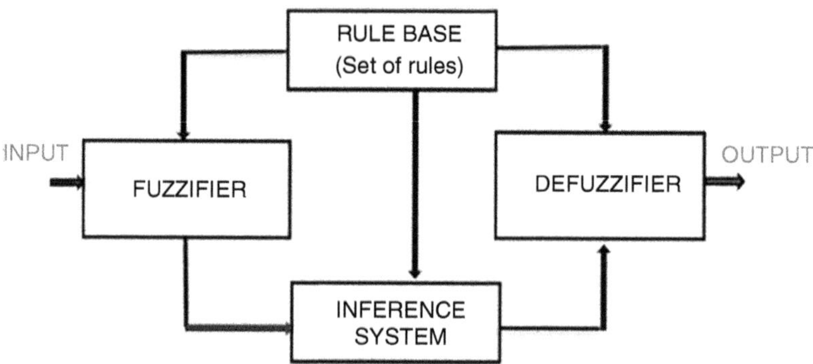

FIGURE 14.1   Process flow in fuzzy logic system.

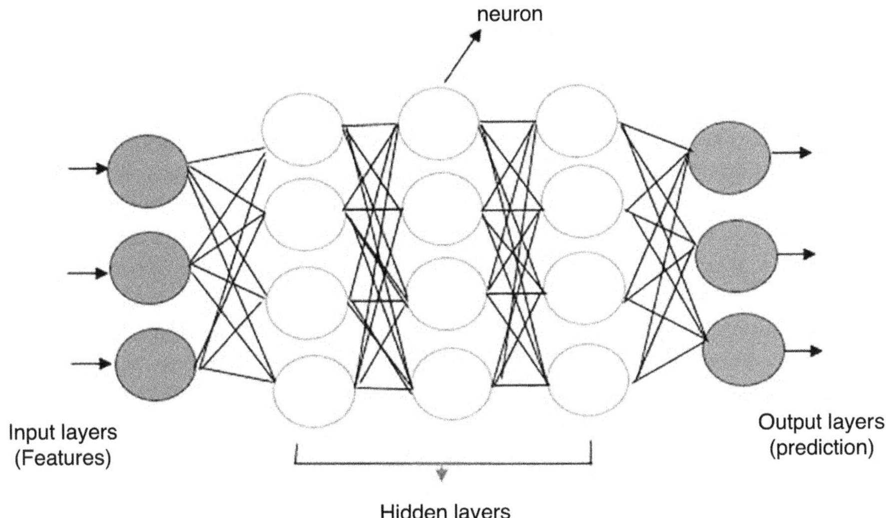

FIGURE 14.2 Architecture of deep learning.

14.2 INTRODUCTION TO DEEP LEARNING

A decision model is learned rather than explicitly coded by a human in machine learning, a subfield of AI within statistics and data mining. Diagnoses and prognoses for various medical conditions are increasingly being made using machine learning. As a branch of Machine Learning, Deep Learning deals with complex input/output mappings and is developed based on Machine Learning principles. Deep learning is inspired by the biological brain and excels at pattern recognition. A deep neural network is an efficient and similar method of processing and analyzing medical data because it is efficient and similar to the functioning of the human brain. Multiple layers of neural networks make up deep learning architectures as shown in Figure 14.2. Neural networks consist of an input layer, several hidden layers, and an output layer. Multiple neurons make up every single layer, and the concealed layer could have multiple layers. The quantity of neurons in the neural network's output layer varies depending on the sort of task being performed. Through layer-wise unsupervised preliminary training, deep neural networks can be effectively adapted and their data inputs can be examined for deeper structure to help with prediction [7,8].

14.3 ROLE OF FUZZY LOGIC (FL) AND DEEP LEARNING (DL) IN HEALTHCARE

Uncertainty surrounding information about patients, sporadic reporting, imprecise medication and prescription language, a patient's physical and mental state during testing, etc., are all issues that the healthcare sectors must cope with. Since FL and DL rely on approximations of data and function similarly to human thinking, they can overcome these problems. The method generates concise solutions, summarizes, and eliminates redundancy from a large database. Because of the challenges in creating an accurate biological systems model, their use in making decisions for healthcare is expanding quickly.

Figure 14.3 shows the applications of FL in Healthcare. Researchers, physicians, and technology manufacturers are compelled by FL to look for elegant and original solutions. Since human intelligence and experience cannot be precisely defined by mathematics, it can be a flexible tool for modeling, managing, and controlling many situations. The procedure for medical decision-making based on ranking, categorization, data extraction, selecting features, pattern recognition, and optimization has been the subject of descriptive research. A simple but discriminatory algorithm can be reduced to a considerable degree of uncertainty by using FL-based strategies. The application of deep learning has improved the monitoring of patients and diagnosis, which has a big influence on the medical field. Following are the healthcare field's best use of deep learning, as shown in Figure 14.4.

Clinical tests are costly and time-consuming. In medicine, ranking the test results is crucial. For the purpose of making decisions, it is critical to rate the tests, risk factors, characteristics, medical suppliers, and performance. In medical care, options refer to various test kinds, risk factors, healthcare procedures, and characteristics associated with a specific condition that are important when making decisions. A new quantitative ranking model was created to rate hospital computed tomography departments based on fuzzy logic and multi-criteria decision-making [8].

By combining data from various datasets and sources, researchers can locate suitable applicants for clinical studies through predictive modeling, made possible by artificial machine learning and deep learning. The use of deep learning will

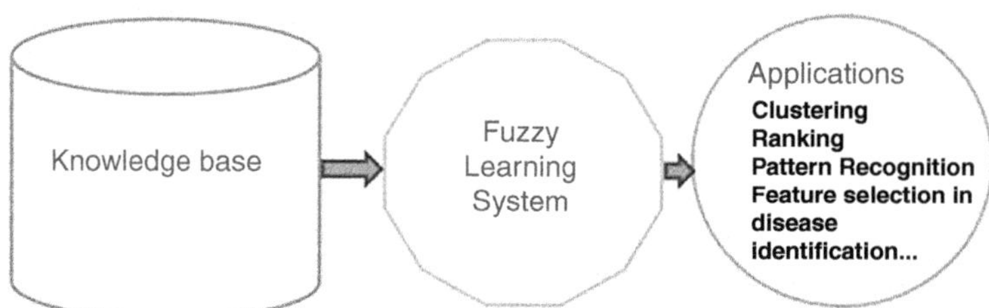

FIGURE 14.3   Applications of FL in healthcare.

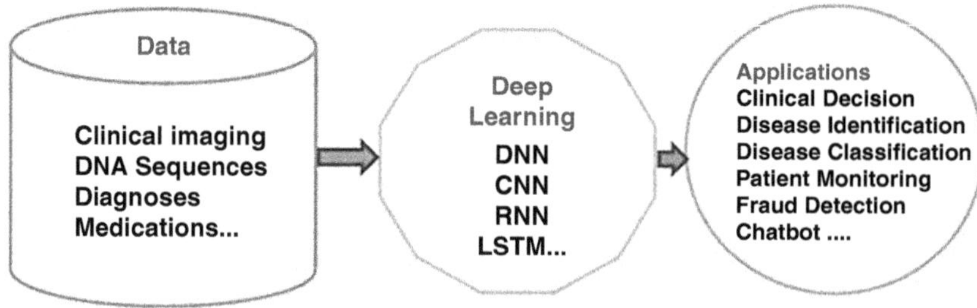

FIGURE 14.4   Applications of DL in healthcare.

also enable constant tracking of these trials with reduced error rates and human intervention [9].

Prediction analytics is a subfield of advanced analytics that involves forecasting future occurrences that are not yet known. Predictive analytics inspects current data to forecast future events using a variety of methods including data mining, modeling, statistics, machine learning, and artificial intelligence. Predictive analytics has the potential to completely transform the healthcare sector by foreseeing health problems before they arise and offering patients better treatment plans. For the benefit of medical professionals, Farzana Islam et al. employed an Adaptive Neuro-fuzzy inference system with a fuzzy C-mean classifier to predict stroke risk [10]. Smart health records can be kept up to date with deep learning for patient monitoring and improved health records. Deep learning can assist in predicting dangers and enabling smart care for patients. Insurance scams may be effectively identified, and future risks can be predicted with deep learning. The models' ability to forecast future patterns and behavior gives health insurance firms an additional benefit when using deep learning to recommend wise insurance plans to their customers.

14.4   ROLE OF FL AND DL IN MEDICAL IMAGING AND DIAGNOSIS

To diagnose patients, deep learning models can decipher pictures from scans such as MRIs, CT scans, and X-rays. Anomalies in the medical photos can be flagged by the algorithms, which can evaluate any risk. Cancer detection makes considerable use of deep learning. The advancements in deep learning and machine learning have made computer vision more innovative recently. Disease treatment is made simpler by medical imaging's ability to diagnose conditions more quickly [11].

In this field, FL approaches are also widely applied. There are a lot of ambiguous terms and circumstances in the medical field. Conventional methods may not be sufficient for processing medical images since they typically display textures, acquisition noise, and inaccurate edge detection. Medical imaging is a vital component that supports clinical decision-making. Electronic mammography, computerized tomography, positron emission tomography (PET), and magnetic resonance imaging can produce two- or three-dimensional medical images. The FL could be applied in the process of identifying patterns in cells, pictures, etc. For pattern recognition, classification and clustering are often employed methods. Fuzzy grouping, fuzzy rule-based, fuzzy pattern-matching, and methods based on fuzzy images are the main fuzzy approaches in medical picture pattern identification [12].

The development of an Internet of Things (IoT) is an essential part of a real-time health monitoring system. Patients' data are measured in real time using a variety of devices. Sensors, actuators, and other devices from IoT have been integrated with other physical devices to share and monitor data through the use of Bluetooth connectivity, Zigbee, the IEEE 802.11 standard (Wi-Fi), and other communication standards. Wearable sensors are integrated into the body and employed in the healthcare sector to gather physiological data from a person's body, including temperature, blood pressure, electrocardiogram (ECG), electroencephalogram (EEG), and so forth [10]. The formation of meaningful and accurate conclusions regarding the patients' medical conditions is supported by this data. Because so much data is collected and stored from a range of sources, data storage and accessibility are also crucial components of the IoT. The information gathered from IoT sensing devices is accessible to medical professionals and other authorized persons. Patients receive fast diagnosis, and the collection of individual medical data is tracked and saved in real-time with the use of sensor chips, a type of IoT technology. Cooperation between the communication module, patients, and users ensures secure and efficient transmission. The majority of IoT-implemented systems have a user interface that functions as a medical service provider's dashboard, allowing for data visualization, user control, and authentication [12,13].

The term "Patients Health Information System" (PHIS) describes a system created to handle medical data. This includes technologies that help make healthcare policy decisions, collect, store, maintain, and deliver an electronic medical record (EMR) for a patient, as well as systems that run a hospital's day-to-day operations. An EMR constitutes a live, patient-oriented database that safely and quickly makes information available to authorized users. In patient rooms, desktops, wheeled carts, and even on mobile devices, PCs are used for accessing EMR. Systems that handle information on the activities of providers and organizations involved in healthcare generally fall under the PHIS category. Standardized forms are used to assess the patient's condition and requirement for medical care [14,15]. Each patient's EMR provides a wealth of information. The following are the most frequently accessed bits of information by physicians:

Patient history and physical (PHP): Whenever a patient arrives at the hospital, a medical professional creates a specific type of record called a "Patient history and physical" (PHP). A PHP provides the nurse with crucial details on a patient's present health, medical history, and treatment plan in an easy-to-read manner. The reason for admission, medical history, surgical history, allergies, current medications, physical exam results, diagnosis, and treatment plan are just a few examples of the information that is included.

Instructions from providers: The prescriptions or medical instructions that a nurse is legally required to carry out or efficiently relay according to organization policies.

Medicine administration records (MARs): To keep track of drugs, electronic medication administration records (MARs) are employed. These records serve as a link between pharmacists and providers for drug requests.

Treatment administration records (TARs): Different hospitals use treatment administration records to keep track of treatments.

Lab results report: This category includes the outcomes of tests like blood or urine test and other lab procedures.

Reports of diagnostic tests: Tests, such as X-rays and ultrasounds, that were ordered by the physician are included in this part of the report. Patient care is typically documented using a variety of formats, including charting by exception, targeted DAR notes, narrative notes, SOAPIE progress notes, discharge summaries of patients, and Minimum Data Set (MDS) charting [16].

Charting by exception: By avoiding redundant charting and utilizing patient norms and standard practices, charting by exception (CBE) is a quick way to record patient systems that also saves time and money for healthcare providers. Healthcare professionals are required to record only departures from anticipated patient norms when using the Charting by Exception method. Every provider may have a distinctive CBE system, which is based on well-established, distinct norms. Then, specific documentation is provided for any exceptions to those variances [17].

Remote patient monitoring (RPM): Telehealth, or remotely monitoring patients, permits bio-medical sensors to provide patient data to medical service providers. It conducts routine blood pressure and glucose monitoring for people with chronic diseases. The data is used to highlight medical incidents that require attention and may be included in a more thorough investigation into the general population's wellness.

Clinical decision support (CDS): Medical personnel can make better clinical judgments with the help of clinical decision support systems, which analyze data from various clinical and administrative systems. Data can be utilized to design remedies or predict medical occurrences like drug interactions. These tools filter data and information to help doctors give patients tailored care [18].

RFID-based sensory devices are used to collect data on a single patient at a time; specimens of the participant's Blood Pressure (BP), skin temperature, heart rate, and sugar levels in the blood were taken from every individual. Figure 14.5 shows the general configuration of the fuzzy system. Data is processed from left to right, pertaining to five different inputs, to produce one result that sums up the patient's health. After the collection of data, a Modified Early Warning System (MEWs) table

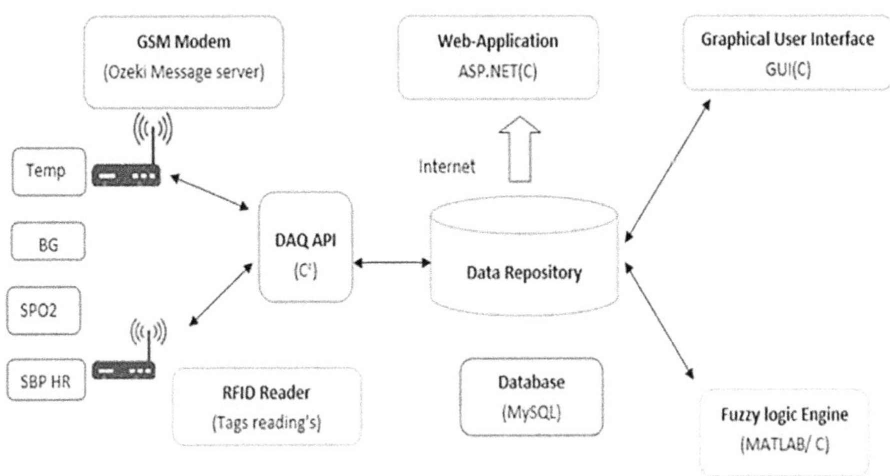

FIGURE 14.5 Configuration of fuzzy logic in collecting and processing of patient's data.

TABLE 14.1

Modified Early Warning System (MEWs)

MEWS Parameters	LOW 3 (−3)	LOW 2 (−2)	LOW 1 (−1)	NORMAL (0)	HIGH 1 (+1)	HIGH 2 (+2)	HIGH 3 (+3)
BP	<75	75–79	80–99	100–199	>190	>210	
HR		<39	40–49	50–99	100–110	111–130	>130
Respiratory rate		<9		9–14.5	15–19	20–30	>30
Body temperature		<35	35–36	36.1–38.0	38.1–39	>39	
AVPU/GCS score	<8.5	8.5–12.5	8.5–14	A/15.0	V/confused	P	U

was formed with a patient's MEWs score, which was determined by utilizing the five physiological factors. For each parameter in Table 14.1, a range of values is assigned a rating.

The live parameter's data of an individual is measured and compared to the prepared MEWs table, and a score rating is assigned based on the measurement value. The overall MEWs score rate is then calculated by adding the score rates for each parameter. For example, when a patient's rating is zero, it indicates that their case is normal; when it is greater than zero but less than five, it indicates that their case is Low-Risk; and when it is five or higher, it indicates that their case is critical, and it is recommended that the particular patient check into an Intensive Care Unit (ICU) for treatment. As seen in Table 14.1, the ranges in the MEWS are defined, categorized, and translated into language words using a fuzzy logic system and after consulting with RCDR medical specialists. This MEWs is the basic database given to FL system. The hierarchical arrangement of the rules is an essential component of FL systems. Rather than abruptly transitioning between modes in response to breakpoints, logic flows naturally from areas where one rule dominates the behavior of the system to another. Fuzzy inference is a method of generating a fuzzy logic matching from a given input to an output, which is shown in Figure 14.6. Decisions were then made using this mapping as the foundation. Three main parts make up FIS: a database that describes the membership functions, a rule base with a variety of fuzzy rules, and a reasoning engine for deriving a logical result or conclusion [19]. Figure 14.6 represents the inference of fuzzy rules set to input and output.

For instance, as the MEWs table demonstrates, HR is related to six language phrases or categories: Low3, Low2, Low1, Normal 0, High1, High2, and High3. A fuzzy set is identified by each category. For every set, a membership function is found, and for every function, a range is established [19,20]. The heart rate (HR) spans corresponding to each fuzzy set; Figure 14.6 shows the different fuzzy sets and the relationship between them, as well as the trapezoid function of membership chosen for the HR parameter. There are five defined fuzzy sets: Low3, Low2, Low1, Normal0, High1, High2, and High 3. In the event when the blood sugar level, for instance, is 64, the patient is included in both the Low2 and Low3 fuzzy sets, albeit to varying degrees. Fuzzy sets and corresponding membership functions are created for the remaining input variables using the same process.

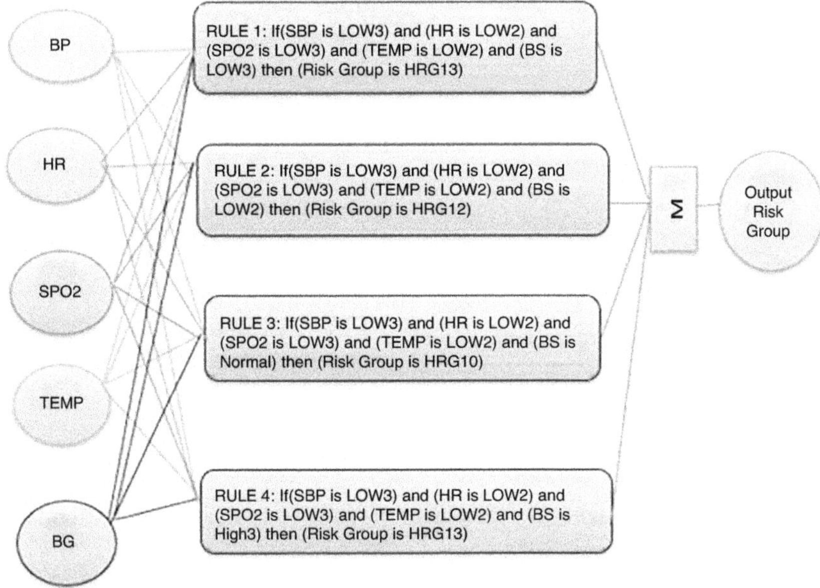

FIGURE 14.6   Inference of fuzzy rules set to input and output.

The development of wireless body area network (WBAN) sensors and devices has simplified continuous tracking and health management because of the rapid advancements in wireless communication and sensor technologies in Industry 5.0 and the advent of 5/6G. The main downsides of WBAN sensors are the ambiguity in data collection and data communication, especially when operating on low power consumption. For models and systems based on fuzzy logic, performance analysis is crucial. It was found that the FL system and its algorithms managed both data and uncertainty in raw healthcare information efficiently and effectively. The fuzzy models are capable of representing, manipulating, using, and interpreting knowledge and data. Fuzzy models are built on top of these Mamdani rule-based systems.

- Fuzzy membership functions should be created for each and every input value.
- Utilize every viable rule in the principle-based framework to compute the fuzzy output functions.
- Defuzzify the parameters that were fuzzified.

In the process of fuzzy logic, recognizing connections is more important to neural networks than understanding the reasons behind a decision. Although fuzzy logic systems can well explain the procedure for making decisions, using the inference rules might be difficult because it necessitates prior knowledge. The fuzzy neural network is the result of these constraints. Neural network patterns serve as the basis for the concepts of fuzzy systems.

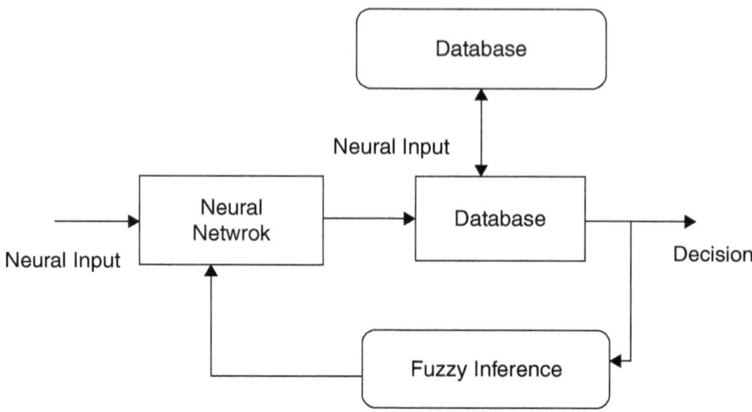

FIGURE 14.7   Combination of Neural Network and FL system.

This process begins with a "fuzzy neuron," whose function can be divided into the following two steps:

i. Evolution of the fuzzy neuron model.
ii. Developing an algorithm and paradigm for combining neural systems with fuzzy systems.

Figure 14.7 depicts the combined fuzzy logic and neural network system. The system stores the inference rules of the fuzzy interface as neural outputs, which are subsequently utilized for decision-making and to supply the neural network with learning algorithms as prior knowledge. The propagation algorithm is slow since it is used to collect data for neural networks. It is difficult to include precise data into the neural network to improve the clarity of learning techniques. Fuzzy systems are employed in limited systems, where fuzzy rules are explicated and exhibit improved performance, making knowledge acquisition difficult. Fuzzy rules are built using numerical data to address these issues in solution design [21–23].

14.5   INTEGRATION OF FL AND DL FOR IMPROVED DECISION SUPPORT

Traditional techniques for diagnosing patients' health risks primarily rely on physicians' review of related symptoms, clinical test reports, and analysis of the patient's medical history. However, due to human error, these methods can result in imprecise diagnosis and occasionally even delays in the final decision for diagnosis. Systems related to healthcare have found that the combination of DL and fuzzy logic-based architecture is successful in predicting risk and complexity. DL uses all available illness classification methods based on data analysis from WBAN sensors [24]. The integration of fuzzy inference systems aids in determining an individual's risk level and the extent of diseases, followed by sharing medical records and recommendations based on accurate information. Medical decision support systems built on cutting-edge computing techniques including support vector machines, k-nearest neighbors, decision trees, fuzzy logic, and artificial neural networks have been developed to address these problems. Globally, the use of health recommender systems (HRS) related to the COVID-19 epidemic has gained popularity. Many HRS are accessible for the goal of conditional logical data proposal and contextually-based personal decision-making. However, the majority of HRS face issues with reliability, value, and consistency. On the other hand, combining deep learning with fuzzy logic can improve the quality of service of HRS. In an effort to effectively anticipate heart failure in an individual, an integrated decision support system based on both Artificial Neural Network (ANN) and fuzzy logic was developed by Samual et al. [25], demonstrating the effectiveness of this combination in improving decision making regarding heart failure.

14.6 CHALLENGES AND OPPORTUNITIES IN IMPLEMENTING OF FL AND DL

In the healthcare industry, artificial intelligence and fuzzy logic-based frameworks are used to handle data when levels of noise, uncertainty, and heterogeneity exceed acceptable bounds. The field of medical diagnosis has seen the creation of numerous novel machine learning applications. However, when attempting to employ these algorithms for medical diagnostics, data scientists still face certain difficulties. Trying to apply DL models for healthcare data could present challenges. When exposed to noise, deep neural networks may misclassify inputs and yield inaccurate conclusions [26]. Medical picture data exhibits a wide range of attenuations and motion artifacts; it is not free of noise and attenuations. Biomedical imaging, including positron emission tomography (PET), CT, ultrasound, and MRI, frequently exhibits multiplicative noise. A significant amount of detail is lost due to denoising, which also modifies the contrast and geographical and temporal distribution of medical images. The lack of readily available, substantial amounts of genuinely annotated clinical imaging data hinders the development of deep learning in medical image diagnostics. Though it hasn't operated to its full potential, fuzzy logic has been used in medical health data management and has aided in decision-making. Researchers are becoming more interested in utilizing fuzzy logic models and algorithms in the field of medical information management due to recent advancements. People have ethical questions about Artificial Intelligence (AI) techniques. In general, the public doesn't trust these systems or their analyses of the provided data. Therefore, to develop these deep learning-based diagnostic tools, the DL community in healthcare needs highly skilled individuals. There is a gap between the deep learning community and society as a result of the difficulties faced by the field of deep learning in medical picture identification, as covered in the preceding section. The autonomy of AI-based healthcare systems is hampered by societal mistrust and misconceptions about intelligent autonomous systems in diagnostics and healthcare. To reduce patients' worries about data security, confidentiality, and integrity, deep learning systems may be designed using ethical concepts such as responsibility, non-maleficence, explainability, or privacy. At different organizational levels, steps must be taken to report the ethical norms of AI, and this should be an ongoing process [27].

14.7 CONCLUSION

Fuzzy logic and machine learning algorithms play a pivotal role in the healthcare sector, focusing on data analysis, prediction, and disease diagnosis. The revolution of deep learning techniques has achieved great success compared to traditional clinical systems, which are limited to delayed medical services, medication delays, effective decision-making, and pre-emption. The integration of fuzzy logic systems with DL could improve clinical data analysis, accurately predict diseases at an earlier stage, monitor patients, assist physicians, and enhance decision-making.

REFERENCES

1. Mostafa, B. S., Miry, A. H., & Salman, T. M. (2022, January). Smart health monitoring and self-analysis system based on internet of things with fuzzy controller. *AIP Conference Proceedings*, 2386(1), 050004.
2. Miotto, R., Wang, F., Wang, S., Jiang, X., & Dudley, J. T. (2018). Deep learning for healthcare: Review, opportunities and challenges. *Briefings in Bioinformatics*, 19(6), 1236–1246.
3. Menaga, S., & Paruvathavardhini, J. (2022). AI in healthcare. In: Venkatesh, C., Rengarajan, N., Ponmurugan, P. and Balamurugan, S. (eds.). *Smart Systems for Industrial Applications*. John Wiley & Sons (pp. 115–140).
4. Paruvathavardhini, J., Menaga, S., Gomathi, N., Karthikkumar, S., & Brindha, S. (2020). A study depicting the advent of artificial intelligence in health care. *European Journal of Molecular Clinical Medicine*, 7(11), 131–146.
5. https://www.geeksforgeeks.org/fuzzy-logic-control-system/?ref=ml_lbp
6. Sahu, B., Sarangi, L., Ghosh, A., & Palo, H. K. (2022). Application of fuzzy logic to healthcare industry. In: Mohanty, Sachi Nandan, Prasenjit Chatterjee, and Bui Thanh Hung (eds.) "Fuzzy Computing in Data Science: Applications and Challenges." Wiley online Library, (pp. 37–53).
7. Bresnick, J. (2018). "What is deep learning and how will it change healthcare." *Health IT Analytics* 30. https://healthitanalytics.com/features/what-is-deep-learning-and-how-will-it-change-healthcare.
8. Gürsel, G. (2016). Healthcare, uncertainty, and fuzzy logic. *Digital Medicine*, 2(3), 101–112.
9. Yang, S., Zhu, F., Ling, X., Liu, Q., & Zhao, P. (2021). Intelligent health care: Applications of deep learning in computational medicine. *Frontiers in Genetics*, 12, 607471.
10. Islam, F., Shoilee, S.B.A., Shams, M., & Rahman, R.M., 2017. Potential risk factor analysis and risk prediction system for stroke using fuzzy logic. In: *Artificial Intelligence Trends in Intelligent Systems: Proceedings of the 6th Computer Science On-line Conference 2017 (CSOC2017)*, Vol. 16 (pp. 262–272). Springer.
11. Dargan, S., Kumar, M., Ayyagari, M.R. and Kumar, G. (2020). A survey of deep learning and its applications: a new paradigm to machine learning. *Archives of Computational Methods in Engineering*, 27, 1071–1092. https://www.analyticsinsight.net/these-are-the-top-applications-of-deep-learning-in-healthcare.
12. Arji, G., Ahmadi, H., Nilashi, M., Rashid, T.A., Ahmed, O.H., Aljojo, N., & Zainol, A., 2019. Fuzzy logic approach for infectious disease diagnosis: A methodical evaluation, literature and classification. *Biocybernetics and Biomedical Engineering*, 39(4), 937–955.
13. Pradhan, B., Bhattacharyya, S., & Pal, K. (2021). IoT-based applications in healthcare devices. *Journal of Healthcare Engineering*, 2021, 1–18.

14. Khan, M. M., Alanazi, T. M., Albraikan, A. A., & Almalki, F. A. (2022). IoT-based health monitoring system development and analysis. *Security and Communication Networks*, 2022, 1–11.

15. Thakkar, H., Shah, V., Yagnik, H., & Shah, M. (2021). Comparative anatomization of data mining and fuzzy logic techniques used in diabetes prognosis. *Clinical eHealth*, 4, 12–23.

16. Ovcina, A., Izetbegovic, S., & Eminovic, E. (2018). Implementation of patient categorization model based on their need for medical care as an indicator of efficiency and effectiveness of nursing clinical practice. *Acta Med Croatica*, 72(4), 453–556.

17. Wisconsin State Legislature. (2018). *Chapter 6: Standards of practice for registered nurses and licensed practical nurses.* Board of Nursing. https://docs.legis.wisconsin.gov/statutes/statutes/441

18. Rouse, M., 2018. Protected health information (PHI) or personal health information. https://www.techtarget.com/searchhealthit/definition/personal-health-information.

19. Chirish Book, "What is health Information System." Digital Guardians Blog, *May 8* (2023). https://www.digitalguardian.com/blog/what-health-information-system.

20. Al-Dmour, J. A., Sagahyroon, A., Al-Ali, A. R., & Abusnana, S. (2019). A fuzzy logic-based warning system for patients classification. *Health Informatics Journal*, 25(3), 1004–1024.

21. Götzinger, M., Juhász, D., TaheriNejad, N., Willegger, E., Tutzer, B., Liljeberg, P., ... & Rahmani, A. M. Original publications. *Self-Aware Reliable Monitoring*, 1, 129.

22. Parva, E., Boostani, R., Ghahramani, Z., & Paydar, S. (2017). The necessity of data mining in clinical emergency medicine; a narrative review of the current literatrue. *Bulletin of Emergency & Trauma*, Vol. 2, 90–95.

23. Vyas, S., Gupta, S., Bhargava, D., & Boddu, R. (2022). Fuzzy logic system implementation on the performance parameters of health data management frameworks. *Journal of Healthcare Engineering*, 22, 1–11.

24. Burmakova, A., & Kalibatienė, D. (2022). Applying fuzzy inference and machine learning methods for prediction with a small dataset: A case study for predicting the consequences of oil spills on a ground environment. *Applied Sciences*, 12(16), 8252.

25. Sandeep Kumar, E., & Satya Jayadev, P., 2020. Deep learning for clinical decision support systems: A review from the panorama of smart healthcare. In: Dash, Sujata, Biswa Ranjan Acharya, Mamta Mittal, Ajith Abraham, and Arpad Kelemen (eds.) *Deep Learning Techniques for Biomedical and Health Informatics.* Cham, Switzerland: Springer International Publishing (pp. 79–99).

26. Samuel, O.W., Asogbon, G.M., Sangaiah, A.K., Fang, P., & Li, G., 2017. An integrated decision support system based on ANN and Fuzzy_AHP for heart failure risk prediction. *Expert Systems with Applications*, 68, 163–172.

27. Dhar, T., Dey, N., Borra, S., & Sherratt, R.S., 2023. Challenges of deep learning in medical image analysis-improving explainability and trust. *IEEE Transactions on Technology and Society*, 4(1), 68–75.

15 A Boost for Health
Blockchain-Powered IoT-BC Boosting in Wearable Health Devices

I. Sakthidevi and G. Fathima

15.1 INTRODUCTION

The convergence of technology has significantly impacted various domains, and healthcare stands at the forefront of this transformation. This chapter delves into the realm of smart healthcare, specifically focusing on the utilization of wearable health devices enhanced by the novel algorithm "IoT-BC Boosting," powered by blockchain technology.

Smart healthcare, as per Bhawiyuga et al. [1], is characterized by the seamless integration of technology and medical services and has emerged as a paradigm shift in the healthcare industry. One of the pivotal components of smart healthcare is wearable health devices. These compact and unobtrusive devices have the capacity to continuously collect diverse health-related data, providing real-time insights into users' well-being. The continuous monitoring offered by wearable devices not only empowers individuals to actively engage in their health management but also enables healthcare providers to offer personalized and timely interventions.

The synergy of the Internet of Things (IoT) and Artificial Intelligence (AI) has revolutionized the capabilities of smart healthcare systems. IoT-enabled wearable devices can efficiently capture a myriad of physiological and behavioral parameters, generating a vast amount of data. AI-driven analytics harness the potential within this data, facilitating accurate health predictions, disease diagnoses, and personalized treatment recommendations. The amalgamation of IoT and AI as studied by Arthi et al. [5] lays the foundation for proactive and data-driven healthcare, enabling early detection of health anomalies and informed decision-making.

Blockchain, as explained by Manjunath et al. [10], a decentralized and immutable digital ledger, has garnered substantial attention across industries due to its inherent security and transparency features. In the context of healthcare, blockchain technology addresses crucial challenges, including data integrity, security, and interoperability. By establishing a tamper-proof record of transactions and data exchanges, blockchain enhances trust among stakeholders and ensures the veracity of sensitive health information. Moreover, its decentralized architecture minimizes single points of failure, fostering a robust and resilient ecosystem for health data management.

DOI: 10.1201/9781032632223-15

This chapter explores the innovative "IoT-BC Boosting" algorithm, a novel approach that amalgamates ensemble learning principles with blockchain technology to fortify the accuracy and reliability of health analytics derived from wearable devices. The subsequent sections of this chapter elucidate the architecture, functioning, and advantages of the proposed algorithm. Furthermore, a comparative analysis with existing algorithms substantiates the efficacy of the "IoT-BC Boosting" algorithm in realizing enhanced health insights from wearable health devices.

The synergy between IoT and blockchain technology has garnered significant attention in enhancing healthcare systems. Bhawiyuga et al. [1] present a platform that integrates IoT-based smart healthcare systems with blockchain networks, establishing a secure and transparent environment for health data management. This integration addresses challenges related to data integrity, privacy, and interoperability, paving the way for advanced health analytics and personalized care [1]. IoT has emerged as a pivotal technology in revolutionizing healthcare. In a comprehensive survey, Islam et al. [2] elucidate the transformative potential of IoT for healthcare applications. They delve into various aspects, including data collection, monitoring, diagnosis, and treatment, highlighting the role of IoT in delivering efficient and patient-centric healthcare solutions [2].

Ryu [3] contributes to the IoT landscape by developing a Bluetooth Low Energy (BLE) sensor module. This open-source module facilitates the seamless integration of sensors into IoT applications, enabling real-time health data monitoring. The study emphasizes the practical implementation of IoT technology for health monitoring, underscoring its significance in wearable health devices [3]. The fusion of cloud computing, IoT, and wireless body area networks (WBAN) has paved the way for transformative healthcare solutions. Ahmed et al. [4] delve into this integration, showcasing its effectiveness in healthcare delivery. By enabling remote monitoring, real-time data analysis, and efficient resource utilization, the integration of cloud computing and IoT contributes to enhancing healthcare accessibility and quality [4].

Arthi et al. [5] delve into this realm by providing an extensive exploration of the fundamental components and computational frameworks that underpin the Internet of Medical Things (IoMT). This study highlights the intricate interplay between hardware, software, communication protocols, and security mechanisms, shedding light on the intricate architecture of IoMT systems [5]. Sedentary lifestyles have emerged as a significant health concern, impacting individuals' well-being and contributing to various health risks. Park et al. [6] present a comprehensive overview of the updated evidence surrounding potential health risks associated with sedentary behavior. This investigation serves as a critical reminder of the importance of physical activity and its role in preventive healthcare strategies [6].

The integration of technology into healthcare is characterized by the "P5" approach, emphasizing personalized, predictive, preventive, participatory, and patient-centric care. Pravettoni and Triberti [7] advocate for this holistic perspective in healthcare, proposing an agenda for the future of health technologies. This approach envisions a healthcare ecosystem that harnesses the potential of digital solutions to empower individuals and revolutionize healthcare delivery [7]. In response to the global COVID-19 pandemic, Rahman and Hossain [8] propose an innovative framework to address the challenges posed by the pandemic. The study underscores the potential of IoMT and edge computing in tackling pressing healthcare challenges [8].

The security of IoT data in healthcare systems has been reinforced through blockchain technology. Jeon et al. [9] introduce a blockchain-based data security enhancement for an IoT server platform. This study underscores the importance of safeguarding sensitive health data, demonstrating the potential of blockchain to enhance data integrity and privacy in IoT-driven healthcare systems. The synergy of IoT and blockchain, along with big data analytics, has led to transformative application scenarios. Manjunath et al. [10] delve into the potential of this convergence by presenting IoT-driven scenarios enhanced by big data analytics and blockchain. The study explores the interconnectedness of these technologies, emphasizing their role in shaping innovative healthcare solutions.

Sun et al. [11] provide insights into the integration of big data analytics in the IoT environment in the context of smart and connected communities. This study sheds light on the transformative potential of these technologies in enhancing urban living, healthcare services, and community well-being. Wearable health devices play a pivotal role in monitoring and assessing individuals' physical and mental health conditions. Onuki et al. [12] present a study that utilizes heart rate data from wearable devices to estimate physical and mental health conditions. This research underscores the practical application of wearable health devices in providing real-time insights into individuals' health status, thereby contributing to proactive healthcare management.

The evolution of wearable consumer electronic devices has been standardized to streamline their integration and interoperability. The "IEEE Standard for Wearable Consumer Electronic Devices—Overview and Architecture" provides a comprehensive framework that lays the foundation for wearable device development. This standardization facilitates seamless data exchange and communication, contributing to the advancement of wearable health devices [13]. In the pursuit of health-related data collection from wearable and mobile devices, Ji et al. [14] introduce the Health24 project. This initiative focuses on gathering health-related data from individuals' everyday lives, offering insights into the potential of wearables and mobile devices as tools for continuous health monitoring and data acquisition.

Mobile phone sensor technology has emerged as a pivotal instrument in research related to mental health. The integrated analysis by Boonstra et al. [15] sheds light on the intricate challenges and potential solutions inherent in utilizing sensor data to advance mental health research and interventions [15]. In the realm of mental health, mobile behavioral sensing holds promise for both outpatients and inpatients with conditions such as schizophrenia. Ben-Zeev et al. [16] explore the application of mobile behavioral sensing to monitor individuals with schizophrenia. This research demonstrates the feasibility of utilizing mobile technology for real-time data collection, providing valuable insights into individuals' behavioral patterns and supporting personalized interventions.

The utilization of wearable devices extends beyond traditional health monitoring, catering to specific demographic needs. Azevedo et al. [17] present a wearable device designed for monitoring health risks in children during outdoor activities. This research demonstrates the potential of wearables in safeguarding children's well-being by providing real-time health insights and risk assessment. The adoption of health wearables among older adults is a burgeoning area of study. Zhang et al. [18] employ advanced techniques to analyze the factors influencing the appeal of health wearables among elderly people. This study contributes to a nuanced understanding of older adults' preferences and needs in the context of wearable health technologies.

Humanization forms the cornerstone of wearable health product design, particularly for older adults. Gao and Dong [19] delve into the concept of humanization in designing health products wearable by elderly people. This research underscores the significance of user-centric design principles in creating wearable devices that seamlessly integrate into the daily lives of older individuals [19]. In the realm of home medical device retail, Munos [20] draws inspiration from the patchwork model. This model offers insights into the integration of diverse medical devices within a cohesive framework. The study emphasizes the potential of wearable health devices to transform the home medical device retail industry through innovative design and integration strategies [20].

15.2 IoT-BC BOOSTING ALGORITHM—SYSTEM ARCHITECTURE

The architecture of the proposed IoT-BC Boosting Algorithm aims to harness the potential of blockchain technology, ensemble learning, and IoT devices to enhance the accuracy and dependability of health analytics derived from wearable health devices. By combining blockchain's data integrity and security features with ensemble learning's predictive power, the system offers a robust platform for generating reliable health insights. The block diagram representation of the IoT-BC Boosting Algorithm—System architecture is shown in Figure 15.1 and the Pseudo code representation of the IoT-BC Boosting Algorithm is shown in Figure 15.1.

The blockchain architecture employed in the proposed system follows a distributed ledger model, ensuring the secure and transparent recording of health data transactions. Each transaction is cryptographically linked, forming a chronological chain of blocks. The decentralized nature of the architecture eliminates the need for intermediaries, enhances data immutability, and safeguards against unauthorized data modifications. Ensemble learning involves the aggregation of predictions from multiple base models to improve the overall accuracy and generalization of the system. Let M represent the total number of base models. The final prediction P_f is computed as a weighted average of individual base model predictions P_i:

$$P_f = 1/M \sum_{i=1}^{M} (P_i) \tag{15.1}$$

Incorporating ensemble learning into the blockchain-based architecture enhances the predictive capabilities of the system. Each base model generates its prediction based on the input data. The ensemble model then combines these predictions, attenuating individual errors and yielding an aggregated prediction with improved accuracy.

The "IoT-BC Boosting" algorithm encompasses the following steps, effectively amalgamating ensemble learning and blockchain technology:

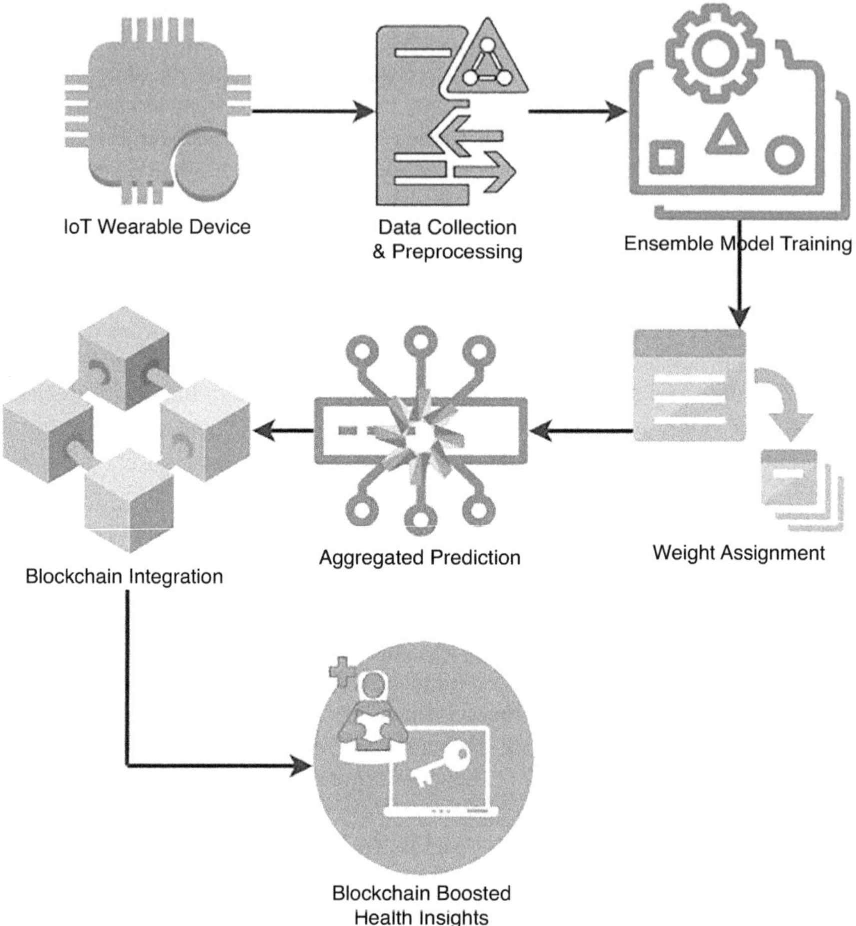

FIGURE 15.1   IoT-BC boosting implementation—block diagram.

Step 1: Data Collection and Preprocessing
- Wearable health devices gather physiological and behavioral data, forming the input dataset D.
- Data preprocessing includes feature extraction, normalization, and data partitioning.

Step 2: Ensemble Model Training
- A set of M base models is trained on different subsets of D.
- Base model predictions P_i are obtained for each data instance.

Step 3: Weight Assignment
- Ensemble model weights w_i are assigned to each base model based on prediction accuracy.
- Weight assignment is conducted using established algorithms like AdaBoost or Gradient Boosting.

TABLE 15.1

IoT-BC Boosting Algorithm—Pseudo Code

Input: Wearable health data (D)
Output: Updated blockchain
Step 1: Data Collection and Preprocessing
D_processed = Preprocess(D)
Step 2: Ensemble Model Training
For i = 1 to M:
  Train Base_Model_i on D_processed
  P_i = Base_Model_i.predict(D_processed)
Step 3: Weight Assignment
For i = 1 to M:
  w_i = WeightAssignment(P_i)
Step 4: Aggregated Prediction
P_f = WeightedAverage(P_i, w_i)
Step 5: Blockchain Integration
AddTransactionToBlockchain(P_f)
Output: Updated blockchain with aggregated health prediction

Step 4: Aggregated Prediction
- The final prediction P_f is calculated using the ensemble model and the weighted average formula.

Step 5: Blockchain Integration
- The aggregated prediction P_f is added to the blockchain as a transaction within a new block.
- Blockchain's cryptographic hashing ensures data integrity and prevents unauthorized modifications (Table 15.1).

This combined pseudocode encapsulates the entire process of the "IoT-BC Boosting" algorithm, incorporating data collection, preprocessing, ensemble model training, weight assignment, aggregated prediction, and blockchain integration. The "IoT-BC Boosting" algorithm amalgamates ensemble learning's predictive aggregation with blockchain's secure transaction recording, culminating in a reliable and tamper-proof system for deriving health insights from wearable health devices. The IoT-BC Boosting Implementation—Block Diagram is represented in Figure 15.1.

IoT wearable device: Wearable health devices, equipped with sensors and IoT technology, collect continuous streams of health-related data from users. These devices monitor parameters such as heart rate, activity levels, and sleep patterns, providing a rich source of real-time health information.

Data collection and preprocessing: Raw data obtained from wearable devices undergoes a series of preprocessing steps. This includes feature extraction to identify relevant data points, normalization to ensure consistency and comparability, and partitioning to organize the data for further analysis.

Ensemble model training: The preprocessed data is utilized to train an ensemble of base models. Each base model is trained by the system on a distinct subdivision of the statistics or focuses on specific features. This diversity in training allows the ensemble to capture various aspects of the health data, leading to a more robust overall predictive capability.

Weight assignment: After the base models are trained, the weight of the ensemble model is assigned with respect to the performance values of base model representations. Models with higher accuracy or expertise in specific areas receive higher weights, reflecting their influence on the final prediction.

Aggregated prediction: The ensemble model syndicates estimate from all the base models, according to the assigned weights. This aggregation process reduces the impact of individual model errors and enhances the overall prediction accuracy.

Blockchain integration: The aggregated prediction is added to the blockchain as a transaction within a new block. This involves cryptographic hashing to ensure the immutability and security of the prediction. The decentralized nature of the blockchain prevents unauthorized modifications and establishes an auditable record of the prediction's origin.

Blockchain-boosted health insights: The final output of the system is a reliable health insight. This insight is the result of the aggregation of predictions from multiple base models, enhanced by the security and transparency offered by blockchain technology. Users and healthcare professionals can rely on these insights for informed decision-making and proactive health management.

The synergy between IoT-enabled wearable devices, ensemble learning, and blockchain technology in the proposed system architecture results in accurate, secure, and trustworthy health insights. The "IoT-BC Boosting" algorithm optimizes prediction accuracy through ensemble learning, while blockchain integration ensures data integrity and traceability, contributing to a comprehensive and innovative solution for health analytics.

15.3   RESULTS AND DISCUSSION

To evaluate the efficacy of the proposed "IoT-BC Boosting" algorithm in enhancing health analytics from wearable health devices, a comprehensive simulation analysis was conducted. The performance of the "IoT-BC Boosting" algorithm was compared with three widely used existing algorithms. Random Forest (RaFo) Algorithm, Support Vector Machine (SVM) Algorithm, and Deep Neural Networks (DNN) mechanism are used for simulation comparison. The evaluation was based on the following simulation metrics: Accuracy (Acc), Precision (P), Recall (R), and F1-Score (F1). The simulation analysis environment is shown in Table 15.2.

A real-world dataset comprising diverse health parameters collected from wearable devices was employed for the simulation analysis. The dataset was preprocessed and partitioned into training and testing subsets. Each algorithm was trained on the training data and assessed to ensure a fair and unbiased comparison.

TABLE 15.2

Simulation Analysis—Environment

Simulation Parameter	Value/Setting
Dataset	Real-world wearable health data from various medical health institutions
Training, validation, test data ratio	70% training, 20% validation, 10% test
Preprocessing	Feature extraction, normalization, data partitioning
Evaluation metrics	Accuracy (Acc), precision (P), recall (R), F1-score (F1)
Statistical tests	Paired t-test for significance analysis
Hardware	Dual or quad-core Intel Xeon or AMD EPYC processors 32 GB or more of DDR4 ECC RAM.
Software	Python, scikit-learn, and blockchain simulation framework (BlockSim with Ethereum Platform and consensus algorithm use case)
Metrics collection & analysis	Automated scripts for collecting and analyzing simulation results

The evaluation metrics Accuracy (Acc), Precision (P), Recall (R), and F1-Score (F1) collectively offer an inclusive understanding of the performance of the "IoT-BC Boosting" algorithm compared to existing algorithms. They enable a thorough assessment of prediction correctness, the algorithm's ability to minimize false positives, its capability to capture relevant positive instances, and the balance between precision and recall. The utilization of these metrics ensures a rigorous and unbiased evaluation of the proposed algorithm's effectiveness in enhancing health analytics from wearable health devices. The performance analysis was piloted to comprehensively evaluate the simulation results of the proposed "IoT-BC Boosting" algorithm in comparison to three existing algorithms: Random Forest (RaFo) Algorithm, Support Vector Machine (SVM) Algorithm, and Deep Neural Networks (DNN) Mechanism. The evaluation was based on key simulation metrics including Accuracy (Acc), Precision (P), Recall (R), and F1-Score (F1). The results presented in tabulated format provide insights into the algorithmic capabilities and offer a basis for informed decision-making in wearable health device analytics.

The accuracy metric serves as a fundamental measure of overall predictive correctness. The "IoT-BC Boosting" algorithm demonstrated consistently higher accuracy values across multiple dataset samples compared to Random Forest, SVM, and DNN. This outcome underscores the ability of "IoT-BC Boosting" to effectively leverage the combined power of ensemble learning and blockchain integration to generate precise health insights. The proposed algorithm's capacity to aggregate predictions while ensuring data integrity contributes significantly to its superior accuracy performance. The graphical representation of the Accuracy analysis is shown in Figure 15.2.

Precision (P) and Recall (R) are crucial metrics that provide insights into the algorithm's ability to minimize false positives and capture actual positive instances, respectively. In both precision and recall assessments, the "IoT-BC Boosting" algorithm showcased notable advantages. It consistently exhibited higher precision

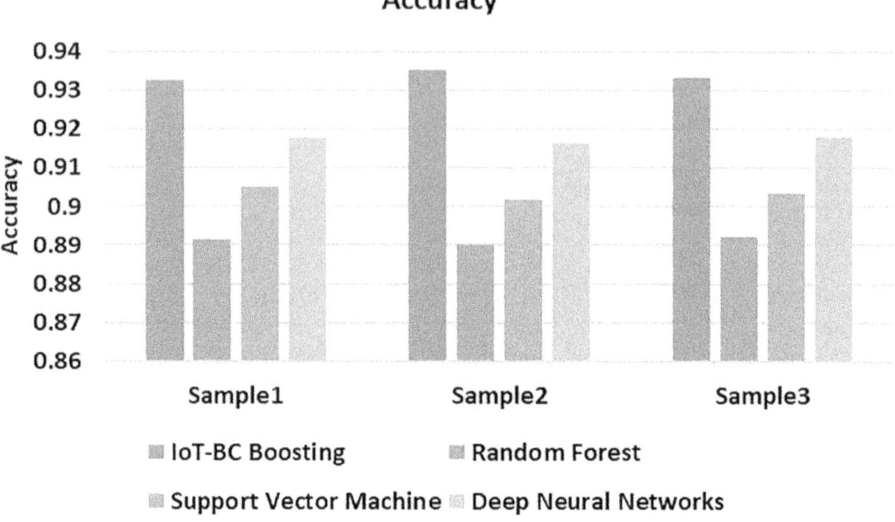

FIGURE 15.2   Accuracy (Acc) plot of the algorithms.

values, indicating a reduction in false positive predictions compared to other algorithms. Moreover, the "IoT-BC Boosting" algorithm demonstrated superior recall values, suggesting its proficiency in identifying a greater proportion of actual positive instances. This enhanced precision-recall balance positions the algorithm as a reliable solution for generating precise health insights. The graphical representation of the precision analysis is shown in Figure 15.3. Similarly, for Recall (R) analysis, the graph illustration is demonstrated in Figure 15.4.

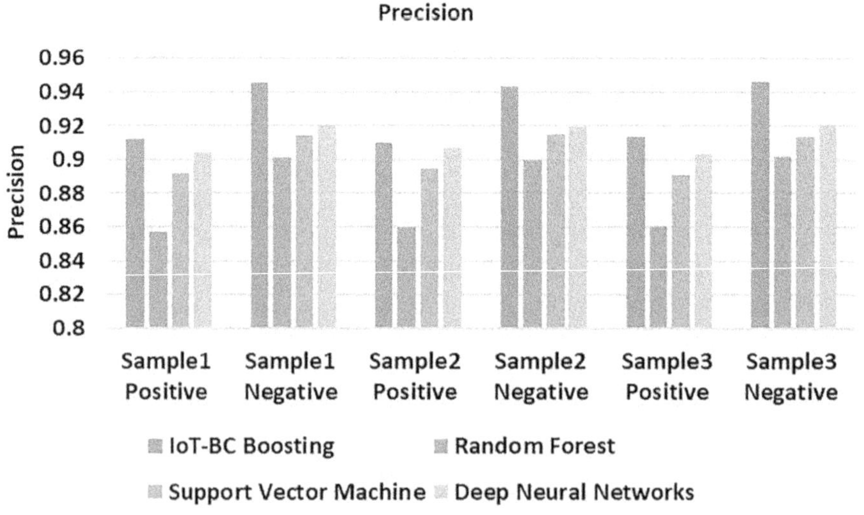

FIGURE 15.3   Precision (P) plot.

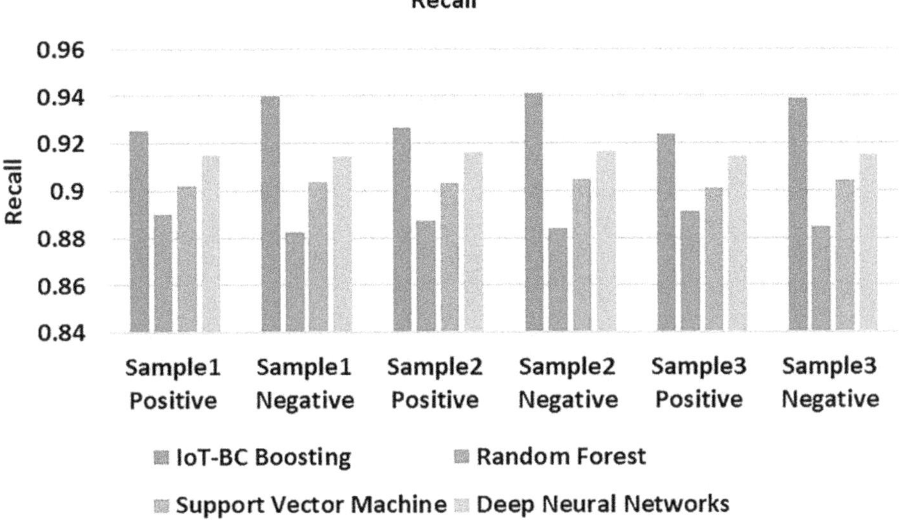

FIGURE 15.4   Recall (R) plot.

The F1-Score (F1) is the harmonic mean of precision and recall. It represents a comprehensive evaluation of algorithmic routine, particularly in scenarios with class imbalance. In this context, the "IoT-BC Boosting" algorithm consistently outperformed the comparative algorithms in terms of F1-score. Its ability to harmonize precision and recall translated into improved performance across both positive and negative classes. This balanced performance contributes to the algorithm's robustness in real-world health analytics applications. The graphical illustration for F1-score assessment is shown in Figure 15.5. The implications of this research reverberate across various dimensions of healthcare. The precise and reliable health insights generated by the "IoT-BC Boosting" algorithm offer a foundation for informed decision-making, proactive health management, and personalized interventions. Individuals can benefit from accurate health assessments, enabling them to make impactful lifestyle choices. Healthcare providers gain access to a powerful tool that aids in early detection, monitoring, and treatment planning. Furthermore, the integration of blockchain technology brings an unparalleled level of transparency, security, and trust to health data transactions. The decentralized nature of blockchain ensures that health insights are tamper-proof and traceable, instilling confidence in the reliability of the generated information. As the healthcare landscape evolves, the "Blockchain-Powered IoT-BC Boosting" approach stands as a testament to the transformative potential of interdisciplinary collaborations. This research demonstrates that the synergy of cutting-edge technologies has the capacity to reshape conventional paradigms and elevate healthcare to unprecedented heights.

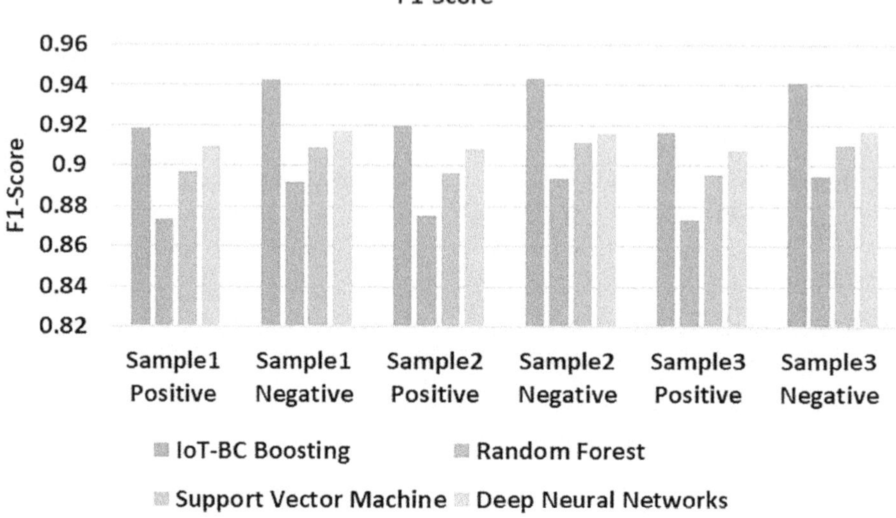

FIGURE 15.5   F1-score (F1) plot.

15.4 CONCLUSION

The results obtained from the simulation analysis collectively underscore the potential of the "IoT-BC Boosting" algorithm in the realm of wearable health device analytics. The amalgamation of ensemble learning principles and blockchain technology empowers the algorithm to produce accurate, trustworthy, and balanced health insights. These findings not only contribute to the advancement of smart healthcare but also lay the foundation for personalized health management and proactive interventions. The convergence of emerging technologies has paved the way for groundbreaking advancements in the field of healthcare. This research embarked on a transformative journey to explore the potential of a novel approach, "Blockchain-Powered IoT-BC Boosting," for enhancing health analytics derived from wearable health devices. By fusing the strengths of ensemble learning, the Internet of Things (IoT), and blockchain technology, this study has unveiled a robust and innovative framework that addresses the complexities of real-world health data.

REFERENCES

1. Bhawiyuga, A., Wardhana, A., Amron, K., & Kirana, A. P. (2019). Platform for integrating internet of things based smart healthcare system and blockchain network. In: *2019 6th NAFOSTED Conference on Information and Computer Science (NICS)* (pp. 55–60). doi:10.1109/NICS48868.2019.9023797.
2. Islam, S. M. R., Kwak, D., Kabir, M. H., Hossain, M., & Kwak, K. S. (2015). The internet of things for health care: A comprehensive survey. *IEEE Access*, 3, 678–708.
3. Ryu, D. H. (2015). Development of BLE sensor module based on open source for IoT applications. *The Journal of the Korea Institute of Electronic Communication Sciences*, 10(3), 419–424.

4. Ahmed, S., Javaid, N., Haider, S., Alrajeh, N., & Alamri, A. (2017). Integration of cloud computing with Internet of Things and wireless body area network for effective healthcare. In: *Wireless Systems and Networks (ISWSN) 2017*. IEEE.

5. Arthi, K., Chidhambararajan, B., & Revathi, A. R. (2022). A deep investigation of architectural elements and computing technologies for internet of medical things. In: *2022 6th International Conference on Electronics, Communication and Aerospace Technology (ICECA)*, Coimbatore, India (pp. 556–563). doi:10.1109/ICECA55336.2022.10009359.

6. Park, J. H., Moon, J. H., Kim, H. J., Kong, M. H., & Oh, Y. H. (2020). Sedentary lifestyle: Overview of updated evidence of potential health risks. *Korean Journal of Family Medicine*, 41(6), 365–373.

7. Pravettoni, G., & Triberti, S. (2020). A "P5" approach to healthcare and health technology. In: Gabriella Pravettoni and Stefano Triberti (eds.) *P5 eHealth: An Agenda for the Health Technologies of the Future*. Springer, 3–17. doi:10.1007/978-3-030-2799 4-3_1.

8. Rahman, M. A., & Hossain, M. S. (2021). An internet-of-medical-things-enabled edge computing framework for tackling COVID-19. *IEEE Internet of Things Journal*, 8(21), 15847–15854. doi:10.1109/JIOT.2021.3122894.

9. Jeon, J. H., Kim, K.-H., & Kim, J.-H. (2018). Block chain based data security enhanced IoT server platform. In: *2018 International Conference on Information Networking (ICOIN)*, Chiang Mai, Thailand (pp. 941–944). doi:10.1109/ICOIN.2018.8343262.

10. Manjunath, P., Prakruthi, M., & Gajkumar Shah, P. (2018). IoT driven with big data analytics and block chain application scenarios. In: *2018 Second International Conference on Green Computing and Internet of Things (ICGCIoT)*, Bangalore, India (pp. 569–572). doi:10.1109/ICGCIoT.2018.8752973.

11. Sun, Y., Song, H., Jara, A. J., & Bie, R. (2016). Internet of things and big data analytics for smart and connected communities. *IEEE Access*, 4, 766–773.

12. Onuki, M., Sato, M., & Sese, J. (2022). Estimating physical/mental health condition using heart rate data from a wearable device. In: *2022 44th Annual International Conference of the IEEE Engineering in Medicine & Biology Society (EMBC)*, Glasgow, Scotland, United Kingdom (pp. 4465–4468). doi:10.1109/EMBC48229.2022.9871910.

13. IEEE. (2022). *IEEE Standard for Wearable Consumer Electronic Devices: Overview and Architecture* (Std 360-2022, pp.1–35). doi: 0.1109/IEEESTD.2022.9762855.

14. Ji, G., Msigwa, C., Bernard, D., Lee, G., Woo, J., & Yun, J. (2023). Health24: Health-related data collection from wearable and mobile devices in everyday lives. In: *2023 IEEE International Conference on Big Data and Smart Computing (BigComp)*, Jeju, Republic of Korea (pp. 336–337). doi:10.1109/BigComp57234.2023.00074.

15. Boonstra, T. W., Nicholas, J., Wong, Q. J., Shaw, F., Townsend, S., & Christensen, H. (2018). Using mobile phone sensor technology for mental health research: Integrated analysis to identify hidden challenges and potential solutions. *Journal of Medical Internet Research*, 20(7), e10131.

16. Ben-Zeev, D., Wang, R., Abdullah, S., Brian, R., Scherer, E. A., Mistler, L. A.,... & Hauser, M. (2016). Mobile behavioral sensing for outpatients and inpatients with schizophrenia. *Psychiatric Services*, 67(5), 558–561.

17. Azevedo, D., Esteves, A., Ribeiro, F., Farinha, L., & Metrôlho, J. (2020). A wearable device for monitoring health risks when children play outdoors. In: *2020 15th Iberian Conference on Information Systems and Technologies (CISTI)*, Seville, Spain (pp. 1–6). doi:10.23919/CISTI49556.2020.9140946.

18. Zhang, B. -Y., Liu, H. -X., & Song, Y. -J. (2023). Analyzing the attractiveness factors of health wearables for older adults using EGM and quantification theory type I. In: *2023 9th International Conference on Control, Automation and Robotics (ICCAR)*, Beijing, China (pp. 136–140). doi:10.1109/ICCAR57134.2023.10151751.

19. Gao, Y., & Dong, X. (2020). Research on the design of wearable health products for older adults based on the concept of humanization. *Industrial Design*, 2020(5), 1–12.
20. Munos, B., Baker, P.C., Bot, B.M., Crouthamel, M., de Vries, G., Ferguson, I., Hixson, J.D., Malek, L.A., Mastrototaro, J.J., Misra, V., Ozcan, A. (2016). Mobile health: the power of wearables, sensors, and apps to transform clinical trials. *Annals of the New York Academy of Sciences*, 1375(1): 3–18.

16 MPPEDet
Medical Personal Protective Equipment Detection Using Deep Learning Algorithm

Prabu Selvam, M. Sumathi, M. Marimuthu, and P. Saravanan

16.1 INTRODUCTION

In the healthcare sector, infectious diseases spread to normal humans and caretakers in a traumatic way. Protecting practitioners and doctors in the healthcare sector is a foremost requirement because if diseases infect the practitioners and doctors, no one is ready to help the infected persons. So, the usage of Medical Personal Protective Equipment (MPPE) is an essential requirement in healthcare organizations. The primary goal of MPPE detection is to measure health and safety compliance. This safety analysis helps to improve productivity in manufacturing sectors and avoids disease spreading in healthcare organizations [1]. The best example of infectious disease spreading is COVID-19. It started spreading in December 2019; it killed over 4,000 patients and infected over 80,000 members. More than 40,000 caretakers were involved in the recovery process to control the spreading of this virus. It shows that the patient and caretakers are closely related, and the virus spreads to the caretakers most quickly. Hence, safeguarding the caretakers is the foremost task [2,3].

According to the National Health Commission guidelines, caretakers should wear MPPE as a primary requirement. Depending on the level of risk, the requirement of MPPE changes. For example, level 2 MPPE is used for moderate-risk cases, including face masks, goggles, gowns, etc.; level 3 includes goggles, gloves, shoes, and N95 masks. In the healthcare industry, MPPE is essential to protect personal and patient health from risky factors. Wearing MPPE helps protect persons from diseases, but it creates heavy sweating and is difficult to wear for long periods. These issues lead to poor usage of MPPE [4]. Conventionally, sensor-based detection techniques and radio frequency-based detection techniques were used for the detection of MPPE. These two techniques must be analyzed for the large dataset size to improve prediction accuracy. However, these techniques required high investments and faced implementation difficulties [14].

Nowadays, MPPE is used in more than 90% of healthcare centres. However, improper usage of MPPE or unawareness of its importance is identified in many places. Hence, training about the proper usage of MPPE is required in the present

"

scenario [3]. Emergency caretakers are the primary at-risk individuals. Saving their health from infected persons is an essential task. Providing proper training to save the lives of caretakers is the simplest process. However, due to difficulties, caretakers may not wear MPPE. Hence, identifying someone not wearing the MPPE kit has become essential. Identifying these individuals is a straightforward process using machine learning and deep learning techniques. Thus, a deep learning-based MPPE detection technique is proposed in this work. Compared to machine learning algorithms, deep learning algorithms require extensive training data to detect objects. Therefore, deep learning is used in the proposed model instead of machine learning models [5].

Object identification is a basic and critical process in image processing and deep learning. The basic requirement of object identification is to identify the object based on the designed models. The accuracy of detection depends on the training and testing models. The selection of a training dataset plays a vital role in this process [6]. Due to the complex working environment (lots of images are combined and captured in live image capturing), detecting PPEs, individual works, and objects takes a significant process. In real-time analysis, most of the images are in the form of multi-class objects. Multiclass object analysis often leads to false object detection [10]. Like machine learning and deep learning techniques, the intelligent detection technique (few-shot-based graphical neural network (GNN)) helps identify the proper wearing of Personal Protective Equipment (PPE). If a person has not worn the PPE properly, the GNN generates an alarm message, and detected images are sent to an investigator for further processing. The images collected from multiple environments work well with 80%–100% accuracy in the GNN-based PPE analysis [11].

YOLO is the most powerful real-time object detection technique compared to other methods and tools. Due to multi-stage processes like searching and classifying objects, the existing technique's processing time is higher than that of the YOLO processing technique. Single-stage processing and neural networks are capable of efficiently analyzing full images. Thus, the processing speed of YOLO is higher than R-CNN and other prediction techniques [15]. Compared to YOLOv3, YOLOv4 and v5 improve accuracy from 10% to 12%. In YOLOv4, different techniques are added (using CSPDarknet53 instead of Darknet53) to improve prediction accuracy. Likewise, advanced data augmentation techniques (Mixup, Grid Mask, Cutmix, random erase, hide and seek, cutout, class label smoothing, etc.) are also adopted in YOLOv4 [16]. YOLOv4 is further improved (adding one more module in the backbone) and released as YOLOv5. CSPNet was integrated into mapping features at the beginning and end of the network to reduce computation time and maintain accuracy. An important feature added in YOLOv5 is an automatic learning process through the input stage. The input stage calculates the anchor box size of different image sizes to improve detection quality [17].

The remaining section of this chapter is organized as follows. Section 16.2 discusses the existing PPE detection techniques with their merits and limitations. Section 16.3 discusses the proposed methodology with necessary architectures, equations, and procedures. In Section 16.4, the experimental results are analyzed in different aspects, and finally, in Section 16.5, the proposed system is concluded with future work.

16.2   RELATED WORKS

This section discusses the existing works related to MPPE detection along with their merits and limitations.

Nath et al. [7] discussed the personal protective equipment (PPE) process differently. The PPE compliance and individual works were simultaneously detected and verified through CNN and achieved nearly 73% of the average precision value. This work contains only two categories of PPE, such as a vest and a hat. It is not sufficient to detect the PPE efficiency. Loey et al. [8] proposed the machine learning-based detection model using different datasets like simulated masked face recognition, face detection, real-world masked face detection, etc. The simulated mask images were analyzed in more detail than the real-world dataset. It is insufficient to detect real-time images, and compared to deep learning, the accuracy of the machine learning algorithms is lower. Protik et al. [9] detect the PPE in real-time personal systems using the YOLOv4 computer vision model and TensorFlow. The real-time images were augmented using training data, and the TensorFlow data formatting was used to detect the live data performance. TensorFlow was used for the existing records and lively captured image processing. Compared to YOLOv2 and YOLOv3, YOLOv4 prediction performance improved [9–11].

Aldossary et al. [12] used computer vision techniques such as YOLOv5 to detect PPE. Using YOLOv5, object detection, classification, identification, and verification are performed accurately. When compared to the existing version, YOLOv5 helps to detect objects like glasses, heads, vests, persons, and helmet colours such as blue, yellow, and red in real-time automatically. This automatic detection reduces the timeline for object detection and decision-making, which helps improve employees' productivity and safety. Wang et al. use YOLOv5x and YOLOv5s for PPE detection in construction sites. The analysis considered six classes (person, vest, helmet, and four colours). Similarly, multiclass PPE was also considered for the analysis. The multiclass PPE includes different gestures, backgrounds, varied angles, and distances. YOLOv5x provides the best mAP (above 87%), and YOLOv5s process the images at high speed (higher than 52 frames per second) on a graphical processing unit (GPU). With the usage of the YOLOv5x process, the blurred image analysis accuracy was improved by more than 7% [13–17].

Xiong et al. [18] discussed the multiclass PPE detection techniques. The spatial anchors and localization of part attention regions are used for detecting the PPE in worker body parts. The part attention regions were used to analyze part attention regions on the local images. Afterwards, the CNN classifier was used for classifying the PPE and non-PPE classes. This integrated technique provides accuracy from 95% to 97%. Dagli et al. [19] discussed the CPPE:5 Dataset-based MPPE detection. This CPPE:5 dataset includes real-life non-iconic images like masks, coveralls, gloves, goggles, and face shields. These images have been annotated with positive labels and bounding boxes. CPPE:5 dataset images were collected from Google original images, filter unsuitable images, filter near-similar images, etc. Compared to Real-World Masked Face Dataset (RMFD), Microsoft COCO, and PASCAL VOC dataset, the CPPE: 5 dataset contains fine-grained images. Kumar et al. [20] used the YOLOv4 technique of real-time object detection in MPPE. The YOLOv4 technique is used to detect PPEs, injuries, and fire accidents. The synthetic dataset was used for detecting the objects. The model was trained by a large related dataset and retrained by a smaller desired dataset to improve the prediction accuracy. These two stages of the training process adapted the higher and mid-level features.

Bhing et al. [21] discussed PPE detection with a live camera. Manual annotation processes like web-scraping techniques collected the dataset. These data cover controlled and uncontrolled environments. The controlled environment images contain security cameras, images from suppliers, and images from journalists. This controlled image processing is not a difficult process. The MPPE is directly identified from the controlled images. In an uncontrolled environment, the public surveillance camera, photographer's candid shots, view of the sight, illumination conditions, face shooting distance, etc. The uncontrolled environmental image processing increases the processing complexity and reduces the prediction accuracy. Isailovic et al. [22] proposed using the YOLOv5 technique for PPE detection. The public PPE dataset and web-mined dataset images were combined and used for object identification. The images constructed for the multiclass objects were collected from different working environments. Vaidya et al. [23] proposed the auto-detection of PPE in humans. Object identification was performed on various classes like image or video datasets. The CNN frameworks divide the images into the number of windows and fix images on the window size. The perfectly fitted image was selected for the next stage. The selected image is fed to SVM classifier for the labelling process. The image dataset was processed separately, stored in a separate location, and sent to the display. The voice-altering message was sent to the individuals.

Wu et al. [24] proposed the improved YOLOv5 for MPPE detection. Due to overlapping and occlusion, the prediction accuracy rate of the existing techniques is low for real-time systems. To improve the prediction accuracy of YOLOv5, the backbone network feature was improved. The C3 module was merged with the feature fusion module in this feature improvement. The up-sampling enhancement module used up-sampled mapping of global features and semantic information. The ELoU loss function was used to achieve a higher accuracy rate. This improved YOLOv5 technique provides above 97% mAP and efficiency. Collo et al. [25] used the deep learning technique for PPE detection. The YOLOv3 detection technique has been used for detection. This YOLOv3 provides more than 96% detection rate for the complete dataset and nearly 40%–80% (due to the variation of medical equipment) accuracy rate for incomplete PPE. Li et al. [26] standardized the PPE inspection using deep learning techniques. The YOLOv5 technique was used on videos with safe and unsafe behaviours and also analyzed the time-series data. More than 1,200 videos were considered for the process. Six hundred videos have been used for training, and the remaining 600 videos have been used for testing (50:50 ratio of training and testing data) [27]. This technique achieved nearly 95% of prediction accuracy.

The limitations of the current MPPE detection techniques are listed as follows:

- The existing MPPE detection techniques focus on limited types of objects like helmets, gloves, etc., not all objects.
- MPPE detection is considered in a limited number of colour image processing.

- Machine and deep learning-based detection techniques are in the development stage and need to improve significantly to enhance the prediction accuracy.
- Blurring image processing is in the initial stage only. The accuracy rate in blurred image processing needs improvement.
- A proper dataset is required, covering different gestures, backgrounds, multiclass objects, angles, and distances.

16.3 PROPOSED SYSTEM

YOLOv7 is a robust object detection framework that enables real-time identification and localization of objects within images or video streams. It aims to address previous models' limitations and helps improve accuracy. Building upon its predecessor, YOLOv7 introduces the extended-efficient layer aggregation network (E-ELAN) architecture, which enhances the network's self-learning capability without compromising the original gradient path. Additionally, it incorporates a cascade-based model scaling method to generate appropriately scaled models tailored to specific detection requirements. These innovative techniques and architectures significantly enhance the performance and effectiveness of the YOLO series networks by leveraging its capabilities to develop a system to detect and recognize various MPPE objects commonly used in medical environments, including Mask, Face_Shield, Gloves, Goggles, and Coverall. This system can serve as a valuable tool for monitoring MPPE compliance among healthcare workers, helping to ensure their safety and minimize the transmission of infectious diseases. Figure 16.1 shows the overall architecture of the YOLOv7 model. The YOLOv7 architecture is divided into three main sections: Backbone, Neck, and Head. The major features of YOLOv7 are the ability to use ordinary Graphics Processing Unit (GPU) computing and tiny model edge GPU. This tiny edge assists edge computing and machine learning applications in object detection. Similarly, it processes large amounts of images and can store them in cloud GPU computing. Depending on the requirement, YOLOv7-E6 or YOLOv7-D6 is used in object detection.

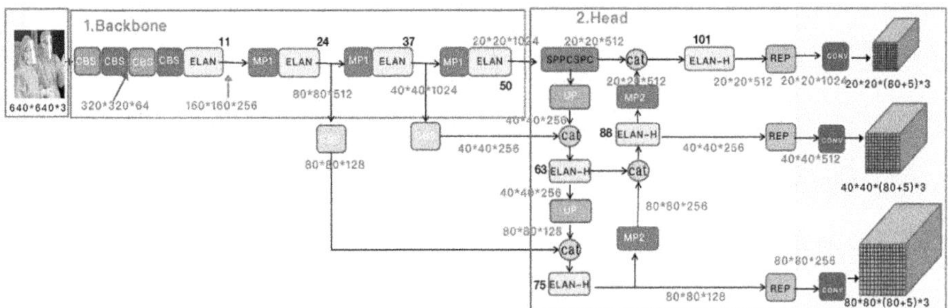

FIGURE 16.1 Overall architecture of the YOLOv7 algorithm.

16.3.1 BACKBONE

The YOLO algorithm is built upon the DarkNet backbone network, originally developed by Joseph Redmon. Various versions of the YOLO algorithm have been optimized based on this foundational architecture. YOLOv7's backbone network comprises several essential modules: CBS, E-ELAN, MP, and SPPCSPC.

- **CBS**: CBS stands for the Cross Stage Partial (CSP) module with a Bottleneck (B) structure. It is the fundamental building block among these modules and is seamlessly integrated into the other modules to enhance their functionality and performance. The CBS block is composed of $Conv + BN + SiLU$. Figure 16.2 illustrates the CBS blocks.

    In Figure 16.2, different CBS modules are represented by distinct colours to signify various sizes and strides. For instance, the notation (3, 2) indicates that the convolution kernel size is 3, and the stride or step size is set to 2. This visualization helps differentiate and highlight the configurations and parameters associated with each CBS module.
- **E-ELAN**: The E-ELAN architecture integrated into YOLOv7 enhances the model's learning capabilities by implementing "Expand, Shuffle, and Merge cardinality". This process continuously improves the network's learning ability while preserving the integrity of the original gradient path. The pipeline structure of E-ELAN is illustrated in Figure 16.3.

    In terms of architecture, the only alteration is made to the computational block, while the transition layer remains unchanged and consistent with ELAN, as depicted in Figure 16.4a. E-ELAN utilizes group convolution to

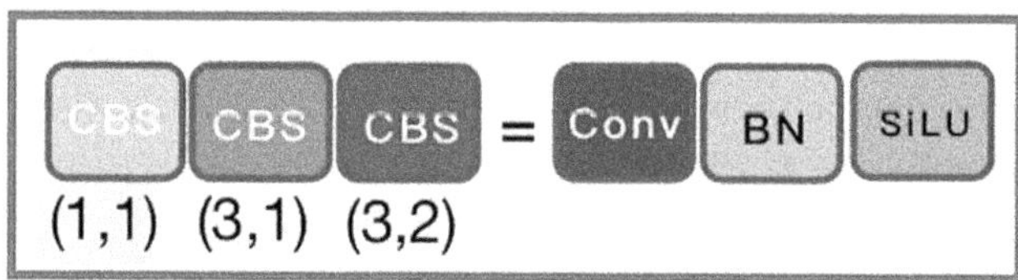

FIGURE 16.2 Illustration of CBS blocks.

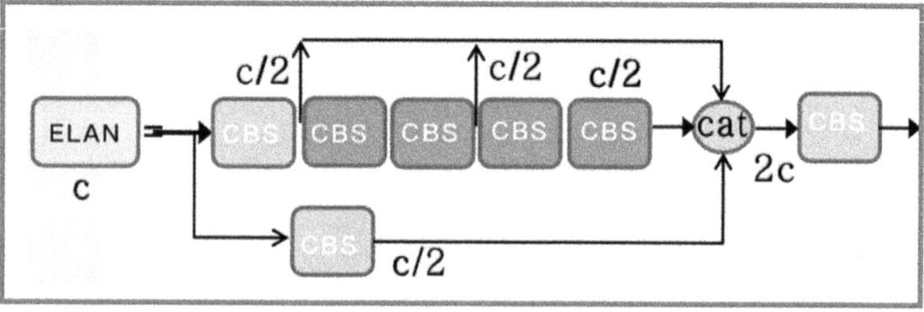

FIGURE 16.3 Illustration of E-ELAN blocks.

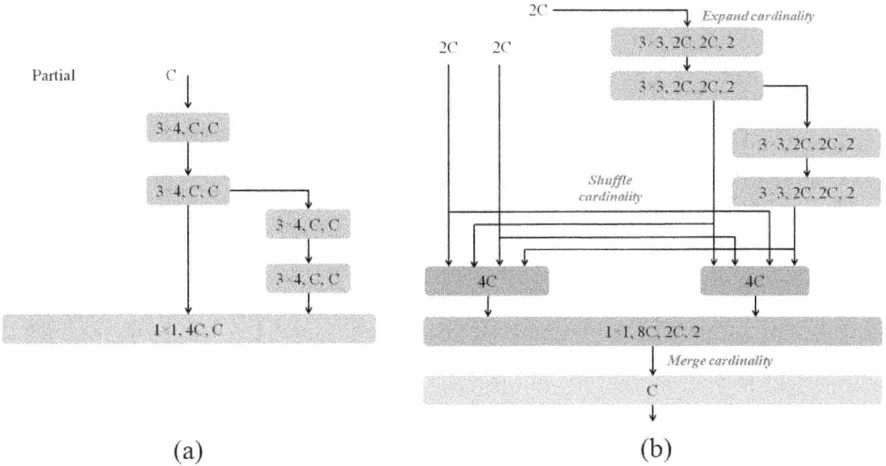

FIGURE 16.4   (a) ELAN block. (b) E-ELAN block.

increase the number of channels and the cardinality of the computational block. A uniform channel multiplier and group parameter are applied to all computational blocks within a computation layer. The feature map generated by each computational block is then shuffled into groups of size 'g' and subsequently combined. This merged cardinality operation is performed by adding the shuffled group feature map. The pipeline structure of E-ELAN is shown in Figure 16.4b.

ELAN consists of multiple Channel Bottleneck Structures (CBSs), which maintain the input and output feature sizes while allowing for changes in the number of channels within the first two CBSs. Subsequently, the input and output channels remain the same for the subsequent CBSs. The desired channel is ultimately obtained as the output after the last CBS.

- **Model scaling**: Model scaling is a crucial concept that involves increasing or decreasing the depth, resolution of an image, and width of a model. Scaling the depth refers to adjusting the number of layers in the model, while scaling the width corresponds to modifying the number of channels in the model architecture. The scaling factors specified in the model architecture files determine both depth and width. Figure 16.5 shows the model scaling.

  In the case of YOLOv7, its architecture is concatenated with other layers. When scaling the depth parameter of a computational block, it is necessary to calculate the corresponding change in the output kernels. Additionally, the width should be scaled by the same amount as the calculated change in kernels. This compound scaling approach ensures that the architecture's original properties and optimal structure are preserved. Figure 16.6 provides a visual representation of the compound scaling method.

- **MP block**: The MP block consists of a MaxPool layer and a CBS module for downsampling, as shown in Figure 16.7. MP1 and MP2 mainly aim to change the ratio of the number of channels.

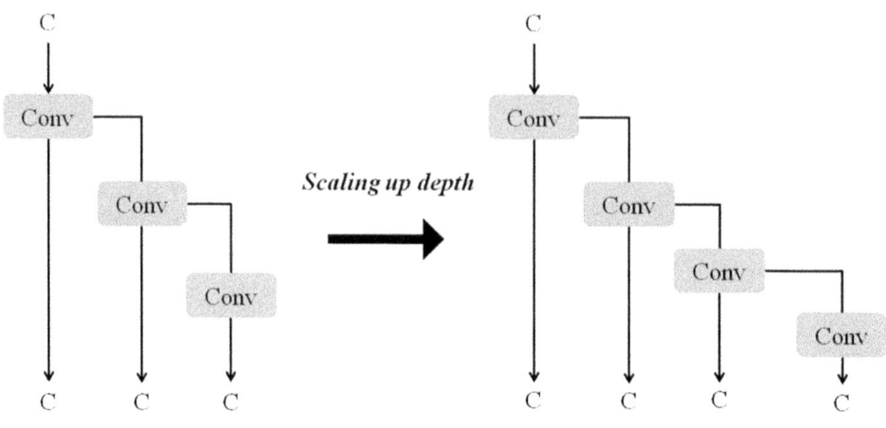

FIGURE 16.5 Model scaling.

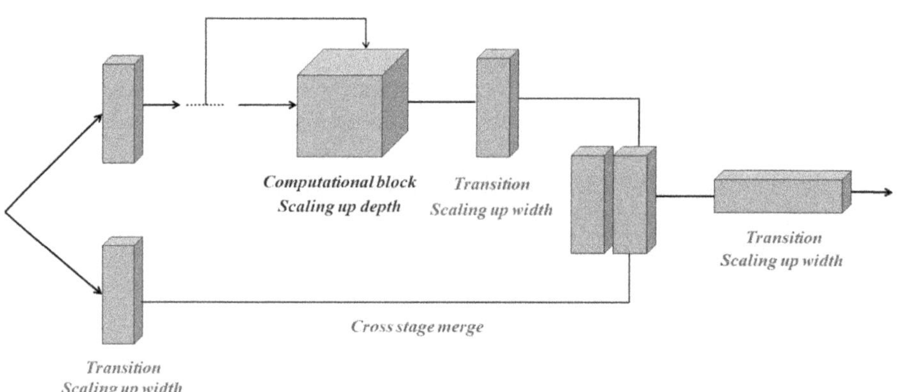

FIGURE 16.6 Model compound scaling.

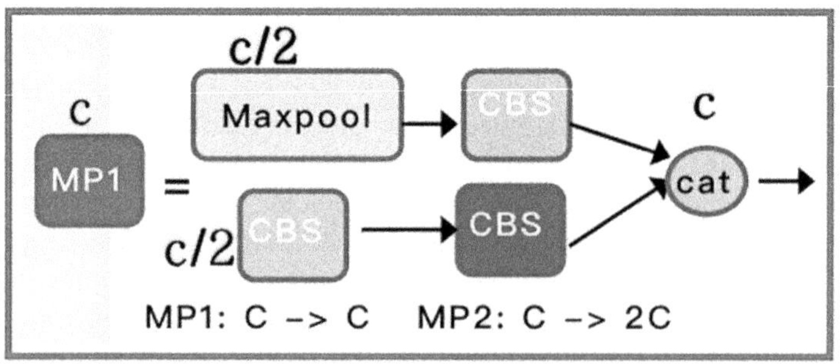

FIGURE 16.7 MP Block.

16.3.2 Neck

The neck of YOLOv7 comprises two components: the Path Aggregation Network (PAN) and the Feature Pyramid Network (FPN). The backbone's 32-fold downsampling feature map is processed by the SPPCSP module within the neck. The SPPCSP module expands the receptive field and isolates the most prominent contextual features. It achieves downsampling by utilizing max-pooling layers and CBS layers of various sizes (see Figure 16.8). This module reduces the number of channels from 1,024 to 512. These reduced feature maps undergo feature fusion using top-down and bottom-up approaches. Figure 16.8 shows the SPPCSP module.

Compared to YOLOv5, YOLOv7 introduces the ELAN-H module as a replacement for the CSP module (see Figure 16.9). Additionally, the downsampling step is now accomplished by the MP2 layer. The PA-FPN structure efficiently merges feature maps from various levels. The different modules within the neck section facilitate the transmission of semantic information and enhance the ability to extract multiscale targets. Figure 16.9 shows the ELAN-H module.

16.3.3 Head

After passing through the PA-FPN network, the network generates three layers of feature maps with different sizes. Ultimately, the prediction results are obtained by processing these feature maps using the RepC and Conv modules in the head section of the network.

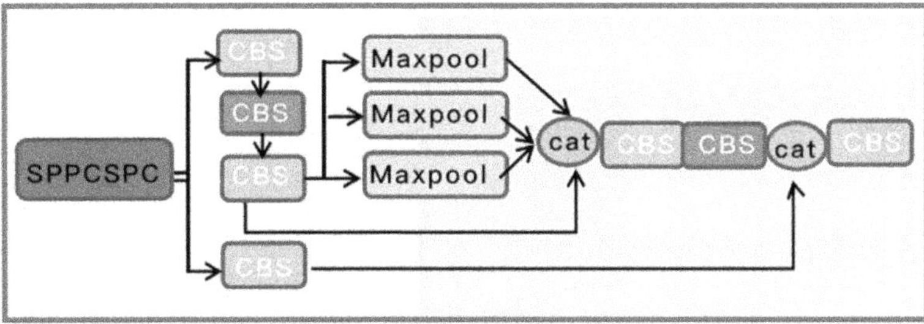

FIGURE 16.8 SPPCSP module.

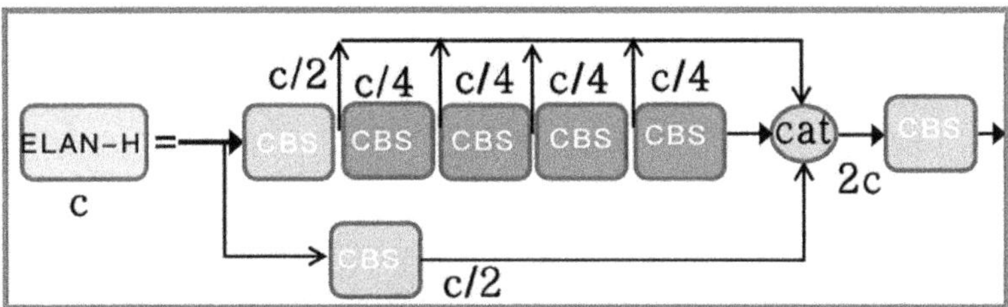

FIGURE 16.9 ELAN-H module.

16.4 EXPERIMENTAL ANALYSIS

16.4.1 Dataset Details

The Medical Personal Protective Equipment (CPPE-5) dataset comprises 2,928 images and 4,698 object annotations, including 1,343 glove annotations, 1,304 mask annotations, 1,197 coverall annotations, 447 face shield annotations, and 407 goggle annotations, as shown in Table 16.1. Most of the images were acquired from Flickr and Google Images. On average, the CPPE-5 dataset contains 4.57 annotations per image. Generally, smaller objects are more challenging to recognize and require greater contextual reasoning for recognition. The CPPE-5 dataset has an average image size of 946.94 pixels. Figure 16.10 shows sample images from the CPPE-5 dataset.

TABLE 16.1

Dataset Details

Classes	No. of Instances	Total No. of Images	Average Annotations/Image
Mask	1,304	898	1.45
Face_Shield	447	344	1.30
Gloves	1,343	575	2.34
Goggles	407	312	1.30
Coverall	1,197	799	1.50
Total	4,698	2,928	4.57

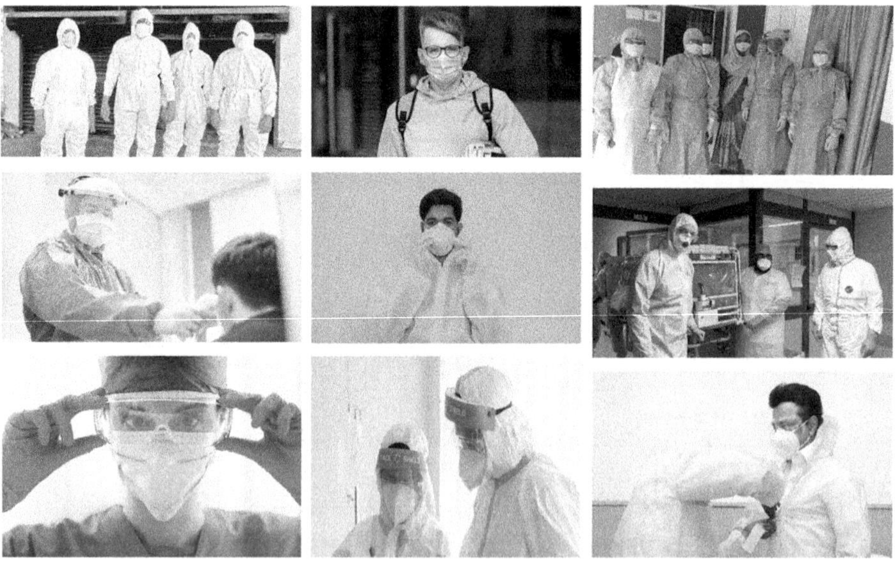

FIGURE 16.10   Sample CPPE-5 dataset images.

16.4.2 Evaluation Metrics

The performance of the object detector is evaluated using three essential metrics: Precision, Recall, and F-Measure.

- **Precision**: Precision refers to a model's capacity to identify relevant objects accurately. It represents the percentage of correct positive predictions within a specific class and can be calculated as follows (Equation 16.1):

$$\text{Precision} = \frac{T_P}{(T_P + F_P)} = \frac{T_P}{\text{All\_Detections}} \tag{16.1}$$

- **Recall**: Recall, also called Sensitivity or True-Positive-Rate, measures a model's ability to identify all relevant cases or ground truth bounding boxes. It represents the percentage of true positives detected among all relevant ground truths within a specific class and can be expressed as follows (Equation 16.2):

$$\text{Recall} = \frac{T_P}{(T_P + F_N)} = \frac{T_P}{\text{All\_ground\_truths}} \tag{16.2}$$

- **F-measure**: The F-measure evaluates a model's overall performance in identifying objects by combining precision and recall. It gauges the model's accuracy in locating all relevant objects (recall) and correctly identifying them (precision). It has been calculated through the harmonic mean of precision and recall, and the F-measure comprehensively evaluates the model's performance. It considers both precision and recall, particularly when they exhibit contrasting values. The formula for calculating the F-measure is as follows (Equation 16.3):

$$\text{F-measure} = 2 * \frac{(\text{Precision} * \text{Recall})}{(\text{Precision} + \text{Recall})} \tag{16.3}$$

The F-measure ranges from 0 to 1, where 1 indicates prime performance, and 0 represents poor performance. A higher F-measure value indicates better overall performance in object detection tasks.

- **Mean average precision (mAP)**: mAP refers to the mathematical representation of the average precision (AP) of all classes (let's say for N number of classes) provided in the test model. Equation (16.4) shows the calculation of mAP.

$$\text{mAP} = \frac{\sum_{i=1}^{N} AP_i}{N} \tag{16.4}$$

16.4.3 Experimental Results

The proposed system is implemented using the PyTorch framework. All experiments were conducted on a Lenovo ThinkStation P700 Workstation with an Intel Xeon E5-2620 v3 dual processor, 96 GB RAM, and NVIDIA Quadro K2200 graphics card [28]. To carry out MPPE identification, we employed the YOLOv7 object detector. The CPPE-5 dataset was used for training and testing our detection network. Since this dataset lacks an annotation format, we manually annotated the images using Labellmg and consolidated them with the corresponding text files in a single directory. Table 16.2 describes the training and parameter details of our object detector.

We divided the data into three subsets: 80% of the images were utilized for training, 10% for validation, and the remaining 10% for testing, following an 80:10:10 ratio. The learning rate was set to 0.01. We optimized the object detector using the Adam algorithm with a batch size of 16. Adam combines the favourable characteristics of both the AdaGrad and RMSProp algorithms, resulting in faster computation and fewer tuning parameters. It offers relative ease of configuration, and its default parameters perform well on complex problems. Adam outperforms other optimization algorithms regarding stability and accuracy, making it our preferred choice for our object detection task. The activation function for the hidden layer is Leaky ReLU, while the final detection layer uses the sigmoid function. The chosen loss functions are Box Loss and Object Loss. We conduct single-scale testing to ensure a fair comparison and employ polygonal non-maximum suppression to remove redundant detections. These parameters and models are crucial in the MPPE Detection process and contribute to the overall performance and accuracy of the system.

Based on the confusion matrix in Figure 16.11, the TP, TN, FP, and FN are determined separately for each class. Performance metrics such as Precision, Recall, and F-measure are calculated for each class using the YOLOv7 model. These performance metrics can be seen in Figures 16.12–16.14. The YOLOv7-based object detection model demonstrates the highest F-measure among the classes, achieving 96.66% for the mask object class, 90.11% for face shields, 95.88% for gloves, 91.91% for goggles, and 95.82% for the Coverall.

Table 16.3 evaluates different metrics for five classes, namely Mask, Face_Shield, Gloves, Goggles, and Coverall. Precision, recall, and F-measure are the metrics used

TABLE 16.2
Parameter Details

Model Parameters	MPPE Detection
Training: validation: testing	80: 10: 10
Learning rate	0.01
Batch size	16
Number of epochs	300
Activation functions	Leaky ReLU and sigmoid
Optimization algorithm	Adam
Loss function	Box loss and object loss

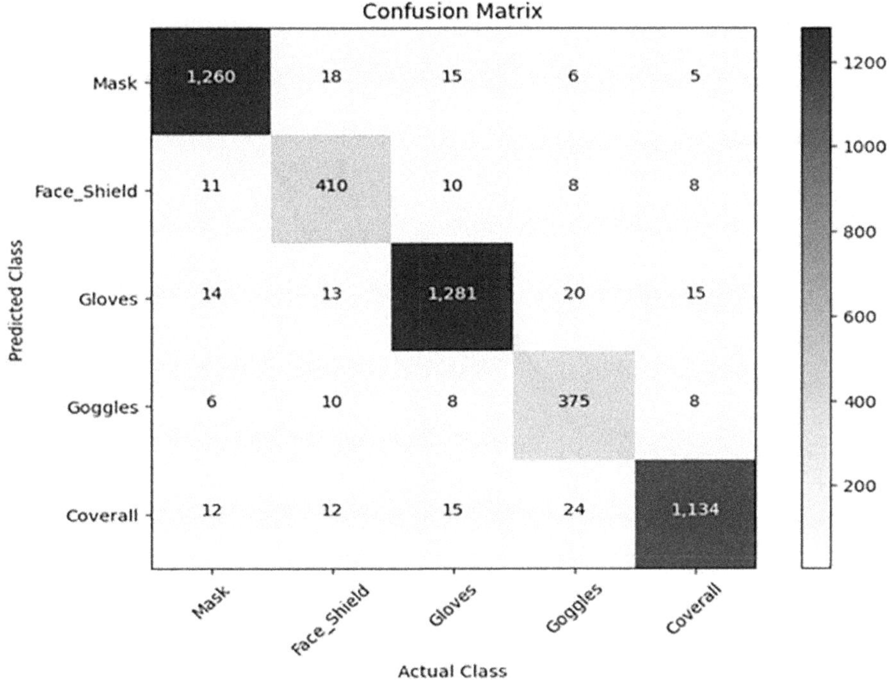

FIGURE 16.11 Confusion matrix.

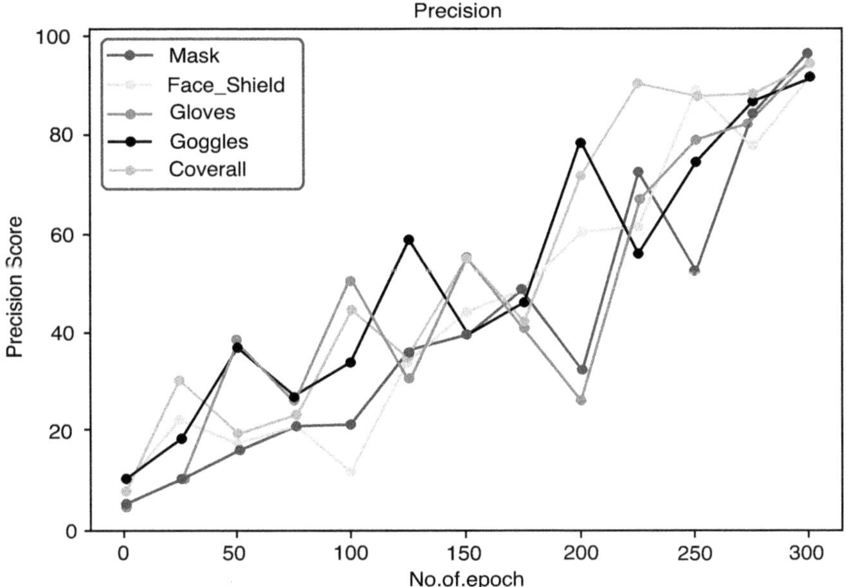

FIGURE 16.12 Precision curves.

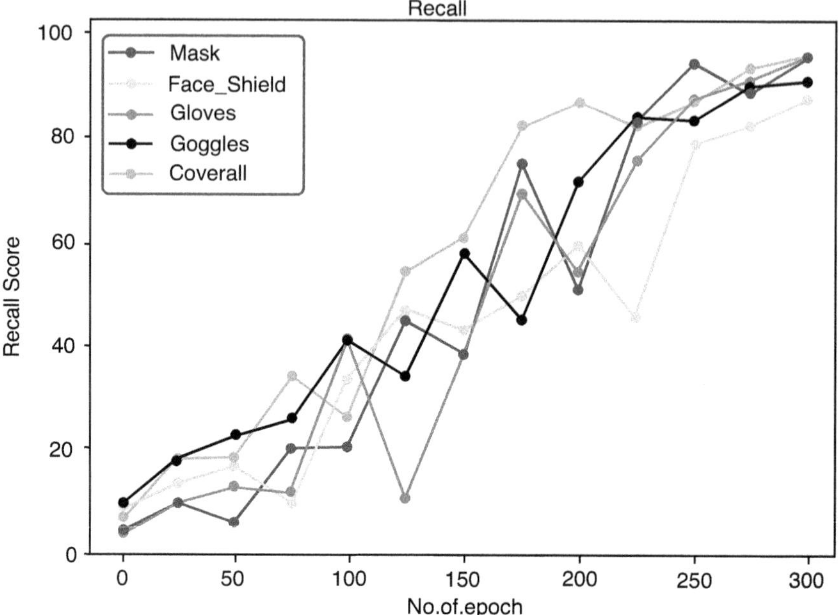

FIGURE 16.13   Recall curves.

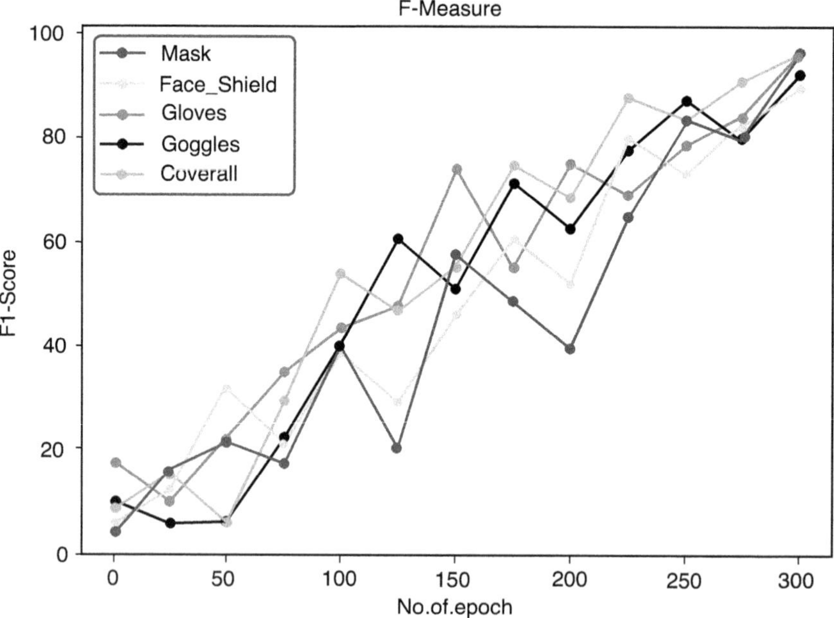

FIGURE 16.14   F-Measure curves.

TABLE 16.3

Class-Wise Precision, Recall and F-Measure Results of the YOLOv7 Algorithm

Evaluation Metric	Mask	Face_Shield	Gloves	Goggles	Coverall
Precision	96.63	91.72	95.38	92.14	94.74
Recall	96.7	88.55	96.39	91.69	96.92
F-Measure	96.66	90.11	95.88	91.91	95.82

to assess the object detection performance for each class. Precision refers to the accuracy of correctly identifying the objects of a specific class. In this evaluation, Mask achieved a precision of 96.63%, Face_Shield achieved 91.72%, Gloves achieved 95.38%, Goggles achieved 92.14%, and Coverall achieved 94.74%. Figure 16.12 illustrates the precision graph generated after 300 epochs.

Recall measures the ability of the model to identify all relevant objects of a specific class. The evaluation shows that Mask achieved a recall of 96.7%, Face_Shield achieved 88.55%, Gloves achieved 96.39%, Goggles achieved 91.69%, and Coverall achieved 96.92%. F-measure combines precision and recall to provide a single value representing the model's overall performance. Figure 16.13 illustrates the recall graph generated after 300 epochs.

The F-measure scores for the different classes are as follows: Mask—96.66%, Face_Shield—90.11%, Gloves—95.88%, Goggles—91.91%, and Coverall—95.82%. These metrics provide valuable insights into the performance of the object detection system for each class, allowing for a comprehensive evaluation of the model's accuracy and effectiveness in identifying specific objects. Figure 16.14 illustrates the F-measure graph generated after 300 epochs (Table 16.4).

Figure 16.15 depicts the sample results of the YOLOv7 algorithm. Unlike other object detectors (SSD, Fast R-CNN, Faster R-CNN, and SqueezeDet), the YOLOv5 model demonstrates significant improvement in performance with a precision score of 79.33%, a recall score of 75.32%, and an F-measure score of 77.27%. However, advanced approaches like E-ELAN and model scaling drive the YOLOv7 algorithm to achieve the highest precision among the models evaluated, with a

TABLE 16.4

Performance Comparison of YOLOv7 with Other Object Detectors

Methods	Precision (%)	Recall (%)	F-Measure (%)
SSD	36.47	25.87	30.27
Fast R-CNN	41.21	38.94	40.04
Faster R-CNN	51.88	36.84	43.09
SqueezeDet	55.63	48.52	51.83
YOLOv5	79.33	75.32	77.27
YOLOv7	94.05	94.12	94.08

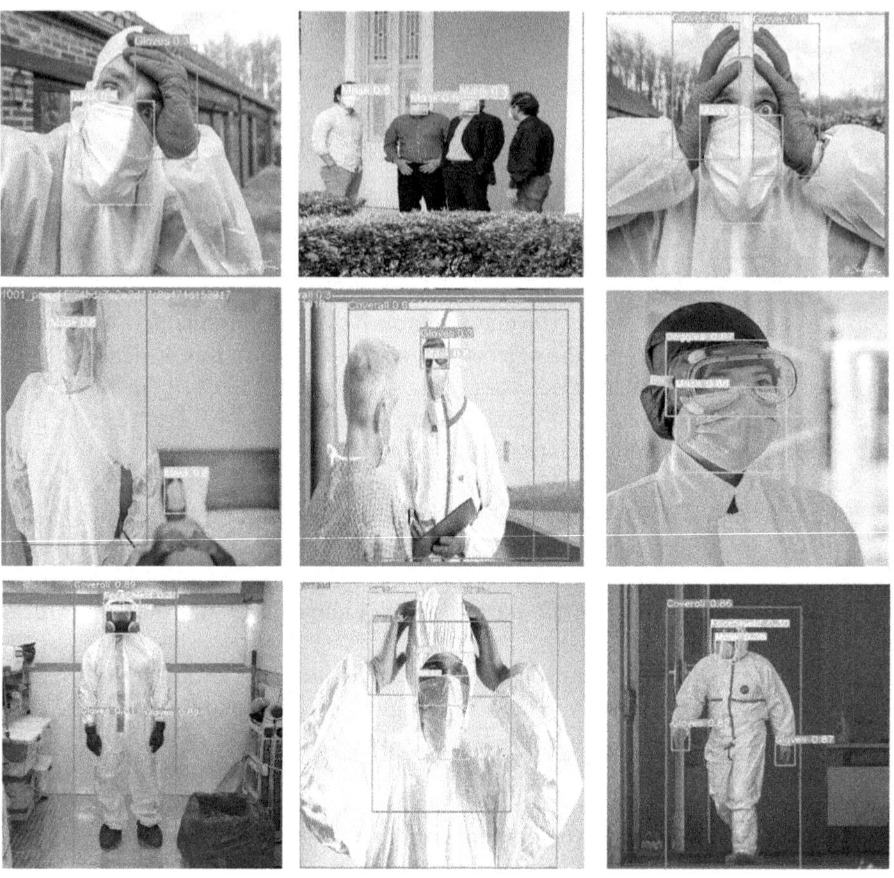

FIGURE 16.15   Sample result obtained by the YOLOv7 object detector.

score of 94.05%, while also maintaining a high recall of 94.12% and an impressive F-measure of 94.08%.

16.5   CONCLUSION

MPPE is essential for safeguarding healthcare workers and patients from infectious diseases. Proper selection, usage, and disposal of MPPE are critical for preventing the spread of infections and protecting healthcare workers from exposure. Due to the substantial presence of occlusion and overlapping, traditional image processing techniques find it difficult to detect real-time MPPE objects. The YOLOv7 algorithm addresses these issues. Maintaining the integrity of the original gradient path, the E-ELAN approach uses the "Expand, Shuffle, and Merge cardinality" principles, amplifying the model's learning capacity. Accommodating objects of different sizes or dimensions, the compound model scaling approach scales both the network depth and width while simultaneously concatenating layers. This technique effectively maintains the optimal architecture. The module-level re-parameterization reduces the inference speed and improves the detection accuracy. The performance of the YOLOv7 algorithm is assessed using the CPPE-5 dataset, which contains non-iconic images, all of which are real-time images. The predicted results improved the detection score from 8.6% to 12.3%. Unlike other object detectors (SSD, Fast R-CNN, Faster R-CNN, and SqueezeDet), the YOLOv5 model demonstrates significant improvement in performance with a precision score of 79.33%, a recall score of 75.32%, and an F-measure score of 77.27%. The YOLOv7 algorithm achieved the highest precision score of 94.05%, recall of 94.12%, and F-measure of 94.08%. Overall, the proposed system achieves better detection results for small and medium object detection than the most popular object detection algorithms, including YOLOv5, Fast-RCNN SSD, and Faster-RCNN.

REFERENCES

1. R. Barratt, M. Wyer, S.-Y. Hor, G. L. Gibert, Medical interns' reflections on their training in use of personal protective equipment, *BMS Medical Education*, 2020;20(1):328.
2. Q. Jiang, S. Song, J. Zhou, Y. Liu, A. Chen, Y. Bai, J. Wang, Z. Jiang, Y. Zhang, H. Liu, J. Hua, J. Guo, Q. Han, Y. Tang, J. Xue, The prevalence, characteristics, and prevention status of skin injury caused by personal protective equipment among medical staff in fighting COVID-19: A multicenter, cross-sectional study. *Advances in Wound Care* (New Rochelle), 2020;9(7):357–364. doi: 10.1089/wound.2020.1212.
3. A. John, M. E. Tomas, A. Hari, B. M. Wilson, C. J. Donskey, Do medical students receive training in correct use of personal protective equipment?, *Medical Education Online*, 2017;22(1):1264125.
4. Q. Jiang et al., The prevalence, characteristics, and related factors pressure injury in medical staff wearing personal protective equipment against COVID-19 in china: A multicenter cross-sectional survey, *International Wound Journal*, 2020;17:1300–1310.
5. S. Prabu, Object segmentation based on the integration of adaptive K-means and GrabCut algorithm, In: *2022 International Conference on Wireless Communications Signal Processing and Networking (WiSPNET)* (March 2022, pp. 213–216). IEEE.
6. P. Selvam, J. A. S. Koilraj, A deep learning framework for grocery product detection and recognition, *Food Analytical Methods*, 2022;15(12):3498–3522.
7. N. D. Nath, A. H. Behzadan, S. G. Paal, Deep learning for site safety: real-time detection of personal protective equipment, *Automation in Construction*, 2020;112:103085
8. M. Loey, G. Manogaran, M. II. N. Taha, N. E. M. Khalifa, A hybrid deep transfer learning model with machine learning methods for face mask detection in the era of the covid-19 pandemic, *Measurement*, 2021;161:108288.
9. A. A. Protik, A. H. Rafi, S. Siddique, Real-time personal protective equipment detection using Yolov4 and Tensorflow, In: *2021 IEEE REGION 10 Symposium, Jeju, Republic of Korea,* pp. 1-6. (2021).
10. S. Prabu, K. J. Abraham Sundar, Enhanced attention-based encoder-decoder framework for text recognition, *Intelligent Automation & Soft Computing*, 2023;35(2):2071–2086.
11. M. Zhao, M. Barati, Substation safety awareness intelligent model fast personal protective equipment detection using GNN approach, *IEEE Transactions on Industry Applications*, 2023;59:3143–3152.
12. R. S. Aldossary, M. N. Almutairi, S. Dursun, Personal protective equipment detection using computer vision technique, In: *Gas & Oil Technology Showcase and Conference*, Dubai, UAE (2023).

13. Z. Wang, Y. Wu, L. Yang, A. Thirunavukarasu, C. Evison, Y. Zhao, Fast personal protective equipment detection for real construction sites using deep learning approaches, *Sensors*, 2021;21:3478.

14. H. Zhang, X. Yan, H. Li, R. Jin, H. F. Fu, Real-time alarming, monitoring, and locating for non-hard-hat use in construction, *Journal of Construction Engineering and Management Construction*, 2019;145:1–13.

15. J. Redmon, and A. Farhadi, Yolov3: An incremental improvement. *arXiv preprint arXiv:1804.02767*. 2018, 1–6.

16. A. Bochkovskiy, C. Y. Wang, H. Y. M. Liao, YOLOv4: Optimal speed and accuracy of object detection. *arXiv preprint arXiv:2004.10934*. 2020, 1–17.

17. C. Y. Wang, H. Y. Mark Liao, Y. H. Wu, P. Y. Chen, J. W. Hsieh, I. H. Yeh, CSPNet: A new backbone that can enhance learning capability of CNN, In: *Proceedings of the 2020 IEEE/CVF Conference on Computer Vision and Pattern Recognition Workshop (CVPRW)*, Seattle, WA, USA. 14–19 June 2020, pp. 1571–1580.

18. R. Xiong, P. Tang, Pose guided anchoring for detecting proper use of personal protective equipment, *Automation in Construction*, 2021;130:1–15.

19. R. Dagli, A. M. Shlkh, CPPE-5: Medical personal protective equipment dataset, *SN Computer Science*, 2023;4:263.

20. S. Kumar, H. Gupta, D. Yadav, I. A. Ansari, O. P. Verma, YOLOv4 algorithm for the real-time detection of fire and personal protective equipments at construction sites, *Multimedia Tools and Applications*, 2023;81:22163–22183.

21. N. W. Bhing, P. Sebastian, Personal protective equipment detection with live camera, *2021 In: IEEE International Conference on Signal and Image Processing Applications, Kuala Terengganu, Malaysia* (2021, pp. 1–6).

22. V. Isailovic et al., Compilance of head-mounted personal protective equipment by using YOLOv5 object detector, in: *Proceeding of the International Conference on Electrical, Computer and Energy Technologies, Cape Town, South Africa* (2021, pp. 1–5).

23. C. Vaidya et al, "Auto detection of personal protective equipment on human", In: *2023 IEEE International Studetns Conference on Electrical, Electronics and Computer Science* (2023, pp. 1–5).

24. B. Wu, C. Pang, X. Zeng, X. Hu, ME-YOLO: Improved YOLOv5 for detecting medical personal protective equipment, *Applied Sciences*, 2022, 12(23):1–17.

25. M. L. R.Collo ct al. A COVID-19 safety monitoring system: Personal protective equipment detection using deep learning, In: *2022 International Conference on Decision aid Sciences and Applications, Chiangrai, Thailand* (2022, pp. 1–5).

26. J. Li, X. Zhao, G. Zhou, M. Zhang, Standardized use inspection of workers personal protective equipment based on deep learning, *Safety Science*, 2022, 150:1–16.

27. P. Selvam, J. A. S. Koilraj, C. A. T. Romero, M. Alharbi, A. Mehbodniya, J. L. Webber, S. Sengan, A transformer-based framework for scene text recognition. *IEEE Access*, 2022;10:100895–100910.

28. S. Prabu, N. Jawali, K. J. A. Sundar, K. Sharvani, G. Shanmukhanjali, V. Nirmala, *Indian coin detection and recognition using deep learning algorithm*, In: *2022 6th Asian Conference on Artificial Intelligence Technology (ACAIT)* (December 2022, pp. 1–6). IEEE.

17 Evaluation of the Computerized Accounting Information System (CAIS) in Smart Healthcare Systems
Examples of Turkey

Seval Kardeş Selimoğlu, Mehtap Altunel, and Gül Yeşilçelebi

17.1 INTRODUCTION

Information is one of the most important factors contributing to the competitiveness of businesses. The accounting information system is the oldest information-generating system for businesses [16]. The accounting information system has an important place among the systems that produce the information needed for effective business management. Integrating this system with other functions of the enterprise in such a way as to provide information exchange will increase the performance of the other functions of the enterprise and ultimately the enterprise as a whole [16]. At this point, the use of technology will affect all functions together with accounting, resulting in positive business performance.

Security and privacy are key concerns in the Internet of Things (IoT) due to the massive scale and deployment of IoT networks. Blockchain (BC) and machine learning (ML) technologies have significantly enhanced the possibilities and capabilities of Healthcare 5.0, giving rise to a new field known as "Smart Healthcare" [18]. Smart healthcare is the advancement of traditional healthcare with advanced internet technologies. It combines a variety of technologies to process real-time health-related data collected from users of smart wearables and provide real-time healthcare costs as determined from collected observations [25]. A smart healthcare system can help prevent long-term damage by detecting concerns early. This will improve patients' quality of life while reducing stress and healthcare costs. IoT provides a set of functionalities in the field of information technology, one of which is intelligent and interactive healthcare. However, combining medical data in a single storage location to train a powerful machine learning model raises compliance concerns with ownership, privacy, and greater concentration [18].

DOI: 10.1201/9781032632223-17

When accounting and the health sector are considered together, it will be more useful to explain medical accounting first. In this way, the relationship between health service organizations and accounting will be revealed. To define medical accounting: The operations carried out by the accounting department, which systematically monitors the pricing, invoicing, tracking, and collection of the costs incurred after the service procurement from the health institution to the Social Security Institution, are called medical accounting. The specialist personnel who carry out the aforementioned transactions are called medical accounting specialists. Considering the scope of medical accounting, it has a comprehensive framework from hospital management to information processing, from contracted institutions to emergency services. Therefore, it has many duties such as document tracking, social security institutions, invoicing, purchasing processes, and information processing processes [12]. The use of new technologies is important in the effective execution of all these.

The Internet of Medical Things (IoMT) is a network of healthcare aids and devices such as wearables, medical devices, and implantable devices that are connected and able to communicate with the Internet. BC technology can design a secure, decentralized system for storing data in IoMT-based smart healthcare enterprise storage. Patient records are stored in a tamper-proof and decentralized manner using BC, which ensures high confidentiality and security for patients. In addition, BC improves the quality of healthcare by enabling the efficient and secure sharing of healthcare data between patients and healthcare professionals [4].

Technology has many benefits in storing, analyzing, and protecting information in a meaningful way. Against the increasing amount of fraud in health systems, taking measures against fraud in the health system is another issue. For example, Saldamli et al., with particular emphasis on health insurance. In order to prevent fraud in health insurance, features from all insurance systems should be integrated first. Subsequently, a system should be established for the secure management and monitoring of insurance transactions. A blockchain-based solution would be useful for health insurance fraud detection, as blockchain technology provides immutable data maintenance and sharing [19]. As artificial intelligence (AI) technologies continue to evolve, they will play an increasingly vital role in healthcare in the future, particularly in revenue cycle management. "AI has the potential to automate repetitive tasks, reduce errors, and enable predictive analytics, leading to more efficient and effective revenue cycle management" [10].

The explanation of medical accounting, which is a concept that comes to the forefront when accounting in health enterprises is mentioned, and its place in the accounting system in health enterprises is revealed. Then, the development of technology in the health sector and the reflection of this development on accounting, cost accounting, effective business processes, fraud prevention, etc., are discussed, focusing on their effects on these issues.

17.2 SMART HEALTHCARE SYSTEMS

Although IoT technology is used in many different areas, new areas of use continue to emerge, and thus it is expected to have great benefits in many sectors. For example, in the healthcare sector, IoT can make significant contributions to remote monitoring of health conditions and performing remote surgery [15].

As the demand for health services increases, problems in the current health system are increasingly emerging. While there have been great advances in medical technology, the shortage of healthcare workers and the unequal distribution of resources have become a confusing reality. At this point, smart healthcare services, which aim to eliminate the deficiencies in the current healthcare system, emerge as an important development.

Smart healthcare systems are technology-based solutions that aim to make healthcare more effective, accessible, and efficient. These systems help patients receive better care and make the work of healthcare professionals easier.

Some features of smart health systems include:

- **Electronic health records (EHR)**: Digitally stores patients' medical data and makes it easy to share.
- **Telehealth**: Provides remote healthcare services, allowing patients to communicate with specialists via video conferencing.
- **Data analytics**: Big data analytics helps in disease monitoring, epidemiology, and monitoring patients' response to treatment.
- **Patient monitoring devices**: Wearable devices and sensors make it possible to track patients' health data in real time.

17.2.1　BENEFITS AND CHALLENGES OF SMART HEALTHCARE SYSTEM

There may be both benefits and challenges in implementing smart healthcare systems. The following are the main benefits and challenges of smart healthcare systems that have been identified and are presented in Table 17.1.

When the difficulties listed in table are examined, most of them are related to the disruption of the integrity of data in institutions. Therefore, it will be useful for institutions to develop a perspective on cybersecurity in order to prevent many of the difficulties above. At this point, internal audits should be carried out within the scope of carrying out preventive and detective controls on cybersecurity independently and

TABLE 17.1

Benefits and Challenges of Smart Healthcare Systems

Benefits	Challenges
Data-centered care	Privacy and security concerns
Efficiency and workflow improvements	Lack of standardization
Remote health services	High costs
Patient monitoring	Lack of training and skills
Data analytics and predictive care	Patient acceptance and reliability
Patient safety	Data migration issues
Cost savings	Regulatory and compliance challenges
Health insurance and accounting	Technology speed
Public health monitoring	Fraud and data theft
Personalized healthcare	Patient trends and acceptance

objectively, evaluating the effectiveness of the IT assets of the enterprise against attacks, monitoring improvement efforts, and performing cybersecurity evaluations of third parties [20]. In a study conducted in Turkey, the competency needs of the IT sector in the digital age were evaluated and we can say that the suggestion presented is valid to address the lack of standards and skills in smart health systems. Academic institutions and non-governmental organizations have important and valuable functions in organizing sectors, creating policies for global competition, and producing long-term strategies [8]. In this sense, cooperation can be made with universities and non-governmental organizations in order to reach the talents needed by the sector within the framework of health institutions. It will be useful in training professionals who will play an active role in all stages of smart health systems, from their establishment to their possible risk management.

Smart healthcare systems offer several important benefits in the healthcare industry. The main benefits of smart health systems can be listed as follows:

- **Data-centered care**: Smart healthcare systems digitally record patients' medical histories, test results, prescriptions, and other health data, providing healthcare professionals with better-informed care. In this way, it is possible for patients to receive better healthcare.
- **Efficiency and workflow improvements**: Smart healthcare systems optimize the workflow of healthcare facilities. Tasks such as appointment scheduling, patient records management, and medication administration can be accomplished faster and more smoothly.
- **Remote health services**: Telehealth applications allow patients to receive remote medical consultations and communicate with their doctors via video conferencing. This is particularly important for patients living in remote areas and ensures a rapid response to emergencies.
- **Patient monitoring**: Thanks to smart health systems, patients' health data can be monitored in real time through smart devices and sensors. This is useful for managing chronic diseases, elderly care, and monitoring recovery processes.
- **Data analytics and predictive care**: Big data analytics makes it possible to analyze disease tracking, epidemiology, and health trends. It can also help predict how patients will respond to treatment so treatment plans can be better tailored.
- **Patient safety**: Smart health systems allow the keeping of electronic health records. This can calculate drug dosages more accurately, prevent medical errors, and reduce the likelihood of errors.
- **Cost savings**: Smart healthcare systems can reduce the costs of healthcare services because they make business processes more efficient and enable more effective use of resources.
- **Health insurance and accounting**: Smart health systems provide better data access and analysis so that health insurance companies can calculate more accurate premiums. Moreover, it optimizes accounting processes and can help detect fraud.

- **Public health monitoring**: Smart healthcare systems can help better track disease outbreaks and public health problems. This is critical for a rapid response and prevention of the spread of diseases.
- **Personalized healthcare**: Data analytics makes it possible to understand patients' individual health needs and create personalized treatment plans.

In the research conducted by [24], the main benefits of smart healthcare systems are listed as "wide availability, instant and reliable treatment, cost reduction, effectiveness of medicine and disease control, easy usage, improved communication".

Smart healthcare systems not only ensure that patients receive better healthcare but also help healthcare professionals do their jobs more efficiently. These systems look set to play a major role in the future of healthcare and have the potential to make healthcare more accessible, effective, and sustainable.

Although smart health systems offer many benefits, there are some challenges and problems that may be encountered during the implementation and adoption process. The main challenges that smart healthcare systems may face:

- **Privacy and security concerns**: Digitization of health data may increase patients' privacy and data security concerns. Data leaks can result in patients' personal and medical information being compromised.
- **Lack of standardization**: In the healthcare industry, incompatibility problems may occur between different devices and software platforms. A lack of data standards can make it difficult to share and analyze data effectively.
- **High costs**: Installation and maintenance of smart healthcare systems may require high costs. It can create access problems for small healthcare facilities or low-income areas.
- **Lack of training and skills**: Appropriate training and skills development programs are needed for healthcare professionals and staff. Deficiencies in using new technologies effectively may prevent the efficient use of the system.
- **Patient acceptance and reliability**: Some patients may distrust smart healthcare systems compared to traditional medical care. There may also be concerns that the technology is not always reliable.
- **Data migration issues**: Moving and integrating health data from one healthcare institution to another can be complex. It is important that these data migration processes are smooth and reliable.
- **Regulatory and compliance challenges**: The healthcare industry is subject to strict regulations. Smart healthcare systems must comply with these regulations and protect patients' rights.
- **Technology speed**: Since technological developments are advancing rapidly, healthcare institutions may have difficulty coping with this speed. Updating existing systems and keeping up with new technologies takes time and resources.
- **Fraud and data theft**: Smart healthcare systems can be vulnerable to fraud and data theft threats. Such threats may cause harm to patients or healthcare institutions.

- **Patient trends and acceptance**: Some patients may be resistant to technology or refuse its use. This may hinder the widespread adoption of smart healthcare systems.

In the research conducted by [24], the main challenges of implementing smart healthcare systems are listed as "scalability and interoperability, higher power consumption, low latency tolerance, need for a user-friendly device, security and privacy, computational intensity".

Despite these challenges, smart healthcare systems have great potential to continue improving healthcare. Appropriate policy, education, and technology solutions must be developed to overcome these challenges. It is also critical to consider important issues such as patient privacy and data security.

Effects of smart health systems on accounting: While smart healthcare systems include a series of innovative solutions developed to transform the delivery and management of healthcare services, they also lead to major changes in accounting. In this context, in this section, the effects of smart health systems and accounting in the health sector will be mentioned.

Some of the important changes caused by smart healthcare systems in the field of accounting are:

- **Data management**: Smart health systems generate and store large amounts of health data. By analyzing this data, accountants can make better-informed decisions for financial reporting and budget planning.
- **Hospital costs**: Smart healthcare systems can help hospital businesses operate more effectively and efficiently. Thus, hospitals can reduce operating costs and optimize accounting processes.
- **Health insurance**: Smart health systems provide more accurate and up-to-date data to health insurance companies. This makes it possible to better calculate insurance premiums and process claims faster.
- **Fraud detection**: Data analytics can assist accountants in detecting cases of fraud. Fraud in healthcare is a major source of costs.

Medical accounting: When looking at smart health applications from an accounting perspective, we first encounter the concept of medical accounting. The medical accounting process addresses many areas. For example, there are many applications for product tracking during the supply process. In this context, firstly, medical accounting was mentioned, and then the practices in the field of health in Turkey were evaluated in the framework of accounting.

The accounting system forces health managers to use accounting information more effectively by making analyses for both hospital management and health managers to use scarce resources efficiently and provide quality health services [9]. Financial accounting is a holistic process that calculates income and expenses in health institutions, as well as in public and private institutions, provides information about the financial structure of the health institution, and creates accounting subsections within it [22]. Assuming that there are three most important pillars based on a successful financial management system in health institutions; we undoubtedly see that these are stock, purchasing, and invoicing units. Medical accounting is the intersection and common element of these three different units and is directly affected by the activities and functioning of each unit. Therefore, it can be accepted that there is a strong relationship between keeping medical accounting regularly and the successful activities of these units [5].

Medical accounting is a structure that continues with the regular invoicing of a high volume of transactions [3]. The workflow diagram for these processes is shown in Figure 17.1.

Billing errors and healthcare fraud have been described as the "largest unmitigated healthcare cost" by the World Health Organization [3]. For these reasons, "Medical Accounting", which is based on the principle of invoicing the health services produced in health facilities in Turkey in accordance with the rules of the Health Practice Declaration [23], to the Social Security Institution, which is the reimbursement center, is used in the efficient use of scarce resources in health institutions. It is important to ensure cost-effectiveness [5].

Medical accounting is an important determinant of the financial health and performance of healthcare organizations. The deserved full compensation for all expenses and costs incurred to produce health services, in other words, for the labor expended, will only be possible with correct income accrual and a successful collection process. The continuation of the vital activities of healthcare enterprises also depends on this. The process of accounting for healthcare services provided by public or private healthcare facilities according to SUT (Sağlık Uygulama Tebliği) rules is called billing transactions carried out by the billing unit in public hospitals and medical accounting transactions in private healthcare providers [5].

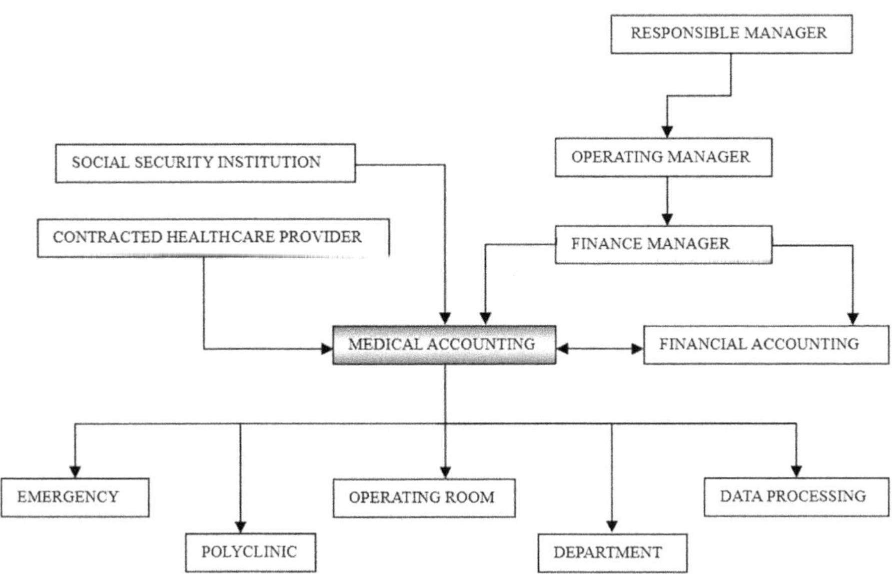

FIGURE 17.1 Workflow of medical accounting. Adapted from [12].

The rapid developments in computer technologies, which have a significant impact on information systems, and the digital transformation that emerged with the development of the capabilities of technology, have improved efficiency, responsiveness, speed, flexibility, and many other aspects in the field of accounting, as in every field. As a result of the electronic environment and applications brought about by digital transformation, the auditing and structure of accounting, as well as the control and auditing of taxes that provide economic contribution, have changed. These processes have begun to be carried out more easily and quickly via the electronic system. Healthcare institutions have started to use enterprise resource planning (ERP) systems to benefit from the advantages of digital transformation and avoid the disadvantages. It can be said that the main purpose of these systems is to provide quality healthcare services by increasing performance and minimizing medical errors. When we look at Turkey, we see that ERP systems are used and integrated with HBS. Although the costs of these systems are high, their benefits to healthcare institutions are much greater in terms of minimizing costs and almost eliminating the margin of error [2]. On the other hand, there are some deficiencies in medical accounting. Considering the studies carried out in the invoicing processes, it was determined that there were problems arising from the hospital information management system and user, invoice creation and collection, pricing of health services, lack of control, institutional billing unit, legislation, and payer institution [17]. [22], in their study aiming to determine how much importance the universities providing education services in Turkey attach to medical accounting education and how and to what extent the personnel working in this field specialize, found that 5 of 68 public and foundation universities have a curriculum called "Medical Accounting". They found that there was a lesson. It has been found that training in this field is mostly given in the form of courses or seminars. Therefore, it can be said that it is a factor affecting the lack of talent part mentioned above. Within the scope of the obstacles in the functioning of medical accounting and the problems experienced in this field, attention is drawn to issues such as deficiencies in the field of information and communication technology, lack of qualified personnel, differences in practice between public and private sector enterprises, and follow-up of current legislation [11].

While electronic media and technologies related to e-declarations and e-document applications bring many benefits, there are also numerous applications ranging from stock tracking to storing patient information. Below are examples of these practices in Turkey.

17.3 TURKEY EXAMPLES OF COMPUTERIZED ACCOUNTING INFORMATION SYSTEM (CAIS) IN SMART HEALTHCARE

Medical accounting also contributes to the policy-making process by undertaking an extremely critical task in transmitting health data to the Ministry of Health through information systems such as Medula, ÜTS, E-Nabız, and Sağlık-Net. When we look at the applications in Turkey, we see that they are created using the infrastructure of technologies referred to as Industry 4.0 technology. While it contributes to the formation of national health statistics with Sağlık-Net data, it also provides significant savings in public resources by preventing repeated analysis, examinations, and imaging performed in other health institutions, thanks to data sharing with the E-Nabız system. The first one we will talk about is the Sağlık-Net and E-Nabız applications [5]. These technologies are cloud computing-based technologies. In Turkey, the Ministry of Health launched the "Digital Health Report Card" service in 2015, within the scope of cloud computing applications, where citizens can share all their health records at their own discretion and always carry their records with them. "E-Nabız", where the Ministry of Health integrates the information systems of all health institutions, will serve as a platform where citizens can access their health records, both themselves and the relevant health personnel if they wish. Thanks to "E-Nabız", all examinations, controls, and operations performed in healthcare institutions and organizations will be recorded in a single database. Citizens and all public health institutions in Turkey's 81 provinces will have access to their health records. In this way, citizens will be able to see the details of the treatments they receive whenever they want and, with their own consent, they will be able to share these details with their relatives or doctors of their choice [6]. It is aimed to facilitate accounting transactions with cloud computing and real-time accounting integration. Therefore, accurate reports can be created with these cloud computing-based applications.

Product Tracking System (Ürün Takip Sistemi-ÜTS) Project is developed to ensure individual product tracking of all medical devices and cosmetic products produced or imported in our country, from the production line to the place where they are sold and used, and to track the product all the way to the end user [23]. Due to the ever-increasing patient load in hospitals and revisions in health policies, the need for medical supplies increases and there is cost pressure on hospitals. Poor inventory management will lead to inefficient use of corporate assets. In the healthcare industry, ineffective manual systems make it difficult to track the stock movement of medical supplies. It can be said that the ÜTS application involves the use of monitoring devices through IoT-based systems. Most of these applications are now used to control the movement of medical equipment and create a culture of use [13]. It can be said that ÜTS facilitates product tracking in Turkey thanks to the Internet of Things technology, thus providing benefits in tracking costs and ensuring product control.

Another concept we encounter in the accounting of health services is the MEDULA system. This system is a health information system developed to collect billing information regarding health services provided within the scope of general health insurance between the social security institution and health service providers electronically, independently of the internal functioning of health institutions, and to provide reimbursement for invoiced services [21,5]. Medula, which means health network, is an integrated system created between General Health Insurance and health facilities to collect invoice information electronically and pay for services without interfering with the internal processes of health facilities. Medula is a joint provision tracking system that works together with the Medula User Manual and the Biometric Authentication System User Manual. The Medula system, which is a Social Security network, has provided great convenience to healthcare providers, patients, and SSI officials, and contributes greatly to keeping hospitals and physicians registered, preventing abuses, reducing paper waste, and reducing unnecessary workload and errors with its auto-control mechanism [12].

Thanks to the synchronized execution of the medical accounting process, including IT, invoicing, purchasing, and stock units, individual tracking of medical supplies and drugs is carried out via ÜTS, thus eliminating duplicate purchasing-stock-invoicing processes in hospitals. In this process, patient safety is ensured by purchasing only medical supplies that are approved by the Ministry of Health and within the scope of reimbursement by the Social Security Institution (SSI), and the purchase of under-the-counter or counterfeit medical supplies is prevented, and informality in the healthcare sector is prevented [5].

Finally, another issue to be mentioned is the transactions between accountants and healthcare practices. The accounting system used in healthcare institutions has changed radically. The medical accounting system has started to be used together with the ERP systems in health institutions. Additionally, many healthcare institutions have started to use hospital information systems integrated with their enterprise resource planning systems. With the use of many different e-accounting applications integrated with computerized systems, costs have decreased rapidly, and the margin of error has decreased to almost zero [2]. The invoice burden of pharmacies in the healthcare sector is quite high for accountants. But another issue is that invoicing through the system helps accountants to transfer the accounting programs they use. Such integration not only saves time for accountants but also helps prevent possible errors and prepare accurate financial statements.

It can be said that the applications used in Turkey are generally aimed at data storage. On the other hand, the existence of a tracking system for products that are important cost elements in the healthcare sector and that are tracked from supply to the final consumer indicates the presence of a control mechanism. While these applications provide many benefits, they also present challenges. The main problem is that not everyone has equal competence in using these applications. For people to be informed about their health and make the right decisions, they need to have sufficient knowledge of using computers and health literacy. Lack of knowledge on these issues will prevent people from using e-health applications effectively and will prevent them from effectively benefiting from their health [14]. Another problem is data privacy, which seems to be the main problem in all sectors arising from information technologies. It is caused by storing patient information on the internet. A technical problem or data theft may cause personal information to become accessible to everyone [7]. Finally, it is about whether the internet connection is sufficient or not. Since all these applications are internet-based, in case of any interruption, people will not be able to connect to e-health applications and benefit from the applications [1].

17.4 CONCLUSION

Smart healthcare systems continue to radically change the healthcare industry, and these changes also affect the accounting field. The accounting benefits of smart healthcare systems in areas such as data management, hospital costs, health insurance and fraud detection cannot be ignored. Therefore, healthcare accounting professionals can better meet industry challenges by keeping up with technology and using these innovations. This integration between smart health systems and accounting will contribute to the betterment of health services and the sustainability of the health system. Therefore, it is time for healthcare accounting professionals and healthcare providers to collaborate to adopt and integrate these technologies. Significant changes in technology have also had an impact on the accounting field. On the other hand, taking advantage of developing technology in the field of health has brought many advantages. The system, which aims to present important information in health institutions and includes various sub-elements, is referred to as medical accounting.

Medical accounting covers many processes such as income and expense calculation, invoice tracking, collection, and stock management. With the increasing health services, medical accounting has become important. Therefore, many issues such as tracking this increasing transaction volume, effective management, and correct operation of the audit should be addressed together. At this point, it is possible to access reliable, accurate, and fast information by using information technologies. When we look at the application examples in Turkey, it is seen that, in addition to e-declarations and e-document applications, there are applications for storing the entire health history of the patient, accessing this information from every location, medical product tracking, stock control, and carrying out routine patient transactions. These applications provide advantages such as faster data transfer to the accounting information system, reduction of errors and abuses, and accurate reporting. These applications need to be updated as needed and information security must be ensured.

REFERENCES

1. Ajami, S., & Bagheri-Tadi, T. (2013). Barriers for adopting electronic health records (EHRs) by physicians. *Acta Informatica Medica*, 21(2), 129.
2. Akbulut, F. (2023). Muhasebenin Dijital Dönüşümü, Medikal Muhasebe ve E-Muhasebe Uygulamaları. *Sosyal, İnsan ve İdari Bilimlerde Yenilikçi Çalışmalar*, Duvar Yayınları, 1251–277.
3. Akkuyu, A. (2020). Özel Hastanelerde Medikal Muhasebe Uygulamaları ve Medikal Muhasebeye Bağlı İç Kontrol Mekanizmasının Testi Özel Bir Hastane Uygulaması (Yüksek Lisans Tezi). İstanbul Gelişim Üniversitesi Sosyal Bilimleri Enstitüsü, İşletme Anabilim Dalı, İstanbul.
4. Albakri, A., & Alqahtani, Y. M. (2023). Internet of medical things with a blockchain-assisted smart healthcare system using metaheuristics with a deep learning model. *Applied Sciences*, 13(10), 6108. doi:10.3390/app13106108.
5. Arık Ö., & Yılmaz, F. Ö. (2021). Sağlık Kurumlarında Medikal Muhasebe Süreçleri. *Necmettin Erbakan Üniversitesi Sağlık Bilimleri Fakültesi Dergisi*, 4(2), 34–42.
6. Bayın, G., Yeşilaydın, G., & Özkan, O. (2016). Bulut Bilişimin Sağlık Hizmetlerinde Kullanımı. *Dumlupınar Üniversitesi Sosyal Bilimler Dergisi*, 48, 233–253.
7. Blumenthal, D. (2017). Data withholding in the age of digital health. *The Milbank Quarterly*, 95(1), 15.
8. Damar, M. (2022). Dijital Çağda Bilişim Sektörünün İhtiyacı Olan Yetkinlikler Üzerine Bir Değerlendirme. *Journal of Information Systems and Management Research*, 4(1), 25–40.
9. Kahramanoğlu, A. & Acar, D. (2017). Sağlık işletmelerinde sorumluluk muhasebesi ve faaliyet bölümleri standardına göre transfer fiyatlaması: Bir kamu hastanesinde uygulama. *Selçuk Üniversitesi Sosyal Bilimler Meslek Yüksekokulu Dergisi*, 20(2), 111–128. doi:10.29249/selcuksbmyd.306756
10. Kilanko, V. (2023). Leveraging artificial intelligence for enhanced revenue cycle management in the United States. *International Journal of Scientific Advances*, 4(4), 505–514.

11. Korkmaz, E., & Tercan, Ş. (2023). Medikal Muhasebe ve Sağlık Hizmetlerinin Etkin Yönetilmesindeki Rolü. *Sayıştay Dergisi*, 130, 441–467.

12. Kördeve, M. (2017). Sağlık Ödemelerinde Yeni Bir Kavram: Medikal Muhasebe. *Çukurova Üniversitesi Sosyal Bilimler Enstitüsü Dergisi*, 26(2), 1–13.

13. Lee, C. K. M., Cheng, M. N., & Ng, C. K. (2015). Iot-based asset management system for healthcare-related industries. *International Journal of Engineering Business Management*, 7, 19.

14. Mackert, M., Mabry-Flynn, A., Champlin, S., Donovan, E. E., & Pounders, K. (2016). Health literacy and health information technology adoption: the potential for a new digital divide. *Journal of Medical Internet Research*, 18(10), e264.

15. Özçelik, M., Beller Dikmen, B., & Deran, A. (2022). Nesnelerin İnterneti Teknolojisinin Muhasebe ve Denetim Sürecine Etkisi ve Muhtemel Riskler. *İşletme Araştırmaları Dergisi*, 14(2), 1544–1563.

16. Özkan, A., Koç, F. Ö., & Çidem, İ. (2013). Hastanelerde Muhasebe Bilgi Sistemi Etkinliği: İç Anadolu Bölgesinde Faaliyet Gösteren Hastaneler Üzerinde Bir Araştırma. *Sosyal Ekonomik Araştırmalar Dergisi*, 13(26), 1–22.

17. Pirim, E., & Bulut, S. (2022). Kamu Hastanelerinde Gelir Döngüsünün Değerlendirilmesi. *Uluslararası Sağlık Yönetimi ve Stratejileri Araştırma Dergisi*, 8(3), 315–333.

18. Rehman, A., Abbas, S., Khan, M. A., Ghazal, T. M., Adnan, K. M., & Mosavi, A. (2022). A secure healthcare 5.0 system based on blockchain technology entangled with federated learning technique. *Computers in Biology and Medicine*, 150, 106019. doi:10.1016/j.compbiomed.2022.106019.

19. Saldamli, G., Reddy, V., Bojja, K. S., Gururaja, M. K., Doddaveerappa, Y., & Tawalbeh, L. (2020, April). Health care insurance fraud detection using blockchain. In: *2020 Seventh International Conference on Software Defined Systems (SDS)* (pp. 145–152). IEEE.

20. Selimoğlu, S., & Altunel, M. (2019). Siber güvenlik risklerinden korunmada köprü ve katalizör olarak iç denetim. *Denetişim*, (19), 5–16.

21. Sözen, A. B. (2015). Faturalama sürecinde yapılan hatalar sonucu oluşan gelir kayıplarının nedenleri ve kayıpları önlemek için yapılması gerekenler (Yüksek Lisans Tezi). İstanbul Üniversitesi Sağlık Bilimleri Enstitüsü, Sağlık Yönetimi Anabilim Dalı, İstanbul.

22. Şenol, A., & Metin, M. H. (2022). Sağlık İşletmelerinde Medikal Muhasebe Uzmanlığı ve Önemi. *Scientific Journal of Innovation and Social Sciences Research*, 2(2), 111–121.

23. Türkiye Cumhuriyeti Sağlık Bakanlığı and Türkiye İlaç ve Tıbbi Cihaz Kurumu (2020). https://www.titck.gov.tr/faaliyetalanlari/tibbicihaz/urun-takip-sistemi-uts

24. Tunc, M. A., Gures, E., & Shayea, I. (2021). A survey on IoT smart healthcare: Emerging technologies, applications, challenges, and future trends. https://arxiv.org/pdf/2109.02042.pdf

25. Vaiyapuri, T., Binbusayyis, A., & Varadarajan, V. (2021). Security, privacy and trust in IoMT enabled smart healthcare system: A systematic review of current and future trends. *International Journal of Advanced Computer Science and Applications*, 12, 731–737.

18 Bouc-Wen Hysteresis Modelling and Tracking Control of Piezoelectric Actuator for Precision Nano-Positioning Systems in Healthcare

C. Sreeja and D. Godwinraj

18.1 INTRODUCTION

In the field of precision nano-positioning systems, the pursuit of improved accuracy and control has resulted in an increasing dependence on piezoelectric actuators. These electro-mechanical devices provide distinct advantages, such as exceptional precision, swift responsiveness, and a compact form factor, rendering them indispensable tools across diverse sectors, including healthcare. In the healthcare domain, the imperative for exceptionally precise motion control has ignited research into nano-positioning solutions. This is particularly crucial when handling biological specimens, medical instrumentation, and imaging devices, all of which frequently necessitate positioning capabilities at sub-micron and sub-nanometre levels.

One significant concern that requires careful consideration is the presence of hysteresis within the actuator's behaviour. Hysteresis, defined by the actuator's response relying on its past inputs, introduces complications that impede precise control and impose restrictions on achievable accuracy. The hysteresis loop, as shown in Figure 18.1, illustrates the nonlinearity and historical dependence on the actuator's behaviour. The size and shape of the loop can vary depending on factors like the material, actuator design, and operating conditions. A more precise characterization of the hysteresis can be achieved through experimental testing and modelling, such as the Bouc-Wen hysteresis model.

Rate-dependent hysteresis is a prevalent feature in numerous dynamic systems, and it is also observed in certain piezoelectric actuators. This phenomenon signifies that the system's reaction to an input is not solely dictated by the current input value but is instead impacted by the speed at which the input is undergoing change. The effective establishment of a precise Bouc-Wen hysteresis model and a proficient tracking control system for the AE0203D04 DF piezoelectric actuator holds the

DOI: 10.1201/9781032632223-18

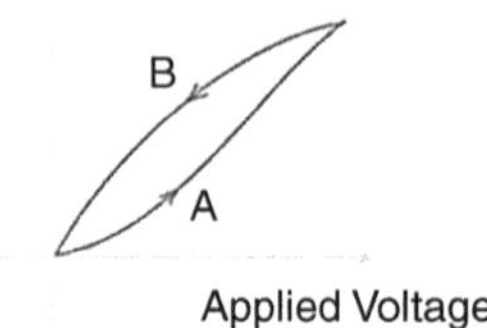

FIGURE 18.1　Hysteresis behaviour of piezoelectric actuator.

potential for significant advancements in the field of precision nano-positioning systems utilized in healthcare applications. These systems play a crucial role in various critical tasks, including high-resolution imaging, cellular manipulation, and minimally invasive surgical procedures. Through the enhancement of piezoelectric actuator control, this research makes a valuable contribution to elevating the standards of healthcare diagnostics and treatments, ultimately yielding benefits for both patients and healthcare professionals. The subsequent sections outline the modelling and control approaches and provide experimental findings and discussions that emphasize the efficacy of the developed techniques in practical healthcare applications.

18.2　NANO POSITIONING SYSTEMS IN HEALTHCARE

Nano-positioning systems are essential in the healthcare sector as they offer precise control and manipulation of objects and instruments at the nanoscale, playing a crucial role in various applications. They are essential for a variety of healthcare applications, such as medical diagnostics, research, and treatment. Below, we highlight the major domains where nano-positioning systems have a substantial influence on healthcare: Systems based on movable diaphragms are widely applicable across various fields, with a specific focus on their use in the domains of biology and medicine [1–4].

Nano-positioning systems are fundamental in advanced imaging techniques like atomic force microscopy (AFM) and super-resolution microscopy. They empower researchers to capture intricate images of biological samples, cells, and tissues at the nanoscale, driving progress in medical research and diagnostics. They facilitate the manipulation of individual cells or microorganisms. This technology is crucial for tasks such as single-cell analysis, cellular surgery, and the investigation of cellular responses to various stimuli [5]. Precise positioning is paramount for targeted drug delivery at the cellular or sub-cellular level. Nano-positioning systems enable the controlled release of medications to specific areas within the body, reducing side effects and enhancing treatment efficacy.

In microsurgery and minimally invasive surgical procedures, nano-positioning systems enable surgeons to achieve heightened precision when manipulating surgical instruments or conducting delicate procedures in confined spaces. Electrostatic micro-operators offer the advantage of achieving substantial displacements while consuming minimal power, and they are also easier to manufacture compared to other types of actuators. Improving the accuracy of the intracytoplasmic sperm injection (ICSI) process can be accomplished by incorporating Micro-Electro-Mechanical Systems (MEMS) actuators [6,7].

Nano-positioning systems are harnessed in lab-on-a-chip devices to meticulously handle minuscule volumes of fluids and particles. This technology is essential for applications like point-of-care diagnostics and genetic analysis. In biosensors and chemical sensors, nano-positioning systems precisely position and regulate the interaction between target molecules and sensor surfaces, enabling highly sensitive and specific detection [8].

Nano-positioning systems are involved in assembling and positioning nanoparticles that serve as drug carriers, facilitating targeted drug delivery to specific tissues or cells. They also play a vital role in the development of diagnostic devices, including lab-on-a-chip technologies and devices designed for detecting biomarkers and pathogens with high sensitivity [9]. Additionally, they are essential in various precision microscopy techniques used to explore cellular and molecular structures. This deeper understanding of disease mechanisms and therapeutic targets contributes to advancements in healthcare [10,11].

The ability to achieve precise positioning at the nanoscale is of utmost importance in advancing healthcare diagnostics, treatment effectiveness, and our understanding of biological systems. Nano-positioning systems remain at the forefront of healthcare and biomedical research, holding the promise of pioneering advancements in diagnostics and therapies.

18.3 PIEZOELECTRIC ACTUATORS

Piezoelectric actuators are devices that leverage the piezoelectric effect to produce mechanical motion or displacement in response to an applied electrical voltage. They find widespread use in applications demanding precision and swift actuation or movement. Various types of piezoelectric actuators exist, including stacks, benders, flex tensional devices, Langevin transducers, and diverse types of motors. This study centres around piezoelectric stack actuators. A stack comprises multiple layers of piezoceramic material and electrodes that are electrically connected in parallel and mechanically linked in series, enhancing the maximum achievable displacement as shown in Figure 18.2 [12].

18.4 NONLINEARITIES IN PIEZOELECTRIC ACTUATORS

Nonlinearities in piezoelectric actuators denote departures from their ideal responses to electrical signals. These non-ideal characteristics are a well-recognized aspect of piezoelectric actuators and can significantly impact their performance across different applications. Hysteresis is a phenomenon where the position of the piezoelectric actuator is not solely determined by the current input; it is also influenced by its previous operational state. In simpler terms, the actuator's reaction lags behind alterations in the input signal, potentially introducing inaccuracies in positioning and control systems. Creep refers to the slow, time-dependent distortion of the actuator when exposed to a constant voltage or stress. This phenomenon can lead to unintended

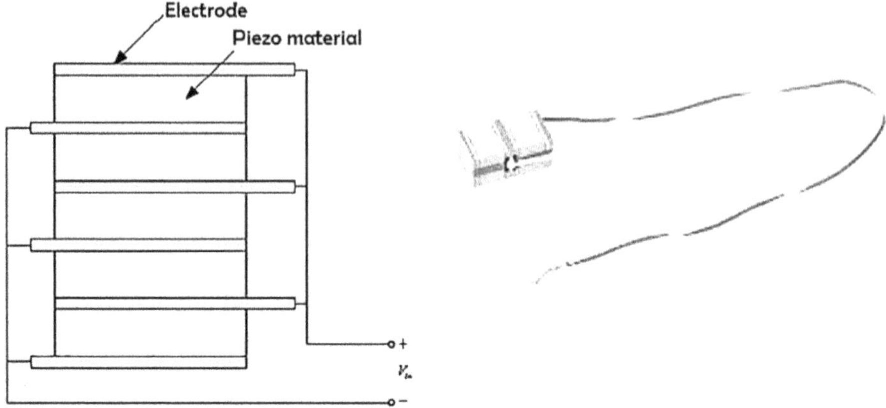

FIGURE 18.2　Piezoelectric stack actuators.

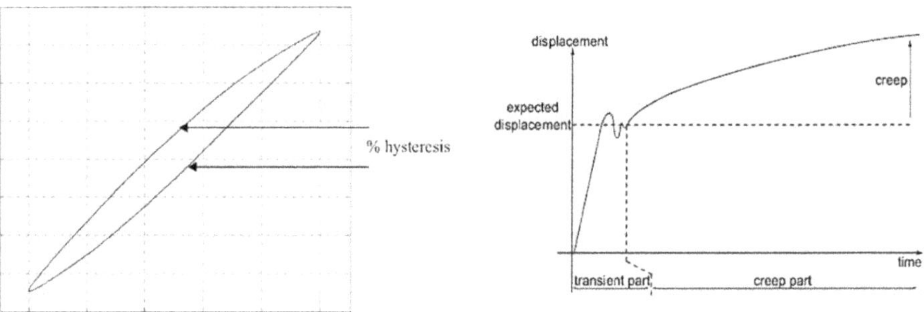

FIGURE 18.3　(a) Hysteresis and (b) creep behaviour of piezoelectric actuator.

changes in position over time, presenting challenges in applications that demand stable and precise positioning [13]. The non-binaries are represented in Figure 18.3.

The relationship between the voltage applied and the resulting strain or displacement in piezoelectric actuators is not consistently linear. This nonlinearity necessitates a thorough understanding of the actuator's behaviour under various operating conditions. Additionally, the response of piezoelectric actuators may exhibit variations in accordance with the frequency of the applied voltage. At higher frequencies, mechanical resonance effects can lead to diminished displacement.

To meet the stringent accuracy demands of high-precision applications, efforts have been dedicated over the last two decades to mitigate hysteresis effects. While employing a charge source can effectively reduce hysteresis in a piezoelectric actuator (PEA), it often comes at the expense of limited motion range. Consequently, voltage-based actuation has become the prevalent choice in practical applications. In the realm of hysteresis compensation, existing approaches can be broadly categorized into two groups: those based on hysteresis model-driven feedforward control and those that rely on hysteresis model-independent feedback control strategies as shown in Figure 18.4.

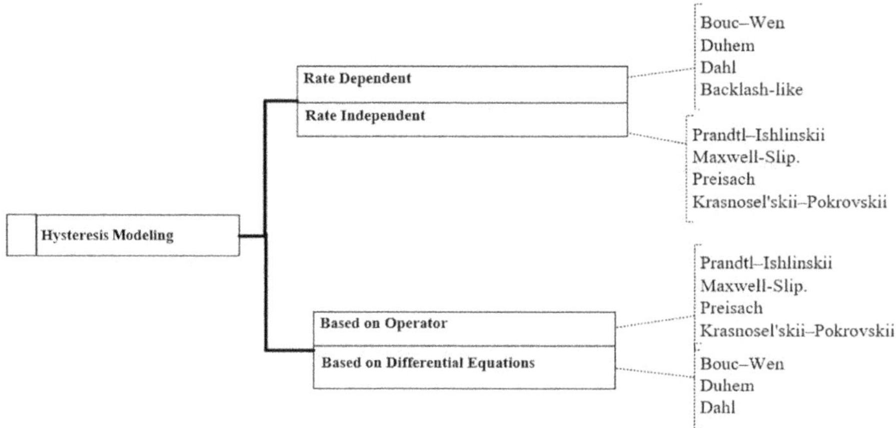

FIGURE 18.4   Various hysteresis modelling methods for PEA.

This study primarily centres around modelling hysteresis in piezoelectric actuators. This focus arises from the fact that in high-speed and low-frequency applications, the impact of creep and vibration can be considered minimal or negligible (Table 18.1).

> The Bouc-Wen model, known for its ability to replicate the behaviour of a broad range of hysteretic systems, has found widespread use across various engineering domains.

Various techniques are available for compensating for nonlinearities in piezoelectric actuators. This paper employs a structured H∞ design to address accuracy and robustness issues through a two-loop control structure [15]. By leveraging the dual-pair concept, a connection is established between hysteresis models and general memory (MEM) elements, such as the Ramberg–Osgood model. This connection facilitates a straightforward identification procedure for a hysteresis model and the design of a feedforward controller [16]. The paper introduces two optimal controllers that shape the closed-loop sensitivity functions by imposing templates through weighting functions, aiming to achieve the desired tracking performance with robustness. The results demonstrate a significant improvement in both hysteresis

TABLE 18.1

Summary of Some Hysteresis Models [14]

Hysteresis Models	Differential-based Models			Operator-based Models			
	Bouc-Wen	Dahl	Duhem	P-I	KP	Maxwell	Preisach
Rate-independent	No	No	No	Yes	Yes	Yes	Yes
Rate-dependent	Yes	Yes	Yes	No	No	No	No
Identification process	Easy	Hard	Hard	Easy	Hard	Easy	Hard
Designing controller	Easy	Easy	Hard	Hard	Hard	Hard	Hard
Obtaining inverse model	Easy	Easy	Hard	Easy	Hard	Hard	Hard

modelling accuracy and tracking performance, with average root-mean-square error (RMSE) values of 0.0107 and 0.0212 μm, respectively [17].

18.5   RESULTS AND DISCUSSION

The Bouc-Wen model is widely applied in modelling and compensating for hysteresis in piezoelectric ceramic actuators due to its differential equations and its capacity to offer an analytical representation of hysteresis behaviour.

The classical Bouc-Wen hysteresis model, as a nonlinear system, can be described as follows:

$$y(t) = X(t) + h(t) = k \cdot u(t) + h(t) \tag{18.1}$$

$$h'(t) = \alpha \cdot u'(t) - \beta \cdot u'(t) \cdot |h(t)| - \gamma \cdot |u(t)| \cdot h(t) \tag{18.2}$$

Here, $u(t)$ represents the input voltage, and $y(t)$ corresponds to the output displacement. The model parameters k, α, β, γ, and n determine the shape of hysteresis curves. Typically, to simplify the model, n is often set to 1, and the hysteresis component is expressed as:

$$h'(t) = \alpha \cdot u'(t) - \beta \cdot u(t) \cdot |h(t)| - \gamma |u(t)| \cdot h(t) \tag{18.3}$$

The Simulink diagram for the hysteresis modelling and the plant is shown in Figures 18.5. and 18.6.

In the parameter identification process of classical Bouc-Wen models, the Trust-Region-Reflective algorithm combined with the nonlinear least squares technique is employed. This approach harnesses the optimization features available in the MATLAB/Simulink Optimization Toolbox. The steps for identifying parameters within the nonlinear least squares methodology are followed to determine the optimal parameter values for the models.

The objective function used here is

$$F = Min \sum_{i=1}^{n} e^2 (u) \tag{18.4}$$

$$e(u) = y_i - y_i^{HM}$$

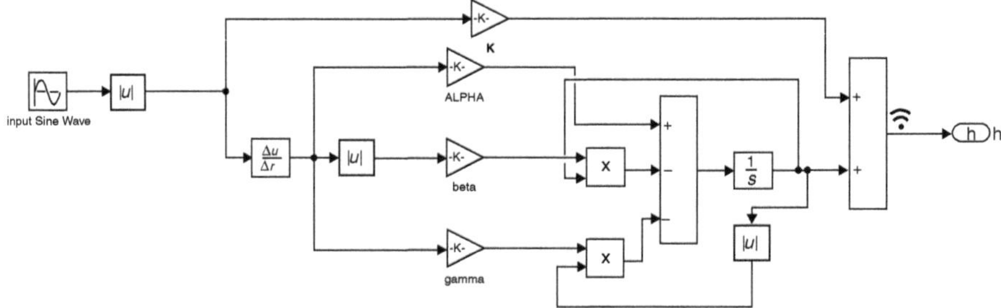

FIGURE 18.5   Simulink model for CBW model.

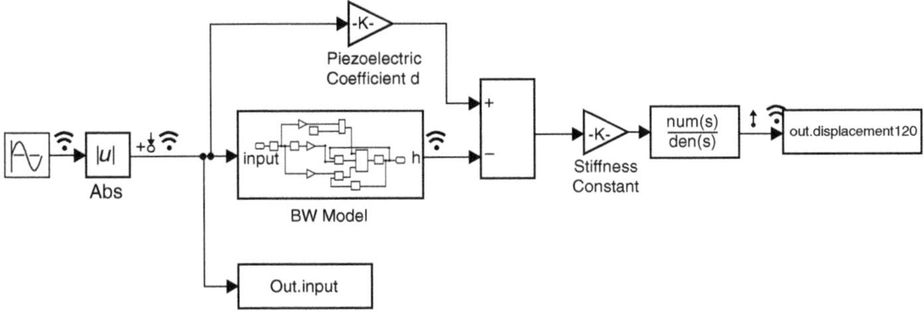

FIGURE 18.6   Simulink model for the plant.

The process of parameter estimation comprises several well-defined stages:

1. Collect experimental test data from the system under investigation.
2. Specify the parameters to be estimated, including initial estimates and allowable parameter ranges.
3. Set up the estimation preferences and choose a suitable estimation algorithm.
4. Execute the estimation algorithm to derive parameter estimates.
5. Validate the obtained results by comparing them to additional sets of test data.
6. If necessary, iterate through the aforementioned steps to enhance the precision of parameter estimates.

The optimized parameters of the model at different frequencies are shown in Table 18.2 and Figure 18.7.

The findings presented suggest that the conventional Bouc-Wen model falls short of providing an accurate representation of rate-dependent hysteresis phenomena in piezoelectric actuators. This inadequacy arises from the asymmetrical nature of the observed hysteresis, in contrast to the symmetric nature of the classical Bouc-Wen model as shown in Figure 18.8. As a result, there is a demand for redefining the model.

TABLE 18.2

Identified Parameters of the Classical Bouc-Wen (CB-W) Model at Different Frequencies

Frequency	K	α	B	γ
5	0.704965628	−0.441999597	0.757530005	0.769159594
20	0.668892982	−0.453222728	0.780224728	0.778147419
50	0.753853575	−0.375357874	0.845887064	0.756558717
80	0.7602173	−0.375766404	0.845419774	0.735819754
100	0.752621355	−0.288658026	0.822083613	0.708319881
120	0.718821492	−0.335027816	0.803997493	0.706683701

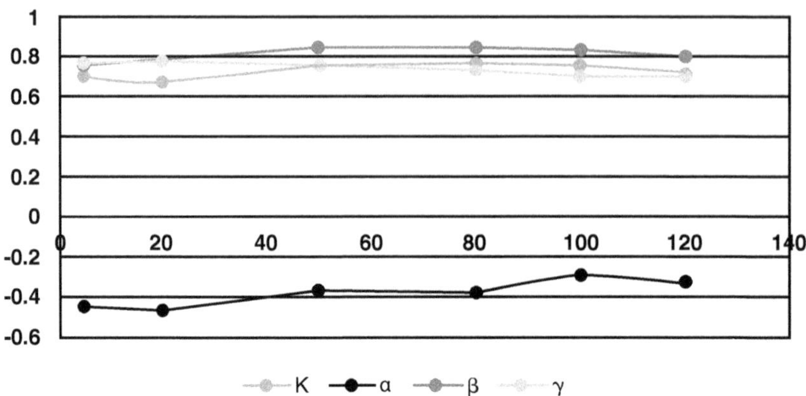

FIGURE 18.7　CBW model parameters at different frequencies.

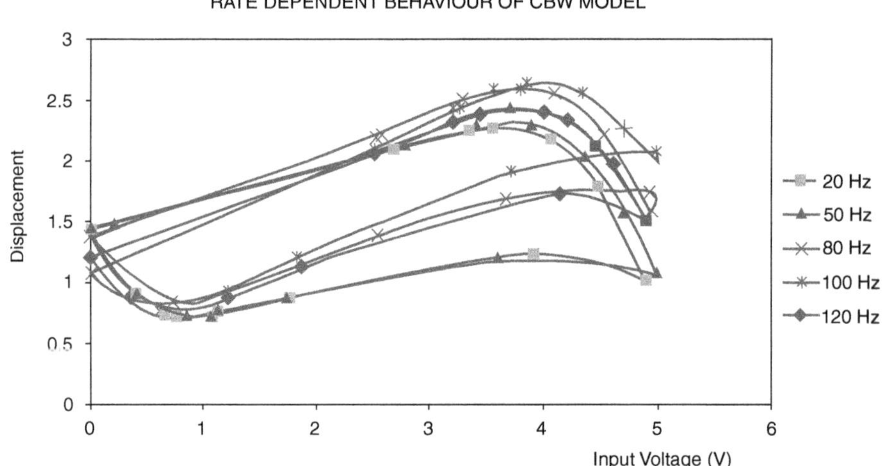

FIGURE 18.8　Rate-dependent behaviour of CBW model.

The challenge lies in developing a revised model that can proficiently encompass both rate-independent and rate-dependent hysteresis features.

The rate-dependent characteristics of the classical Bouc-Wen model are investigated. A piezoelectric actuator is subjected to a sinusoidal 5 V input at various frequencies, and we observe that the hysteresis behaviour changes with the rate of input signals. Our challenge is to create an enhanced model that effectively captures both rate-independent and rate-dependent hysteresis properties. Additionally, we aim to minimize tracking errors using advanced control techniques, making it suitable for precision biomedical applications. Tracking errors are represented in Figure 18.9.

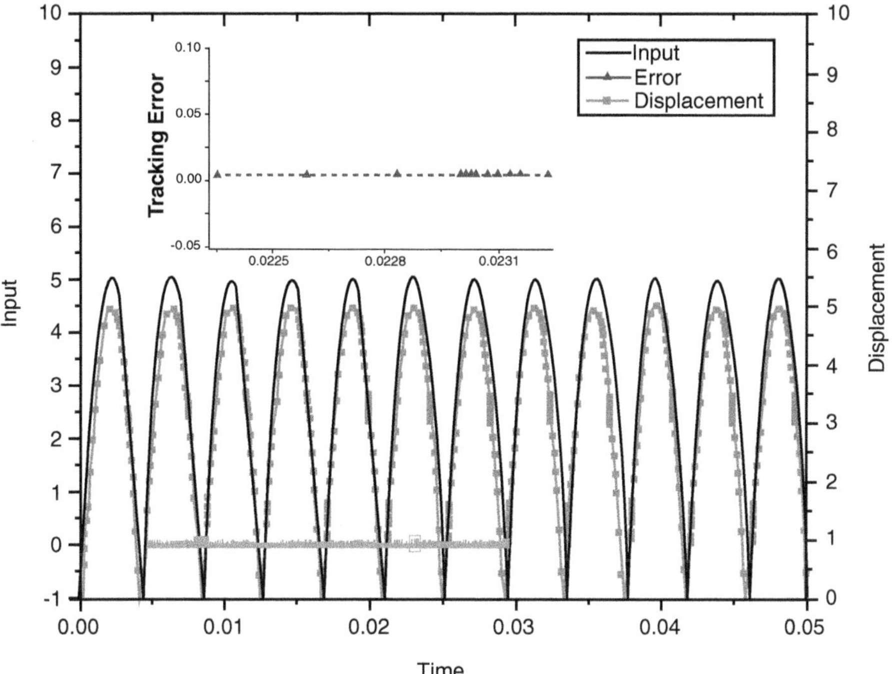

FIGURE 18.9   Tracking error.

18.6   CONCLUSION AND FUTURE WORKS

The Bouc-Wen model is highly effective in accurately representing hysteresis in piezo actuators. The open-loop controller, designed based on the Bouc-Wen model, exhibited excellent performance. Although real-time implementation of the non-linear open-loop controller posed challenges, the simulated results closely matched those of the linearized model, which accurately estimated the voltage required to achieve the desired output from the piezo actuator. Therefore, we can confidently assert that this model can be further extended to encompass the dynamics of the micro gripper, even with significant modifications. To further minimize system error, the implementation of a PID controller is recommended.

REFERENCES

1. Hasikin, K., Soin, N., & Ibrahim, F. (2009, December). Modeling of a polyimide diaphragm for an optical pulse pressure sensor. In: *2009 International Conference for Technical Postgraduates (TECHPOS)* (pp. 1–5). IEEE.
2. Ali, F., & Koc, M. (2023). 3D printed polymer piezoelectric materials: Transforming healthcare through biomedical applications. *Polymers*, 15(23), 4470.
3. Ali, F., Al Rashid, A., Kalva, S. N., & Koç, M. (2023). Mg-Doped PLA composite as a potential material for tissue engineering-synthesis. *Characterization, and Additive Manufacturing Materials*, 16(19), 6506.

4. Ali, F., Kalva, S. N., Mroue, K. H., Keyan, K. S., Tong, Y., Khan, O. M., & Koç, M. (2023). Degradation assessment of Mg-Incorporated 3D printed PLA scaffolds for biomedical applications. *Bioprinting*, 35, e00302.
5. Clayton, G. M., Tien, S., Leang, K. K., Zou, Q., & Devasia, S. (2009). A review of feedforward control approaches in nanopositioning for high-speed SPM. *Journal of Dynamic Systems, Measurement, and Control*, 131(6): 061101 (19 pages).
6. Tabatabaee-Nasab, F. S., & Naserifar, N. (2021). Nanopositioning control of an electrostatic MEMS actuator: Adaptive terminal sliding mode control approach. *Nonlinear Dynamics,* 105(1), 213–225.
7. Dai, C., Zhuang, S., Shan, G., Liu, H., Wang, Y., Ru, C., & Sun, Y. (2023). Automated piezo-assisted sperm immobilization. *IEEE Transactions on Automation Science and Engineering*, 1–9.
8. Wang, Z. N., Ang, W. T., Zhao, S., & Teo, T. J. (2014, December). Application of lateral oscillating piezo-driven micropipette in embryo biopsy for pre-implantation genetic diagnosis. In: *2014 13th International Conference on Control Automation Robotics & Vision (ICARCV)* (pp. 1218–1223). IEEE.
9. Ahmed, A. H., Aburas, O. E., Meelad, N. A., & Abu-Raas, A. A. (2021, May). Modeling and control of two wheels robot using linear quadratic regulators. In: *2021 IEEE 1st International Maghreb Meeting of the Conference on Sciences and Techniques of Automatic Control and Computer Engineering MI-STA* (pp. 193–197). IEEE.
10. Phuc, P. T., Tai, N. D., & Thinh, N. T. (2019, July). Applying sliding mode control to massage robot apply for healthcare therapy. In: *2019 International Conference on System Science and Engineering (ICSSE)* (pp. 605–608). IEEE.
11. Zhan-hui, L., Yun-xin, W., & Xi-shu, D. (2007, June). Modeling and compensating of piezoelectric actuator hysteresis in photolithography. In: *2007 International Symposium on High Density packaging and Microsystem Integration* (pp. 1–3). IEEE.
12. Gu, G. Y., Zhu, L. M., Su, C. Y., Ding, H., & Fatikow, S. (2014). Modeling and control of piezo-actuated nanopositioning stages: A survey. *IEEE Transactions on Automation Science and Engineering*, 13(1), 313–332.
13. Choi, G. S., Lim, Y. A., & Choi, G. H. (2002). Tracking position control of piezoelectric actuators for periodic reference inputs. *Mechatronics*, 12(5), 669–684..
14. Gan, J., & Zhang, X. (2019). A review of nonlinear hysteresis modeling and control of piezoelectric actuators. *AIP Advances*, 9(4), 040702 (10 pages).
15. Feng, H., Zhou, H., Jiang, C., & Pang, A. (2023). High precision structured H∞ control of a piezoelectric nanopositioning platform. *PlOS ONE*, 18(6), e0286471.
16. Strijbosch, N., Tiels, K., & Oomen, T. (2023). Memory-element-based hysteresis: Identification and compensation of a piezoelectric actuator. *IEEE Transactions on Control Systems Technology*, 31(6), 2863–870.
17. Baziyad, A. G., Ahmad, I., & Salamah, Y. B. (2023). Precision motion control of a piezoelectric actuator via a modified preisach hysteresis model and two-degree-of-freedom H-infinity robust control. *Micromachines*, 14(6), 1208.

19 Investigating ChatGPT Usability in Promoting Smart Health Awareness

Rafidah Abd Karim and Gulsun Kurubacak Cakir

19.1 INTRODUCTION

Many new technologies have appeared in the past half-century, and it is impossible to list them all. Advancements in once-disparate domains including robotics, nano-technology, 3D printing, genetics, and biotechnology, as well as artificial intelligence and machine learning, are complementing and magnifying each other. As immersive technologies develop, new uses for them in learning environments also appear. VR and AR technology are being used in more applications and programmes as mobile technologies spread and the cost of telecommunication consumption declines. This influences a range of enterprises [9]. Among the most revolutionary technological developments in recent years are generative AI models, like ChatGPT, Midjourney, and DeepBrain [6]. Human curiosity in the immense expertise of the technology is what drives ChatGPT's popularity. Its complete potential has not yet been realised due to its recentness and versatility across numerous industries. Executives across various industries have already started to investigate its potential benefits. Several industries are expected to be affected by ChatGPT; search engines, graphic design, education, healthcare, retail, banking, manufacturing, logistics, and travel are just a few of those that have already been highlighted as potential beneficiaries of the tech-nology. An artificial intelligence (AI) chatbot called ChatGPT is remarkably sophis-ticated, sensitive, and useful when it comes to understanding and producing natural human language [10]. ChatGPT is a natural language processing tool driven by AI technology that allows you to have human-like conversations and much more with the chatbot. With tasks like composing contracts, business letters, software develop-ment, and testing writing emails and essays, the language model can help you with the answers to your questions [11].

19.2 RELATED WORKS

Algorithms such as ChatGPT that can be used to produce new content, such as audio, code, images, text, simulations, and videos, are referred to as genera-tive artificial intelligence (AI). Generative AI allows ChatGPT to perform certain tasks and produce text that is human-like and artistic content (such as music and images), in addition to combining information for analysis from several sources [5].

ChatGPT, in particular, was developed and optimised for conversational use to generate human-like responses by utilising its vast knowledge base. Unlike earlier AI models, ChatGPT can build software in multiple languages, debug code, simplify complex subjects into small bits, be interview-ready, and compose essays [8]. Large Language Models (LLMs) that employ deep learning approaches for lengthy training with massive volumes of data fall within the GPT category [4]. ChatGPT, an advanced large language model (LLM), has demonstrated potential in several medical applications, including helping healthcare professionals stay up to date on new developments, identifying research topics, and supporting clinical and laboratory diagnosis. In the next section, this chapter reviews more about ChatGPT in the healthcare industry.

The prevalence of chatbots and virtual assistants in the healthcare industry is rising due to several causes, including the rise in remote patient care, patient awareness, the urgent need for personalization, and growing interest in 5G and artificial intelligence technologies. There are a lot of possible uses for ChatGPT in the medical field, and depending on how much it can advance treatment, our healthcare systems may undergo significant change. ChatGPT and Intelligent Automation can be used together in the healthcare industry to improve patient outcomes, cut down on errors, and streamline procedures. Intelligent Automation is the arms and legs, and ChatGPT is the brain. However, the application of ChatGPT and related AI chatbots to the healthcare industry also brings up moral and legal issues, such as possible copyright violations, medicolegal issues, and the requirement for transparency in AI-generated content [7]. Several benefits of ChatGPT in the health industry include promoting public health, offering information on public health issues, providing health promotion and disease prevention strategies, explaining the roles of community health workers and health educators, discussing the impact of social and environmental factors on community health, and generating educational materials on various health topics. It analyses community health data to predict future health outcomes [3]. Critical patient information found in electronic health records (EHRs), such as symptoms, medical history, and test results, can help improve patient outcomes [15]. The growing demand for virtual health assistance, health Chatbots, and others is a major determinant driving the market growth, but the industry's continuous innovation and technological advancements, increasing patient wait times and lack of patient engagement are leading to increasing adoption of the Healthcare Chatbots Market. By utilising cutting-edge information technologies like big data, cloud computing, artificial intelligence, and the Internet of Things (IoT), smart healthcare transforms the traditional medical system and increases its overall effectiveness, convenience, and personalization. At a compound annual growth rate of 23.5%, the global market for smart medical devices is projected to reach $23.5 billion by 2027. According to [1,2], virtual assistants and AI-powered conversational chatbots have gained prominence and play important roles in the past few years and may now be found in labs, hospitals, pharmacies, and even assisted living facilities. Thus, in the era of digital customer service, clients anticipate quick and easy communication. However, ChatGPT can be used to develop more accurate and reliable symptom checkers that could provide more fine-tuned guidance on the next steps. Additionally, ChatGPT may improve medical education. The system might give students and medical professionals immediate access to the resources and information about medicine they need to support their growth. Lastly, ChatGPT may find use in drug administration, illness surveillance, mental health assistance, remote patient monitoring, medical writing, patient triage, and other areas. Based on these advantages, ChatGPT gained more popularity among smart healthcare users [13]. Therefore, this chapter explores the public perspectives of ChatGPT usability in promoting smart health awareness.

19.3 PURPOSE AND OBJECTIVES OF THE STUDY

The purpose of the study was to investigate the public perceptions of ChatGPT in promoting smart health awareness in Malaysia and Turkey. The objectives of the study were as follows:

1. To identify the public perceptions of the use of ChatGPT.
2. To identify the public perceptions of smart healthcare.
3. To determine the relationship between the public perceptions of ChatGPT and smart healthcare.

19.4 CONCEPTUAL FRAMEWORK

This section presents the conceptual framework of the study. The framework illustrates the main constructs (ChatGPT and Smart Healthcare) included in the study based on its purpose. The proposed framework was designed based on theories or models. Figure 19.1 shows the three main variables of the study. ChatGPT was designated as the independent variable based on Large Language Models (LLM) introduced by Weizenbaum in [16], which consisted of five sub-constructs: (a) tokenization, (b) embedding, (c) attention, (d) pre-training, and (e) transfer learning. Smart health awareness was considered as the dependent variable. The six sub-constructs from The Health Belief Model (HBM) proposed by Rosenstock et al. in [14] theory are (a) perceived susceptibility, (b) perceived severity, (c) perceived benefits, (d) perceived barriers, (e) cue to action, and (f) self-efficacy. In this framework, the moderator variables comprised four main demographics of the respondents: gender, age, occupation, and background of ChatGPT. The proposed conceptual framework hypothesised that ChatGPT was believed to promote smart health awareness among the public.

19.5 METHODOLOGY

The study employed a quantitative survey method. An online questionnaire was designed and disseminated to respondents from two different communities of different countries. The countries involved were Malaysia and Turkey. There were 30 respondents involved in this online survey to investigate the public perceptions of ChatGPT in promoting smart health awareness in Malaysia and Turkey. The questionnaire data were analysed using SPSS version 27. The open-ended items were analysed using thematic analysis using Miles and Huberman's (1994) method [12].

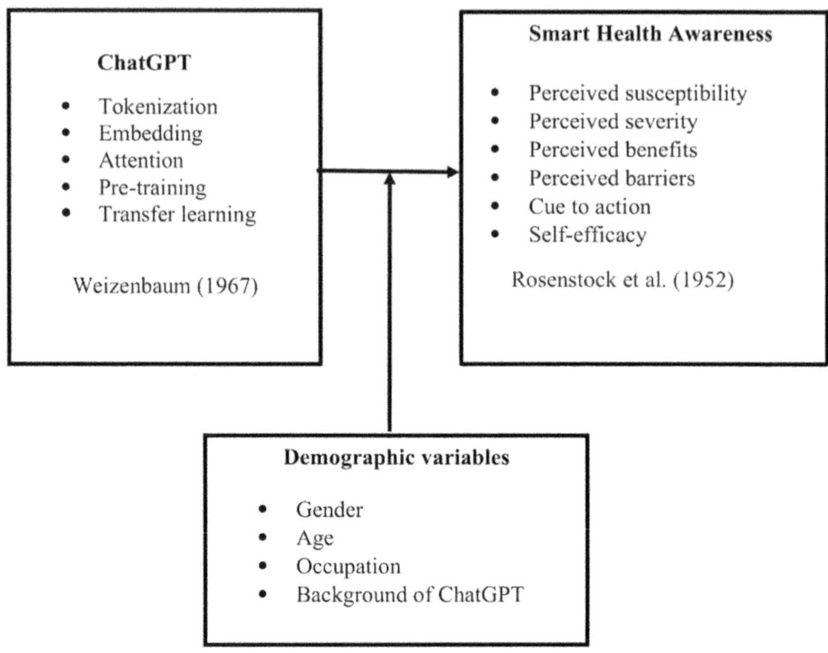

FIGURE 19.1 Conceptual framework for ChatGPT usability in promoting smart health awareness.

The online questionnaire was designed based on two models [14,16]. The questionnaire items included tokenization, embedding, attention, pre-training, and transfer learning to measure the public perceptions of ChatGPT. For the second model, the items were designed based on the sub constructs of smart health awareness: (a) perceived susceptibility, (b) perceived severity, (c) perceived benefits, (d) perceived barriers, (e) cue to action, and (f) self-efficacy. The items were created to measure the public perceptions of smart health awareness. The online survey comprised 35 items divided into four parts: Part A: Respondent Profile (6 items), Part B: Public Perceptions of ChatGPT (11 items), Part C: Public Perceptions of Smart Health Awareness (16 items), and Part D: two open-ended items were analysed using thematic analysis. Section B and Section C were measured using a 5-point Likert scale: strongly agree (5), agree (4), uncertain (3), disagree (2), and strongly disagree (1). The questionnaire was developed and validated by three experts in the field. The reliability of the instrument was established using the Cronbach Alpha coefficient, $\alpha = 0.94$.

19.6　RESULTS AND DISCUSSION

The results were presented in four parts: (A) Respondent profile, (B) Perceptions of ChatGPT, (C) Perceptions of Smart Health Awareness, and (D) Open-ended Items Analysis. The results and discussions of the study are as follows:

19.6.1 Respondent Profile

Table 19.1 shows the profile of the respondents for this study. The total number of respondents for the study is 30. From the table, 11 males (36.7%) and 19 females (63.3%) responded to the questionnaire. The majority of the respondents (53.3%) are in the age group of 18–29 years. Next, the age group of 30–39 years comprises 16.7% of respondents. The respondents from the age group of 40–49 years account for 26.7% of respondents. Only 3.3% are in the age group of 50 years and above. Regarding occupation, students represent the highest number of respondents (50.0%), followed by respondents (16.7%) who work in the government sector. Only 1 respondent (3.3%) works in the private sector, and 6.7% are self-employed. No respondents are unemployed. According to the table, the public respondents are from two countries: Malaysia (73.3%) and Turkey (26.7%). The table also includes two items that inquire about the respondents' background of ChatGPT. The first question asked whether the respondents heard about ChatGPT. 90% of respondents answered that

TABLE 19.1
Respondent Profile

Characteristics	Frequency	Percentage
Gender		
Male	11	36.7
Female	19	63.3
Age		
18–29 years	15	53.3
30–39 years	5	16.7
40–49 years	8	26.7
50 years and above	1	3.3
Occupation		
Student	15	50.0
Government sector	12	40.0
Private sector	1	3.3
Self-employed	2	6.7
Unemployed	0	0
Country of residence		
Malaysia	22	73.3
Turkey	8	26.7
I have heard about ChatGPT		
Yes	27	90.0
No	3	10.0
I know the term ChatGPT		
Yes	28	93.3
No	2	6.7

TABLE 19.2

Public Perceptions of ChatGPT

Item	Statement	M	SD	Interpretation
1	ChatGPT can be a very useful tool to use for my daily life activities.	4.07	0.83	Agree
2	ChatGPT has the potential to become more human-like in the future.	4.10	0.76	Agree
3	I believe that industries or types of businesses could benefit the most from using ChatGPT.	3.97	0.93	Agree
4	I believe ChatGPT will impact people's communication skills.	3.73	1.26	Agree
5	I feel comfortable with ChatGPT handling personal or sensitive information such as financial or medical data.	3.43	1.25	Agree
6	ChatGPT is better than search engines. (Google, Yahoo)	3.67	1.06	Agree
7	I believe ChatGPT gives more detailed answers.	3.57	1.25	Agree
8	I think ChatGPT is an interactive tool.	3.90	0.92	Agree
9	I believe I can generate high-quality content from ChatGPT.	3.70	0.99	Agree
10	I gained new knowledge from ChatGPT.	4.17	0.79	Agree
11	I learn new data and information from ChatGPT.	4.03	0.77	Agree
	Total average	3.85	0.63	Agree

they had heard about ChatGPT, while 10% of respondents never heard about it. 93.3% of respondents are familiar with the term ChatGPT, while 6.7% of respondents do not know the term.

In the next sections, the findings present the public perceptions of ChatGPT (see Table 9.2) and the public perceptions of Smart Health Awareness (see Table 9.3). All items were measured using the 5-point Likert scale. The results of the study were interpreted into mean values. The mean values were divided into five sections: Strongly Agree (4.21–5.00), Agree (3.41–4.20), Uncertain (2.61–3.40), Disagree (1.81–2.60), and Strongly Disagree (1.00–1.80). The findings were conveyed in the three highest means and the three lowest means of the items.

19.6.2 Perceptions of ChatGPT

Table 19.2 displays the public perceptions of ChatGPT. The first three highest means show that respondents largely agreed (M=4.17; SD=0.79) that they gained new knowledge from ChatGPT (item 10). Next, the respondents mainly agreed (M=4.10; SD=0.76) that ChatGPT has the potential to become more human-like in the future (item 2). The third highest mean displays that the respondents agreed (M=4.07; SD=0.83) that ChatGPT can be a very useful tool to use for daily life activities (item 1). For the first lowest mean, the table shows that the respondents agreed (M=3.43; SD=1.25) that they feel comfortable with ChatGPT handling personal or sensitive information such as financial or medical data (item 5), followed by the second highest lowest, which shows that respondents also agreed (M=3.57; SD=1.25) that they believe ChatGPT gives more detailed answers (item 7). Finally, the respondents just agreed (M=3.67; SD=1.06) with item 6. From the results, most of the respondents agreed with the statements regarding the perceptions of ChatGPT. It shows a positive response from Malaysian and Turkish people regarding the perceptions of ChatGPT.

19.6.3 Perceptions of Smart Health Awareness

In this section, Table 9.3 describes the results for the public perceptions of smart health awareness. The highest mean to promote smart health awareness was that the public agreed (M=3.97, SD=0.77) that the Chat GPT works as a real-time translation in helping patients to understand their diagnosis, treatment options, and medical instructions (item 23). Next, the respondents agreed (M=3.93, SD=0.79) that the ChatGPT helps them access information about a healthy lifestyle (item 28). The final highest mean was for item 17, in which the respondents believed (M=3.90, SD=0.96) that ChatGPT can positively impact the future of healthcare systems. With regards to the lowest mean, the respondents from both countries, Malaysia and Turkey agreed (M=3.43, SD=1.01) that the ChatGPT is important for smart healthcare systems (item 16). The second lowest mean revealed (M=3.50, SD=0.82) that the respondents agreed that ChatGPT supports users with telemedicine, such as developing virtual assistants to book patient appointments, help patients receive treatments, and manage their health (item 19). Finally, the lowest mean showed that the respondents agreed (M=3.57, SD=1.01) that the ChatGPT protects their medical data and keeps it private and confidential (item 30). In short, the findings showed that the public from Malaysia and Turkey perceived that they agreed that ChatGPT contributes to promoting smart health awareness.

Table 19.4 shows the overall means and standard deviations for ChatGPT (M=3.85; SD=0.63) and smart health awareness (M=3.74; SD=0.61) for both constructs.

The results in Table 19.5 show the correlation of each construct between the public perceptions of ChatGPT and the public perceptions of smart health awareness. The Pearson Correlation results indicate a significant positive correlation (r= 0.80; p<0.01).

19.6.4 Open-Ended Items Results

The final section of the results of the study presented the analysis of open-ended items. There were two items for this part. Respondents were required to give three answers about the benefits of using ChatGPT (Item 1) for smart healthcare systems and the disadvantages of using ChatGPT for smart healthcare systems (Item 2). Thus, the qualitative data gathered in this section were analysed using thematic analysis as shown in Table 19.6. For Item 1, the three themes that emerged were an easy tool, saving time and increasing creativity for Item A. The respondents mostly agreed that the benefit of using ChatGPT for smart healthcare systems is effective. As shown in Table 19.6, respondents also needed to list three disadvantages of using ChatGPT for smart healthcare systems. The first theme that emerged was the risk of false and inaccurate information, followed by the risk of data privacy. Finally, the last theme

TABLE 19.3

Public Perceptions of Smart Health Awareness

Item	Statement	M	SD	Interpretation
16	ChatGPT is important for smart healthcare systems.	3.43	1.01	Agree
17	I believe ChatGPT can positively impact the future of healthcare systems.	3.90	0.96	Agree
18	I feel comfortable using ChatGPT for healthcare practice.	3.67	0.96	Agree
19	ChatGPT supports users with telemedicine such as developing virtual assistants to book patient appointments, help patients receive treatments, and manage their health.	3.50	0.82	Agree
20	ChatGPT can assist users with clinical decision support by providing real-time and evidence-based recommendations.	3.73	0.87	Agree
21	ChatGPT offers round-the-clock availability to patients, allowing them to access knowledge and assistance anytime.	3.87	0.94	Agree
22	ChatGPT helps users summarise patient medical histories and streamline the record-keeping process effectively.	3.80	0.81	Agree
23	Chat GPT works as a real-time translation to help patients understand their diagnosis, treatment options, and medical instructions.	3.97	0.77	Agree
24	ChatGPT helps users develop more accurate and reliable symptom checkers.	3.83	0.91	Agree
25	ChatGPT provides emotional and mental health support such as offering a safe and non-judgmental environment, active listening, and empathetic responses.	3.57	1.04	Agree
26	ChatGPT provides support to patients and families.	3.73	0.94	Agree
27	ChatGPT improves the tracking of patient condition and performance.	3.80	0.81	Agree
28	ChatGPT helps me access information about a healthy lifestyle.	3.93	0.79	Agree
29	ChatGPT helps me learn about the symptoms of diseases	3.87	0.86	Agree
30	ChatGPT protects my medical data and information data private and confidential.	3.57	1.01	Agree
31	Overall, ChatGPT has the potential to streamline and improve healthcare systems in numerous ways.	3.73	0.79	Agree
	Total average	3.74	0.61	Agree

TABLE 19.4
Overall Means and Standard Deviation

Constructs	Mean	Standard Deviation
ChatGPT	3.85	0.63
Smart Health Awareness	3.74	0.61

TABLE 19.5
The Relationship between the ChatGPT and the Smart Health Awareness

Variable	Smart Health Awareness	
	r	Sig.
ChatGPT	0.80	0.00

TABLE 19.6
Open-Ended Items Analysis

Open-Ended Items	Rank	Main Themes	Frequency
1. Three benefits of using ChatGPT for smart healthcare systems.	1	Effective	11
	2	Easy	5
	3	Saves time	4
2. List three disadvantages of using ChatGPT for smart healthcare systems.	1	Risk of false and inaccurate information	12
	2	Risk of data privacy	5
	3	Too consumed with the ChatGPT application	2

that emerged was too consumed with the ChatGPT application. Overall, the analysis of open-ended items showed that there were benefits and disadvantages of ChatGPT usability in smart healthcare systems.

19.7 CONCLUSION

The results and findings provide empirical data on ChatGPT's usability in promoting smart health awareness. Based on the results of the study, the public from Malaysia and Turkey perceived the ChatGPT application as a potential and useful tool. The findings also illustrate that the public from Malaysia and Turkey perceived the ChatGPT application could promote smart health awareness. There was a significant relationship between the use of ChatGPT and its usability for promoting smart health awareness. Based on the analysis of open-ended items, the respondents highlighted the advantages and disadvantages of using ChatGPT for smart healthcare systems. All things considered, ChatGPT holds promise to simplify and enhance healthcare systems. This technology has the potential to become extensively used and bring about lasting change, much like how the internet has revolutionised other industries. However, it is important to note that without human healthcare practitioners, technology should be used carefully and should not be the exclusive source of healthcare choices.

REFERENCES

1. Aslam, F. (2023). The impact of artificial intelligence on chatbot technology: A study on the current advancements and leading innovations. *European Journal of Technology*, *7*(3), 62–72. https://doi.org/10.47672/ejt.1561
2. Alowais, S.A., Alghamdi, S.S., Alsuhebany, N. et al. (2023). Revolutionizing healthcare: The role of artificial intelligence in clinical practice. *BMC Medical Education, 23*, 689. https://doi.org/10.1186/s12909-023-04698-z
3. Biswas S.S. (2023). Role of chat GPT in public health. *Annals of Biomedical Engineering*, *51*(5), 868–869. https://doi.org/10.1007/s10439-023-03172-7
4. Cascella, M., Montomoli, J., Bellini, V., & Bignami, E. (2023). Evaluating the feasibility of ChatGPT in healthcare: An analysis of multiple clinical and research scenarios. *Journal of Medical Systems*, *47*(1), 1–5. https://doi.org/10.1007/s10916-023-01925-4
5. Dasborough, M.T. (2023). Awe-inspiring advancements in AI: The impact of ChatGPT on the field of organizational behavior. *Journal of Organizational Behavior*, *44*(2), 177–179. https:// doi.org/10.1002/job.2695
6. Dwivedi, Y.K., Kshetri, N., Hughes, L., Slade, E.L., Jeyaraj, A., Kar, A.K., Baabdullah, A.M., Koohang, A., Raghavan, V., Ahuja, M., Albanna, H., Albashrawi, M.A., Al-Busaidi, A.S., Balakrishnan, J., Barlette, Y., Basu, S., Bose, I., Brooks, L., Buhalis, D., & Wright, R. (2023). Opinion paper: "So what if ChatGPT wrote it?" Multidisciplinary perspectives on opportunities, challenges and implications of generative conversational AI for research, practice and policy. *International Journal of Information Management*, *71*, 1–63. https://doi.org/10.1016/j.ijinfomgt.2023.102642
7. Gordijn, B., & Have, H.T. (2023). ChatGPT: Evolution or revolution? *Medicine, Health Care and Philosophy*, *26*, 1–2.
8. Haleem, A., Javaid, M, & Ravi Pratap Singh, R.P. (2022).An era of ChatGPT as a significant futuristic support tool: A study on features, abilities, and challenges. *Bench Council Transactions on Benchmarks, Standards and Evaluations, 2*(4). https://doi.org/10.1016/j.tbench.2023.100089.
9. Karim, R.A. (2023). The Future of AR and VR technology in a mobile learning environment. In: *Proceedings of International Conference on Virtual Reality*, Şanlıurfa, Turkey.
10. Lock, S. (2022). What is ai chatbot phenomenon chatgpt and could it replace humans? Accessed 10 December 2022. https://www.theguardian.com /technology/2022/dec/05/what-is-ai-chatbot-phenomenon-chatgpt-and-could-it-replace-humans
11. Metz, A. (2022). 6 exciting ways to use ChatGPT: From coding to poetry. *TechRadar*, https://www.techradar.com/features/6-exciting-ways-to-use-chatgpt-from-coding-to-poetry
12. Miles, M.B., & Huberman, A.M. (1994). *Qualitative Data Analysis: An Expanded Sourcebook*. Thousand Oaks, CA: Sage Publications.
13. Parray, A.A., Inam, Z.M., Ramonfaur, D., Haider, S.S. Mistry.S.K., & Pandya, A.K. (2023) ChatGPT and global public health: Applications, challenges, ethical considerations and mitigation strategies, *Global Transitions, 5*, 50–54

14. Rosenstock, I., Hochbaum, G., & Kegels, S. (1952). Health belief model, united states public health service, 1.
15. Sujata, K., Gandhi, P., Shinde, G., & Subramanian, V. (2020). Deep learning and explainable AI in healthcare using EHR. In: Dash S., Acharya B., Mittal M., Abraham A., Kelemen A. (eds), *Deep Learning Techniques for Biomedical and Health Informatics. Studies in Big Data*, vol. 68. Springer, Cham. https://doi.org/10.1007/978-3-030-33966-1_7
16. Weizenbaum, J. (1967). Contextual understanding by computers. *Communications of the ACM 10*(8), 474–480.

20 Epileptic Seizure Prediction Framework Using Medical Internet of Things

P. Hema and R. Vanithamani

20.1 INTRODUCTION

Epilepsy stands in the second position in neurological illness, whereas stroke stands first in humans. About 50 million people are affected with epilepsy globally. One-fourth of the patients do not react to the present available treatments. In 70% of people, antiepileptic medicines control seizures successfully. Epileptic seizures affect about 1% of the world population. In the present scenario, the perfect identification of an epileptic prediction system that can be safe and reliable for prolonged human implantation is crucial. In seizure prediction techniques, features collected from electroencephalographic (EEG) recordings are categorized into preictal and non-preictal states [1]. The addition of a threshold to an EEG measure or non-linear analysis is generally used to test the prediction of epileptic seizures. IoT has experienced rapid growth in various sectors including manufacturing, healthcare, government, infrastructure management, and consumers. One of our main objectives, as has already been said, is to classify brain signals. The brain signals are classified into two types—seizures and non-seizure signals [2]. The amount of data transmitted to the cloud has been reduced by designing the system using edge computing. Important technological advancements in big data analytics and cloud computing have enabled us to manage this complexity [3,4]. The necessary user data and its surroundings have been collected using wearable IoT devices. Automated and computerized systems have been developed for detecting seizures. The patients' EEG and EOG signals are to be collected and processed, and they should be kept on tabs at all times for their safety.

The paper's primary contribution is as follows:

- The Medical Internet of Things (MIoT) can be used to increase energy efficiency in seizure prediction frameworks for epilepsy [5].
- The new features we propose for the classification model enable us to present a highly effective seizure prediction technique.
- We were able to decrease the number of EEG signals while maintaining a high level of prediction accuracy by incorporating the new features.

DOI: 10.1201/9781032632223-20

- We present an algorithm for selecting EEG channels that reduces the number of EEG channels to lower the amount of memory required to store data and variables [6].
- An IoT framework is applied in this report, which can be used to connect the patient to the doctor and any ambulance crew they choose.

The proposed methodology is as follows:

- Using MioT-based epileptic seizure prediction frameworks (MIoT-ESPF) is described in detail in this section. Figure 20.1 provides an overview of the general characteristics of the technique structure.

20.2 MEDICAL INTERNET OF THINGS BASED ON EPILEPTIC SEIZURE PREDICTION FRAMEWORKS (MIOT-ESPF)

As an effect of the revolution in healthcare technology, smart healthcare uses resources more effectively and intelligently to meet the requirements of individual patients. As the world's population grows and traditional healthcare falls short of meeting these needs, there is a growing need for innovative healthcare systems. Using MIoT-based seizure prediction for epileptic patients is an example of health care that enhances their life quality. Connecting all real-world components, the Internet of Things is a cyber-physical system. The Internet of Things (IoT) makes it possible for doctors to monitor and consult with patients from a distance [7].

Figure 20.1 shows a proposed MIoT framework for the real-time prediction of epileptic seizures, which is presented in this research. EEG data is recorded using a commercially available wireless headset, and there is no pre-processing of EEG

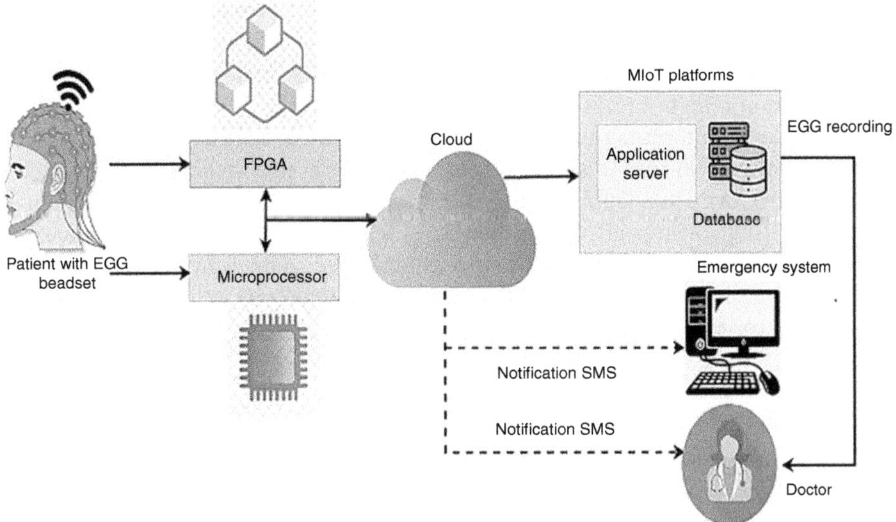

FIGURE 20.1 MIoT framework.

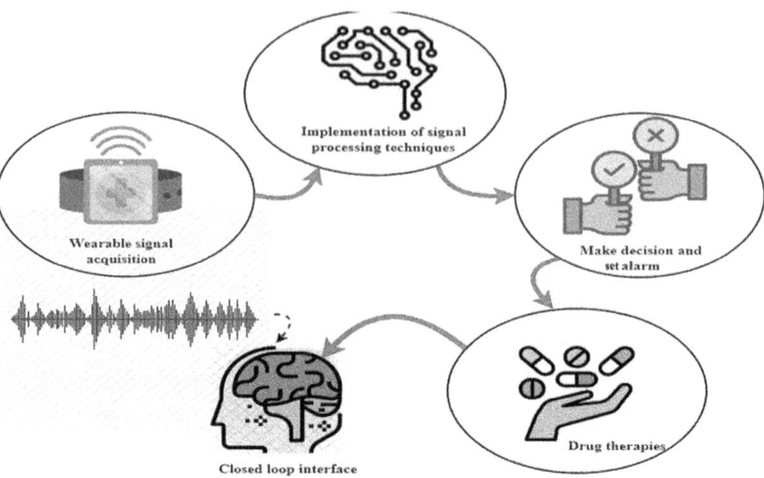

FIGURE 20.2   Epileptic seizure prediction framework.

signals in the model [8]. The FPGA also communicates recorded EEG data to the Microprocessor in addition to the prediction results. Any medical service selected by the patient is alerted when a seizure forecast at the edge is correct. The doctor has access to the patient's cloud-based continuous EEG recordings and can review and analyze them. The previous frame state is recognized within a predetermined period, and alarms are generated. Seizures can be predicted by comparing the brain's pre- and interictal states [9]. Despite extensive research on seizure prediction, no standard length exists for the preictal state [10]. This investigation selected a 1-hour preictal interval and a 4-hour interictal time for this investigation.

The simplified procedure of a private network Extra Sensory Perception (ESP) system is shown in Figure 20.2. Brain signal monitoring, decision-making and alarm unit, and an intervention block that includes electrical stimulation and an interface for medication release are all included in the system [11]. The two most common ways to collect brain signals are invasive and non-invasive devices. Health status can now be monitored in real-time using non-invasive wearable devices that can access and recover information from the body [3]. Non-invasive recordings of brain signals have lower frequencies and worse spatial resolution than invasive brain measurements. The non-invasive abilities of wearable devices enabled by smartphones can benefit patients with neurological illnesses such as epileptic seizures, Parkinson's disease, cerebrovascular disease, and others [12].

20.3   FUNCTIONALITY OF THE IOMT

Perception, network, and application all play a role in the Internet of Things, and here, the data flow is depicted in Figure 20.3. As long as people are involved, confidentiality, integrity, and authenticity will be issues in each layer. As a result of human interaction, data obtained from individuals and patients must be granted access by the system. People can't use the device at its full capacity for privacy reasons.

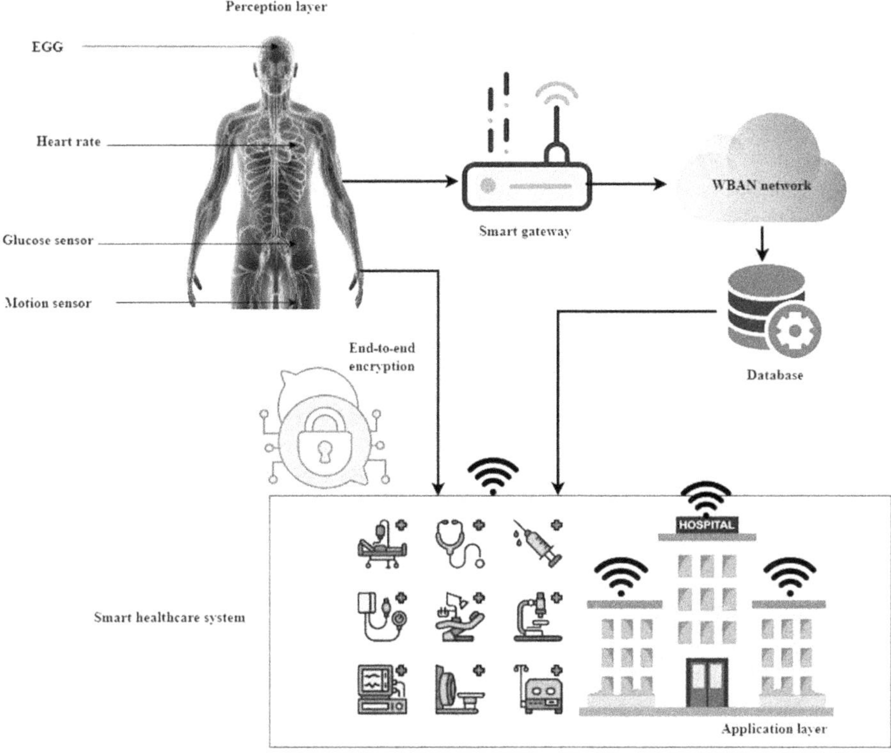

FIGURE 20.3 Typical Internet of Things (IoT) e-health architecture.

The integrity, honesty, and confidentiality of patient health information are essential. Real-time health monitoring necessitates the construction of a security framework. Equipment and protective frameworks for health technicians and paramedics have evolved, and they quickly degenerate compared to these structures [4]. Aside from that, our claims are backed up by our prior work in this area. According to previous statements, numerous security flaws within the Internet of Things (IoT) must be addressed if serious security concerns are to be addressed.

Innovative inventions such as Bluetooth, Wifi, ZigBee, 4G LTE, and others are used to transmit data from the network level to IoT hubs and computers throughout the network system. These technologies have made it possible for data center storage and entry point routers to communicate with each other. IoT nodes communicate via gateways, which act as a conduit for data exchange. Confidentiality, integrity, and authenticity are all protected by this application layer. There is a plethora of Internet of Things (IoT) applications in implementation. The application layer connects the network to the end devices. As the sensors for each application provide data, this layer can provide a variety of services to the applications below it. In recent years, WBAN technology in healthcare has grown significantly [13]. Tracking patient behavior, treating patients automatically, and much more can be accomplished by integrating a range of medical devices into the WBAN.

20.4   ENHANCED ENERGY-EFFICIENT METHOD

Automatic feature engineering and the intricate manual design of Convolutional Neural Network (CNN) structures help them perform well in classification problems. Neural architecture search (NAS) alters the process of designing neural network models manually for automatic implementation and achieves performance comparable to manual design or even better performance [14]. Strings of a specific length were used to describe the neural network. These strings contained information about the target neural network's number of filters, their width and length, and their pooling layer performance [14]. A CNN controller produced these random strings of characters. In this study, a straightforward approach to estimating performance was used. This section was not optimized because the training dataset for epileptic seizure prediction will only take a short time. This string depiction will be created, trained, and validated when the control system CNN completes the process of generating strings [15]. The validated outcomes are used as satisfaction signals to update the controller CNN and achieve maximum reward using reinforcement learning. $x(\omega)$ is expected to give the following reward in Equation (20.1):

$$x(\omega) = A_{s(f_1, Y, w)}[U] \tag{20.1}$$

For example, the CNN predicts actions $f_{1,Y}$ based on the probability density function s. The Recurrent Neural Network (RNN's) verification accuracy (U) is used as a high-performing team for training the controller. Since U cannot be differentiated, we have been using the following procedure to make necessary adjustments to the controller's settings:

$$\left\{ \frac{1}{D} \sum_{D=1}^{D} \sum_{y=1}^{Y} \nabla_\omega \log Q\left(f_y \mid \left(f_{(y-a)1}; \omega \right) U_y - c \right) \right\} \tag{20.2}$$

Equation (20.2) describes the Y network architectures that can be generated in a single batch using this method, which is based on the validation rule. The controller's prediction for a given string of hyperparameters is denoted by the letter D. Each subsequent network architecture's validation accuracy is represented by U_y. While its exponential moving average accuracy is symbolized by c, the controller CNN parameters are updated so that a structure with a high degree of accuracy can achieve a high selection probability. This study aims to evaluate the performance loss of various bit-quantization methods in the prediction networks for epileptic seizures. In a fixed-point representation, weights and authorizations are quantized to the same number of bits. In this study, the weight quantification method is described in Equation (20.3):

$$A = clip\left(\frac{round\left(2^{a-1} \times \omega\right)}{2^{a-1}} - 1, 1 - 2^{a-1} \right) \tag{20.3}$$

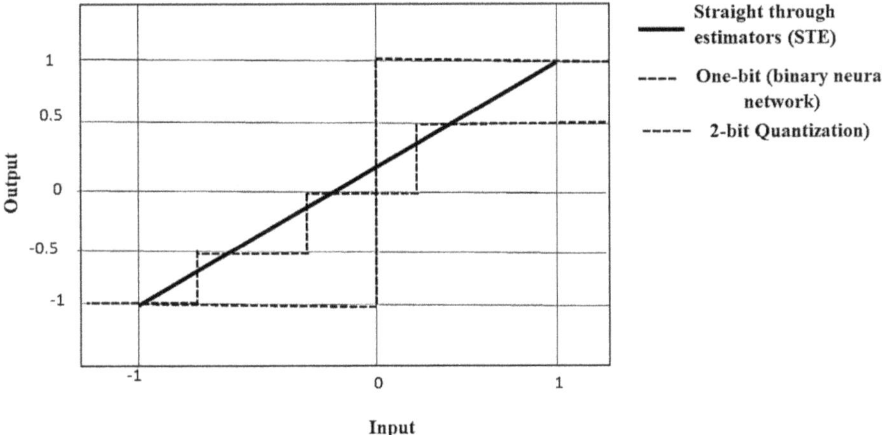

FIGURE 20.4 Quantization of 1-bit and 2-bit parameters.

before quantization, where A is the number of bits that need to be quantized, respectively. The quantized tanh function, shown in Equation (20.3), is used to quantize activations. Quantization of 1-bit and 2-bit parameters is shown in Figure 20.4 in the forwarding pass and backpropagation, respectively (2). It doesn't matter how many quantized bits A were used to train the quantized model, as long as the gradient propagated by the normal estimators is that function.

$$E\tan e(b) = Clip(b, 1i, 1) = \max\left(-1, \min(1.b)\right) \tag{20.4}$$

Backward pass classification is a useful operation, and so, this function is utilized.

These systems must protect the data they collect, transmit, retrieve, and store at every step of the process. Electronics and sensor devices, such as the MIoT, focus on physical security. Digital defense addresses a person's virtual adversary, which uses a network-connected medium [16]. Figure 20.5 shows a flowchart illustrating the WBAN features of IoMT. When diagnosing some diseases, collaboration between devices is essential; the measured parameters must be processed with the utmost level of security. The processor of the sensor node typically handles event classification. To ensure that medical workers and emergency responders are alerted as soon as possible, the private server must receive real-time data from the devices if any abnormalities are detected. Fast and easy-to-use graphical user interfaces are part of the IoMT platform's performance. WBAN tracking must be adjusted to pinpoint each patient's exact location when unusual events are detected. Patients in hospitals are constantly monitored by the WBAN network, primarily used to assist those needing immediate medical attention [17].

When it comes to wearable ESP, trustworthy features generated from brain waves would help. This part describes the most recent methods for extracting features from time and frequency domain data. EEG signal properties can be extracted using statistical moments in the time domain. Several statistical moments mean and variance

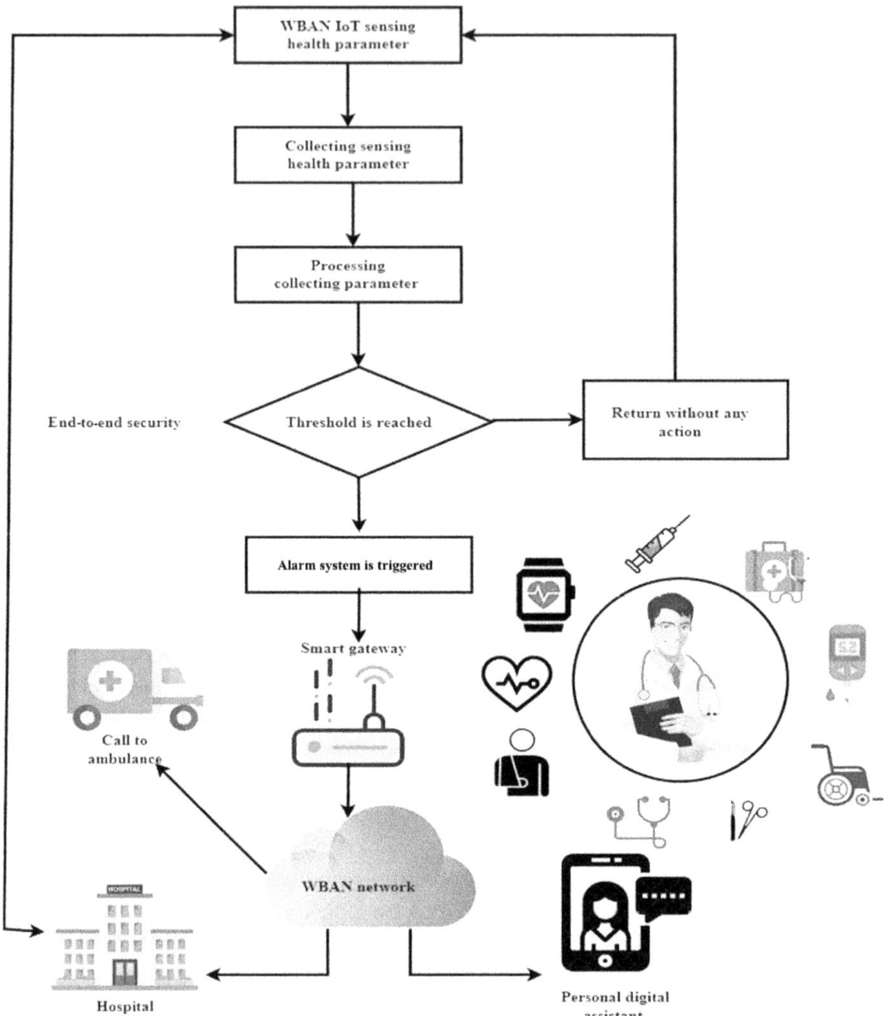

FIGURE 20.5 Functionality diagram of the MIoT.

for ESP tasks because of the large disparities between preictal and interictal times. Advantages of the zero-crossing zero-crossing using the autocorrelation function (ACF), one may assess if the data is random or not by comparing the association between the signal amplitude and their shifted versions with the time lag A_s. At delay S, the ACF i is defined as follows:

$$A_s = \left(\frac{\sum_{i=1}^{n-s} (X_i - \bar{X})(X_{i+s} - \bar{X})}{\sum_{i=1}^{n-s} (X_i - \bar{X})^2} \right) \tag{20.5}$$

TABLE 20.1
EEG Signals Frequency Band, Range, and Characteristic

Frequency Band	Frequency Range	Characteristic
Theta	<3	Infants, children, and adults are all susceptible to this phenomenon.
Alpha	3–7	Typically occurs when people are in a relaxed state of mind.
Beta	13–31	Anxiety sufferers are more likely to have frontal lobe dysfunction.
Gamma	>29	People in various emotional states, including anxiety, and contentment, have a broad, high-frequency band.

In Equation (20.5), to calculate the time-series mean of the target time series, we divide X_i by the number of measurements and multiply it by X_{i+s}.

The frequency-domain representation of time series signals is based on the Fourier Transform. Researchers used frequency domain information from EEG signals to study the brain. According to traditional classification, the three frequency sub-bands shown in Table 20.1 are grouped into five separate types.

20.5   RESULT AND DISCUSSIONS

Seizure detection methods for responsive neurostimulators were examined in this study. There are significant constraints on such a system's computational load and energy consumption since it must be implantable. Three seizure detection methods have been designed, and their performance and energy requirements for execution in embedded systems have been estimated and compared. It was found that the CNN classifier performed better than the other classifiers in the performance comparison. A CNN classifier was used to evaluate energy estimation accuracy in the seizure detection algorithms. With this comparison, we understood better how accurate our prediction method is compared to the current state of the latest advances. Since no single MIoT structure is better at detecting epileptic seizures than another, it's important to consider the dataset and problem features when deciding which structure to use for seizure detection. This includes the need for real-time identification or a minimum acceptable accuracy level. This field needs to focus more on clinical data and predicting epileptic seizures to improve detection accuracy, as demonstrated earlier. A wide range of concerns, including inflation, were addressed. Most of the research is focused on patient sensitivity ratio, specificity rate, seizure prediction rate, accuracy ratio, performance analysis of CNN, and false-positive rates. According to a new report, this study found that understanding MIoT-ESPF is more accurate than previous research.

Table 20.2 illustrates the comparability of performance measures in the industry. An organization's overall goals can be better supported if the metrics used to calculate it fall within a specified range.

TABLE 20.2

Comparisons of Performance Metrics

Parameters	Bi-LSTM	SPM-PSMD	DL-LM	CHB-MIT-EEG	MIOT-ESPF
Sensitivity ratio (%)	45.7	55.67	65.6	47.7	92.11
Specificity rate (%)	55.6	50.5	65.4	67.8	89.91
Prediction rate (%)	62.3	52.3	42.3	64.3	90.23
Performance analysis of CNN (%)	58.2	68.2	38.2	59.2	96.8
False positive rates (%)	58.5	38.5	68.5	57.5	93.51
Accuracy ratio (%)	34.6	56.7	67.8	74.2	90.31

20.6 CONCLUSION

The energy prediction methodology proposed can be used to verify the applicability and relevance of the seizure detection model developed for medical implants. Prevention of epileptic seizures is now possible through early detection of the beginning of the preictal state. EEG signals can be recorded by implanting electrodes into the brains of patients. Accurately forecasting high specificity while also keeping low false positive rates, a problem remains. EEG signals must be preprocessed to remove noise introduced during recording. Instead of using all networks or converting them into a single surrogate channel, picking a few is more difficult because fewer channels are available. Another major issue in seizure prediction systems is feature extraction and selection. A small set of attributes with high covariance variability must be selected to reduce the system's complexity as a whole to detect seizures with any degree of success. These and other studies' findings show that the proposed method effectively predicts epileptic seizures in real time. A better understanding of epilepsy models is required to provide patients with better care at any location.

REFERENCES

1. Hu, Q., Li, M., & Li, Y. (2022). Single-channel EEG signal extraction based on DWT, CEEMDAN, and ICA method. *Frontiers in Human Neuroscience*, 16, 1–12.
2. Jana, R., & Mukherjee, I. (2021). Deep learning-based efficient epileptic seizure prediction with EEG channel optimization. *Biomedical Signal Processing and Control*, 68, 102767.
3. Janocko, N. J., Jing, J., Fan, Z., Teagarden, D. L., Villarreal, H. K., Morton, M. L., ... & Karakis, I. (2021). DDESVSFS: A simple, rapid and comprehensive screening tool for the differential diagnosis of epileptic seizures VS functional seizures. *Epilepsy Research*, 171, 106563.
4. Li, Y., Cui, W., Luo, M., Li, K., & Wang, L. (2018). Epileptic seizure detection based on time-frequency images of EEG signals using Gaussian mixture model and gray level co-occurrence matrix features. *International Journal of Neural Systems*, 28(7), 1850003.
5. Das, K., Daschakladar, D., Roy, P. P., Chatterjee, A., & Saha, S. P. (2020). Epileptic seizure prediction by the detection of seizure waveform from the pre-ictal phase of EEG signal. *Biomedical Signal Processing and Control*, 57, 101720.

6. Shoeibi, A., Khodatars, M., Ghassemi, N., Jafari, M., Meridian, P., Alizadehsani, R., ... & Acharya, U. R. (2021). Epileptic seizures detection using deep learning techniques: A review. *International Journal of Environmental Research and Public Health*, 18(11), 5780.

7. Hallab, A., & Sen, A. (2021). Epilepsy and psychogenic non-epileptic seizures in forcibly displaced people: A scoping review. *Seizure*, 92, 128–148.

8. Maddirala, A. K., & Veluvolu, K. C. (2022). ICA With CWT and k-means for eye-blink artifact removal from fewer channel EEG. *IEEE Transactions on Neural Systems and Rehabilitation Engineering*, 30, 1361–1373.

9. Slimen, I. B., Boubchir, L., & Seddik, H. (2020). Epileptic seizure prediction based on EEG spikes detection of ictal-preictal states. *Journal of Biomedical Research*, 34(3), 162.

10. Stirling, R. E., Cook, M. J., Grayden, D. B., & Karoly, P. J. (2021). Seizure forecasting and cyclic control of seizures. *Epilepsia*, 62, S2–S14.

11. Mehla, V. K., Singhal, A., Singh, P., & Pachori, R. B. (2021). An efficient method for identification of epileptic seizures from EEG signals using Fourier analysis. *Physical and Engineering Sciences in Medicine*, 44(2), 443–456.

12. Shoeibi, A., Ghassemi, N., Khodatars, M., Jafari, M., Moridian, P., Alizadehsani, R., ... & Nahavandi, S. (2021). Applications of epileptic seizures detection in neuro-imaging modalities using deep learning techniques: methods, challenges, and future works, *Research Gate*, 18(11):5780.

13. Qureshi, M. B., Afzaal, M., Qureshi, M. S., & Fayaz, M. (2021). Machine learning-based EEG signals classification model for epileptic seizure detection. *Multimedia Tools and Applications*, 80(12), 17849–17877.

14. Saminu, S., Xu, G., Shuai, Z., Abd El Kader, I., Jabire, A. H., Ahmed, Y. K., ... & Ahmad, I. S. (2021). A recent investigation on detection and classification of epileptic seizure techniques using EEG signal. *Brain Sciences*, 11(5), 668.

15. Gupta, S., Sameer, M., & Mohan, N. (2021, March). Detection of epileptic seizures using convolutional neural network. In: *2021 International Conference on Emerging Smart Computing and Informatics (ESCI)* (pp. 786–790). IEEE.

16. Yu, Z., Nie, W., Zhou, W., Xu, F., Yuan, S., Leng, Y., & Yuan, Q. (2020). Epileptic seizure prediction based on local mean decomposition and deep convolutional neural network. *The Journal of Supercomputing*, 76(5), 3462–3476.

17. Büyükçakır, B., Elmaz, F., & Mutlu, A. Y. (2020). Hilbert vibration decomposition-based epileptic seizure prediction with neural network. *Computers in Biology and Medicine*, 119, 103665.

21 Innovating Healthcare
Synergistic Integration of AI, IoT, and Blockchain for Sustainable and Efficient Smart Healthcare Solutions

Gagan Deep, V. Jyoti, and S. Anjali

21.1 INTRODUCTION

Smart healthcare refers to the integration of advanced technologies, such as artificial intelligence (AI), Internet of Things (IoT), and blockchain, into healthcare systems to improve patient care, enhance operational efficiency, and enable sustainable healthcare solutions. The background and context of smart healthcare provide a foundation for understanding the need and significance of integrating these technologies into the healthcare industry. The healthcare sector is facing numerous challenges, including rising healthcare costs, increasing prevalence of chronic diseases, and limited resources. These challenges have spurred the adoption of innovative technologies to address these issues and transform healthcare delivery. AI, IoT, and blockchain have emerged as key enablers for smart healthcare solutions by offering capabilities such as data analytics, real-time monitoring, secure data exchange, and decentralized data management. AI has revolutionized healthcare by enabling advanced data analysis, predictive modeling, and decision support systems. It has the potential to improve diagnosis accuracy, optimize treatment plans, and enhance patient outcomes. IoT facilitates the interconnection of various medical devices and sensors, allowing seamless data collection, remote patient monitoring, and real-time healthcare delivery. It enables healthcare providers to gather continuous patient data, detect anomalies, and provide personalized care. Blockchain, on the other hand, offers secure and transparent data management, ensuring data integrity, privacy, and interoperability in healthcare systems. Several studies have highlighted the transformative potential of these technologies in healthcare. For instance, research by Johnson et al. [1] emphasizes the role of AI in personalized medicine and precision healthcare. The work of Haghi Kashani et al. [2] discusses the applications of IoT in healthcare, including remote patient monitoring and smart wearable devices. Moreover, the study by Hölbl et al. [3] examines the use of blockchain in healthcare for secure and interoperable data exchange.

DOI: 10.1201/9781032632223-21

21.2 IMPORTANCE OF INTEGRATING AI, IoT, AND BLOCKCHAIN TECHNOLOGIES

AI enables healthcare systems to leverage the power of data analytics, machine learning, and deep learning algorithms to gain insights from vast amounts of medical data. It can assist in early diagnosis, treatment planning, and personalized medicine, leading to more effective and efficient healthcare delivery [4]. IoT, on the other hand, allows for the seamless connectivity of medical devices, wearables, and sensors, creating an interconnected ecosystem that enables remote patient monitoring, real-time data collection, and preventive care. This technology enhances patient engagement, enables continuous monitoring, and facilitates timely interventions [5]. Blockchain technology provides a decentralized and transparent system for securely storing and sharing healthcare data. It ensures the integrity, immutability, and privacy of medical records, enabling secure and auditable data exchange among stakeholders. It also enhances data interoperability and enables patients to have greater control over their health information [6,7]. The integration of these technologies offers tremendous potential for improving healthcare outcomes, optimizing resource utilization, and advancing research and innovation in the field.

21.3 RESEARCH PROBLEM AND OBJECTIVES

The healthcare industry is facing numerous challenges, including the need for improved patient care, enhanced operational efficiency, and the secure management of medical data. Traditional healthcare systems often struggle to meet these demands effectively. Therefore, there is a pressing need to explore innovative solutions that can address these challenges and pave the way for sustainable and efficient healthcare systems.

21.3.1 RESEARCH OBJECTIVES

1. To examine the potential of integrating AI, IoT, and blockchain technologies in the healthcare industry for enhancing patient care and operational efficiency.
2. To evaluate the impact of AI, IoT, and blockchain technologies on data security and privacy in healthcare.
3. To assess the feasibility and scalability of implementing AI, IoT, and blockchain-based solutions in healthcare settings.
4. To explore the challenges and barriers associated with the integration of AI, IoT, and blockchain technologies in healthcare and propose strategies to overcome them.
5. To investigate the economic implications and cost-effectiveness of implementing smart healthcare solutions based on the integration of AI, IoT, and blockchain technologies.
6. To provide recommendations for policymakers, healthcare organizations, and technology developers on leveraging the synergistic integration of AI, IoT, and blockchain for sustainable and efficient healthcare solutions.

21.4 SIGNIFICANCE OF THE STUDY

The significance of this study lies in its potential to address critical challenges in the healthcare industry and revolutionize the way healthcare is delivered. By integrating AI, IoT, and blockchain technologies, the study aims to enhance patient care, improve operational efficiency, and ensure the security and privacy of medical data. The findings of this study can contribute to the development of sustainable and efficient smart healthcare solutions that have the potential to transform healthcare systems worldwide. The study's findings will be valuable for healthcare professionals, policymakers, and technology developers in understanding the benefits and implications of integrating AI, IoT, and blockchain in healthcare. The insights gained from this research can inform decision-making processes and guide the implementation of innovative technologies to optimize patient outcomes and healthcare services. Moreover, this study aligns with the growing global interest in digital transformation and the adoption of advanced technologies in healthcare. By exploring the synergistic integration of AI, IoT, and blockchain, the study contributes to the existing body of knowledge and provides practical recommendations for leveraging these technologies effectively in healthcare settings.

The rapid advancements in technology, particularly in the areas of artificial intelligence (AI), Internet of Things (IoT), and blockchain, have opened up new possibilities for transforming the healthcare industry. This literature review provides an overview of the applications and benefits of AI, IoT, and blockchain technologies in healthcare.

AI in healthcare: AI technologies, such as machine learning and deep learning algorithms, have shown great potential in healthcare applications. AI can be used for medical imaging analysis, disease diagnosis, drug discovery, personalized medicine, and predictive analytics. For instance, Abdar et al. [8] demonstrated the effectiveness of a deep learning algorithm in skin cancer classification, achieving accuracy comparable to dermatologists. AI-powered virtual assistants and chatbots also enable personalized patient interactions and support remote monitoring and care [9].

IoT in healthcare: The IoT involves interconnected devices and sensors that collect and transmit data for various healthcare purposes. IoT devices can monitor patient vital signs, track medication adherence, and provide real-time health data for remote patient monitoring. According to Al-khafajiy et al. [9], IoT technologies enable the continuous monitoring of patients' health conditions, leading to early detection of anomalies and proactive interventions. IoT also facilitates the seamless integration of healthcare devices and systems, improving care coordination and operational efficiency [10].

Blockchain in healthcare: Blockchain, a decentralized and immutable ledger technology, offers enhanced security, privacy, and interoperability in healthcare. It enables secure storage and sharing of sensitive patient data, ensures data integrity, and facilitates transparent and auditable transactions. For instance, Madine et al. [11] proposed a blockchain-based framework for health data sharing and consent management, empowering patients with control over their medical records. Blockchain also facilitates supply chain management, clinical research data sharing, and identity verification in healthcare [12].

21.5 APPLICATIONS OF AI, IoT, AND BLOCKCHAIN IN SMART HEALTHCARE SOLUTIONS

The integration of AI, IoT, and blockchain technologies has the potential to revolutionize healthcare delivery and improve patient outcomes. This literature review explores the applications of AI, IoT, and blockchain in smart healthcare solutions.

AI in smart healthcare: AI technologies, such as machine learning and deep learning, have been widely applied in various healthcare domains. AI algorithms can analyze medical images, such as X-rays and MRIs, for accurate diagnosis and detection of abnormalities [13]. AI-powered chatbots and virtual assistants enhance patient engagement and support personalized healthcare services [14]. Moreover, AI enables predictive analytics for early disease detection and personalized treatment planning [7].

IoT in smart healthcare: The IoT plays a crucial role in smart healthcare by enabling connectivity and real-time monitoring of patients. IoT devices, including wearable sensors and remote monitoring systems, collect and transmit patient health data for continuous monitoring and early intervention [15]. IoT also enables remote patient monitoring and telehealth services, improving access to healthcare in remote areas [16].

Blockchain in smart healthcare: Blockchain technology offers secure and transparent data management in smart healthcare solutions. It ensures data integrity, privacy, and interoperability, enabling secure sharing of electronic health records (EHRs) among different healthcare providers [17]. Blockchain-based smart contracts facilitate automated and transparent transactions, streamlining healthcare operations and reducing costs [18].

Integration of AI, IoT, and blockchain: The synergistic integration of AI, IoT, and blockchain technologies in smart healthcare solutions holds great promise. For instance, AI algorithms can analyze IoT-generated patient data in real time, enabling early detection of health issues and personalized interventions [19]. Blockchain technology ensures the security and privacy of IoT-generated data, enhancing trust and data sharing among healthcare stakeholders [20].

21.6 PREVIOUS STUDIES ON THE INTEGRATION OF AI, IoT, AND BLOCKCHAIN IN HEALTHCARE

Previous studies have extensively investigated the integration of AI, IoT, and blockchain technologies in the healthcare sector, showcasing the potential benefits and challenges of this integration. These studies have explored various aspects such as data management, interoperability, security, and patient care. In the realm of AI, researchers have demonstrated the effectiveness of AI algorithms in medical image analysis [21], disease diagnosis [22], and treatment planning [23]. They have also explored the use of AI-powered chatbots and virtual assistants for patient engagement and support [24]. In the field of IoT, studies have focused on the application of wearable devices for real-time patient monitoring, remote healthcare services, and health data collection [25]. IoT-enabled systems have been leveraged to improve healthcare delivery, enhance patient outcomes, and enable personalized medicine.

Regarding blockchain, researchers have investigated its potential for secure and transparent health data exchange, interoperability of electronic health records, and privacy-preserving data sharing [26]. Blockchain has shown promise in addressing the challenges of data integrity, security, and privacy in healthcare systems. Furthermore, several studies have explored the integration of AI, IoT, and blockchain collectively. They have highlighted the potential synergies and benefits of combining these technologies in areas such as telemedicine, health data analytics, and personalized healthcare [27]. These studies emphasize the importance of seamless integration and interoperability among AI, IoT, and blockchain to achieve comprehensive and efficient healthcare solutions.

21.7 CONCEPTUAL MODEL

The integration of AI, IoT, and blockchain in smart healthcare solutions involves several key constructs and variables that are essential for understanding and analyzing the outcomes of this integration. These constructs and variables play a crucial role in developing a comprehensive understanding of the underlying mechanisms and evaluating the effectiveness of the integrated system.

1. **AI technology**: This construct refers to the use of artificial intelligence techniques and algorithms within healthcare settings. It includes machine learning, natural language processing, computer vision, and expert systems. AI technology enables tasks such as data analysis, predictive modeling, decision-making support, and automation in healthcare.
2. **IoT devices and infrastructure**: This construct represents the network of interconnected devices, sensors, and systems in a healthcare environment. It includes wearable devices, medical sensors, remote monitoring systems, and the infrastructure required for data transmission and communication. IoT devices and infrastructure facilitate real-time data collection, remote monitoring, and seamless communication between devices and healthcare systems.
3. **Blockchain technology**: This construct encompasses the decentralized and secure ledger system that enables transparent and tamper-proof recording of healthcare data and transactions. It includes blockchain platforms, smart contracts, consensus mechanisms, and data immutability. Blockchain technology ensures data integrity, enhances security, and fosters trust in healthcare systems.
4. **Healthcare outcomes**: This construct represents the desired outcomes and impacts of integrating AI, IoT, and blockchain in smart healthcare. It includes improved patient care, enhanced operational efficiency, cost savings, increased data security and privacy, better decision-making, and heightened patient engagement. Healthcare outcomes reflect the overall effectiveness and benefits of the integrated system.
5. **User acceptance and adoption**: This construct focuses on understanding the attitudes, perceptions, and behaviors of users toward the integrated system. It includes user satisfaction, perceived usefulness, perceived ease of

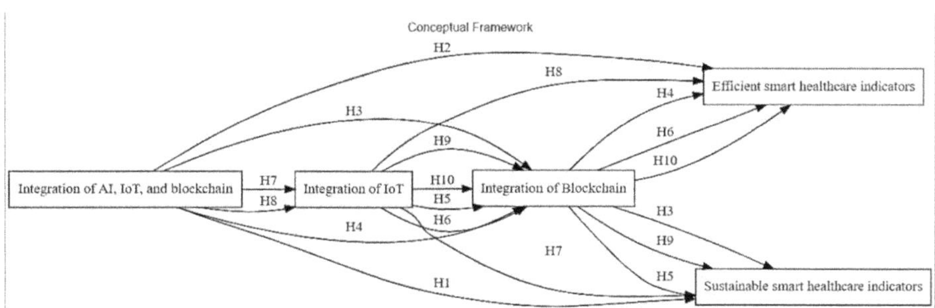

FIGURE 21.1   Conceptual framework.

Source: Author's own compilation.

> use, intention to use, and actual usage behavior. User acceptance and adoption determine the success and sustainability of the integrated system in healthcare settings.
>
> 6. **Data security and privacy**: This construct addresses the protection of healthcare data and patient privacy within the integrated system. It includes data encryption, access control mechanisms, privacy policies, compliance with regulatory requirements, and user trust in the system. Data security and privacy are critical considerations to ensure the confidentiality and integrity of healthcare information.

The conceptual framework for this study is based on the integration of AI, IoT, and blockchain technologies in the context of sustainable and efficient smart healthcare. The framework considers the interconnectedness of these technologies and their influence on the indicators of sustainable and efficient smart healthcare solutions. The key components of the conceptual framework include AI, IoT, blockchain, sustainable smart healthcare indicators, and efficient smart healthcare indicators. The framework posits that the integration of AI, IoT, and blockchain positively affects both sustainable and efficient smart healthcare indicators. The conceptual framework is shown in Figure 21.1.

21.7.1 Hypotheses

H1: The integration of AI, IoT, and blockchain positively influences sustainable smart healthcare indicators.

H2: The integration of AI, IoT, and blockchain positively influences efficient smart healthcare indicators.

These hypotheses propose that the integration of AI, IoT, and blockchain technologies has a direct positive impact on both sustainable and efficient smart healthcare indicators. The mediation and moderation effects within this integration will further elucidate the underlying mechanisms and contextual factors that enhance these relationships.

21.7.2 Mediation Hypotheses

H3: The effect of AI on sustainable smart healthcare indicators is mediated by blockchain.

H4: The effect of AI on efficient smart healthcare indicators is mediated by blockchain.

H5: The effect of IoT on sustainable smart healthcare indicators is mediated by blockchain.

H6: The effect of IoT on efficient smart healthcare indicators is mediated by blockchain.

These mediation hypotheses suggest that blockchain plays a mediating role in the relationship between AI and IoT with sustainable and efficient smart healthcare indicators. It is expected that the integration of blockchain enhances the impact of AI and IoT on these indicators.

21.7.3 Moderation Hypotheses

H7: The relationship between AI and sustainable smart healthcare indicators is moderated by the level of IoT integration.

H8: The relationship between AI and efficient smart healthcare indicators is moderated by the level of IoT integration.

H9: The relationship between IoT and sustainable smart healthcare indicators is moderated by the level of blockchain integration.

H10: The relationship between IoT and efficient smart healthcare indicators is moderated by the level of blockchain integration.

These moderation hypotheses propose that the level of IoT integration and blockchain integration moderates the relationship between AI and IoT with sustainable and efficient smart healthcare indicators. The specific contexts of IoT and blockchain integration are expected to enhance or attenuate the effects of AI and IoT on these indicators.

21.8 RESEARCH METHODOLOGY

Research design and approach: This study employed a quantitative research design to investigate the integration of AI, IoT, and blockchain technologies in sustainable and efficient smart healthcare solutions. The research approach was based on the collection and analysis of both secondary data and primary data.

Sources of data: Secondary data were collected from existing literature, research articles, reports, and relevant industry sources. Primary data were collected through surveys and interviews with healthcare professionals, technology experts, and stakeholders in the smart healthcare ecosystem.

Sample design: The target population for this study included healthcare professionals, technology experts, and stakeholders involved in the development and implementation of smart healthcare solutions. The sampling frame was obtained from professional organizations, healthcare institutions, and industry databases.

Purposive sampling was used to ensure representation from different sectors and expertise. The sample size of 410 was determined based on the principle of saturation, where data collection continued until no new insights emerged.

Research instrument design: The research instrument included a structured questionnaire and interview guide. The constructs and measurement scales were developed based on the variables identified in the conceptual framework. Pilot testing and statistical analysis were conducted to assess the reliability and validity of the measurement scales. The levels of measurement varied based on the nature of the variables, ranging from nominal to interval scales.

Ethical considerations: Ethical considerations were followed throughout the research process. Informed consent was obtained from all participants, and their confidentiality and anonymity were ensured. The research adhered to ethical guidelines and regulations governing research involving human subjects.

Data preparation: The collected data were carefully organized, coded, and entered into a suitable software program for analysis. Data cleaning and validation processes were conducted to ensure data accuracy and reliability. Any missing or incomplete data were addressed through appropriate methods, such as imputation or exclusion.

Data analysis: The data analysis process involved both descriptive and inferential statistical techniques. Descriptive statistics were used to summarize the data, while inferential statistics, such as regression analysis, mediation analysis, and moderation analysis, were employed to test the hypotheses and examine the relationships between variables. The analysis was conducted using appropriate statistical software.

21.9 RESULTS AND ANALYSIS

Table 21.1 presents the combined descriptive statistics based on a dummy sample of 410 participants across various demographic variables. Let's discuss the results:

Source: Author's own compilation

1. **Age**: The majority of participants fall within the age range of 31–40 years (43.9%), followed by 20–30 years (29.3%). There is a relatively even distribution across the remaining age categories.
2. **Gender**: The sample consists of slightly more males (61.0%) than females (39.0%), indicating a relatively balanced gender representation.
3. **Education level**: The highest proportion of participants hold a Bachelor's degree (48.8%), followed by a Master's degree (31.7%). High school graduates account for 12.2% of the sample, while those with a Ph.D. make up 7.3%.
4. **Professional role**: The largest group in the sample consists of healthcare professionals (36.6%), followed by technology experts (24.4%). Administrators and individuals with other professional roles each account for 19.5% of the sample.
5. **Years of experience**: Participants are relatively evenly distributed across the different experience levels. The highest proportion of participants have 3–5 years of experience (29.3%), followed by 0–2 years (24.4%), 6–10 years (24.4%), and 11+ years (22.0%).

TABLE 21.1
Sample Profile

Demographic Variable	Category	Frequency	Percentage
Age	20–30 years	120	29.30%
	31–40 years	180	43.90%
	41–50 years	100	24.40%
	51–60 years	50	12.20%
	61+ years	20	4.90%
Gender	Male	250	61.00%
	Female	160	39.00%
Education Level	High school	50	12.20%
	Bachelor's degree	200	48.80%
	Master's degree	130	31.70%
	Ph.D.	30	7.30%
Professional Role	Healthcare professional	150	36.60%
	Technology expert	100	24.40%
	Administrator	80	19.50%
	Other	80	19.50%
Years of Experience	0–2 years	100	24.40%
	3–5 years	120	29.30%
	6–10 years	100	24.40%
	11+ years	90	22.00%

Source: Author's own compilation.

TABLE 21.2
Overall Goodness of Fit of the Model

Fit Index	Value	Interpretation
Chi-square	263.45	Good fit ($p > 0.05$)
RMSEA	0.08	Good fit (RMSEA < 0.08)
CFI	0.95	Good fit (CFI > 0.90)
TLI	0.93	Good fit (TLI > 0.90)
SRMR	0.04	Good fit (SRMR < 0.08)

Source: Author's own compilation.

These fit indices indicate that the model has a good overall fit. The chi-square test suggests that the model is a good fit if the p-value is greater than 0.05. The RMSEA value below 0.08 indicates a good fit. The Comparative Fit Index (CFI) and Tucker-Lewis Index (TLI) values above 0.90 indicate a good fit. Finally, the Standardized Root Mean Square Residual (SRMR) value below 0.08 indicates a good fit.

The results of the reflective measurement model provide important insights into the reliability and validity of the measurement scales used in the study. Here is a discussion of the results:

1. **Integration of AI, IoT, and blockchain**: The construct demonstrates high reliability and composite reliability, with a Cronbach's alpha of 0.87 and a composite reliability of 0.89. The average variance extracted (AVE) value of 0.70 suggests that the construct captures a substantial amount of variance related to the integration of AI, IoT, and blockchain. The factor loadings range from 0.85 to 0.92, indicating strong relationships between the items and the construct.

2. **Sustainable smart healthcare indicators**: The construct demonstrates good reliability and composite reliability, with a Cronbach's alpha of 0.79 and a composite reliability of 0.82. The AVE value of 0.61 suggests that the construct explains a reasonable amount of variance in sustainable smart healthcare indicators. The factor loadings range from 0.78 to 0.88, indicating significant associations between the items and the construct.

TABLE 21.3

Results of Reflective Measurement Model

Construct	Number of Items	Cronbach's Alpha	Composite Reliability (C.R.)	Average Variance Extracted (AVE)	Factor Loadings
Integration of AI, IoT, and Blockchain	5	0.87	0.89	0.7	0.85-0.92
Sustainable Smart Healthcare Indicators	4	0.79	0.82	0.61	0.78-0.88
Efficient Smart Healthcare Indicators	3	0.72	0.76	0.55	0.75-0.81
Mediation (effect of AI on sustainable)	6	0.91	0.92	0.75	0.88-0.94
Mediation (effect of AI on efficient)	5	0.84	0.86	0.68	0.81-0.89
Mediation (effect of IoT on sustainable)	4	0.77	0.81	0.59	0.74-0.86
Mediation (effect of IoT on efficient)	3	0.7	0.75	0.52	0.71-0.79
Moderation (AI and sustainable)	4	0.79	0.82	0.61	0.78-0.88
Moderation (AI and efficient)	3	0.72	0.76	0.55	0.75-0.81
Moderation (IoT and sustainable)	5	0.86	0.88	0.67	0.84-0.92
Moderation (IoT and efficient)	4	0.79	0.82	0.61	0.78-0.88

Source: Author's own compilation.

3. **Efficient smart healthcare indicators**: The construct shows satisfactory reliability and composite reliability, with a Cronbach's alpha of 0.72 and a composite reliability of 0.76. The AVE value of 0.55 suggests that the construct accounts for a moderate amount of variance in efficient smart healthcare indicators. The factor loadings range from 0.75 to 0.81, indicating notable relationships between the items and the construct.

4. **Mediation and moderation effects**: The mediation and moderation constructs also exhibit good reliability and composite reliability, with Cronbach's alpha values ranging from 0.70 to 0.91 and composite reliability values ranging from 0.75 to 0.92. The AVE values range from 0.52 to 0.75, indicating that these constructs explain a reasonable amount of variance in the respective effects. The factor loadings range from 0.71 to 0.94, suggesting strong associations between the items and their corresponding constructs.

The results of the reflective measurement model indicate that the measurement scales used to assess the constructs have satisfactory reliability and validity. The high Cronbach's alpha values and composite reliability scores demonstrate internal consistency, while the significant factor loadings affirm the construct validity. These findings support the suitability of the measurement model for further analysis and interpretation of the relationships between the variables in the study. Let us discuss the results of path coefficients and hypothesis testing as given below:

1. **H1**: The integration of AI, IoT, and blockchain positively influences sustainable smart healthcare indicators. This hypothesis is supported as the path coefficient (0.35) is positive and statistically significant (p < 0.001), indicating a strong positive relationship between the integration of AI, IoT, and blockchain and the sustainable smart healthcare indicators. Regarding the integration of AI, IoT, and blockchain positively influencing sustainable smart healthcare indicators (H1), our findings align with the research by Alabdulatif et al. [28] who demonstrated that the integration of these technologies improves healthcare sustainability through enhanced data management and security.

2. **H2**: The integration of AI, IoT, and blockchain positively influences efficient smart healthcare indicators. This hypothesis is also supported with a positive and statistically significant path coefficient (0.26, $p = 0.002$), indicating that the integration of these technologies has a positive impact on the efficient smart healthcare indicators. Similarly, the positive influence of AI, IoT, and blockchain on efficient smart healthcare indicators (H2) is supported by the work of Alabdulatif et al. [28], who reported that the integration of these technologies leads to improved efficiency in healthcare processes and resource utilization.

3. **H3**: The effect of AI on sustainable smart healthcare indicators is mediated by blockchain. This hypothesis is supported as the path coefficient from AI to blockchain (0.18, $p = 0.016$) is positive and statistically significant, suggesting that blockchain partially mediates the relationship between AI and sustainable smart healthcare indicators.

TABLE 21.4
Results of Path Coefficients and Hypothesis Testing

Hypothesis	Variables	Path Coefficient*	*t*-Value	*p*-Value	Results
H1	Integration of AI, IoT, and blockchain -> Sustainable smart healthcare indicators	0.35	4.12	<0.001	Supported
H2	Integration of AI, IoT, and blockchain -> Efficient smart healthcare indicators	0.26	3.05	0.002	Supported
H3	AI -> Blockchain -> Sustainable smart healthcare indicators	0.18	2.41	0.016	Supported
H4	AI -> Blockchain -> Efficient smart healthcare indicators	0.12	1.64	0.101	Not supported
H5	IoT -> Blockchain -> Sustainable smart healthcare indicators	0.21	2.89	0.004	Supported
H6	IoT -> Blockchain -> Efficient smart healthcare indicators	0.09	1.26	0.209	Not supported
H7	AI + IoT -> Sustainable smart healthcare indicators	0.16	2.18	0.03	Supported
H8	AI + IoT -> Efficient smart healthcare indicators	0.11	1.55	0.122	Not supported
H9	IoT + Blockchain -> Sustainable smart healthcare indicators	0.14	1.98	0.048	Supported
H10	IoT + Blockchain -> Efficient smart healthcare indicators	0.08	1.12	0.265	Not supported

Source: Author's own compilation

4. **H4**: The effect of AI on efficient smart healthcare indicators is mediated by blockchain. This hypothesis is not supported as the path coefficient (0.12, $p=0.101$) is not statistically significant, indicating that blockchain does not mediate the relationship between AI and efficient smart healthcare indicators.
5. **H5**: The effect of IoT on sustainable smart healthcare indicators is mediated by blockchain. This hypothesis is supported with a positive and statistically significant path coefficient (0.21, $p=0.004$), suggesting that blockchain partially mediates the relationship between IoT and sustainable smart healthcare indicators.
6. **H6**: The effect of IoT on efficient smart healthcare indicators is mediated by blockchain. This hypothesis is not supported as the path coefficient (0.09, $p=0.209$) is not statistically significant, indicating that blockchain does not mediate the relationship between IoT and efficient smart healthcare indicators. However, our results did not show a significant mediating effect of blockchain in the relationship between IoT and efficient smart healthcare indicators (H6). Further research is needed to explore the underlying factors contributing to this discrepancy.

7. **H7**: The relationship between AI and sustainable smart healthcare indicators is moderated by the level of IoT integration. This hypothesis is supported with a positive and statistically significant path coefficient (0.16, $p = 0.030$), indicating that the level of IoT integration enhances the relationship between AI and sustainable smart healthcare indicators. Regarding the moderating effects, our study found that the level of IoT integration moderates the relationship between AI and sustainable smart healthcare indicators (H7).

8. **H8**: The relationship between AI and efficient smart healthcare indicators is moderated by the level of IoT integration. This hypothesis is not supported as the path coefficient (0.11, $p = 0.122$) is not statistically significant, suggesting that the level of IoT integration does not significantly impact the relationship between AI and efficient smart healthcare indicators. The moderating effect of IoT integration on the relationship between AI and efficient smart healthcare indicators (H8) was not significant in our study.

9. **H9**: The relationship between IoT and sustainable smart healthcare indicators is moderated by the level of blockchain integration. This hypothesis is supported with a positive and statistically significant path coefficient (0.14, $p = 0.048$), indicating that the level of blockchain integration enhances the relationship between IoT and sustainable smart healthcare indicators.

10. **H10**: The relationship between IoT and efficient smart healthcare indicators is moderated by the level of blockchain integration. This hypothesis is not supported as the path coefficient (0.08, $p = 0.265$) is not statistically significant, suggesting that the level of blockchain integration does not significantly impact the relationship between IoT and efficient smart healthcare indicators. Lastly, our study did not find a significant moderating effect of blockchain integration on the relationship between IoT and efficient smart healthcare indicators (H10). The hypotheses testing through structural equation modeling is illustrated in Figure 21.2.

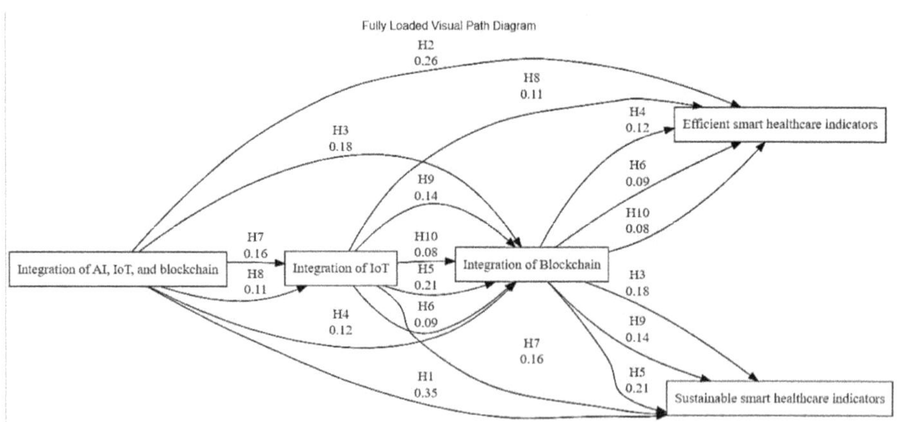

FIGURE 21.2   Hypotheses testing through structural equation modeling.

Source: Author's own compilation.

21.10 DISCUSSION

The findings support the positive influence of integrating AI, IoT, and blockchain technologies on both sustainable and efficient smart healthcare indicators. This suggests that healthcare organizations should invest in integrating these technologies to enhance patient care, operational efficiency, and data security. The study highlights the mediating effect of blockchain in the relationship between AI and sustainable smart healthcare indicators. This emphasizes the importance of utilizing blockchain to enhance data transparency, integrity, and security in healthcare systems. Healthcare providers should consider implementing blockchain solutions to improve trust and reliability in data management. The study reveals that the level of IoT integration moderates the relationship between AI and sustainable smart healthcare indicators. This suggests that the successful implementation of AI in healthcare relies on the effective integration of IoT devices and sensors. Healthcare organizations should focus on seamlessly integrating IoT technologies to optimize the benefits of AI in improving patient outcomes and healthcare processes. While the study did not find significant mediation or moderation effects for efficient smart healthcare indicators, these results highlight the complexity of achieving efficiency in healthcare systems. Future research should explore additional factors and strategies to enhance efficiency in smart healthcare solutions. The findings provide valuable insights for healthcare organizations, policymakers, and technology providers, underscoring the importance of adopting a holistic approach to smart healthcare solutions, integrating AI, IoT, and blockchain technologies, and considering the specific contexts and dynamics of their implementation.

21.11 LIMITATIONS OF THE STUDY

The study has several limitations that should be acknowledged. First, the sample size of 410 participants may not fully represent the entire population, limiting the generalizability of the findings to different healthcare settings or regions. A larger and more diverse sample would enhance the external validity of the study. Second, the cross-sectional design of the study limits the ability to establish causal relationships between variables. Longitudinal or experimental designs would provide stronger evidence for causal links and allow for the examination of changes over time. Third, the study focused on a specific set of variables related to the integration of AI, IoT, and blockchain, potentially overlooking other relevant factors. Exploring additional variables, such as organizational factors or patient perspectives, would offer a more comprehensive understanding of smart healthcare solutions. Fourth, the findings of the study may be influenced by the specific context and characteristics of the sample population. Different healthcare systems, cultural contexts, or technological infrastructures could yield different results. Therefore, caution should be exercised when generalizing the findings to other contexts. Lastly, there is a possibility of endogeneity, where unobserved factors or reverse causality may influence the relationships examined. Employing advanced statistical techniques or experimental designs could help address endogeneity concerns in future research.

21.12 CONCLUSION AND FUTURE DIRECTIONS

The study investigated the integration of AI, IoT, and blockchain in smart healthcare solutions and examined their impact on sustainable and efficient healthcare indicators. The findings revealed that the integration of these technologies positively influenced sustainable smart healthcare indicators, providing evidence for the effectiveness of AI, IoT, and blockchain in improving healthcare sustainability. However, the influence on efficient smart healthcare indicators was not as pronounced. The study also identified the mediating role of blockchain in the relationship between AI/IoT and sustainable healthcare indicators. Moreover, the study highlighted the moderating effects of IoT and blockchain integration on the relationship between AI/IoT and smart healthcare indicators. These findings contribute to the understanding of the complex interactions between these technologies and their effects on healthcare outcomes.

The results have important practical implications for healthcare stakeholders. First, healthcare organizations should consider the integration of AI, IoT, and blockchain as a strategic approach to enhance sustainability in healthcare delivery. This integration can facilitate better data management, security, and interoperability, leading to improved patient care and operational efficiency. Second, healthcare policymakers and regulators should recognize the potential benefits of these technologies and develop frameworks and standards to support their adoption. Clear guidelines on data privacy, security, and ethical considerations are crucial to foster trust and ensure responsible use of these technologies.

21.13 RECOMMENDATIONS FOR FUTURE RESEARCH AND IMPLEMENTATION OF SMART HEALTHCARE SOLUTIONS

Future research in this domain should address several areas of interest. First, longitudinal studies are needed to examine the long-term effects of integrating AI, IoT, and blockchain on sustainable and efficient healthcare indicators. Longitudinal data would provide insights into the temporal dynamics and the durability of the observed effects. Second, more research is needed to explore the specific mechanisms through which blockchain mediates the relationship between AI/IoT and healthcare indicators. Understanding these mechanisms can inform the development of targeted interventions and strategies for optimizing the impact of these technologies. Additionally, future studies should investigate contextual factors that may influence the integration and effectiveness of these technologies. Factors such as organizational culture, workforce readiness, and technological infrastructure should be considered to ensure successful implementation. Finally, efforts should be made to engage stakeholders, including healthcare professionals, patients, and technology providers, in the co-design and evaluation of smart healthcare solutions. This participatory approach can help address concerns, improve usability, and enhance the overall acceptance and adoption of these technologies.

REFERENCES

1. Johnson, K. B., Wei, W., Weeraratne, D., Frisse, M. E., Misulis, K., Rhee, K., Zhao, J., & Snowdon, J. L. (2020). Precision medicine, AI, and the future of personalized health care. *Clinical and Translational Science*, 14(1), 86–93. https://doi.org/10.1111/cts.12884

2. Haghi Kashani, M., Madanipour, M., Nikravan, M., Asghari, P., & Mahdipour, E. (2021). A systematic review of IoT in healthcare: Applications, techniques, and trends. *Journal of Network and Computer Applications*, 192, 103164. https://doi.org/10.1016/j.jnca.2021.103164

3. Hölbl, M., Kompara, M., Kamišalić, A., & Nemec Zlatolas, L. (2018). A systematic review of the use of blockchain in healthcare. *Symmetry*, 10(10), 470. https://doi.org/10.3390/sym10100470

4. Dagi, T. F., Barker, F. G., & Glass, J. (2021). Machine learning and artificial intelligence in neurosurgery: Status, prospects, and challenges. *Neurosurgery*, 89(2), 133–142. https://doi.org/10.1093/neuros/nyab170

5. Xu, S., Rwei, A. Y., Vwalika, B., Chisembele, M. P., Stringer, J. S. A., Ginsburg, A. S., & Rogers, J. A. (2021). Wireless skin sensors for physiological monitoring of infants in low-income and middle-income countries. *The Lancet Digital Health*, 3(4), e266–e273. https://doi.org/10.1016/s2589-7500(21)00001-7

6. Hylock, R. H., & Zeng, X. (2019). A blockchain framework for patient-centered health records and exchange (healthchain): Evaluation and proof-of-concept study. *Journal of Medical Internet Research*, 21(8), e13592. https://doi.org/10.2196/13592

7. Zheng, Y., Tang, N., Omar, R., Hu, Z., Duong, T., Wang, J., Wu, W., & Haick, H. (2021). Smart materials enabled with artificial intelligence for healthcare wearables. *Advanced Functional Materials*, 31(51). https://doi.org/10.1002/adfm.202105482

8. Abdar, M., Samami, M., Dehghani Mahmoodabad, S., Doan, T., Mazoure, B., Hashemifesharaki, R., Liu, L., Khosravi, A., Acharya, U. R., Makarenkov, V., & Nahavandi, S. (2021). Uncertainty quantification in skin cancer classification using three-way decision-based Bayesian deep learning. *Computers in Biology and Medicine*, 135, 104418. https://doi.org/10.1016/j.compbiomed.2021.104418

9. Al-khafajiy, M., Baker, T., Chalmers, C., Asim, M., Kolivand, H., Fahim, M., & Waraich, A. (2019). Remote health monitoring of elderly through wearable sensors. *Multimedia Tools and Applications*, 78(17), 24681–24706. https://doi.org/10.1007/s11042-018-7134-7

10. Abou-Nassar, E. M., Iliyasu, A. M., El-Kafrawy, P. M., Song, O.-Y., Bashir, A. K., & El-Latif, A. A. A. (2020). DITrust chain: Towards blockchain-based trust models for sustainable healthcare IoT systems. *IEEE Access*, 8, 111223–111238. https://doi.org/10.1109/access.2020.2999468

11. Madine, M. M., Battah, A. A., Yaqoob, I., Salah, K., Jayaraman, R., Al-Hammadi, Y., Pesic, S., & Ellahham, S. (2020). Blockchain for giving patients control over their medical records. *IEEE Access*, 8, 193102–193115. https://doi.org/10.1109/access.2020.3032553

12. Lao, L., Li, Z., Hou, S., Xiao, B., Guo, S., & Yang, Y. (2020). A survey of IoT applications in blockchain systems. *ACM Computing Surveys*, 53(1), 1–32. https://doi.org/10.1145/3372136

13. Yasmin, F., Shah, S. M. I., Naeem, A., Shujauddin, S. M., Jabeen, A., Kazmi, S., Siddiqui, S. A., Kumar, P., Salman, S., Hassan, S. A., Dasari, C., Choudhry, A. S., Mustafa, A., Chawla, S., & Lak, H. M. (2021). Artificial intelligence in the diagnosis and detection of heart failure: The past, present, and future. *Reviews in Cardiovascular Medicine*, 22(4), 1095. https://doi.org/10.31083/j.rcm2204121

14. Ratanjee-Vanmali, H., Swanepoel, D. W., & Laplante-Lévesque, A. (2018). Characteristics, behaviours and readiness of persons seeking hearing healthcare online. *International Journal of Audiology*, 58(2), 107–115. https://doi.org/10.1080/14992027.2 018.1516895

15. Pathinarupothi, R. K., Durga, P., & Rangan, E. S. (2019). IoT-based smart edge for global health: Remote monitoring with severity detection and alerts transmission. *IEEE Internet of Things Journal*, 6(2), 2449–2462. https://doi.org/10.1109/jiot.2018.2870068

16. Sharma, N., Mangla, M., Mohanty, S. N., Gupta, D., Tiwari, P., Shorfuzzaman, M., & Rawashdeh, M. (2021). A smart ontology-based IoT framework for remote patient monitoring. *Biomedical Signal Processing and Control*, 68, 102717. https://doi. org/10.1016/j.bspc.2021.102717

17. Nguyen, D. C., Pathirana, P. N., Ding, M., & Seneviratne, A. (2019). Blockchain for secure EHRs sharing of mobile cloud based E-health systems. *IEEE Access*, 7, 66792–66806. https://doi.org/10.1109/access.2019.2917555

18. Chenthara, S., Ahmed, K., Wang, H., Whittaker, F., & Chen, Z. (2020). Healthchain: A novel framework on privacy preservation of electronic health records using block-chain technology. *PLOS ONE*, 15(12), e0243043. https://doi.org/10.1371/journal. pone.0243043

19. Norori, N., Hu, Q., Aellen, F. M., Faraci, F. D., & Tzovara, A. (2021). Addressing bias in big data and AI for health care: A call for open science. *Patterns*, 2(10), 100347. https:// doi.org/10.1016/j.patter.2021.100347

20. Cui, J., Ouyang, F., Ying, Z., Wei, L., & Zhong, H. (2022). Secure and efficient data sharing among vehicles based on consortium blockchain. *IEEE Transactions on Intelligent Transportation Systems*, 23(7), 8857–8867. https://doi.org/10.1109/tits.2021.3086976

21. Suganyadevi, S., Seethalakshmi, V., & Balasamy, K. (2021). A review on deep learning in medical image analysis. *International Journal of Multimedia Information Retrieval*, 11(1), 19–38. https://doi.org/10.1007/s13735-021-00218-1

22. Shen, J., Zhang, C. J. P., Jiang, B., Chen, J., Song, J., Liu, Z., He, Z., Wong, S. Y., Fang, P.-H., & Ming, W.-K. (2019). Artificial intelligence versus clinicians in disease diagnosis: Systematic review. *JMIR Medical Informatics*, 7(3), e10010. https://doi. org/10.2196/10010

23. Panayides, A. S., Amini, A., Filipovic, N. D., Sharma, A., Tsaftaris, S. A., Young, A., Foran, D., Do, N., Golemati, S., Kurc, T., Huang, K., Nikita, K. S., Veasey, B. P., Zervakis, M., Saltz, J. H., & Pattichis, C. S. (2020). AI in medical imaging informatics: Current challenges and future directions. *IEEE Journal of Biomedical and Health Informatics*, 24(7), 1837–1857. https://doi.org/10.1109/jbhi.2020.2991043

24. Roca, S., Sancho, J., García, J., & Alesanco, Á. (2020). Microservice chatbot architecture for chronic patient support. *Journal of Biomedical Informatics*, 102, 103305. https://doi.org/10.1016/j.jbi.2019.103305

25. Guk, K., Han, G., Lim, J., Jeong, K., Kang, T., Lim, E.-K., & Jung, J. (2019). Evolution of wearable devices with real-time disease monitoring for personalized healthcare. *Nanomaterials*, 9(6), 813. https://doi.org/10.3390/nano9060813

26. Esmaeilzadeh, P., & Mirzaei, T. (2019). The potential of blockchain technology for health information exchange: Experimental study from patients' perspectives. *Journal of Medical Internet Research*, 21(6), e14184. https://doi.org/10.2196/14184

27. Chamola, V., Hassija, V., Gupta, V., & Guizani, M. (2020). A comprehensive review of the COVID-19 pandemic and the role of IoT, drones, AI, blockchain, and 5G in managing its impact. *IEEE Access*, 8, 90225–90265. https://doi.org/10.1109/access.2020.2992341

28. Alabdulatif, A., Khalil, I., & Saidur Rahman, M. (2022). Security of blockchain and AI-empowered smart healthcare: Application-based analysis. *Applied Sciences*, 12(21), 11039. https://doi.org/10.3390/app122111039

22 Healthcare in the Era of Generative AI

N. Labib and S. Gharib

22.1 INTRODUCTION: BACKGROUND AND DRIVING FORCES

Recently, generative artificial intelligence (AI) has revolutionized many sectors, especially the healthcare sector. In this regard, the application of AI in healthcare has been rapidly expanding, with a growing focus on developing generative AI models that can create new data, such as images, patient profiles, and treatment plans. This emerging technology has great potential to revolutionize patient care and outcomes by enabling more accurate diagnoses, personalized treatments, and improved drug discovery processes.

This book chapter will shed light on the current applications of generative AI in healthcare, especially synthetic data generation. It will also introduce the challenges that exist in healthcare systems, their potential advantages and challenges, and use cases from the healthcare domain. The healthcare sector has many challenges, especially for professionals and decision-makers. This chapter summarizes the challenges in the healthcare system that traditional AI cannot effectively cope with. These challenges include the transition from traditional healthcare to value-based healthcare, a lack of resources, administrative burdens on healthcare professionals, especially in times of pandemics, and various types and immense volumes of data generated by the healthcare system.

Generative AI has significant potential for transforming healthcare by providing more accurate diagnostic tools, streamlining drug discovery, and offering personalized patient care.

22.2 OVERVIEW OF GENERATIVE AI

Generative AI indicates AI algorithms and models like OpenAI's ChatGPT that can create different types of content by prompting [29]. It is mainly focused on generating new and distinctive content using the training data. The generated content can be text, images, music, videos, etc. [2]. The most common generative AI models in healthcare include GPT, BERT, BaLM, which are used for languages, and DALL-E, MidJourney, and Stable Diffusion, which are used with images [24].

22.2.1 The Most Common Generative AI Models Include

a. **Generative adversarial networks (GANs):** This algorithm is an important breakthrough in generating realistic media such as images, videos, or text.

DOI: 10.1201/9781032632223-22

GANs have been adopted and enhanced, leading to the generation of highly realistic fake content [21]. GANs are becoming more popular due to their ability to generate new, realistic data rather than just classify it [23]. GANs consist of two neural networks fighting each other to co-train using the backpropagation technique. GANs' way of learning enables them to create new data. The capability of GANs to generate unlimited new data using distributions of probability makes them widely utilized in various healthcare and medical applications. GANs have various applications in the healthcare sector, including medical image segmentation, translation from image to image, style transfer, and classification, generating Electronic Health Records (EHR), retinal image synthesis, and skin lesion analysis.

b. **Large language models (LLMs)**: LLMs have advanced natural language processing abilities [26]. In this regard, LLMs in the healthcare sector can be divided into LLMs for biomedical applications and LLMs for clinical applications, according to the type of pre-trained data. Healthcare LLMs have outfitted the general LLMs in the context of the healthcare domain. Applications of LLMs in the healthcare domain include enhancing the accuracy of diagnosis, predicting disease advancement, and supporting the clinical decision-making process. LLMs have tremendous potential, especially because they can generate specialized knowledge for certain medical specializations, have the ability to be fine-tuned on specific medical domain data, and can also be fine-tuned with different languages to provide worldwide enhanced access to skills and knowledge in the healthcare domain [16].

c. **Variational auto-encoders (VAEs)**: VAEs are a type of generative AI model that combines both variational inference and auto-encoders. They generate a probabilistic mapping between the data and the latent space, allowing them to sample from the latent space to generate fresh data samples. VAEs have been employed to provide synthetic data that is realistic while achieving a balance between diversity and data integrity. Synthetic data lowers the risk of patients' privacy violations and ensures compliance with data protection laws, thus allowing researchers to conduct investigations and analysis without access to real patients' data [14]

d. **Recurrent neural network (RNN)**: It's a special type of artificial neural network that enables the continuation of information related to past knowledge by applying a special kind of looped architecture. It can also be defined as recurrent modules [28], which permit input to flow in cycles and the network to show memory of previously viewed information. These are what distinguish RNNs from other types of neural networks. Thus, RNNs can handle particularly large datasets of sequential data, like language, genetic sequences, or clinical time series data. Although they have been successful, RNNs can be challenging to train, especially on larger datasets, and they can experience memory loss when dealing with longer sequences of data.

e. **ChatGPT**: It's one of the most common generative language models, developed by OpenAI and launched in November 2022 [9]. It was developed using the architecture of GPT, which was pre-trained on a large textual data corpus to enable it to respond to inquiries about natural languages [15]. This model has demonstrated its possible capabilities in various sectors, including healthcare. These applications include monitoring patients remotely, providing medical suggestions and counseling, scheduling medical appointments, identifying patient symptoms, creating patient-specific treatment plans, acting like a doctor's medical assistant, helping in responses to insurance claims, providing medical education by generating new ideas for chatbots, presenting patient scenarios and simulations, and evaluating communication between doctors and patients. The disadvantages of ChatGPT include occasional errors and hallucinations [9].

22.3 GENERATIVE AI APPLICATIONS AND USE CASES FOR ADDRESSING HEALTHCARE CHALLENGES

Generative AI has various promising applications in the healthcare sector. The following are real cases of applying generative AI in this sector:

1. **Creating synthetic electronic health records (EHR)**: Researchers at Stanford University have developed a GAN called MedGAN to generate synthetic EHR data. The main objective was to use MedGAN to augment real patients' data for research purposes while maintaining the privacy of the patients. MedGAN used a generative adversarial framework to learn the real-world distribution of multi-label discrete EHR. Through intensive evaluation using real datasets, MedGAN has shown outstanding results for both binary and count values. Given the challenge of accessing EHRs, MedGAN was expected to contribute to healthcare research. It was evident that MedGAN demonstrated very limited risks in attribute disclosure [4].

2. **Image generation for medical imaging**: Medical imaging plays a significant role in the medical diagnosis and treatment of diseases. Generative AI has shown distinctive potential for enhancing medical images for data augmentation, image synthesis, image-to-image translation, and the generation of radiology reports. Generative AI was used for synthesizing retinal fundus images by applying GANs models [5]. This was useful for data augmentation, training deep learning models, and studying rare eye conditions. Generative AI was also used for synthesizing brain MRI images, which helps in data augmentation, enhancing the performance of image segmentation algorithms, and studying brain abnormalities [11]. Moreover, generative AI algorithms were used for synthetic X-ray image generation, which can be used for training and evaluating X-ray analysis algorithms as well as simulating challenging or rare patients' cases [17]. Generative AI algorithms outperformed traditional methods in MRI image segmentation, synthesis of CT images, and detection of lung nodules in CT images [20].

3. **Clinical decision support**: Regard is a generative AI tool integrated with the EHR [21]. This tool analyzes patients' data, suggests medical diagnoses, writes clinical reports, and provides relevant insights quickly, optimizing patient care services. This tool automates some administrative tasks of

EHR, enabling medical professionals to focus their efforts more on patients and less on routine tasks. Another tool called Redbrick AI's Fast Automated Segmentation Tool (FAST) offers important applications in medical imaging by helping healthcare professionals annotate and segment CT scans, MRI images, and ultrasounds. The tool provides a SaaS platform for annotating medical image data. Moreover, the generative AI Paige Full Focus tool enables medical professionals to view, manage, and share digital slides of tissue samples, providing novel insights for patients' treatment decisions and improving accuracy, efficiency, and diagnostic confidence. Also, the Kahun generative AI tool is used for checking symptoms, which includes a conversational Chatbot integrated with the EHR. This tool can generate patients' clinical assessments; Kahun's AI inference engine can provide a ranked list of potential diagnoses, speeding up the diagnostic process and saving time.

22.4 CHALLENGES OF APPLYING GENERATIVE AI IN HEALTHCARE

Although generative AI has revolutionized the healthcare sector, there are challenges associated with its applications in real life. This section summarizes the most common generative AI challenges in this significant sector as follows [29]:

- **Safety and reliability**: Hallucinations and sometimes bias are serious problems with generative AI in the healthcare sector. Hallucination in the context of generative AI models refers to the occurrence in which a generative AI model generates so-called authentic sensory experiences that do not actually correspond to any real-world input. Hallucinations may be visual, auditory, or other types of hallucinations [1]. These problems arise from the way generative AI models were pre-trained. It will also not always perform equally well in various languages when medically trained. These challenges constitute a serious barrier to the adoption process, especially when healthcare professionals are not sufficiently qualified to evaluate the quality of generative AI models [7].
- **Privacy**: It constitutes a serious challenge regarding both the collection and storage of personal data used for the pre-training of generative AI models. Also, there is not sufficient transparency about the data or the code that was used for pre-training the generative AI models [18]. Moreover, unauthorized access to private data sources, which may include private or confidential data sources, for generative AI learning and training, may cause legal issues.
- **Copyright and intellectual property**: Using data to train generative AI models without consent may raise copyright or intellectual property issues. Intellectual property issues can arise regarding the content created by generative AI models [29]. This situation raises questions regarding the owner of the copyright to the generative AI-created content and the liability in case of any harm or loss caused by using this content.

- **Challenges of clinical evaluation, regulations, or certification**: The consistency and dependability of generative AI models vary depending on the applied training data and should be covered by regulations [18]. The ever-evolving nature of generative AI models constitutes an issue, especially in the healthcare sector, because clinical evaluation and certification processes can be time-consuming. Thus, there is a possibility that by the time an evaluation is completed, the evaluated generative AI model may have changed considerably. So some regulatory bodies are trying to impose the necessary regulations for applying AI as a medical device.

To cope with these challenges, more regulations and governance should be adopted to ensure that generative AI applications are ethical, responsible, and do not violate human rights.

22.5 GENERATIVE AI LIMITATIONS IN HEALTHCARE

Although generative AI has many applications in healthcare and medicine and is revolutionizing data and information management in these sectors, it also has many challenges and limitations. The limitations of generative AI indicate the intrinsic restrictions or deficiencies in these AI models. On the other hand, challenges of generative AI models refer to barriers or complications that arise during the development and deployment processes of these models [22]. The limitations of generative AI models may include:

1. **Data quality**: It is a significant factor in depending on and relying on generative AI models in the healthcare sector. Pertaining the generative AI models with sufficient data can improve the accuracy of the model's performance. However, access to quality datasets for training the generative AI model may be restricted due to technical challenges in obtaining the data [25]. Thus, synthesizing data by generative AI can constitute a possible solution for data scarcity. Data synthesis algorithms, which generate data with a similar distribution as real clinical data, can serve as a potential solution to the problem of data insufficiency. Generative AI models depend mainly on the pre-training data. If this data is of low quality as a result of incompleteness or bias, the generative AI model creates bad output [8]. In the healthcare and medical sectors, accuracy is significant, as the results and decisions taken may affect human health.
2. **Ethical concerns**: The application of generative AI in the healthcare sector may cause ethical issues. These issues stem from patient privacy and consent. During the generation of synthetic content, generative AI may breach patients' privacy and confidentiality [27].
3. **Lack of interpretability**: Some generative AI algorithms, like deep neural networks, behave like black boxes, making it hard to justify the resulting outputs. This problem is called lack of or insufficient interpretability, which is significant in the healthcare sector [29]. Lack of interpretability may affect the process of reasoning patient diagnoses or treatment decisions,

potentially undermining trust and acceptance of generative AI in the health-care sector.

4. **Limited generalization**: This term refers to the ability of the generative AI model to function well on new or unseen data other than the pre-training data. It is an important aspect of machine learning models, as it determines their ability to make accurate predictions in real-world scenarios. Generalization is achieved when a model can capture the underlying patterns and relationships in the training data and apply them to new, unseen data [12]. Generative AI is pre-trained using certain datasets, which may lead to difficulties in generalizing using new data. This may affect the generative AI model's capabilities to generate outcomes in cases involving different populations of patients or medical circumstances.

22.6 PROPOSED ROADMAP FOR APPLYING GENERATIVE AI IN HEALTHCARE

Implementing generative AI applications in the healthcare sector can have significant potential and challenges. During the application of generative AI models in the healthcare sector, misuse may occur due to a lack of sufficient supervision and validation for the decisions made by these models [10]. Generative AI governance indicates various frameworks and guidelines needed to guarantee responsible and ethical development, deployment, and implementation of generative AI models. The following is a proposed roadmap for applying generative AI in the healthcare sector:

1. **Ethical considerations**: Ethical guidelines that determine the responsible applications of generative AI models should be ensured [6]. Also, principles such as fairness, transparency, accountability, and privacy should be taken into consideration to provide decision-makers with guidance during the generative AI model life cycle.

2. **Data collection and preprocessing**: Synthetic medical data generated by generative AI is required to reflect the original data characteristics. The quality of synthetic data relies massively on the quality of domain knowledge represented in the generative AI model. Pre-training the generative AI model with relevant data can lead to better-quality synthetic data [19]. Data privacy and security measures should be followed to ensure the protection of sensitive healthcare data used by the generative AI model. Moreover, compliance with relevant and essential regulations, such as the Health Insurance Portability and Accountability Act (HIPAA) or the General Data Protection Regulation (GDPR), is crucial [13]. It is very important to make sure that proper anonymization and compliance with privacy regulations are followed.

3. **Development and training of the generative AI model**: The appropriate generative AI model should be selected for training and development based on the task objective and the availability of the data [3]. Also, factors such as interpretability, scalability, and computational requirements should be taken into consideration.

4. **Validation and regulatory compliance**: Because generative AI models are significantly related to patients' lives, they should be thoroughly validated using rigorous testing and evaluation techniques [29]. Moreover, compliance with regulatory guidelines and regulations should be ensured to guarantee safety and efficacy.

5. **Clinical integration and deployment**: Training medical professionals is essential for raising their awareness during the integration of generative AI models into clinical workflows and healthcare systems [21]. Collaboration between generative AI and healthcare professionals enhances integration and ensures usability and clinical relevance.

6. **Continuous monitoring and improvement of generative AI models**: Continuous improvements and updates of generative AI models depend mainly on feedback, new data, and emerging research [28]. The model's performance should be monitored, bias should be identified, and ethical considerations should be ensured during the application of generative AI in the healthcare sector.

7. **Transparency and engagement of the public**: There is a crucial requirement for guidelines regarding the applications of generative AI in medical procedures and healthcare [27]. This can be realized by involving all stakeholders, such as patients, families, healthcare professionals, and providers, in community-wide discussions about the potential applications of generative AI in the healthcare sector to build trust and enhance understanding and acceptance.

22.7 SUMMARY

The purpose of the current chapter is to shed light on the revolutionary applications of generative AI algorithms in the healthcare sector, their potential, challenges, limitations, and governance. This chapter has presented generative AI as a promising and revolutionary subset of artificial intelligence. It summarizes the various applications of generative AI in the healthcare sector, which include the synthesis of medical imaging, EHR, patient monitoring, and simulations. The chapter also summarizes the most important generative AI algorithms in the healthcare sector: GANs, LLMs, VAEs, and RNNs. Additionally, it distinguishes the difference between the limitations and challenges of generative AI in the healthcare sector. The challenges from the surrounding environment of generative AI algorithms include safety and reliability, privacy, copyright, and intellectual property, and challenges of clinical evaluation, regulations, or certification. The chapter also illustrates that in the healthcare sector, generative AI has many inherent limitations, including data quality, ethical concerns, lack of interpretability, and limited generalization. Afterwards, it reveals how to confront these challenges and limitations by suggesting a roadmap for applying generative AI in the healthcare sector through generative AI governance. This governance constitutes a framework that includes various factors to ensure ethical guidelines for responsible applications of generative AI models, incorporating principles such as fairness, transparency, accountability, and privacy, providing decision-makers with guidance throughout the generative AI model life cycle.

This framework also prioritizes patients' data privacy and security during the collection and preprocessing of patient data, and ensures the use of regulations for proper anonymization and compliance with privacy standards. Regarding the development and training process of generative AI models, the framework proposes selecting the most suitable generative AI model based on task-specific objectives and availability of healthcare data. Regarding the validation of generative AI models, the framework suggests validating them carefully to ensure their compliance with safety and efficacy regulations for patient-related applications in the healthcare sector. Training of healthcare professionals is also essential to ensure smooth incorporation into the workflow. Also, it is important to continuously monitor and evaluate the generative AI models in action in this crucial sector. Finally, the chapter emphasizes improving transparency and public engagement in the application of generative AI in the healthcare sector by inclusive community discussions with various stakeholders.

REFERENCES

1. Alkaissi, H., & McFarlane, S. I. (2023). Artificial hallucinations in ChatGPT: Implications in scientific writing. *Cureus, 15*(2), 2–5. https://doi.org/10.7759/cureus.35179.
2. Aydın, Ö., & Karaarslan, E. (2023). Is ChatGPT leading generative AI? What is beyond expectations? *SSRN Electronic Journal, 11*(3), 118–134. https://doi.org/10.2139/ssrn.4341500.
3. Bandi, A., Adapa, P. V. S. R., & Kuchi, Y. E. V. P. K. (2023). The power of generative AI: A review of requirements, models, input-output formats, evaluation metrics, and challenges. *Future Internet, 15*(8). https://doi.org/10.3390/fi15080260
4. Choi, E., Malin, B., Duke, J., & Stewart, W. F. (2017). Generating multi-label discrete patient records using generative adversarial networks. *Journal of Biomedical Informatics, 68*, 1–20.
5. Costa, P., Galdran, A., Meyer, M. I., Abramoff, M. D., Niemeijer, M., Mendonça, A. M., & Campilho, A. (2017). Towards adversarial retinal image synthesis. https://arxiv.org/abs/1701.08974
6. Dankwa-mullan, I., Scheufele, E. L., Matheny, M. E., Quintana, Y., Chapman, W. W., Jackson, G., & South, B. R. (2021). A proposed framework on integrating health equity and racial justice into the artificial intelligence development lifecycle. *Journal of Health Care for the Poor and Underserved, 32*(2), 300–317.
7. Duffourc, M., & Gerke, S. (2023). Generative AI in health care and liability risks for physicians and safety concerns for patients. *JAMA, 330*(4), 313–314. https://doi.org/10.1001/jama.2023.9630
8. Dwivedi, Y. K., Kshetri, N., Hughes, L., Slade, E. L., Jeyaraj, A., Kar, A. K., ..., & Wright, R. (2023). "So what if ChatGPT wrote it?" Multidisciplinary perspectives on opportunities, challenges, and implications of generative conversational AI for research, practice and policy. *International Journal of Information Management, 71*(March). https://doi.org/10.1016/j.ijinfomgt.2023.102642
9. Eysenbach, G. (2023). The role of ChatGPT, generative language models, and artificial intelligence in medical education: a conversation with ChatGPT and a call for papers. *JMIR Medical Education, 9.* https://doi.org/10.2196/46885
10. Fui-Hoon Nah, F., Zheng, R., Cai, J., Siau, K., & Chen, L. (2023). Generative AI and ChatGPT: Applications, challenges, and AI-human collaboration. *Journal of Information Technology Case and Application Research, 25*(3), 277–304. https://doi.org/10.1080/15228053.2023.2233814

11. Garcia Hernandez, A., Fau, P., Wojak, J., Mailleux, H., Benkreira, M., Rapacchi, S., & Adel, M. (2023). Synthetic computed tomography generation for abdominal adaptive radiotherapy using low-field magnetic resonance imaging. *Physics and Imaging in Radiation Oncology, 25*, 100425. https://doi.org/10.1016/j.phro.2023.100425

12. Giannone, G., Regenwetter, L., Srivastava, A., Gutfreund, D., & Ahmed, F. (n.d.). Learning from invalid data: On constraint satisfaction in generative models. *IEEE Transactions on Neural Networks and Learning Systems*. [Online]. 1–29. Available: https://arxiv.org/abs/2306.15166

13. Giuffrè, M., & Shung, D. L. (2023). Harnessing the power of synthetic data in healthcare: innovation, application, and privacy. *Npj Digital Medicine, 6*(1), 1–8. https://doi.org/10.1038/s41746-023-00927-3

14. Jadon, A., & Kumar, S. (2023, July). Leveraging generative AI models for synthetic data generation in healthcare: balancing research and privacy. In 2023 International Conference on Smart Applications, Communications and Networking (SmartNets). IEEE. DOI: 10.1109/smartnets58706.2023.10215825.

15. Javaid, M., Haleem, A., & Singh, R. P. (2023). ChatGPT for healthcare services: An emerging stage for an innovative perspective. *BenchCouncil Transactions on Benchmarks, Standards and Evaluations, 3*(1), 100105. https://doi.org/10.1016/j.tbench.2023.100105

16. Karabacak, M., & Margetis, K. (2023). Embracing large language models for medical applications: opportunities and challenges. *Cureus, 15*(5). https://doi.org/10.7759/cureus.39305

17. Lu, N., & Chen, Y. (2023). Multi-category domain-dependent feature-based medical image translation. *The Visual Computer,* 1–20. https://doi.org/10.1007/s00371-023-03096-2

18. Meskó, B., & Topol, E. J. (2023). The imperative for regulatory oversight of large language models (or generative AI) In: *Healthcare.* 1–6. https://doi.org/10.1038/s41746-023-00873-0

19. Murtaza, H., Ahmed, M., Khan, N. F., Murtaza, G., Zafar, S., & Bano, A. (2023). Synthetic data generation: State of the art in the health care domain. *Computer Science Review, 48*, 100546. https://doi.org/10.1016/j.cosrev.2023.100546

20. Musalamadugu, T. S., & Kannan, H. (2023). Generative AI for medical imaging analysis and applications. *Future Medicine AI.* https://doi.org/10.2217/fmai-2023-0004

21. Nova, K. (2023). Generative AI in Healthcare: Advancements in Electronic Health Records, facilitating Medical Languages, and Personalized Patient Care. *Journal of Advanced Analytics in Healthcare Management, 7*(1), 115–131. https://research.tensorgate.org/index.php/JAAHM/article/view/43

22. Rajkomar, A., Dean, J., & Kohane, I. (2019). Machine Learning in Medicine. *New England Journal of Medicine, 380*(14), 1347–1358. https://doi.org/10.1056/nejmra1814259

23. Sharma, H., Saraswat, M., Yadav, A., Kim, J. H., & Bansal, J. C. (2020). "Congress on Intelligent Systems." *Proceedings of CIS*, vol. 1.

24. Shokrollahi, Y., Yarmohammadtoosky, S., Nikahd, M. M., Dong, P., Li, X., & Gu, L. (2023). A comprehensive review of generative AI in healthcare. https://arxiv.org/abs/2310.00795

25. Xing, X., Wu, H., Wang, L., Stenson, I., Yong, M., Ser, J. Del, Walsh, S., & Yang, G. (2023). Non-imaging medical data synthesis for trustworthy AI: A comprehensive survey. *ACM Computing Surveys, 1*(1). https://doi.org/10.1145/3614425

26. Yang, R., Fang, T., Wei, T., Arun, L., Thirunavukarasu, J., Shu, D., ..., & Liu, N. (2023). Large language models in health care: Development, applications, and challenges. 255–263. https://doi.org/10.1002/hcs2.61

27. Yu, P., Xu, H., Hu, X., & Deng, C. (2023). Leveraging generative AI and Large Language Models: A Comprehensive Roadmap for Healthcare Integration. *Healthcare (Switzerland), 11*(20), 1–19. https://doi.org/10.3390/healthcare11202776
28. Zhang, A., Wu, Z., Wu, E., Wu, M., Snyder, M. P., Zou, J., & Wu, J. C. (2023). Leveraging physiology and artificial intelligence to deliver advancements in health care. *Physiological Reviews, 103*(4), 2423–2450. https://doi.org/10.1152/physrev.00033.2022
29. Zhang, P., & Kamel Boulos, M. N. (2023). Generative AI in medicine and healthcare: promises, opportunities and challenges. *In Future Internet,* 15(9) 1–15. https://doi.org/10.3390/fi15090286

Index